THE TREASURY LINE

For 40 years the federal Treasury has been the single most influential source of economic advice to the Australian Government. Treasury's massive dominance of economic management has led to a widespread conviction that it does not merely implement policy – it creates it and forces it on governments, whatever their political colour. Surprisingly, this is the first historical account of this crucial institution and the claims made about it.

The Treasury Line tells the story of this instrument since World War II. It chronicles how one generation of technocrats adopted the gospel of J.M. Keynes during wartime and turned it into the economic faith of the 1950s and 1960s; how a new generation lost that faith in the late 1960s; and how the unstable and inflation-ridden 1970s saw the rise of a new orthodoxy, 'neo-classical' economics.

Here is the story of how this gradual transformation in the Treasury's 'line' brought with it radical changes in its view of how the economy works and in its attitude to the role of government and of the market.

Written in a straightforward manner, this book will appeal to all those citizens concerned with the complex relationship between the economy and government, the Treasury's decisive role in that relationship.

Greg Whitwell teaches at the University of Melbourne, and is currently researching aspects of Australian economic history since World War II.

Greg Whitwell

The Treasury Line

Allen & Unwin
Sydney   London   Boston

© Greg Whitwell 1986
This book is copyright under the Berne Convention.
No reproduction without permission. All rights reserved.

First published in 1986
Allen & Unwin Australia Pty Ltd
8 Napier Street, North Sydney, NSW 2060, Australia

Allen & Unwin New Zealand Limited
60 Cambridge Terrace, Wellington,
New Zealand

George Allen & Unwin (Publishers) Ltd
Park Lane, Hemel Hempstead, Herts HP2 4TE, England

Allen & Unwin Inc.
8 Winchester Place, Winchester Terrace, Mass 01890, USA

National Library of Australia
Cataloguing in publication entry:

Whitwell, Greg.
The Treasury line.

Bibliography.
Includes index.
ISBN 0 86861 727 X.
ISBN 0 86861 735 0 (pbk.).

1. Australia. Treasury — History.
2. Australia — Economic policy.   I. Title.
354.94062
Library of Congress Catalog Card Number: 85–71982

Set in 10/11.5 Sabon by Graphicraft Typesetters Ltd., Hong Kong
Printed in Singapore by Koon Wah Pte Ltd

Contents

Tables	vi
Abbreviations	viii
Preface	x

I Setting the scene

1	An introduction to the Treasury	3
2	Keynes and neoclassicism	25
3	Australia adopts Keynesianism, 1930–45	53

II The Treasury line, 1945–84

4	Keynesian theory converted into practice, 1945–55	83
5	The problems of continuous growth, 1956–62	111
6	Defence expenditure and efficient resource allocation, 1963–67	144
7	Heightened inflation and the abandonment of Keynesian meliorism, 1967–73	176
8	Economic instability and neoclassical resurgence, 1973–79	205
9	The ascendancy of the market-based approach, 1980–84	236
10	Explaining the transition	262

Appendix: The Treasury's NIF model	276
Notes	280
Bibliography	295
Index	303

Tables

1.1	Academic qualifications of first and second division Treasury officers, 1956–79	12
1.2	Completed tertiary courses by discipline, as of 1975	13
1.3	Graduate or diplomate staff as a proportion of permanent third division staff in selected departments, 1968–74	14
1.4	Honours or higher degrees as a proportion of degrees held by third division permanent staff in selected departments, 1968–74	14
1.5	Second division career service — number of departments served in	18
5.1	Expenditure on gross domestic product at constant prices, 1954–55 to 1962–63	113
5.2	Unemployment and vacancies, 1954–62	114
5.3	Wage rates, 1954–55 to 1962–63	114
5.4	Consumer price index, 1954–55 to 1962–63	115
5.5	Official reserve assets, 1954–55 to 1962–63	116
6.1	Expenditure on gross domestic product at constant prices, 1963–64 to 1967–68	151
6.2	Outlays, receipts and deficit of commonwealth budget 1963–64 to 1967–68	153
6.3	Defence expenditure, 1964–65 to 1967–68	153
7.1	GFEP second division officers, 1970–79	180
7.2	Average weekly earnings, 1968–69 to 1972–73	182
7.3	Consumer price index, 1968–69 to 1972–73	183
7.4	Industrial disputes 1962–70	189
7.5	Expenditure on gross domestic product at constant prices, 1968–69 to 1972–73	195
7.6	Official reserve assets, 1968–69 to 1972–73	197
7.7	Net apparent inflow of capital, 1966–67 to 1972–73	197

8.1	Commonwealth government outlays, receipts and deficit, 1973–74 to 1979–80	208
8.2	Expenditure and production at constant prices, 1973–74 to 1979–80	209
8.3	Consumer price index, 1973–74 to 1979–80	211
8.4	Wages, 1973–74 to 1979–80	212
8.5	Money supply, 1972–73 to 1979–80	213
8.6	Unemployment, 1973–79	218
A.1	NIF model — behavioural equations	278

Charts

1.1	The Australian Treasury, 1974	8

Abbreviations

AA	Australian Archives (Canberra Branch)
ACTU	Australian Council of Trade Unions
AGPS	Australian Government Printing Service
AIPS	Australian Institute of Political Science
AMFSU	Amalgamated Metals, Foundry and Shipwrights' Union
ANU	Australian National University
ANZAAS	Australia and New Zealand Association for the Advancement of Science
CCAC	Commonwealth Conciliation and Arbitration Commission
CGP	Commonwealth Government Printer
CPD	*Commonwealth Parliamentary Debates*
CPI	consumer price index
CPP	*Commonwealth Parliamentary Papers*
CRF	Consolidated Revenue Fund
F&E	Financial and Economic Advisory Committee
GDP	gross domestic product
GFEP	General Financial and Economic Policy (Division)
GNE	gross national expenditure
GNP	gross national product
IAESR	Institute for Applied Economic and Social Research (University of Melbourne)
IMF	International Monetary Fund
LCP	Liberal-Country Party
LGS	liquid assets and government securities
NGB	W.E. Norton, P.M. Garmston and M.W. Brodie *Australian Economic Statistics 1949–50 to 1980–81: 1 Tables* Reserve Bank of Australia, Occasional Paper No. 8A, May 1982
NIF	national income forecasting
OER	Overseas Economic Relations (Division)
OPEC	Organisation of Petroleum Exporting Countries
PJT	Prices Justification Tribunal
PMC	(Department of) Prime Minister and Cabinet
PPB	planning, programming budgeting
RCAGA	Royal Commission on Australian Government Administration
SRD	statutory reserve deposit

TEP	Treasury Economic Paper
UAP	United Australia Party
VDR	variable deposit requirement

Preface

Despite the attention now paid to the Treasury in the press and despite the interest aroused by the public pronouncements of John Stone during his time as secretary to the Treasury and since his retirement, the Treasury remains a somewhat neglected institution. For there has been no attempt to provide any sort of systematic or comprehensive analysis of the evolution of the Treasury's ideas and philosophy on macroeconomic matters. This omission seems all the more remarkable given the department's undoubted influence throughout most of the postwar period in the formulation of economic policy advice.

This book is an attempt to rectify this omission. It has several aims: it sets out to provide a guide to the nature of Treasury thought over the past 40 years, with the focus being mostly on broad topics such as the Treasury's interpretation of the nature of the Australian economy, its views on the sources of the economy's strengths and weaknesses, and its changing attitude toward what sorts of policies can and should be adopted in an attempt to maintain economic stability; it tries to set the Treasury's outlook in context by outlining the changing economic conditions and policy problems which have prevailed since the war; and it uses the Treasury as a vehicle for making some broad comparisons with the dominant ideas and interests of the Australian economics profession so as to draw attention to what is or is not distinctive about the Treasury's approach and to get some of the flavour of economic debate in postwar Australia.

The book also aims to explain the adoption of Keynesianism in Australia and to show that the department's outlook has slowly changed since the war from a predominantly Keynesian model to a predominantly neoclassical one. In tracing this change, it attempts to show that the Treasury's ideas, like those of all economists and economic institutions, are informed by and reflect a whole series of presuppositions about the fundamental nature of the economy and the processes which occur within it.

To say that the Treasury line changed from a Keynesian to a largely neoclassical view is not to say that the department monolithically slid from one philosophical position to another. What needs to be stressed, some will argue, is that a range of opinions exist in the Treasury at any one time. But the key questions are the degree to which opinions diverge and whether the differences are over fundamental issues. In describing such a large-scale change I am, of course, offering a generalisation, and like all generalisations about institutional viewpoints, it does not assume that the Treasury is perfectly harmonious but that there is enough agreement on issues for individual idiosyncracies to be safely ignored.

Even so, it might still be argued that in attempting to show that the Treasury's outlook was either largely Keynesian or largely neoclassical (or a mixture of the two), I have ignored the fact that the department is for the most part responding in its daily activities to pragmatic policy considerations. There is, admittedly, a risk of overphilosophising Treasury activities. But an even greater risk is to ignore the fact that ideas do not exist in a vacuum. Utterances by the Treasury on what powers governments have or do not have in seeking to maintain economic stability, pronouncements on the causes of inflation and unemployment, calls for more attention to be paid to the question of efficient resource allocation, warnings on the deleterious consequences of too much spending and too little saving — such things are of course limited by the need to put forward views that are politically acceptable and by the Treasury's need to be seen as an impartial adviser. But, and this is too often forgotten, such things are informed ultimately by the economic method and philosophy which Treasury officers have learnt at university and in their departmental training. Every economist, every treasury officer makes sense of reality through an interpretative framework (which is itself moulded by a variety of forces). The delineation of this framework is the first step in moving beyond superficial analysis of economic debate.

The tendency in popular discussion is to see debates between economists as arising essentially from different views on the efficacy and consequences of particular policy proposals. The issues are perceived to be essentially technical. For instance, are budget deficits really inflationary? And are price changes the result of changes in the money supply or vice versa? What is insufficiently recognised is that underpinning economic debate are different conceptions of how the economy does and should work. Significantly, the Treasury itself has argued, in a recent paper devoted to structural change, that 'basically different mental pictures of how the Australian economy works underlie different policy prescriptions in this area'.[1] By pointing to the transition from Keynesianism to neoclassicism the importance of this particular aspect of economic debate — the different 'mental pictures' of economists — will I hope become clearer.

As well as this, while the analysis of Treasury thought in terms of two models may involve the risk of overphilosophising the Treasury's approach to economic problems, it is infinitely superior to the alternative of descriptivism. For such constructs are useful for pointing to underlying assumptions, for providing a framework within which to organise the ideas presented in Treasury documents (rather than simply trying to summarise and catalogue them), for making comparisons between one period and another, and for finding the point of departure in the views of different institutions and individuals.[2]

The Treasury line

This book is a completely revised version of my doctoral dissertation. The process of rewriting and reworking the thesis was aided by the comments of Professor G.C. Harcourt, formerly of Adelaide now of Cambridge, and Professor A.W. Coats, of the University of Nottingham. My colleagues at the University of Melbourne, Mrs Marjorie Harper (Economic History) and Dr Robert Dixon (Economics) offered incisive comments on chapter 2. Professor P. Groenewegen, of the University of Sydney, read the entire penultimate draft. I have made many changes in the light of his detailed comments. My greatest intellectual debt is to Professor Boris Schedvin who, as teacher, thesis supervisor and now colleague, has had a marked influence not only on the nature of this book but on my approach to economic history in general. Several former Treasury officers, all with long experience in the department, read either parts of, or the entire, penultimate draft. Their comments were most enlightening and I gratefully acknowledge their assistance. With one exception, I have thought it best not to identify these officers. I would also like to thank the Australian Information Service and the National Library, Canberra, for permission to reproduce photographs. Finally, thanks to my wife, Simone, for her patience and support.

I

Setting the scene

1

An introduction to Lean — Setting the scene

1
An introduction to the Treasury

BEFORE the early 1970s a mood of confidence and optimism pervaded postwar Australia: confidence that knowledge of the Australian economic system was now sufficient (and could be progressively refined) to achieve continuous full employment and thereby banish permanently the economic insecurity of the interwar years; optimism that the future would be yet another step along the path of linear economic progress. A manifestation and a source of this optimism was the fact that from World War II onwards, Australian governments abandoned prewar norms and explicitly acknowledged a responsibility for managing the economy. Keynesian theory and wartime experience had shown that this was both necessary and possible. The task of economic management came to be interpreted as a responsibility for maintaining not only internal and external balance but also continuous economic growth and sustained increases in living standards. In fulfilling these responsibilities the procurement of economic expertise became essential. Demand for the services of economists grew and gave rise to the employment of an ever-increasing number of economists in the public service, often at senior levels. Throughout the 1950s and 1960s, a period often referred to as the Age of Keynes, members of the economics profession had cause for seeing themselves as the architects of material prosperity. Governments made proud comparisons between pre- and postwar conditions and congratulated themselves and their advisers on contributing, primarily by the use of flexible demand management policies, to Australia's record of reasonably high growth, low inflation and very low unemployment.

Eventually, however, optimism was to give way to pessimism, confidence to puzzlement. With the dramatic deterioration in the condition of the Australian economy during the 1970s, the Keynesian wisdom came to be viewed with increasing scepticism. By the mid-1970s mainstream economics was said to be in crisis and began to be derided as an impotent collection of conflicting ideas and policy prescriptions. Its practitioners were criticised for being unable to offer an effective solution to the twin evils of inflation and unemployment. Any semblance of consensus within the discipline vanished, though within official circles the neoclassical school gained the ascendancy.

Yet in the midst of economic difficulties and in the midst of claims that the discipline was intellectually bankrupt, economic policy and economic ideas generated, if anything, more rather than less public interest. And greater, not less, attention came to be given to the institutions responsible for formulating policy recommendations. The Australian Treasury, which throughout most of the postwar period had acted as the government's chief adviser on economic and financial matters, entered the limelight. In the second half of the 1970s federal governmental economic initiatives and attitudes were sometimes referred to as the economics of the Stone Age — an epithet in dubious honour of John Stone, secretary to the Treasury, 1979–84. Such was the perceived influence of the Treasury and such was the growing interest in the nature of its advice.

This book seeks to put the Treasury's present economic philosophy into perspective and to show, among other things, the myopia of those who assume that the Treasury's present outlook is simply a product of the 1970s, something accompanying the onset of stagflation and the rise to importance of John Stone. It is written on the premise that such an exercise is valuable in itself, given the department's influence on economic policy advice, but also on the premise that a study of the Treasury can be used as a vehicle for investigating other rather neglected aspects of Australia's postwar economic history. It can be used, for instance, to chart the major attitudinal changes which have occurred within the Australian economics profession and to explore the interaction between changing economic conditions and problems and changing economic philosophies.

If one is to appreciate fully the evolution of the Treasury line, one needs to have some understanding of the institutional context out of which the department's philosophy has emerged. We start therefore with an account of the character of the department, its responsibilities, its reputation within the public service, its self-image, its organisational structure and its recruitment pattern.

Role and responsibilities

Before the 1930s the Australian Treasury's role was tightly circumscribed and its importance limited. Its role was a reflection in part of the federal government's limited role and powers in the macroeconomic field. Its job was simply to act as the government's accounts keeper, a task which involved overseeing the raising of revenue for government activities, controlling the amount of money going in and out of the public account and, as part of this, controlling departmental spending. The Treasury was also responsible for the note issue — a responsibility taken over from the trading banks (and from the Queensland government) in 1910. Treasury attitudes were likewise circumscribed. Dominated by accounting principles, Treasury officers were imbued with a keen interest to ensure value for money, to prevent profligate spending, to maintain departmental spending within prescribed limits and, if possible, to reduce expenditure.

During the 1930s, however, the Treasury's influence upon financial and economic affairs began to be enlarged, a development linked directly with the establishment at the end of the 1920s of the compulsory Loan Council. The council was significant, first, in that it was a symbol of the growing financial domination of the federal government over the states and, second, in that it gave rise to a measure of centralised decision-making in economic policy, something previously lacking. Unlike the voluntary council, the role of the new statutory council was not merely to coordinate the borrowing programs of the state and federal governments (with the aim of avoiding excessive competition for loan funds), but to exercise control over the scale of these programs. The council, however, did no more than establish the broad principles for loan policies. It was left to the Treasury, which acted as the council's secretariat, to put these principles into effect.[1] The Treasury became increasingly concerned with the day-to-day management of the public debt (including the task of advising on the conversion and repayment of loans) and with assessing and providing for the loan requirements of the various governments, state and federal.

Even greater changes in the department's role were to occur during World War II. The war was associated with a marked increase in the financial power and budgetary obligations of the federal government; the responsibilities of the Treasury increased accordingly. The war saw, in particular, the introduction of uniform tax legislation in 1942, by which the federal government became for the remainder of the war (and after it, through legislation passed in 1946), the sole levier of income and company taxes in Australia. The war saw also the Labor government assume responsibility for a variety of social service benefits, including widows' pensions, funeral benefits, unemployment and sickness benefits, hospital benefits and tuberculosis benefits. And not long after the completion of the war, the Labor government established the Commonwealth Employment Service. The inevitable result of these initiatives was an increase in the importance of the Treasury and a marked extension of the areas over which it had to exercise financial control.

But for the Treasury an even more significant wartime development was the acceptance by the federal government of the notion of economic control or management. The economy was now to be kept under close and continuous surveillance; not only present but prospective trends in spending and the level of economic activity would be under scrutiny. Furthermore, aggregate expenditure was to be consciously and purposively manipulated to iron out boom-slump cycles and maintain full employment. Such activities required a vast array of statistics, especially of the Keynesian aggregate type. They required also personnel capable of interpreting these statistics and recommending appropriate policies. Such tasks became largely the preserve of the Treasury. The department emerged from the war responsible for both financial *and* economic management. Not only did the Treasury have to act as the keeper of the public purse, but now it also had to make recommendations on how budgetary, monetary and other policies could be used to regulate the level of economic activity.

During the war and intermittently afterwards, the argument was raised that it was a mistake to assign to the Treasury responsibility for both of these functions. Financial and economic management, it was argued either explicitly or implicity, were best performed by two separate departments. For instance, in 1943, Harold Holt, then on the opposition front bench, insisted that 'it is notorious that the job of the Treasury is not to put forward progressive schemes, such as we would expect from the Department of Post-War Reconstruction, but to scrutinise closely the proposals of other Departments. Its policy is invariably one of retrenchment and that is the mental approach of its officers in the proper exercise of their duty'. It had been a 'serious administrative blunder', as such, to have appointed Chifley head of both Treasury and Postwar Reconstruction.[2] Six years later, J.J. Dedman, having taken over from Chifley as minister for postwar reconstruction, offered a similar view: 'The Treasury is, by tradition, and rightly so, conservative. It is more concerned with the examination and criticism of policies and proposals formulated elsewhere than it is with the preparation of such policies itself. It has the steady pressure of day-to-day financial business on it all the time. This is not the atmosphere in which we look for the future development of our broad policies.'[3] It was essential therefore that an economic division be established in the Prime Minister's Department which would act as the chief source of advice on economic policy matters.

These sorts of arguments were to re-emerge periodically throughout the postwar period. But in each instance the Treasury was able to withstand the attack. In 1976, however, in a surprise move, the Fraser government decided to split the department — although as it turned out financial management was entrusted not to the Treasury but to the new Department of Finance, the Treasury being left in charge of economic matters. Just why the department was split in 1976 will be discussed in a later chapter. The point to note for now is that the Treasury continued to exercise dual responsibility for financial and economic management for over three decades. While this study focuses on Treasury economic thought, it will be seen that during those three decades the department's traditional role of financial management helped shape in a variety of ways its attitude toward economic issues and policies.

Organisation

Accompanying the change in the Treasury's responsibilities was a change in its administrative structure. In 1946 a major reorganisation took place which involved compressing the existing eleven sections into five divisions:[4] Loans and General Services; Budget and Accounting; Banking, Trade and Industry; Social Services; and General Financial and Economic Policy (GFEP). GFEP, established as a section in 1943, was testimony to the change in the Treasury's responsibilities which occurred during the war. By the end of 1945 GFEP consisted of five officers, all with economics training. As the name suggests, its responsibility was to provide advice on general economic policy issues and their financial implications as well as to undertake economic research. GFEP is the division which is of most concern to this study. It formed the nucleus of economic expertise within the department; the concern of other divisions was essentially financial rather than economic. The power and importance of GFEP was to increase steadily after the war, a reflection of the importance attached to stabilisation policy, both internal and external.

The 1946 organisational structure remained intact for a remarkably long time. During the 1950s and 1960s the department chose to expand by increasing the division of labour within the existing structure rather than by establishing new divisions. Under the 1946 reorganisation the department comprised a secretary, deputy secretary, first assistant secretary, and five assistant secretaries. Though the increase was certainly not dramatic, the department could boast by 1968 a secretary, two deputy secretaries, five first assistant secretaries, and thirteen assistant secretaries.

The expansion of GFEP during this period was particularly noticeable. Having only five officers in 1945, it consisted in 1966 of four branches (Home Finance, Overseas Finance, Research and Information, and Economic and Financial Surveys), each headed by an assistant secretary. Home Finance was made up of two sections: Budget Policy and Commonwealth–State relations. Likewise, Economic and Financial Surveys comprised the Expenditure Survey and Resources sections, while Overseas Finance comprised the Balance of Payments and International Relations sections.

The Treasury's expansion must be seen in perspective. Throughout the postwar period the department's responsibilities and workload tended to increase more rapidly than the additions to available staff, with the result that a shortage of staff became an enduring Treasury phenomenon. In 1964 R.W. Cole of the Treasury could point to 'the continuing, indeed growing, shortage through the 1950s of staff of adequate calibre and attainments'. This problem, he said, was then endemic to the public service.[5] The situation was not much better in the 1960s, as Bruce Juddery testifies: 'In the late 1960s the Treasury was understaffed and over-worked, the more so the closer one approached the top. For many second division officers, the flow of paperwork had become a flood which threatened to engulf them.'[6]

A major reorganisation of the Treasury was made in 1969 to improve this situation. The reorganisation involved the creation of three additional divisions: Overseas Economic Relations (OER), Financial Institutions, and Defence and Works. It involved also a considerable bolstering of the Treasury's upper echelons. Between September 1968 and September 1969 the number of first assistant and assistant secretaries increased from thirteen to twenty-two. Over the same period the number of Class 11 third division officers jumped from 36 to fifty-five.[7] The then secretary, Sir Richard Randall, attempted to gain a third deputy secretaryship but failed to persuade the Public Service Board. This decision, however, was later reversed and in 1971 the position of deputy secretary (economic) was created.

Chart 1.1: The Australian Treasury, 1974

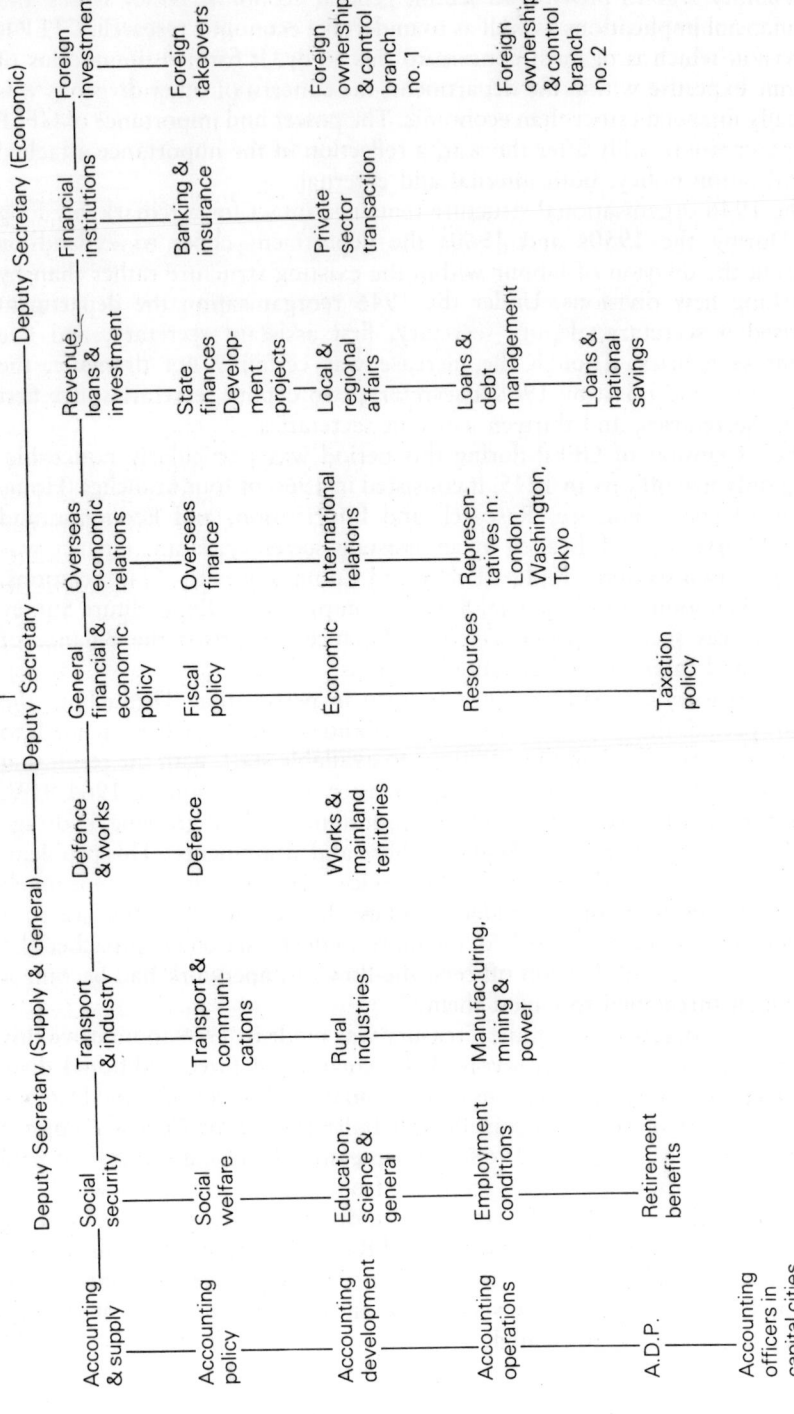

Introduction to the Treasury

As a result of the reorganisation, and with the creation of the Foreign Investment Division in 1972, the number of divisions responsible mainly for economic policy advice expanded from one to four, with responsibility for advice on *general* economic policy matters shared by GFEP and OER, and with Financial Institutions and Foreign Investment acting as 'specialist' divisions. (The organisational structure of the Treasury as it had evolved by 1974 is revealed in Chart 1.1.) GFEP was now formally responsible for the

> continuous assessment of current and prospective conditions and provision of advice on appropriate policies, including: budgetary policy — matters relating to expenditure, revenue and deficit/surplus and means of achieving overall budgetary objectives; monetary policy — matters relating to the control of the money supply, official interest rates etc.; incomes and prices matters — trends in income and price levels and wages policy.[8]

OER's concern was with external financial and economic policy issues, 'including the balance of payments, the exchange rate, the working of international economic and monetary systems, international economic development and aid issues, Australia's role in international financial affairs, economic relations with other countries and Australia's membership of various international organisations'.[9] In short, then, after 1969 GFEP was concerned predominantly with internal (domestic) matters, OER with external matters. But as one would expect, there was a degree of overlap between the concerns of the two divisions. To state the obvious, GFEP could hardly be restrained from taking an active interest in external policy and its implications for the domestic situation. GFEP remained in fact the main division responsible, as one ex-Treasury officer succinctly put it, 'for advising on the broad macroeconomic picture and the overall economic policy framework'.[10] It was GFEP which had the main responsibility for preparing the documents upon which this book is based.

The rise of the Treasury economist

Given the changes in its responsibilites, it is not surprising that World War II marked the beginning of a fundamental transformation in the educational qualifications of Treasury recruits. The most important changes were, first, the appointment of university graduates to the department's upper echelons and, second, an overwhelming preference for economics graduates. These changes, however, were not unique to the Treasury and should be seen as part of a broader revolution in the recruitment patterns of the public service and beyond.

Advancement in the public service traditionally involved a tedious climb from the bottom ranks. Recruits, usually in their early teens, entered by competitive examination. After World War I, however, the vast majority of vacancies were filled by ex-servicemen. Sol Encel says that the educational standards of these recruits were usually 'lower than those prescribed for normal peacetime entrants — themselves not notably high'.[11] By the beginning of the 1930s there was considerable pressure on the Commonwealth Public Service Board to introduce a system of graduate recruitment so as to improve standards within the service. In response to this pressure the Commonwealth Public Service Act was amended in 1933 and section 36A inserted, thereby permitting the recruitment of graduates under the age of twenty-five. But a rider was added restricting the annual intake to no more than 10 per cent of the proposed outside appointments to the third division. It was not long, however, before the scheme was deemed a failure: the number of graduates entering the service under the scheme consistently fell far short of the 10 per cent quota. It would seem that with relatively low wage levels, with little prospect of rapid advancement, and often subjected to menial tasks, graduates looked elsewhere for employment.[12]

With the failure of the graduate recruitment scheme and, more particularly, with the dominance of ex-servicemen, the public service was left ill equipped to handle the administrative strains imposed by World War II. With the onset of war it soon became apparent that outside help was needed if the federal government was to handle its increased responsibilities successfully. An urgent recruitment drive resulted in the appointment of businessmen, academic staff and state public servants to the commonwealth service. In the appointment of outside help, traditional promotional channels were ignored; seniority gave way to skill and expertise. The number of employees employed under the Public Service Act jumped from 47 000 in 1939 to 95 000 in 1946; by 1951 the figure was 147 000. Most of the outside help entering the service during the war were employed on a temporary basis, with the result that over half of the 95 000 employees in 1946 were designated as temporaries. Many of the temporaries, however, elected to retain their positions after the war ended; by virtue of sections 44 and 47 of the Public Service Act they were granted permanent status. In 1953 fourteen of the 29 first division officers in the service had been wartime temporaries.

Of significance to the Treasury, and to the subsequent evolution of the Treasury line, was the fact that the war was associated with an influx of young economics graduates. Perhaps the most notable of the Treasury's economics recruits was H.C. Coombs, a doctoral graduate of the London School of Economics, who was borrowed from the Commonwealth Bank at the outbreak of war. Coombs retained the position of Treasury economist until 1942 when he moved to Melbourne as director of rationing; later he was to head the Department of Postwar Reconstruction. Other economics recruits included Frederick Wheeler and R.J. Whitelaw. Wheeler, who entered the Treasury in 1939 in the new position of research officer, had studied commerce part-time at the University of Melbourne during the 1930s while working at the State Savings Bank. Whitelaw joined the Treasury in 1941 as research officer. Whitelaw, too, was a graduate of the University of Melbourne, holding degrees in both arts and commerce (majoring in economics in both). In 1943 Wheeler and Whitelaw joined with Frank Pryor, an honours arts graduate of the University of Sydney who had entered the Treasury in 1941, and N.F. Stuart, an MA graduate of the University of Melbourne who had joined the department in 1940 after working in the Economist's Department of the Commonwealth Bank and with E.J. Morgan & Co., to form the newly established GFEP section. Wheeler was placed in charge.

Before World War II senior Treasury posts were dominated, as one would expect, by men with accounting backgrounds. In 1944 the Treasury was headed by S.G. McFarlane, the secretary, A.C. Joyce, assistant secretary (Administrative), J. Brophy, assistant secretary (Finance), and W.C. Thomas, assistant secretary (General). Joyce, Brophy and McFarlane were deeply imbued in accounting techniques and conventions. Brophy, for instance, born in 1889, joined the public service in 1908. He was appointed accountant at the Brisbane Sub-Treasury in 1919 and remained there until 1927. From 1927 to 1930 he was accountant at the Melbourne Sub-Treasury. In 1933 he moved to Canberra to become Treasury accountant and in 1943 was appointed assistant secretary in charge of finance. Similarly, both McFarlane and Joyce entered the public service at a relatively young age and spent many years in accounting posts on their way to the higher Treasury echelons.

The influx of economics graduates during the war was the beginning of a noteworthy trend in the recruitment pattern of the public service. In 1948 when section 36A was resumed (it had been suspended in 1941), the various government departments asked for 134 graduates in economics, 23 in economics or arts with a major in economics, 37 in arts and 27 in law. The departments actually received only 56 graduates in arts, 31 in economics and nine in law. Nevertheless, it was becoming clear that Copland was correct in 1944 when he said 'we may dislike this new breed of theorists who masquerade under the name of economists, but they will be with us for a long time'.[13] Four years later S.J. Butlin could comment:

> the last ten years have seen an outstanding new development. The economic adviser has taken the back-seat where he belongs, and where he need not trouble the driver who keeps his eye on the road; in his place is the economic expert who has gone into the public service as a career... Scarcely a department but has its economic division or section, its Principal Economist, its research officers, and its subscription to *Econometrica*. The Public Service Board has established permanent scales of salaries for economists of various grades, with specifications of the required qualifications, and the conditions for climbing the promotion ladder. In Canberra the economist has arrived.[14]

Certainly within the Treasury the economist had arrived. This was evident in 1951 when, with the appointment of Roland Wilson as secretary, the Treasury was headed for the first time by an economist. Wilson's qualifications were impeccable: a Bachelor of Commerce from the University of Tasmania, a Diploma of Economics and Political Science from Oxford, a doctorate from Oxford and a doctorate from the University of Chicago. By the end of the 1950s economics and commerce graduates dominated the second division of the Treasury. Table 1.1 shows that this trend continued and intensified in the 1960s and 1970s. The table is grouped according to the chronological divisions adopted in chapters 5 to 8, and shows the educational qualifications

Table 1.1 Academic qualifications of first and second division Treasury officers, 1956–79

	1956–62	1963–67	1968–72	1973–79
BEc/BCom	11	13	26	34
BA	7	7	9	16
BSc	1	1	2	6
BEng	–	–	–	3
LLB	–	–	1	2
BPhil	–	–	–	1
BEd	–	–	–	1
Diplomas	3	1	1	2
MA	2	2	3	3
MEc	–	1	2	1
MSc	–	–	1	1
LLM	–	1	–	–
MPA	–	–	1	1
MBA	–	–	–	1
PhD	3	5	3	3
Total degrees, diplomas	27	31	49	75
Honours	5	6	14	22
No qualifications	3	3	3	3
Unknown	–	–	5	10
Total officers	22	25	44	62

Source: Compiled from various *Federal Guides* and *Commonwealth Directories*
Notes: 1 Information on educational qualifications comes from the listings in *Who's Who in Australia* and from the Treasury *Submission to the RCAGA*, Attachment (c).
2 The Table does not include officers in the Insurance and Actuarial Branch nor those in the Defence Division. It does include, however, officers in the Defence and Works Division — created in 1969.
3 Four of the five officers who have Masters degrees do not state their first degree.

of first and second division Treasury officers (assistant secretaries, first assistant secretaries, deputy secretaries and secretaries). The dominance of economics and commerce graduates is obvious but is in fact understated as many of the arts graduates and some of the science graduates majored in economics.

It should be noted that the Treasury's eager search for young economics recruits was not simply a response to the department's enlarged responsibilities. It was prompted also by a desire to bring about a more balanced age distribution within the department. In a 1946 memorandum, setting forth proposals on how the department should be organised to cope with its new responsibilities, the Treasury noted that a large proportion of senior officers would soon be retiring, including the secretary and deputy secretary. The lesson drawn was that

> the crux of the Treasury problem is not only that of a suitable organisation to meet peace time requirements. It is vital to recruit as rapidly as possible sufficient high grade officers at varying levels to fill in the gaps caused by recent losses of staff and

the growth of new responsibilities and to develop the present establishment and to provide against the retirements of senior officers within the next five to ten years.[15]

It was essential that there be a 'substantial number' of new appointments. But the department was adamant that these recruits be of the highest standard. The importance of the Treasury's responsibilities was such that 'the calibre of the Treasury staff should be maintained at a very high level and in particular at a higher average level than that which obtains in other departments'. Such staff could only be obtained if the financial rewards were adequate:

> If the right type of men are to be recruited and retained in the future there must be some recasting of the salary structure. This is particularly so because the Treasury now requires a substantial number of young men of outstanding ability and qualifications who would not be attracted by a career in the Treasury involving stage by stage promotion through the ranks. Accordingly the view is held that a percentage of young officers should be recruited under a system of classification different from the normal and the maxima of the salary ranges must be fixed at a level high enough to attract recruits of outstanding ability. In the proposed organization this is provided for in relation to Research Officers.

Some idea of the Treasury's success in obtaining staff of 'outstanding ability and qualifications' can be obtained by comparing total degrees or diplomas with total officers in Table 1.1. More detailed information on this was provided by the evidence submitted by the Treasury in 1975 to the Royal Commission on Australian Government Administration (RCAGA or Coombs Commission). This revealed a high educational standard among Treasury officers. Out of a survey of 685 officers, 497 had completed tertiary qualifications, 96 had incomplete qualifications (such as incomplete degrees) and only 92 had no tertiary qualifications. Of the 497 officers with completed tertiary qualifications, 389 had one qualification, 90 had two qualifications and 54 had three qualifications, giving a total of 623 degrees. Table 1.2 classifies these 623 degrees according to discipline. It shows, as one would expect, that economics and commerce graduates were dominant, not just among senior officers but throughout Treasury ranks.

The high level of educational attainment of Treasury officers is indicated also by the fact that the Treasury has a much higher proportion of graduate and diplomate staff than the public service overall, as can be seen in Table 1.3.

Table 1.2 Completed tertiary courses by discipline, as of 1975

Administration / Management	19
Arts and humanities	52
Economics, commerce and art (economics)	442
Education/teaching	22
Law	10
Science and arts (mathematics)	63
Computing	8
PhD	7
Total Qualifications	623

Source: Reproduced from the Treasury Submission to the RCAGA, Attachment (a).

The large percentage of honours degrees shown in Table 1.1 is also relevant in evaluating the department's educational standards. Although this is evident particularly from 1969 onwards, the fact that the table refers to senior officers means that many of these honours graduates would have entered the Treasury much earlier. Finally, Table 1.4 shows not only a particularly high proportion of honours or higher-degree graduates among Treasury officers but reveals also that the Treasury proportion is well above that of the public service as a whole and has been steadily increasing, whereas that of the service has remained constant.

Table 1.3 Graduate or diplomate staff as a proportion of permanent third division staff in selected departments, 1968–74

	1968	1970	1972	1974
	%	%	%	%
Public Service Board	38.6	45.8	51.1	49.6
Treasury	20.9	33.9	41.8	48.6
Service overall	14.2	23.8	25.8	26.3

Source: Reproduced from Appendix 3.A: 'The Career Service Survey' Paper 11: 'The Co-ordinating Departments' in RCAGA *Appendix* vol. 3, Canberra: AGPS, 1976.

Table 1.4 Honours or higher degrees as a proportion of degrees held by third division permanent staff in selected departments, 1968–74

	1968	1972	1974
	%	%	%
Public Service Board	23.3	30.5	34.3
Treasury	34.8	43.0	45.6
Service overall	27.1	27.8	27.4

Source: As for Table 1.3.

While the evidence is clear that there was a fundamental shift in the department's recruitment pattern after the war and a continuing improvement in its educational standards, the shift neither happened overnight nor occurred uniformly within the various divisions of the Treasury. One officer who joined GFEP at the beginning of the 1950s has pointed out to the author that GFEP stood apart in being 'a new creation staffed with graduates'. The division contrasted markedly with much of the public service and the rest of the Treasury which, as he puts it, 'was non-graduate and dated from the pre-war period'. Right through the 1950s the third division of the public service 'still comprised mainly people who had passed their Leaving Certificates'. Such was the contrast that 'inside GFEP there was an almost quasi-academic atmosphere in which free debate could occur on issues'.[16]

Commenting on the role of GFEP, one of the division's original members has suggested to the author that

> FEP was always an integral part of an administrative machine; it was never an ivory tower or economics debating society, but an area which was concerned with

the formulation *and* execution of Government policy. Within the Treasury, FEP was regarded for many years as, in effect, the 'Secretary's Branch' and the Permanent Head of the day invariably selected his Executive Assistant from personnel in this area... It would not be correct, therefore, to regard FEP as simply an Economist Branch or Division; it was no accident that, after the first year or two, the Head of the area relinquished the title of Economist in favour of the Assistant Secretary and First Assistant Secretary nomenclature.[17]

For this reason, he continued, there needs to be some slight qualification to the argument that with the establishment of GFEP and with Wilson's accession to the secretaryship 'the economist had arrived':

In a broad sense this view is beyond dispute but it would be wrong to infer from this that appointment to the FEP area was open only to economic experts or that economic expertise was a sufficient condition for success in that area. I can recall, for example, graduates with first-class honours economics degrees who had little aptitude for FEP work and, conversely, some graduates with little or no formal training in economics who performed extremely well in FEP. In my experience, a knowledge of and sensitivity to political practicalities was one of the essential requirements in most areas of FEP work and this consideration was important in the recruitment of new appointees.

The departmental line

In performing its role of economic management, the department has often been criticised for presenting and sticking to a single line of advice. Patrick Weller points, for instance, to the department's 'reputation for giving the advice it considers to be correct, regardless of the known policy preferences of ministers and, indeed, sometimes sticking to those views long after an alternative strategy has been adopted by a government'.[18]

A prominent example of the Treasury's determination to see that its single line of advice was accepted occurred in 1974 under the Whitlam government. Whitlam's speech writer, Graham Freudenberg, provided a first-hand account of the department's behaviour:

Treasury weakened its own influence with the Labor Government not because its advice was often unpalatable but because it was always monolithic. Treasury refused to set out the economic options available to the politicians. It presented its advice on an all-or-nothing, take-it-or-leave-it basis. If its first advice was rejected, Treasury volunteered no other. If Cabinet persisted in rejecting the original advice, some Treasury officials then used their contacts with other departments, the press, business, and Opposition spokesmen, to build support for its line.[19]

The advice proffered by Treasury to the Labor government was the now-famous 'short, sharp shock' strategy which aimed, by a series of deflationary measures, to combat inflation by raising unemployment. The strategy was first put forward in July 1974 at a meeting of senior cabinet members. The kitchen cabinet, as it was known, at first accepted the Treasury's proposals. However, full cabinet, and later caucus, rejected them, believing them to be economically irresponsible and morally reprehensible. The Treasury apparently took no heed of this rejection and in August 1974 recommended in its cabinet submission a budget strategy along the lines of its earlier short, sharp shock proposals:

> In the submissions there was no attempt to discuss the issues that had been debated in the previous months. Treasury's only concession to the idea that demand inflation might no longer be the main problem was to suggest that an increase in expenditure would 'restimulate demand pressures'; in the draft [submission written earlier in August] it suggested an increase would 'sustain' them. Otherwise it treated alternative economic strategies with contempt and dismissed them in a line. For instance, *Economic Situation and Prospects* [one of the main Treasury submissions] declared that inflation was the major problem and then stated: 'There is another view-point. That is that over-full employment must be maintained all of the time.' There was little recognition of the fact that alternative strategies might have some value; the submissions provided a blanket dismissal of ideas which, after all, had the support of caucus and of a substantial section of cabinet.[20]

Amid growing concern that cost, rather than demand, pressures were the chief economic problem, the department suggested a tax increase of $400 million and a reduction in government expenditure of $600 million which, it maintained, would result in an overall deficit of around $250 million and a domestic surplus of around $320 million.

There is no suggestion here that the Treasury is somehow unique in pushing a departmental line. The method of presenting a single set of options is a common bureaucratic ploy. There are strong reasons for using such a tactic: 'To show alternatives is to invite debate; to admit weaknesses encourages rejection; to highlight the less welcome alternatives is tactically unwise.'[21] It does not always follow of course that the strategy of discounting options is a necessary preliminary to gaining influence and acceptance. The strategy can sometimes backfire, as the Treasury discovered during the Whitlam years. When advice is offered on a take-it-or-leave-it basis, there is always the possibility that it will indeed be left.

Treasury unity

The Treasury has acquired a reputation for placing a high premium on loyalty, on maintaining a united front. In explaining the basis of this reputation, it is clear that the department's role is of fundamental importance. It is useful here to consider how Richard Randall, then first assistant secretary in charge of GFEP, described in 1954 the Treasury's role:

> Each year the requests for expenditure, coming from Departments and from people outside the Government, add up to a sum considerably greater than the Government is willing to spend. That, however, is not all. The Government, if left to itself, might be willing to spend a certain total sum of money in the year; but whatever that sum might be the taxpayers always think it is far too much and they demand, energetically and specifically, that expenditure be cut down so that taxation can be

reduced. Somehow these competing demands must be reconciled and it is the benign role of the Treasury to reconcile them. It is a benign role because, if someone did not act as mediator, the position would become chaotic, even violent. If all the people who demand additional expenditures were brought together with all those who demand tax reductions and left to fight it out, there could be open strife. Scenes of disorder might disgrace the capital city.

By interposing itself between the contending parties, the Treasury prevents this kind of thing from happening. It is the keeper of the Queen's Peace. It holds the contenders apart and, taking them one by one, with gentle persuasive art induces them to abate their demands until, at some point, the two sides of the account which is the budget add up to the same figure. Unfortunately, though perhaps inevitably, the Treasury shares the fate of all peace-makers in the process. Enthusiasts for this or that policy often mistake the Treasury for the real opposition and vent the strength of their feelings upon it. This accounts for the air of sad resignation which Treasury officers come to acquire in the course of time.[22]

As Randall's comments suggest, the Treasury is sometimes seen by its rivals with unabashed enmity and sometimes at best as a necessary evil. The RCAGA pointed out in its report that the Treasury was often criticised for being 'too privileged, too powerful, and too prone to substitute its own judgements, its own values and its own priorities for those of other departments, ministers and the government itself'.[23] Such criticism is only to be expected, given the Treasury's role. As the report quite correctly pointed out, 'it would be surprising if Treasury were a popular department. The task of drawing attention to the reality of constraints on what ministers, departments, parliamentarians and groups and individuals in the community would like to do or have done is not one which easily wins friends for those who perform it'.

The link between the Treasury's role and its apparent unity lies in this criticism which it is prone to receive and the criticism which it itself is expected to bestow on proposals which come before it. The fact that the Treasury has acquired a negative image breeds camaraderie — in a world of conflict, unity is indeed strength, a shield to deflect persistent attacks. An emphasis on unity springs also from a desire to maintain power. While most if not all departments desire power, in the Treasury's case power is deemed a necessity. For there will inevitably be a conflict between spending proposals and available financial resources, and if the Treasury is to resolve this conflict successfully, which, it is argued, it must, it is necessary that it obtain power and influence. It would be an exercise in reductionism to assign the Treasury's concern with power merely to a pathological or ego-fulfilling desire for power as such. To the Treasury, power is a means to an end: access to power is necessary in order to fulfil its guardianship role. Given this need, unity is crucial. For unity, or at least the appearance of unity, is an essential ingredient in getting and keeping power.

It is a mark of Treasury unity that promotion in the upper echelons of the department is normally an internal affair. Table 1.5 shows that a remarkably high percentage of Treasury officers have served only in that department. Such officers can be expected to have thoroughly accepted and internalised Treasury attitudes and canons of conduct and to be concerned that recruits develop and

Table 1.5 Second division career service — number of departments served in

	Public Service Board N = 9	Treasury N = 37	Service overall (excluding PMG) N = 548
		%	%
One	6	83.8	57.8
Two	2	16.2	26.3
Three or more	1		15.9

Source: As for Table 1.3.
Note: The Table is based upon responses to a career service survey instigated by the RCAGA in 1974.

display a similar temperament. But quite apart from any sort of socialisation process once a recruit joins the department, it is sometimes claimed that, as part of a conscious attempt to encourage departmental cohesion, the Treasury carefully selects recruits from leading universities and by a screening process attempts to choose individuals likely to accept the department's outlook and mores. In evidence before the RCAGA, however, Sir Frederick Wheeler strongly denied this. He insisted that 'I do not in any way accept that there is a doctrinal attitude to which you must conform before you can get entrance to the Treasury. It is demonstrably not so'.[24] Those former Treasury officers who have commented on this chapter firmly endorsed Wheeler's verdict.

The degree of unity in the Treasury is such that it seems reasonable to assume that generalisations can be made about the nature of Treasury thought. But this is not to argue that the department is composed solely of like-minded individuals. Despite the need for unity to ensure the continuation of power, disagreements inevitably occur within the department, as they do in all institutions. Indeed, the main theme of this book, that the Treasury's economic philosophy has changed in the postwar period, is an acknowledgement of the fact that the Treasury is not monolithic. Such change implies an element of disagreement; it implies the rejection of old interpretations and the injection of new ones. It would therefore be foolish to suggest that the views described in later chapters were held by all Treasury officers and all to the same degree.

Treasury rivals

The Treasury's authority in the field of economic policy advice, though considerable, has never been absolute. There is never any guarantee that the departmental line will be accepted. A host of factors are important here, including the 'political muscle' of the Treasurer, the persuasive power of the secretary, the attitude of the Prime Minister and other members of cabinet, and the number and relative strength of rival sources of economic advice.

To deal with the last of these, by 1950, with the Department of Postwar Reconstruction wound up, the Treasury held a clearly dominant position in the provision of economic policy advice. Its main rival was the newly established

Introduction to the Treasury

Economic Division in the Department of Prime Minister and Cabinet (PMC). The Economic Division, however, proved to be an ineffective alternative to the Treasury. L.F. Crisp has commented:

> Though, man for man, it may have matched a like number of Treasury men in native ability and training, if not always in experience, the Division was in fact a mere handful — in the early years a dozen at most. By contrast, the Treasury not only commanded incomparably more 'troops', but both their traditional *and* their relatively newly-developed functions alike presented them in their normal course of business with incomparably wider and more authoritative direct command of the stuff of policies and the most obvious levers of co-ordination.[25]

The division's potential power was nipped in the bud following the change of government late in 1949. Unlike Chifley, the new Prime Minister, R.G. Menzies, was not interested in economic policy-making and its detailed ramifications. Moreover, a major lesson for Menzies arising out of the events of 1941 was the need to maintain a harmonious relationship with the Country Party. Arthur Fadden, the Country Party leader and deputy prime minister, was Treasurer. Thus, any attempt to establish an effective alternative to the Treasury would have run the risk of placing coalition relationships in jeopardy. Under Menzies the Economic Division was left to wither.

The relative weakness of PMC's Economic Division meant that the Treasury had a virtual monopoly on budgetary and monetary matters through the 1950s and 1960s. On commercial matters, however, Treasury authority came to be effectively challenged in the late 1950s and during the 1960s by the Department of Trade (from 1964, Trade and Industry). As Glezer notes, the Department of Trade 'emerged in 1956 from a major departmental reorganization intended to concentrate policy-making on imports and exports in the one department and was intended by its founders to be one of the central economic policy units of the Commonwealth bureaucracy. Trade had the potential for much influence on primary and secondary industries and, with them, the rural and urban economies'.[26] This was a potential often realised, in large part because of the political strength of its minister, Sir John McEwen (Fadden's successor to the head of the Country Party), and the department's highly competent secretaries, Sir John Crawford and Sir Alan Westerman.

John Gorton's prime ministership (1968–71) saw Trade's influence begin to wane. It saw also, however, a rise in the importance of PMC as a source of economic policy advice. Gorton decided to split his department into a department of the Prime Minister and a cabinet office. Sir Lennox Hewitt, a former Treasury official, was placed in charge of the Prime Minister's Department and set about establishing a revitalised economic division which could provide Gorton with an alternative source of economic advice. Hewitt's reign, however, was short-lived. McMahon, Gorton's replacement, quickly set about restoring the department to the same structure and mode of operation as it had enjoyed in the pre-Gorton days and reinstated Sir John Bunting as the department's permanent head. Bunting was not particularly interested in economic issues and was determined that PMC would operate mainly as a secretariat. Treasury was temporarily relieved of a potential rival. Under Whitlam and particularly Fraser, however, PMC's role in economic policy advice was to undergo a resurgence, this despite the fact, as Ainsley Jolley puts it, that PMC 'has a comparatively small number of economists and is largely confined to providing broadbrush comments on policy'.[27] But unlike the Treasury-Trade rivalry of the 1960s, the differences in opinion between Treasury and the economists in PMC have rarely been fundamental (a notable exception being over the 1982–83 budget). This can be explained in part by the fact that a number of the leading economists in PMC have been ex-Treasury officers (in 1976, for instance, the department's two main advisers on macroeconomic policy, Ian Castles and Ed Visbord, were former senior Treasury officers).

The Treasury has long had a close working relationship with the Reserve Bank, the other principal source of advice on monetary policy. Consultation between the bank and the Treasury is frequent. The secretary to the Treasury is an ex officio member of the bank board. It would perhaps be inaccurate therefore to describe the bank as a Treasury rival. Moreover, the bank is not an independent institution: it reports to the Treasurer and legislative provisions exist which could be used by the Treasurer to direct bank policy. On the question of the relative importance of Treasury–Reserve Bank influence, Jolley's judgment is that

> In practice the Treasury has been more influential than the Reserve Bank in determining the main aggregates of monetary policy — the exchange rate, administered interest rate and government debt policy. The Bank is more influential in the day-by-day conduct of monetary policy — intervention in the money markets, the setting of the daily exchange rate, monitoring of the activity of the various financial institutions and informal controls over financial institutions.[28]

The maintenance of Treasury power

Of key significance in understanding how the Treasury was able to establish and maintain a dominant position in economic policy advice is the fact that its traditional function of financial controller enabled it to become involved in the whole gamut of governmental activities. As the Treasury itself noted in 1946, 'there is hardly any governmental activity which does not involve finance and expenditure and consequently involve Treasury consideration'. Similarly, 'there are few aspects of governmental activity which at one time or another do not come before the Treasury for examination and the formation of a considered opinion on the basis of which departmental action may be taken or advice tendered to the Minister'.[29] The Treasury's role of government accountant empowered it to participate in the activities of nearly all departmental and interdepartmental committees which involved expenditure of public funds. This not only enabled the Treasury to have its finger in every financial pie but enabled it also to claim that it was in the unique position of being able to consider spending proposals from a holistic point of view. 'Treasury,' as one senior officer put it, 'does not claim to be the seat of all wisdom, but it is in an advantageous position to see the financial picture as a whole.'[30]

Similarly, the Treasury was able to claim that it was the only department able to see the *economic* picture as a whole. Whereas departments such as Trade, Urban and Regional Development, National Development and so on were concerned only with particular aspects of the economy and represented particular interests, the Treasury could point to the fact that it was concerned with the full range of both domestic and external economic conditions and policies and with their interrelationships and was unencumbered by having to defend any specific interest or sector. Hence it could claim to be in a better position to judge what was or was not in the national interest. The present secretary to the Treasury, Bernie Fraser, has recently emphasised this point:

> Treasury advice is very broad in its perspective. More than other Departments, Treasury endeavours to take an economy-wide view and to be concerned with 'the general interest'. The Treasury does not have a narrow 'clientele' in the sense that most other departments do. It should have no particular sectional barrows to push.
>
> It is this responsibility for looking at the economy as a whole — 'the general interest' — which mainly distinguishes the Treasury from other departments. Treasury people are not necessarily any better or worse than people in other departments. But they do have other responsibilities and different interests to pursue.[31]

The Department of Trade provides a useful contrast with Treasury. Leon Glezer points out that the close identification of Trade with its minister, McEwen, had the eventual result of limiting the department's potential influence:

> During the 1960s the department was widely regarded as having become the minister's personal political machine ... McEwen ... turned Trade into his private bailiwick. His bureaucratic advisors appeared to their Canberra colleagues to be eagerly participating in this process. The minister's wants, rather than policy conviction, were seen to be central in the department's behaviour... Disquiet about the character of bureaucratic responsibility it had adopted reduced Trade's standing.

This situation had the additional effect of weakening departmental unity:

> The virtual abolition within Trade and Industry of the distinction between government policy and the minister's preferences generated tensions within as well as outside the department. While some found the politicized character stimulating, and in line with their conception of their professional role, others found it less palatable. It affected morale, as well as attracting recruiters from private industry. Both were reasons for the departure between 1967 and the end of the 1969 of some eighteen of the department's most senior officers, including three deputy secretaries. No other department had a similar rate of resignation.[32]

Glezer makes the additional point that Trade's role as representative of and adviser on sectional interests had both advantages and disadvantages. It was at first a source of strength for the department to represent both rural and secondary industry and to be entrusted with responsibility for both export and import policy. As the 1960s progressed, however, and as rural and secondary industry grew further apart on their attitude toward tariffs, 'the department found it difficult to maintain the support of those whose interests it had undertaken to promote. When one of these interests saw in the others a source of their troubles, the department came under strain.' As we have seen, the Treasury, unlike Trade, had no sectional barrows to push. It was able therefore to avoid the centrifugal forces which weakened Trade.

Treasury power in the provision of economic advice derived also from the fact that throughout the 1940s and 1950s and beyond the department was headed by treasurers who exercised both power and influence in cabinet. First under Chifley, then Fadden and Harold Holt, the Treasury was able to ensure that its view was accorded weight and (often decisive) influence in cabinet. Chifley, who became Treasurer in 1941, laid the foundations. As described by Paul Hasluck, Chifley was a 'tower of strength ... receptive to his department, strong in the Cabinet, shrewdly practical and quiet moving'.[33] From 1945 Chifley was in the unique position of being both Treasurer and Prime Minister. He was to retain both posts until 1949, and while he did so the Treasury's policy recommendations and analysis were given considerable weight. Fadden, like Chifley, was a powerful force in cabinet. As noted, he enjoyed the advantage of being both leader of the Country Party and deputy prime minister and this was a key reason why the Economic Division in PMC proved to be an ineffective alternative to the Treasury. Fadden remained Treasurer until 1958 and during that time the Treasury consolidated its power. He was succeeded by Harold Holt. Holt, too, was a firm supporter of the Treasury line and an effective advocate of the departmental line, though, as noted, Sir John McEwen proved an increasingly formidable opponent on commercial matters.

Reflecting on Labor's achievements, Chifley congratulated himself in 1950 on having built up a strong Treasury team. He told Fadden:

> Although I do not expect the Treasurer to admit the fact publicly, I feel that he must realise the debt he owes to previous Labour Administrations for having assembled in the Treasury such a group of outstandingly able officers. When Labour was in office it always paid great attention to the selection of officers to fill important positions in the Public Service, and when I was Treasurer I did not pay regard to the personal convictions of prospective appointees but was concerned solely with their competence. I wanted the highest order of ability.[34]

Here is another reason for the Treasury's authoritative position in economic matters: it acquired a reputation for unsurpassed intellectual strength and expertise. The analysis earlier of the department's educational qualifications suggests that there is indeed some substance to the notion that Treasury officers represent an educational elite within the public service. The Treasury is particularly proud of this reputation. One officer, in reply to criticism that the Treasury was 'educated and privileged, cossetted and selfish', answered simply: 'We earn our power by being right. People who get things wrong lose power.' Discussing the problems associated with acquiring staff for the

Introduction to the Treasury

Economic and Financial Surveys Branch, established at the end of 1962, another Treasury officer remarked:

> The fact is that people of the calibre and background training in economics required for this sort of work, if it is to be done at normal Treasury standards, are extremely short within Australia. Although positions at various levels in the Division have been advertised on a number of occasions for application by persons both inside and outside the Public Service, the response has been limited in terms of the quality sought. It would, no doubt, have been possible to fill vacant positions by lowering standards; but no long-term good could come of the acceptance of such a short-term view.[35]

Such comments, especially the reference to there being only a handful of people of the calibre to meet the Treasury's recruitment standards and the insistence that such standards would not be violated, reflect the department's pride in its intellectual expertise. They reflect also Chifley's declaration that he wanted people in the Treasury who were only of 'the highest order of ability' and the Treasury's own declaration in 1946 that it wanted recruits of 'outstanding ability and qualifications' who could raise the calibre of Treasury staff to 'a higher average level than that which obtains in other departments'. This tradition of impeccable intellectual standards, it can be noted, has served to reinforce the Treasury's conviction that its analysis of the economic situation is superior to those of others: not only does the department have a more holistic viewpoint but its analysis is assumed to be necessarily more rigorously analytical than that of rivals because of its greater intellectual depth.

Just as treasurers have been important in establishing and maintaining Treasury economic authority, so too have the secretaries to the department. Treasury was particularly fortunate in having Sir Roland Wilson as its permanent head from 1951 to 1966. Wilson's association with the Treasury began in fact in the 1930s. In 1932 Wilson left his post as lecturer in economics at the University of Tasmania to fill the newly created position of economist in the Commonwealth Bureau of Statistics. In 1936 he was appointed commonwealth statistician. In the same year, in recognition of his importance within the department, he was given the additional title of economic adviser to the Treasury. He held both positions until 1940 and again from 1946 to 1951. To some, Treasury and Wilson were synonymous — something not surprising after such a lengthy stewardship. Wilson was seen to be the epitome of the 'good Treasury man': confident, authoritative, resolute, academically gifted, coldly logical, acerbic and quick-witted. Wilson appears to have had an almost domineering relationship with his treasurers. Coombs recalls that Fadden 'greatly admired Roland Wilson's capacity, and depended heavily on his judgement, but he found Roland too cold and unyielding for a wholly satisfactory partner'. Coombs suggests that Fadden quite possibly 'was a little afraid of Wilson's razor-sharp intellect, his intolerance of human frailty and his acid tongue'.[36] He argues that when Holt was Treasurer he was heavily dependent on Wilson and that in Holt's work as Minister for Labour and National Service during World War II 'his association with Roland Wilson was a source of strength for him and when they came together again at the Treasury it ensured a continuance of that strength'.[37]

Wilson's immediate successors, Sir Richard Randall (1966–71) and Sir Frederick Wheeler (1971–79), were less successful than Wilson in securing acceptance of the Treasury view. This was not, however, so much a reflection of inferior ability or persuasive power but a reflection of the relative weakness and political vulnerability of several of their ministers — particularly Leslie Bury, Frank Crean and Jim Cairns — and more importantly the greater strength of opposition to their advice: Randall faced John Gorton's stubbornness; Wheeler faced the Labor caucus's hostility and distrust. Both men, however, were able to retire at a time when the Treasury was once again 'riding high', Randall in 1971 following the presentation of a budget closely in line with Treasury advice, Wheeler in 1979 when the Fraser government had apparently accepted the Treasury's insistent calls for a balanced budget and for the need to 'fight inflation first'.

Treasury power derives also from its access to, and sometimes monopolisation of, information. In 1975 the Task Force on Economic Policy attached to the RCAGA observed that one of the main criticisms levelled at the Treasury was that the department was 'unnecessarily reticent in providing information on the economic situation, the options available to the government, and the likely implications of exercising any one of those options'. In January 1979 a confidential report by a working party to the Crawford Committee on Structural Adjustment castigated the Treasury for not publishing its quarterly forecasts (which are based on its national income forecasting model — see Appendix). The working party complained: 'At the very least, information of this kind should be generally available within Government agencies and should also be provided to major non-Government economic organisations involved in forecasting and/or assessing the short-term economic outlook.' Such criticism left the Treasury unmoved. A month later, John Stone declared before the Senate Committee on Constitutional and Legal Affairs that the Treasury would be seeking exemption for its forecasts under the proposed freedom of information legislation. A number of factors prompted the department's move to gain exemption for its forecasts. Not least among these was a desire to retain power. For as the Task Force on Economic Policy observed, 'information is strength and the Treasury's control over a large amount of economic information and intelligence puts it in a strong position'.

The essential point to note, then, is that throughout the postwar period, particularly since the early 1950s, the Treasury has enjoyed an authoritative position in the field of economic advice. This is not to say of course that the government has always followed Treasury advice or to suggest that the Treasury is the only source of advice. What cannot be denied, however, is that the department has been a major force since the war in shaping governmental attitudes and policy decisions. To investigate the Treasury's economic philosophy is therefore an exercise of some importance.

2

Keynes and neoclassicism

SINCE the war there has been a gradual shift in Treasury philosophy, a change from something which can be called Keynesianism to something which is best described as neoclassicism. Just what this shift entailed, however, is not self-evident from these labels. For neoclassicism, and in particular Keynesianism, are terms capable of and subject to a wide variety of interpretations. As well as this, there has been a longstanding tendency among economists, one which began as soon as Keynes' *General Theory* was published in 1936, to argue that there are no fundamental differences between Keynes' economics and that of the orthodoxy which preceded him. More precisely, it is often claimed that Keynes' contribution can easily be shown to be a subset of, or a special case within, the neoclassical schema. If my aim is to examine the adoption of Keynesianism in Australia and then to trace the transition in Treasury philosophy away from Keynesianism toward neoclassicism, it is necessary to be clear about the sense in which these terms are being used. It is necessary in particular to consider in which ways Keynes may have departed from the viewpoint of the neoclassical orthodoxy.

We begin by constructing two models. As used here, 'model' refers to a set of mental representations of the economic world. It is similar to what Schumpeter referred to as the economist's 'vision'.[1] In describing the Keynesian and neoclassical models, the predominant concern is with differing beliefs on such things as whether the economy has inherent tendencies and, if so, what sort of tendencies; the nature of the forces producing economic change and directional tendencies; and whether the system can and should be controlled. What is being described is the often unarticulated, if not largely unconscious, assumptions made about the nature of economic agents and how the economy operates.

The purpose in outlining these models is to provide a perspective with which to analyse Treasury thought, a perspective which will provide a deeper understanding of the changing nature of the Treasury line than that obtained by the alternative of descriptivism. In outlining the models, however, no attempt is made to provide a detailed history of the ideas of individual economic theorists. Inevitably, therefore, the description of Keynesianism and neoclassicism involves some distortion and simplification.

The neoclassical model

The neoclassical model in particular is difficult to describe without simplification because it has English and continental variants. The chief nineteenth-century exponent of the former is Alfred Marshall (1842–1924) and of the latter the French economist Léon Walras (1834–1910). Until at least the end of the 1920s Marshallianism dominated Anglo-Saxon economics. Marshall's successor to the chair at Cambridge, A.C. Pigou, remained firmly within the Marshallian tradition. In a spate of publications, on topics such as the economics of welfare, the theory of unemployment, and industrial fluctuations, Pigou attempted to propagate the faith. From the 1930s onwards, however, the views of continental neoclassicists — not only Walras but his successor to the chair at the University of Lausanne, Vilfredo Pareto, and also Austrians such as Ludwig von Mises — began to increase in influence in Great Britain and America through the teaching and writing of a group of individuals, all of whom were at the London School of Economics (LSE) during the first half of the 1930s, and which included Lionel Robbins, Friedrich von Hayek and J.R. Hicks. Hicks recalls that when Robbins took up the chair at LSE in 1929 (Hicks had been there since 1926 and was to remain until 1935), 'he moved me on from Cassel to Walras and Pareto, to Edgeworth and Taussig, to Wicksell and the Austrians with all of whom I was much more at home at that stage than I was with Marshall and Pigou'.[2] Pointing to the gulf which separated the approach prevailing in Cambridge and that which was being formulated at the London School, Hicks notes that 'we were such "good Europeans" in London that it was Cambridge that seemed "foreign"'. Turning his back on Cambridge, Robbins found 'allies' in Chicago (with people such as Frank Knight and Jacob Viner) and in Vienna (notably von Mises). In the introduction to his 1939 publication, *Value and Capital*, Hicks made clear his own allegiance to the continental tradition (an allegiance which had already been revealed in Hicks' 1934 reconsideration of value theory in which he introduced readers to Paretian indifference-curve analysis). He announced that economic theory needed a technique for analysing the interrelations between markets and that one was thus 'naturally impelled' to turn to the writings of Walras and Pareto and also Wicksell. He continued: 'The method of General Equilibrium, which these writers elaborated, was specially designed to exhibit the economic system as a whole in the form of a complex pattern of interrelations of markets. Our work is bound to be in their tradition, and to be a continuation of theirs.'[3]

The point is, then, that to blend the various writers mentioned above, separated geographically and in time and tradition, and call the resulting mixture 'the neoclassical model', is necessarily to create something somewhat artificial. But as with Keynes' decision to lump together a diverse group of writers and label them 'classical', such concoctions are useful as points of reference. My main aim in this chapter is to provide benchmarks, and nothing more, with which to guide our investigation of Treasury documents and with which to point to the ways in which there has been a transformation in the department's outlook.

The neoclassical model, especially in its Walrasian version, is essentially mechanistic and reflects the continuing influence of the Newtonian world view. Writing in the fourth edition of his *Elements of Pure Economics*, Walras envisaged a day when 'mathematical economics will rank with the mathematical sciences of astronomy and mechanics'.[4] He argued that the pure theory of economics 'is a physico-mathematical science like mechanics or hydrodynamics'. The crux of the Walrasian position was that the diverse elements of the entire system tended unceasingly toward a point of general equilibrium which, because of the passage of time and because of market imperfections, was never actually attained:

> Equilibrium in production, like equilibrium in exchange, is an ideal and not a real state. It never happens in the real world that the selling price of any given product is absolutely equal to the cost of the productive services that enter into that product, or that the effective demand and supply of services or products are absolutely equal. Yet *equilibrium is the normal state, in the sense that it is the state towards which things spontaneously tend under a regime of free competition in exchange and production*. In fact, under free competition, if the selling price of a product exceeds the cost of the productive services for certain firms and a profit results, entrepreneurs will flow towards this branch of production or expand their output, so that the quantity of the product [on the market] will increase, its price will fall, and the difference between price and cost will be reduced; and, if [on the contrary], the cost of the productive services exceeds the selling price for certain firms, so that a loss results, entrepreneurs will leave this branch of production or curtail their output, so that the quantity of the product [on the market] will decrease, its price will rise and the difference between price and cost will again be reduced.[5]

The Newtonian underpinnings of the neoclassical model are evident here. As with Newton, the vision is essentially one of order, harmony and determinancy. The economic system is like the Newtonian celestial clockwork in which all the parts, interrelated and interdependent, combine to form a smoothly functioning and efficient machine. The system is self-correcting: it tends 'spontaneously' and predictably toward an optimum point. Just as the planets are held in place by gravity so too do economic units gravitate toward a position of equilibrium. Inherent and irresistible forces ensure that displacement from equilibrium is only a temporary aberration.

It would seem that Walras was a good example of that type of person, described by Simmel, whose 'cognitive ideal is to conceive of the world as a huge arithmetical problem, to conceive events and the qualitative distinction of things as a system of numbers'.[6] According to Walras, 'the world may be looked upon as a vast general market made up of diverse special markets where social wealth is bought and sold'. The discovery of 'the laws to which these purchases and sales tend to conform automatically' was Walras' 'huge arithmetical problem'. To discover these laws he relied upon mathematical techniques. Emphasis was placed upon quantitative, rather than qualitative, differences. Further, the analysis was based upon the abstraction of a perfectly competitive system, 'just as in pure mechanics we suppose, to start with, that machines are perfectly frictionless'.[7] One starts with an abstraction, an ideal type, and from that one deduces the laws governing the operation of the real world.

Walras' pleas for a physico-mathematical economics received little sympathy, however, either from Marshall or Pigou. Certainly Marshall and Pigou stressed the need to dig in the reality of economic life for generalisations and to attempt to formulate economic laws, and they proudly referred to economics as being the most exact of the social sciences. But they were well aware that economics could never match the exactness of the natural sciences. Likewise, Marshall was not as enthusiastic as Walras about the use of mechanistic models. To Marshall, the mecca of the economist lay in biology. But he was willing to indulge in mechanistic analogies as a necessary first step in understanding. Marshall considered mechanistic analogies to be a useful pedagogical device, a way of penetrating the complexities of real life. He relied heavily on mechanistic analogies in his classic introductory text, *Principles of Economics*. The economic analysis which Marshall and Pigou practised and preached differed also from Walras in being much more empirical and more attuned to the reality of everyday existence. Schumpeter was correct when he observed that Walras 'was bent on scraping off everything he did not consider essential to his theoretical schema [while] Marshall, following the English tradition, was bent on salvaging every bit of real life he could possibly leave in'.[8] As Jaffé points out, Walras' *Elements* was concerned with investigating 'a realistic utopia, i.e., a delineation of a state of affairs nowhere to be found in the actual world, independent of time and place, ideally perfect in certain respects, and yet composed of realistic psychological and material elements'.[9] By contrast, Marshall insisted that the economic analysis in his *Principles* represented a 'study of men as they live and move and think in the ordinary business of life'.[10] Similarly, Pigou introduced his *Economics of Welfare* by noting that he was endeavouring 'to elucidate, not any generalised system of possible worlds, but the actual world of men and women as they are found in experience to be'.[11] It is perhaps not surprising that the Marshallian tradition was a literary one. Both Marshall and Pigou saw the possibility of obscurantism in mathematical economics. Though a competent mathematician, Marshall relegated the mathematical exposition of his 'principles of economics' to footnotes and appendixes.

Where Marshall and Walras were one, however, was in their belief that beneath the apparent confusion and indeterminancy of daily experience there existed in fact a sense of order, a determinative, purposive process working inherently and inexorably. The underlying logic of daily economic life was expressed in terms of a persistent tendency toward long-term equilibrium. That this was Walras' conviction is evident in the long quotation above. Likewise, Marshall declared that 'the general theory of the equilibrium of demand and supply is a Fundamental Idea running through the frames of all the various parts of the central problem of Distribution and Exchange'.[12] Similarly, Hicks notes that the group of economists which Robbins gathered around him at LSE in the first half of the 1930s shared a 'common viewpoint' or 'common faith': 'The faith in question was a belief in the free market, or "price-mechanism" — that a competitive system, free of all "interferences", by government or by monopolistic combinations, of capital or of labour, would easily find an "equilibrium".'[13]

As defined by neoclassicists, equilibrium has a number of specific characteristics. In the first place, equilibrium is a situation in which markets are clear — in that demand (whether it be for a particular commodity or for a particular 'factor of production') matches supply. Second, firms maximise profits and consumers maximise utility. Third and implicit in the first two characteristics, productive capacity as well as labour and all other resources are fully utilised: were this not the case, firms would be failing to maximise profits and consumers/workers would not be maximising their utility.[14] Fourth, and again this is implicit in the preceding characteristics, full employment equilibrium is an ideal or optimal point. It is where both consumers and producers want to be. Hence it may be characterised as a state of rest, a situation no economic agent would want to alter or abandon.

In studying the process by which the economic system, or individual markets or industries, moved toward equilibrium, neoclassical writers such as Marshall and Walras shared with classical economists an interest in long-period analysis. By this is meant that they focused on the systematic, persistent and regular forces that pushed the system toward 'normal' or 'natural' conditions and values. Distinguishing the determination of long-period values from those of the short period, Marshall argued that 'the actual value at any time, the market value as it is often called, is often more influenced by passing events and by causes whose action is fitful and short lived, than by those which work persistently. But in long periods these fitful and irregular causes in large measure efface one another's influence; so that in the long run persistent causes dominate value completely'.[15] There was no suggestion here that the short period could be distinguished from the long period by some convenient calendar reference. Marshall acknowledged that there was 'no absolute partition' between the two periods and that 'they shade into one another by continuous gradations'.[16] His belief was simply that there was always a centre of gravitation for the system. Though buffeted by irregular and accidental forces, market or day-to-day values fluctuated around the long-period norm, being irresistibly drawn toward it. Conventionally, the distinction between the short and long period is expressed in terms of whether, for analytical purposes, adjustment to a change in the underlying conditions is permitted to be only partial or full. In a broader sense, short-period analysis involves the investigation of disequilibrium states and in particular the obstacles preventing the establishment of equilibrium. Long-period analysis, on the other hand, and this was what most interested Marshall and Walras, is the study of the attainment of equilibrium and of the forces pushing the system toward it.

Cyclical fluctuations, by definition, fell into the category of short-period analysis, for they represented a deviation from the norm. Booms and slumps (and the unemployment accompanying slumps) were seen as nothing more than transitory phenomena arising from a temporary 'shock' to the system, such as a crop failure or an important technological advance. The root cause of these cyclical aberrations was usually traced, however, to the operation of the credit system. Marshall, for instance, was convinced that recurrent 'reckless inflations of credit' were 'the chief cause of all economic malaise'.[17] He explained this by arguing that the inflation of credit fuelled a sense of optimism in businessmen and induced them to pay high money wages to 'men of but second-rate efficiency'. Here were the seeds of later difficulties. For in the inevitable ensuing period of credit contraction, prices would fall and so too would profit margins, levels of efficiency and the real value of labour. Invariably this would lead to an increase in unemployment (first in investment goods industries and then in consumption goods industries) and eventually to the eradication of the unfortunate consequences of the preceding mood of over-optimism. Marshall took for granted that there were always forces which would come into operation to counteract any cyclical downturn. Thus he could confidently announce: 'though the rapidity of invention, the fickleness of fashion, and above all the instability of credit, do certainly introduce disturbing elements into modern industry; yet ... other influences are working strongly in the opposite direction, and there seems to be no good reason for thinking that inconstancy of employment is increasing on the whole'.

As noted, neither Marshall nor Walras were much interested in explaining transitory cyclical phenomena (though Pigou, by contrast, writing in the depressed conditions of the interwar period, analysed at length the causes of industrial fluctuations and high unemployment). For them, what was of chief importance was the elucidation of the nature and operation of the system's persistent and dominant forces, those that pushed it toward stable equilibrium. What were these forces?

To the neoclassicist, the basic forces operating in any competitive economy are those of supply and demand. These combine to determine relative prices. Price signals, in turn, coordinate the actions of individual economic agents. They indicate whether demand is exceeding supply or vice versa and they thereby act as a guide to decision-making. To the neoclassicist, all markets and hence all commodities and all 'factors of production' are regulated by the forces of supply and demand. The labour market is considered the same as any other market. Thus, provided the price of labour (the real wage rate) is allowed to adjust unhindered to variations in supply and demand, the labour market will tend toward a full employment equilibrium where demand for labour equals supply. The real wage, like other prices, moves inherently toward the market-clearing rate. It does so by eliciting appropriate quantity adjustments: the neoclassicist argues that there is a functional relationship between prices and quantities. For the economy as a whole, the neoclassical view is that at any time there is a unique set of equilibrium prices and equilibrium quantities, which are determined simultaneously and to which the economy is forever tending. The forces of supply and demand operating within a competitive framework produce this tendency.

The idea that economic agents respond readily to price signals is based on a number of behavioural postulates. These postulates relate to how economic agents act, not why they act as they do — the latter does not interest the neoclassicist. The fundamental behavioural assumption of the neoclassical model is that all economic agents are maximisers. Firms maximise profits and individuals maximise utility. Marshall provided numerous examples in his *Principles* of instances where economic agents, whether they be housewives, businessmen, builders, clerks, young couples or farmers, attempt to achieve a subjectively determined optimal position. The young couple, for example, finding that they have to reduce their expenditure, 'compare the (marginal) utilities of different items, weighing the loss of utility that would result from taking away a pound's expenditure here, with that which they would lose by taking it away there; they strive to adjust their parings down so that the aggregate loss of utility that remains to them may be a maximum'.[18] The businessman, similarly, 'will push the investment of capital in his business in each several direction until what appears in his judgement to be the outer limit, or margin, of profitableness is reached; that is, until there seems to him no good reason for thinking that the gains resulting from any further investment in that particular direction would compensate him for his outlay'.[19]

In each of Marshall's examples economic agents pursue the goal of maximisation carefully, consciously, step by step, weighing up the advantages and disadvantages of different courses of action. Economic agents are depicted as essentially calculative creatures. The implication would seem to be that if a firm or industry experiences a loss, that loss need not become cumulative. There is no reason why it should necessarily start a wave of pessimism. The atomistic decision-maker can be expected to interpret the loss merely as an indication that output schedules have to be revised or that profits can be made elsewhere. Economic decision-makers will not panic; they will continue to do that which is commensurate with the goal of maximisation.

Marshall, however, was in fact well aware of the forces of optimism and pessimism — as was shown in his comments on the effect of inflations of credit. Nevertheless, he remained convinced that it was the calculativeness of economic agents that was their outstanding characteristic. In part reacting against the popular notion that economics was based on the utilitarian assumption that people were motivated simply by self-interest (or sheer selfishness), he argued that the dominant characteristics of industrial life were 'a certain independence and habit of choosing one's own course for oneself, a self-reliance; a deliberation and yet a promptness of choice and judgement, and a habit of forecasting the future and of shaping one's course with reference to distant aims... It is deliberateness and not selfishness that is the characteristic of the modern age'.[20] He qualified this by noting that 'it is not to be supposed that we assume every action to be deliberate, and the outcome of calculation ... in ordinary life people do not weigh beforehand the results of every action'. But the sorts of activities which dominated *economic* life were those 'in which man's conduct is most deliberate, and in which he most often reckons up the advantages and disadvantages of any particular action before he enters on it'. Even when decisions in the economic sphere were in accordance with habits and customs and were taken seemingly without calculation, 'the habits and customs themselves are most nearly sure to have arisen from a close and careful watching [of] the advantages and disadvantages of different courses of action'.

Marshall's descriptions of the maximising actions of the young couple and the businessman point to at least two other behavioural assumptions made by neoclassicists. In the first place, it is argued that the process by which economic agents attempt to maximise utility or profits involves focusing on the margin. What a person takes most notice of is not aggregate quantities but the benefits and gains of each marginal increase in the use of any resource. In equilibrium the marginal benefits of any activity will equal the marginal costs. A second assumption is that 'if a person has a thing which he can put to several uses, he will distribute it among these uses in such a way that it has the same marginal utility in all. For if it had a greater marginal utility in one use than another, he would gain by taking away some of it from the second use and applying it to the first'.[21] Closely allied with this notion of distribution of uses is the idea that the rational person is able to, and in fact will, substitute one 'factor of production' (whether it be land, labour or capital) for another so as to yield that combination which maximises utility or profits. The 'alert business man', for instance, 'is ever seeking for the most profitable application of his resources, and endeavouring to make use of each several agent of production up to that margin, or limit, at which he would gain by transferring a small part of his expenditure to some other agent'. In doing so, he 'so adjusts the employment of each agent that, in its marginal application, its cost is proportionate to the additional net product resulting from its use'.[22]

Fundamental to the neoclassical model is the postulate of scarcity — the idea that productive resources are always insufficient in relation to people's wants. The scarcity constraint is implicitly assumed to act as a powerful prompt to maximising behaviour. For it makes critical the efficient allocation of resources. In other words, because the means for satisfying wants are limited and can be used in a variety of ways, people have to make the best of what is available to them. Hence the constant drive, according to Marshall, to distribute means between their uses to achieve uniform marginal utility.

Under the influence of the Austrian school's view of methodology, Robbins attached great importance to the scarcity constraint in his *Essay on the Nature and Significance of Economic Science*, first published in 1932. He defined economics as 'a science which studies human behaviour as a relationship between ends and scarce means which have alternative uses'.[23] To Robbins, perhaps the most significant consequence of the scarcity constraint was that it forced economic agents to make choices. And having to make choices, economic agents necessarily had to rank their preferences or objectives (in a consistent way, it was assumed). They also had to consider the opportunity cost (a concept introduced by the Austrian Friedrich von Wieser) of using resources to meet different ends — that is, they were forced to calculate the value of the alternatives or opportunities which had been foregone in using resources to meet a particular end.

The idea that individuals rank their preferences was considered in more depth in 1934 by Robbins' colleague, J.R. Hicks, in his reconsideration of value theory.[24] Hicks denounced the idea of cardinal or measurable (and hence interpersonally comparable) utility. Utility, he argued, could only properly be viewed as ordinal. Hicks attempted to show how ordinal utility and in particular the concept of indifference curves (which Pareto had discussed in his *Manual of Political Economy*)[25] could be used as the basis for constructing a theory of value. The scarcity constraint was made explicit by superimposing expenditure or budget lines on an indifference map. Equilibrium for the maximising individual was now defined as a tangency solution, being the point where the individual's expenditure line met the highest indifference curve. This approach to demand theory proved extremely popular. It was deemed a marked improvement on Marshallian theory, primarily because it expunged the 'unscientific' tinge associated with the concept of cardinal utility (which both Marshall and Walras had relied on) and because it offered a framework for dealing with income and substitution effects.

Hicks was to play a major role also, from the late 1930s onwards, in the re-evaluation of the foundations of welfare economics. His contribution was to draw attention to the question of which criteria could be used to determine the optimal allocation of resources for the economy as a whole. Borrowing again from Pareto, Hicks noted that a range of obstacles were encountered in each individual's attempt to satisfy preferences. For society as a whole, the obstacles were technical — 'the limited amount of productive power available, and the technical limits to the amount of production that productive power will yield'. For the single individual, the obstacles were not only technical 'but also the wants or tastes of other people'. The problem confronting the individual was that 'he is prevented from being better off than he is, not only because total production is limited, but also because so much of total production is at the disposal of persons other than himself'.[26] Sometimes a person could only improve his or her position at the expense of the satisfaction of others. In other instances, however, the same end could be achieved without any detrimental effects on others. Hicks concluded that it was possible to determine the conditions in which there had been 'an increase in the efficiency of the system as a means of satisfying wants'. Formulating what came to be called the Pareto criterion of allocative efficiency (for it was he who first proposed it), Hicks concluded that an economic system could be said to be optimally organised if 'every individual is as well off as he can be made, subject to the condition that no reorganisation permitted shall make any individual worse off'. Hicks' contribution was to have a lasting effect on the research program of neoclassical economics, stimulating an investigation of the concept of Pareto optimality and its relevance to policy decisions.

With the exception of the Austrian school, neoclassicists have willingly conceded that while there is a tendency in a competitive market framework for resources to be allocated efficiently and hence for societal welfare to be maximised, the activities of self-seeking individuals may in some instances be a cause of inefficiencies and disharmonies. Pigou in particular drew attention to the frequency with which societal and individual interests could diverge when the pursuit of private interest was left unfettered. Pigou discussed at length the problem of externalities — costs or benefits in production and/or consumption not reflected in market prices. An example was the person who decided to breed rabbits. Being a maximiser, this person would invest in this activity up to the point where marginal cost equalled marginal benefit. In doing so, however, he was unlikely to take into consideration the damage to neighbours' crops which the rabbits inflicted every time they escaped.[27] In this case, then, as in the classic example of the manufacturer who does not take into consideration the effect on others of the discharge of his firm's effluent into a nearby river, the social costs of the investment decision were greater than the private costs. Pigou concluded that, given a desire to improve social welfare, there was an obvious justification in such circumstances for governmental regulation of individualistic maximising behaviour to bring individual and societal costs (or benefits) into line — a point which will be considered shortly.

Just as Pigou pointed to the problem of externalities in disrupting the usually beneficial operation of market forces, so too have most neoclassicists pointed to the problem of market imperfections in preventing the attainment of equilibrium (market-clearing) prices and quantities. The existence of imperfections has been used in particular to explain the problem of unemployment. The neoclassicist argues, as noted, that in normal circumstances competition in the labour market will ensure that real wages are driven toward the equilibrium point. Prolonged unemployment can therefore mean only one thing: that real wages are somehow being maintained at levels which are too high; in other words, they are above the equilibrium wage point. As Pigou put it in 1913, unemployment would necessarily occur if wages were 'lacking in plasticity' or were 'artificially raised above that which the free play of economic forces tends to bring about'.[28] As with any other disequilibrium situation, unemployment was blamed on the existence of rigidities or frictions which hampered the operation of market forces. Pigou warned, for instance, that 'any attempt on the part of a particular Trade Union to force up the wages of its members above those current in the general run of similar occupations is a cause of unemployment'. He pointed also to the deleterious effects on unemployment of the establishment of a minimum wage when there existed 'a large body of persons not worth this minimum wage'. Twenty years later, with the depression at its nadir, Pigou was pushing the same line. Capturing the essence of the neoclassical position, he declared that 'there will always be at work a strong tendency for wage-rates to be so related that everybody is employed. Hence, in stable conditions every one will actually be employed'. This was on the proviso, however, that there was perfectly free competition among workers and that labour was perfectly mobile. 'The implication,' he continued, 'is that such unemployment as exists at any time is due wholly to the fact that changes in demand conditions are continually taking place and that frictional resistances prevent the appropriate wage adjustments from being made instantaneously.'[29] Unemployment, from the neoclassical perspective, could only be considered as voluntary.

The argument which Pigou was advancing, one which can be called the 'imperfectionist' view, (to borrow Eatwell and Milgate's term), was that the fact that equilibrium was achieved only infrequently, and perhaps in some markets never, could be attributed soley to the existence of a multitude of imperfections — such as rigid wages, inflexible interest rates and monopoly pricing — which were products of particular social and institutional arrangements. Such imperfections, however, and this was the crux of his argument, did not make the notion of a tendency toward full employment equilibrium any less valid. It was taken for granted that if market imperfections could somehow be expunged, equilibrium would readily be achieved.

It follows that the neoclassicist supports any measure or practice which promotes flexibility and/or unleashes competitive forces. To the neoclassicist, economic efficiency is dependent upon correct pricing signals and appropriate responses to signals. Hence, the more flexible prices are and the more mobile the factors of production, particularly labour, then the smoother and the closer will the system approach equilibrium. Conversely, that which hinders either signal or response is anathema. Monopolistic practices thus usually invite disdain.

This leads to the question of the role of government in the neoclassical schema. Since the system is considered self-regulating, the predisposition of the neoclassicist is to advocate a minimum of state intervention, though what this minimum is and what form it takes tend to vary from one economist to the next. One reason for this variation, as Milgate and Eatwell point out, is that the 'imperfectionist' view held by most neoclassicists renders arbitrary the formulation and justification of economic policy: 'The ultimate superiority of a policy of fiscal expansion *vis-a-vis* a policy of social legislation to, say, "unstick" the wage, is not self-evident. Indeed, if the powerful mechanism of market adjustment via demand and supply *is* present in the economy, then it seems almost perverse not to attempt to harness these (ultimately) beneficial forces.'[30] Another reason for the disparity among neoclassicists on the question of the extent and nature of state intervention is that the policy prescriptions of the neoclassicist are not always strictly related to the logic of his theory. In a famous footnote Keynes complained that 'it is the distinction of Prof. Robbins that he, almost alone, continues to maintain a consistent scheme of thought, his practical recommendations belonging to the same system as his theory'.[31]

It may be useful, then, to consider Robbins' policy recommendations and then, to provide a balanced account, compare them with those of Pigou. Throughout the depression years Robbins remained preoccupied with achieving monetary stability and ensuring that the price mechanism operated efficiently. He strongly opposed increased public works expenditure as a means of reducing unemployment. Commenting on the unorthodox practices being pursued in the United States, Robbins warned that 'the unbalancing of the Budget and the vast expenditures on public works have an inflationary tendency which may ... engender an inflationary boom — a boom which ... would likely to be followed by a deflationary collapse'.[32] Expansionary policies, in other words, were self-defeating.

To Robbins, an essential precondition for economic recovery was the restoration of business confidence. For there would be no revival of the most depressed industries, those producing capital goods, until there was a renewed willingness to take long-term risks. And while confidence languished, so too would the taking of risks. If the restoration of business confidence was a major requirement of economic recovery, then it was necessary to give priority to trying to stabilise foreign exchanges. For Robbins judged that the main threat to confidence was the fear of monetary disturbance. The best way to stabilise foreign exchanges, he argued, was the restoration of an international gold standard. He argued in favour also of the 'removal of the grosser obstacles to trade', including a reduction in tariffs, so as 'to enhance a recovery made possible by a stabilisation of monetary conditions'.[33]

But Robbins stressed that none of these policies would ensure lasting stability 'if the underlying structure of business costs and organisation does not regain its capacity for adaptation to change'. He was particularly critical of the inflexibility of wage rates — more specifically, the unwillingness to reduce wages that were clearly above the equilibrium rate. He declared: 'If it had not been for the prevalence of the view that wage rates must at all costs be maintained in order to maintain the purchasing power of the consumer, the violence of the present depression and the magnitude of the unemployment which has accompanied it would have been considerably less. If the obstacles to cost adjustment in Great Britain had been less formidable the whole history of the last ten years would have been different.' Robbins stressed that there was certainly no need to abolish trade unions to ensure a reasonably free labour market. All that was required was that, like other monopolists, trade unions 'should receive no support from the Government, either direct or indirect'.

This notion of withdrawing governmental support from monopolists was for Robbins a critical step in eliminating inflexibilities not only in the labour market but in other markets. He was convinced that 'the worst cases of market rigidity, or of insecurity of industrial structure, are the creation of Government policy'. For governments had been guilty of sustaining and fostering monopolies. They had been guilty also of propping up inefficient industries. Worst of all, they had crushed the capitalist spirit of enterprise. There was a need, therefore, for a 'complete revision' of the role of the state in relation to industry. 'Nothing must be done which will encourage business men to believe that they will not be allowed to go under if they make mistakes or if the conditions of the market make necessary a contraction of their industry.' The businessman had been hamstrung by administrative rules and regulations. The state had to give him the necessary freedom to perform his essential function — 'the assumption of risk and the planning of initiative'. The same principles had to apply to private property: 'Property must be left to stand on its own legs. Intervention to maintain the value of the existing property — i.e. to frustrate the effects of change in the conditions of demand and supply — must cease. The property owner must learn that only by continually satisfying the demands of the consumer can he hope to maintain intact its value.'

Robbins' message, in brief, was that governmental interference was the root of present difficulties. Governments had been guilty of overstepping their 'proper functions'. They had gone 'outside a certain sphere' of responsibilities which could be handled efficiently. There had been a 'congestion of governmental business'. Insisting that his proposal was not one of *laissez faire*, Robbins nevertheless stressed the need for 'a more radical limitation of State activity'. He declared: 'if recovery is to be maintained and future progress assured, there must be a more or less complete reversal of contemporary tendencies of governmental regulation of enterprise.' The market instead had to be allowed to govern.

Pigou, by contrast, was willing to support a much wider variety of economic policies and regulatory activities and looked more positively at the role of the state. Complaining that the monopolist's pursuit of private interest did not promote the public interest, Pigou argued that there was a 'case for State intervention, whether by way of public control over the conduct of combinations whose range confers on them monopoly powers or, in some circumstances, by direct State or municipal operation of services, which might be expected in the normal course to fall into the hands of private monopolists'.[34] His analysis of externalities led him to recommend the use of taxes (or in some cases subsidies) to bring private costs (benefits) into line with social costs (benefits). The idea essentially was to use legislative initiative to alter or introduce prices and thereby increase the efficiency of market forces. In dealing with the problem of unemployment, Pigou suggested a variety of remedies. Arguing that any device that rendered wages less rigid would reduce unemployment, Pigou supported the establishment of conciliation committees whose role would be to facilitate 'the rapid adjustment of wage-rates to varying conditions'.[35] Since he thought that a reduction in industrial fluctuations would help reduce unemployment, and that fluctuations were primarily related to changes in credit conditions, Pigou recommended among other things the shortening of industrial credits, the adoption of a more 'enlightened' loan policy by bankers, and modifications to the currency system so as to secure greater stability in the general price level. Since 'the volume of unemployment is likely to be diminished by any device which enables workpeople to ascertain where work is wanted, and to move freely towards available vacancies', Pigou supported also the establishment of labour exchanges. On a number of occasions Pigou advocated the use of direct state action to reduce unemployment, arguing in favour of increased public works expenditure. This was on the proviso, however, that it be matched by increased taxation so as to retain budgetary balance. Resting his case on what was to be called the balanced budget multiplier, Pigou reasoned that 'it is probable that only a part of the extra taxes people pay would be taken from funds they would otherwise have devoted at that time directly or indirectly to wage-payments. Hence, the true result of the relief works and so on is not to leave the aggregate amount of unemployment in the country unaltered, but to diminish that amount'.[36]

The Keynesian model

Keynes was convinced that his way of looking at the world was fundamentally different from that of the neoclassical orthodoxy. He considered the *General Theory* a revolutionary work, the culmination of 'a long struggle of escape ... from habitual modes of thought and expression', an escape from the ideas of orthodoxy 'which ramify, for those brought up as most of us have been, into every corner of our minds'.[37] He told German and Japanese readers of the *General Theory* that 'this book represents a reaction, a transition away from the English (or orthodox) tradition'. Similarly, he pointed out in 1939 in the French edition of his book that in writing the *General Theory* he had felt himself 'to be gaining an emancipation' from the orthodoxy which had dominated English political economy for over a hundred years.

These claims have to be treated with some caution. They should not be interpreted to mean that Keynes believed he was offering something completely original, something which had not been influenced to a degree by Marshall's insights. They should be treated with caution also because the *General Theory* was littered with conscious and unconscious concessions to the neoclassical orthodoxy, some of which can and have been used to argue that Keynes' contribution was strictly in the field of short-period or disequilibrium analysis, leaving neoclassical long-period analysis intact. It will be argued here, however, that the general tenor of Keynes' claims are correct. For while he did not entirely succeed in providing a critique of the neoclassical view, he did offer a distinctively different vision of the economic system.

The most important difference between the Keynesian and neoclassical models concerns the self-correcting ability of the capitalist economy. The key to Keynes' 'emancipation' was his rejection of the neoclassical claim that the economic system has an inherent tendency toward full employment equilibrium. Keynes' 1934 BBC broadcast, 'Poverty in Plenty: Is the Economic System Self-Adjusting?', was an unambiguous denial of the idea of a self-regulating system. Keynes drew attention to two competing schools of thought. On the one hand were those who believed that 'the existing economic system is, in the long run, a self-adjusting system, though with creaks and groans and jerks, and interrupted by time lags, outside interferences and mistakes'. Adherents to this faith did not believe the system to be automatically or immediately self-adjusting. But they did maintain that, provided the system 'is not interfered with and if the action of change and chance is not too rapid', there was an inherent tendency leading to the elimination of imbalances between supply and demand. On the other hand was the school of thought which rejected the notion that the system was, 'in any significant sense', self-adjusting. Those who belonged to this school were 'the descendants of a long line of heretics', 'isolated groups of cranks', 'people of practical good sense'. To Keynes, the differences between these two schools were fundamental; the extent of the gap between them had been underestimated. He insisted that the 'essential truth' lay with the viewpoint of the heretics. Keynes declared quite categorically: 'The system is not self-adjusting, and, without purposive direction, it is incapable of translating our actual poverty into our potential plenty.'[38]

Although there is little disagreement that Keynes denied the idea of an inherent tendency toward full employment equilibrium, there exists a range of opinions on the essence of the Keynesian vision. Some economists insist that central to Keynes' outlook was the idea that capitalist economies are plagued by cyclical fluctuations. Hyman Minsky, for instance, argues that Keynes depicted the capitalist economy, equipped with sophisticated financial institutions, as being 'inherently flawed, because it is intractably cyclical'. Keynes' viewpoint, he argues, was that such an economy 'cannot by its own processes sustain full employment, and each of a succession of cyclical states is transitory in the sense that relations are built up which transform the way in which the economy will behave'.[39]

There is much in the *General Theory* to support this interpretation. For instance, one can point to Keynes' characterisation of the economy in chapter 18 of the book (which summarised the theory). Here the system was seen to be constantly fluctuating, prone to instability but not violent instability:

> [The economic system] seems capable of remaining in a chronic condition of sub-normal activity for a considerable period without any marked tendency either towards recovery or towards complete collapse. Moreover, the evidence indicates that full, or even approximately full, employment is of rare and short-lived occurrence. Fluctuations may start briskly but seem to wear themselves out before they have proceeded to great extremes, and an intermediate situation which is neither desperate nor satisfactory is our normal lot.[40]

Fluctuations in output and employment, it was pointed out elsewhere in the *General Theory*, involved passing through a succession of phases. The economy was described as moving in cyclical fashion through boom, crisis, slump and recovery. Though the economy was characterised as being 'not violently unstable' an exception was the transition from boom to slump which 'often takes place suddenly and violently'. In the transition from slump to boom, however, there was generally 'no such sharp turning point'. This particular transition in activity from a downward to an upward trend, characterised for the most part by the underemployment of resources, was a protracted affair and was deemed the usual condition for the economy.

In assessing Minsky's interpretation it could also be noted that Keynes never tired of pointing to the inappropriateness of neoclassical theorising in investigating problems such as unemployment and the trade cycle. He complained in 1933, for example, that

> all our ideas about economics, instilled into us by education and atmosphere and tradition are, whether we are conscious of it or not, soaked with theoretical presuppositions which are only properly applicable to a society which is in

equilibrium, with all its productive resources already employed. Many people are trying to solve the problem of unemployment with a theory which is based on the assumption that there is no unemployment.[41]

Similarly, Keynes complained in 1939 that neoclassical theory was 'clearly incompetent' to deal with the problem of the trade cycle because it subscribed to Say's 'fallacy' that supply created its own demand (which implied that the economy operated at full capacity).[42] By contrast, Keynes was convinced that the principle of effective demand provided a firm basis for understanding cyclical fluctuations. Although the *General Theory* was not itself a theory of the trade cycle, Keynes declared that 'since we claim to have shown in the preceding chapters what determines the volume of employment at any time, it follows, if we are right, that our theory must be capable of explaining the phenomena of the Trade Cycle'.[43]

As noted, Minsky argues that underlying Keynes' vision of cyclical instability was a belief that each stage of the cycle — boom, crisis, slump, recovery — contained (to use a Marxist metaphor) the seeds of its own destruction. That this was Keynes' belief is undeniable. He referred in the *General Theory*, for instance, to the 'tendency of a fluctuation in one direction to reverse itself in due course'.[44] Elaborating on this, Keynes noted that 'even those degrees of recovery and recession, which can occur within the limitations set by our other conditions of stability, will be likely, if they persist for a sufficient length of time and are not interfered with by changes in the other factors, to cause a reverse movement in the opposite direction, until the same forces as before again reverse the direction'. According to the Keynesian conception, then, stability in an unregulated economy occurs only by chance. Having occurred, it will not persist. For the very forces which have led to stability will in time render the system unstable.

But, and this is a key question, are we to infer from this that to Keynes there were no persistent, systematic forces in the economy? In claiming that the economy was not self-adjusting was Keynes arguing that it had no 'centre of gravity'? To put this yet another way, was Keynes forsaking the traditional long-period method?

The answer to all these questions must be no, though the answer to the third question must be qualified. It can readily be demonstrated that Keynes believed that there were persistent forces which produced tendencies in capitalist economies, but tendencies directionally different from those assumed by neoclassical economists. In the earliest drafts of the *General Theory*, those of 1931–32, Keynes announced that he agreed that there were 'forces which one might fairly well call "automatic" which operate ... in the direction of restoring a long-period equilibrium between saving and investment'. But he continued: 'The point upon which I cast doubt — though the contrary is generally believed — is whether these "automatic" forces will, in the absence of deliberate management, tend to bring about not only an equilibrium between saving and investment but also an optimum level of production.'[45] In a 'Historical Retrospect', written around 1932, Keynes took up this theme again, noting that 'the orthodox equilibrium theory of economics has assumed ... that there are natural forces tending to bring the volume of ... output ... back to the optimum level whenever temporary forces have led it to depart from this level'. Commenting on this, Keynes did not deny the existence of 'natural forces'. The point which he wished to establish was simply 'that the equilibrium level towards which output tends to return after temporary disturbances is not necessarily the optimum level'.[46] He went on to argue that in fact it was the 'normal thing' in modern economies 'for output to be below the optimum level', that is, to be below the full employment level. In the *General Theory* Keynes concluded his summary chapter by referring to 'the mean position ... determined by "natural" tendencies, namely, by those tendencies which are likely to persist, failing measures expressly designed to correct them'.[47] Describing this position, Keynes noted 'that we oscillate, avoiding the gravest extremes of fluctuation in employment and in prices in both directions, round an intermediate position appreciably below full employment and appreciably above the minimum employment a decline below which would endanger life'.

The point is, that when Keynes denied the neoclassical claim that the system was self-adjusting he was not denying the idea that there were always forces at work which gave the economy particular tendencies. He was simply denying the idea that the adjustment would be toward some sort of optimal point. Another matter which needs clarification is that while Keynes talked about points of oscillation, tendencies toward equilibrium, and natural and automatic forces — those things, in other words, which are characteristic of the long-period method — it was nevertheless the case that in the *General Theory* Keynes took as given a whole host of factors. These factors included the existing skill and quantity of labour, the existing quality and quantity of available equipment, existing techniques, and the degree of competition. In one sense, then, Keynes was obviously operating in the short period. Nevertheless, it would be a mistake to categorise Keynes' analysis as short-period if that term is being used as it was defined in the discussion of neoclassicism, namely the analysis of disequilibrium states and of the obstacles in the way of the achievement of full employment equilibrium. For Keynes' statements of tendency, and this needs to be stressed, were not derived from assumptions about price rigidities (such as wages being sticky downwards and interest rates being inflexible because of a 'liquidity trap') — although this is frequently claimed to be the case. The most reasonable conclusion, as Eatwell puts it, is that 'while there can be no doubt that Keynes developed his theory within what he saw as a short-period setting ... it is the long-period implications of his analysis, as a theory of employment, which represents the significant contribution'.[48]

The argument advanced in the *General Theory* was that the level of output and total employment is determined by effective demand, this being the point at which aggregate supply intersects aggregate demand. As described by Keynes, aggregate supply is a schedule, representing the estimated labour costs associated with each level of employment. The aggregate demand schedule, on the other hand, represents the revenue which firms expect to receive from the output corresponding to each level of employment. Keynes argued that firms will choose to produce that level of output which they think will maximise profits — a postulate entirely consistent with the neoclassical model. He argued further that if, for a given level of employment, expected revenue exceeds estimated costs, there will an incentive for firms to decide to expand employment and output. Firms will expand employment up to the point where the aggregate demand function intersects the aggregate supply function. At this point, he claimed, firms' expectations of profit would be maximised.[49]

At the risk of repetition, the revolutionary point which Keynes sought to establish was that the level of employment associated with the point of effective demand need not be one of full employment. There was no reason at all why effective demand should tend toward a· value consistent with full employment. Indeed, it was much more likely, as was noted above, that the intersection of aggregate demand and aggregate supply would occur below the full employment level — producing what is often described as an underemployment equilibrium.

Most of the *General Theory* was an investigation of the determination of aggregate demand (as opposed to the question of how firms estimated what demand would be). Keynes' analysis was applied to a closed economy. Further, he abstracted from the public sector. Aggregate demand was, then, simply the aggregation of private consumption and investment expenditure. The first was undertaken by consumers, the second by entrepreneurs.

It was Keynes' view that of the two components of aggregate demand, investment expenditure was by far the more important determinant of changes in output and employment:

> When employment increases, aggregate real income is increased. The psychology of the community is such that when aggregate real income is increased aggregate consumption is increased, but not so much as income. Hence employers would make a loss if the whole of the increased employment were to be devoted to satisfying the increased demand for immediate consumption. Thus, to justify any given amount of employment there must be an amount of current investment sufficient to absorb the excess of total output over what the community chooses to consume when employment is at the given level. For unless there is this amount of investment, the receipts of the entrepreneurs will be less than is required to induce them to offer the given amount of employment. It follows, therefore, that, given what we shall call the community's propensity to consume, the equilibrium level of employment, i.e. the level at which there is no inducement to employers as a whole either to expand or contract employment, will depend on the amount of current investment.[50]

Keynes went on to note that the amount of current investment depended on what he called the inducement to invest, which in turn depended on the relationship between the schedule of the marginal efficiency of capital and the rate of interest. The marginal efficiency of capital was the term Keynes used to refer to the relationship between the prospective yield of a capital asset and its supply price. Keynes argued that there was a marginal efficiency of capital corresponding to each level of current investment. The point he sought to show was that 'whilst there are forces causing the rate of investment to rise or fall so as to keep the marginal efficiency of capital equal to the rate of interest, yet the marginal efficiency of capital is, in itself, a different thing from the ruling rate of interest'.[51] This raised the question of what then determined the rate of interest. Keynes sought an answer in the concept of liquidity preference, arguing that the current rate of interest depended 'not on the strength of the desire to hold wealth, but on the strengths of the desires to hold it in liquid and in illiquid forms respectively, coupled with the amount of the supply of wealth in the one form relatively to the supply of it in the other'.[52] Keynes analysed at length the various motives for wanting to hold money. He identified three such motives: the transactions, precautionary and speculative motives. His conclusion was that it was the demand for money, informed by these motives, in relation to its supply that determined the rate of interest.

Keynes' analysis of liquidity preference was directly counter to the neoclassical account of the role and determination of the rate of interest. Neoclassicists saw the rate of interest as performing the same role as any other relative price: in this case, to bring the supply of investible funds into equilibrium with the demand for them; in other words, to equilibrate investment and saving. Keynes offered a radically different vision. He argued that planned savings were brought into equality with planned investment through changes in the level of income and employment, not through changes in the rate of interest. Here was the nub of Keynes' heresy. He complained: 'The traditional analysis has been aware that saving depends on income but it has overlooked the fact that income depends on investment, in such fashion that, when investment changes, income must necessarily change in just that degree which is necessary to make the change in saving equal to the change in investment.'[53]

Keynes suggested that once it was realised that changes in consumption expenditure and investment determined not the rate of interest but the aggregate volume of employment, 'then our outlook on the mechanism of the economic system will be profoundly changed'. These considerations were 'a matter of the most fundamental theoretical significance and of overwhelming practical importance'. The reasons why are readily apparent. In the first place, 'a decreased readiness to spend will be looked on in quite a different light if, instead of being regarded as a factor which will, *cet. par.*, increase investment [by decreasing the rate of interest], it is seen as a factor which will, *cet. par.*, diminish employment'. Using the same logic, Keynes could argue against the idea that a reduction in money wages might help reduce unemployment. In an individual industry or firm this might be the case, but for the economy as a whole it would simply act to reduce aggregate demand. Second, Keynes offered a different account of the relationship between saving and investment. His point was that it was changes in investment expenditure, through their effect on the level of income, which determined the level of saving. As Meade puts it, 'Keynes's intellectual revolution was to shift economists from thinking normally in terms of a model of reality in which a dog called *savings* wagged a tail labelled *investment* to thinking in terms of a model in which a dog called *investment* wagged his tail labelled *savings*'.[54] It could also be noted that the implicit message in Keynes' comments on saving represented a departure from prevailing ethics. For Keynes' message was both an exaltation of spending and a denouncement of a fundamental Victorian virtue — the ethic of thrift.[55]

Another reason why Keynes placed so much emphasis on investment was that he considered it particularly susceptible to change. As early as 1931 he drew attention to the fact that investment was capable of 'sudden and violent change' and argued that such change was of prime importance in understanding present economic difficulties.[56] To Keynes, the nature of investment was symptomatic of the nature of the system as a whole. He suggested in 1937 that his theory could be summed up as follows: 'given the psychology of the public, the level of output and employment as a whole depends on the amount of investment.' But emphasis was placed not just on the level of investment but on its variability. For he continued: 'I put it in this way, not because this is the only factor on which aggregate output depends, but because it is usual in a complex system to regard as the *causa causans* that factor which is most prone to sudden and wide fluctuation.'[57]

In explaining why fluctuations in investment could have wide-reaching effects, Keynes relied on the multiplier principle. What is interesting about the multiplier principle is that it embodied the notion of cumulative change. The concept of the multiplier refers simply to a situation in which, say, a firm decides to spend a certain sum on capital equipment. This will lead directly to an increase in the income of the firm supplying the capital good and hence also in national income. But the process does not stop there. For the firm whose income has now increased will spend a certain proportion of its receipts on goods and services and retain the rest. This in turn increases the income of those who have provided the goods and services, some of which, once again, is spent, some saved. And so the process goes on, with the result that national income is increased by some multiple of the initial outlay on capital equipment. In the Keynesian model, then, not only is there continuous change but the changes occurring have cumulative effects.

The multiplier effect, however, did not by itself explain the initial fluctuation in aggregate demand. In explaining why investment was prone to sudden change, Keynes placed particular emphasis upon the fact that all investment decisions were taken in the face of an uncertain future. He argued, for instance, that 'the rate of interest and the marginal efficiency of capital [the key determinants of the volume of investment] are particularly concerned with the *indefinite* character of actual expectations; they sum up the effect on men's market decisions of all sorts of vague doubts and fluctuating states of confidence and courage. They belong, that is to say, to a stage of our theory where we are no longer assuming a definite and calculable future'.[58] His point was simply that the root cause of the economy's volatility lay in the capriciousness of community, and especially business, attitudes. The latter, in turn, resulted from the fact that the future was always uncertain.

In the *General Theory* the effects of an uncertain future were stressed. The argument was put forward that the static-state analysis of neoclassical theory, in which the future does not influence the present, broke 'the theoretical link between to-day and to-morrow' and thereby resulted in 'a large element of unreality'. What had been too often forgotten was 'that human decisions affecting the future, whether personal or political or economic, cannot depend on strict mathematical expectation, since the basis for making such calculations does not exist'. Economists had not paid enough attention to the state of business confidence and its influence on the marginal efficiency of capital. Keynes observed: 'Our knowledge of the factors which will govern the yield of an investment some years hence is usually very slight and often negligible.' Such knowledge was notable for its 'extreme precariousness'. Economic instability could arise from the human characteristic that positive action depended largely on 'spontaneous optimism rather than on a mathematical expectation'. Keynes described the 'spontaneous urge to action rather than inaction' as 'animal spirits'. It was animal spirits rather than 'the outcome of a weighted average of quantitative benefits multiplied by quantitative probabilities' which propelled man into action. It was animal spirits which made 'the wheels go round'. Thus, if for some reason or other these spirits were dampened and decision-making was left to depend solely on a mathematical expectation, 'enterprise will fade and die — though fears of loss may have a basis no more reasonable than hopes of profit had before'.

Since the future was incalculable, decision-making involved 'choosing between the alternatives as best we are able, calculating where we can, but often falling back for our motive on whim or sentiment or chance'. People fell back also on what was referred to as a 'convention' by which the unrealistic assumption was made that the present state of affairs would continue into the future. It was highly unlikely, however, that such a convention could be maintained for very long: 'A conventional valuation which is established as the outcome of the mass psychology of a large number of ignorant individuals is liable to change violently as the result of a sudden fluctuation of opinion due to factors which do not really make much difference to the prospective yield; since there will be no strong roots of conviction to hold it steady.' Thus at all times it was possible that the rules and conventions governing economic behaviour could break down and that the 'thin and precarious crust' supporting the economy could crack.[59] There was no inherent protective mechanism akin to the physiological phenomenon of homeostasis. The weakness in the system was fundamental.

Clearly, there was a close connection in the Keynesian model between community psychology and the state of the economy. Keynes, as has been made clear, emphasised the volatility of investment in causing fluctuations in output and employment. But the instability of investment reflected the instability of conventional judgments about the future. Through the level of investment there was a link between expectations and economic performance.

It would be a mistake, however, to argue that the essential novelty of Keynes' approach, his main departure from the neoclassical model, lay in his emphasis on expectations and uncertainty. For this would be to ignore Keynes' own argument that his key contribution was the principle of effective demand. Expectations and uncertainly were important ingredients in his schema only in so far as they influenced effective demand. This was a point, Keynes reflected in 1937, that had too often been ignored or misunderstood by those who had read his book. What most of them had missed, he lamented, was the fact that 'the theory of effective demand is substantially the same if we assume that short-period expectations are always fulfilled'.[60]

Another reason sometimes put forward for not exaggerating the significance of Keynes' emphasis on uncertainty and expectations is the fact that these were things which had long been discussed, or at least acknowledged, by neoclassical writers. While the validity of this point can hardly be denied, it nevertheless glosses over the fact that there were important differences between the way Keynes and neoclassical writers incorporated uncertainty and expectations into their analyses. In the first place, it was Keynes' view that while neoclassical writers such as Marshall, Edgeworth and Pigou did not rule out change or even the possibility of expectations being disappointed, it was nevertheless characteristic of their approach that 'at any given time facts and expectations were assumed to be given in a definite and calculable form; and risks, of which, though admitted, not much notice was taken, were supposed to be capable of an exact actuarial computation. The calculation of probability, though mention of it was kept in the background, was supposed to be capable of reducing uncertainty to the same calculable status as that of certainty itself'.[61] Keynes made no such assumption.

Second, and more significantly, to the extent that neoclassical writers discussed the effects of alternating waves of optimism and pessimism in producing trade cycles, these psychological swings were held to be a function not so much of the inescapable fact of uncertainty as of the man-made (and hence potentially eradicable) problem of variations in credit conditions. This seemed to imply that if credit conditions could be stabilised, so too could waves of pessimism and optimism be flattened. To Keynes, expectations could never be rendered insignificant (though he agreed that they could be made less volatile) so long as the future remained uncertain. Perhaps the more important point is that in neoclassical analysis fluctuating expectations tended to be relegated to the field of monetary theory and delineated from the core of neoclassical economics — the theory of value and distribution. Austin Robinson recalls that when he learnt economics at Cambridge during the 1920s, 'there was complete schizophrenia between value theory and monetary theory; I listened to value theory one hour and bicycled across Cambridge to listen to a wholly unrelated monetary theory the next hour'.[62] In Keynes' analysis, by contrast, there was no such schizophrenia. Monetary and real factors were integrated into a single theory of the determination of employment and output. Moreover, the principle of effective demand, and the effect on it of changing expectations, could be used equally well in the analysis both of long-period tendencies and short-run cyclical movements — a fact, as noted earlier, to which Keynes drew attention.

Alan Coddington has made the point that what is critical in Keynes' depiction of investment behaviour is not the *fact* of uncertainty but the assumptions Keynes made about how economic agents react to uncertainty: 'what is required within Keynes's scheme is not the uncertainty, as such, surrounding private sector investment decisions; it is the wayward and unruly behaviour of the aggregates resulting from the decisions taken in the face of this uncertainty.'[63] But what is also critical in Keynes' analysis is his belief, which stands in contrast to the generally atomistic approach of neoclassical analysis in which economic agents are depicted as self-determining beings, that investors depended not on an individual assessment of future possibilities but on majority opinion — the reason, so Keynes claimed, being that the individual would assume that the majority opinion was better informed. Decision-making, according to Keynes, was essentially an exercise in conformity, in conventionality: 'The psychology of a society of individuals each of whom is endeavouring to copy the others leads to what we may strictly term a *conventional* judgment.'[64] It was here that the instability of investment decisions had its roots. For the 'flimsy' foundation of conventional judgments was such that they were prone to 'sudden and violent' change. The result, as depicted by Keynes, was that

> the practice of calmness and immobility, of certainty and security, suddenly breaks down. New fears and hopes will, without warning, take charge of human conduct. The forces of disillusion may suddenly impose a new conventional basis for valuation. All these pretty, polite techniques, made for a well-panelled board room and a nicely regulated market, are liable to collapse. At all times the vague panic fears and equally vague and unreasoned hopes are not really lulled, and lie but a little way below the surface.[65]

This depiction of the volatility of investment behaviour should not be interpreted to imply, as Shackle claims, that 'a theory of unemployment is necessarily, inescapably, a theory of disorder'.[66] Rather, it lends credence to E.J. Nell's suggestion that Keynes' particular form of long-period analysis was one 'in which some of *the persistent and systematic forces*, always at work and therefore not ignorable, *were inherently volatile*'. He continues: 'The consequence would be a system with an unreliable shifting equilibrium — not a succession of temporary equilibria — but an equilibrium that might never be reached because its determinants would shift before they had adequately exercised their influence.'[67] This accords with Keynes' discussion of expectations in the *General Theory*, where he argued that a given state of expectations was associated with a particular equilibrium level of long-period employment. But before these long-period effects could be worked out the economic system was subjected to a new set of expectations. Thus, the economy's equilibrium point was constantly changing; the economy was forever adjusting to new and unattainable equilibrium points.[68]

Keynes' vision of the economy, like the neoclassical, had particular policy implications. It was entirely consistent with his belief that the economy could not look after itself that Keynes stressed the need for economic control or management. As he explained in 1931: 'I believe that our destiny is in our own hands and that we can emerge from [the slump] if only we choose — or rather if those choose who are in authority in the world.'[69] The argument that instability would persist 'in the absence of deliberate management', 'unless corrective measures are taken', 'without purposive direction', ran throughout his writings. Having denied the neoclassical faith in beneficent natural tendencies, Keynes insisted that economic problems could nevertheless be alleviated by deliberate, purposive action taken by those 'in authority'. The system could not be left alone. It required constant supervision and direction.

Keynes remained a meliorist throughout his life, despite his gradual recognition of 'irrational' springs of action. In his 1938 address, 'My Early Beliefs', Keynes confessed that as a young man he adhered firmly to the belief that people were rational in the sense that they were reasonable, malleable and perfectible:

> We were among the last of the Utopians, or meliorists as they are sometimes called, who believe in a continuing moral progress by virtue of which the human race already consists of reliable, rational, decent people, influenced by truth and objective standards, who can be safely released from the outward restraints of convention and traditional standards and inflexible rules of conduct, and left, from now onwards, to their own sensible devices, pure motives and reliable institutions of the good... In short, we repudiated all versions of original sin, of there being insane and irrational springs of wickedness in most men.[70]

Reflecting on this, he concluded that he had 'completely misunderstood human nature'. He had been guilty of superficiality. He had 'ignored certain powerful and valuable springs of feeling'. In particular, he had ignored 'the spontaneous, irrational outbursts of human nature ... volcanic and even wicked impulses'. Nevertheless, Keynes admitted that 'I still suffer incurably from attributing an unreal rationality to other people's feelings and behaviour'. He remained convinced of the possibility of using patient and logical counselling to induce people to adopt a more reasonable stance, to overcome some of their 'vague panic fears and doubts' and thereby achieve a more orderly and more stable economy. 'I behave,' Keynes explained, 'as if there really existed some authority or standard to which I can successfully appeal if I shout loud enough — perhaps it is some hereditary vestige of a belief in the efficacy of prayer.' This particular idea informed many of the essays in his aptly titled *Essays in Persuasion* (1931). The assumption throughout was that people's outlooks could be changed and some sort of consensus could be established on what was 'proper', 'normal' and 'reasonable'.

Also underlying Keynes' belief in the notion of economic control were (to use Harrod's phrase) 'the presuppositions of Harvey Road', those inviolable assumptions Keynes absorbed in childhood and beyond from his father and mother (who lived in Harvey Road, Cambridge). Of particular importance here was the presupposition that 'the government of Britain was and would continue to be in the hands of an intellectual aristocracy using the methods of persuasion'.[71] The assumption was that economic management would be the responsibility of an enlightened, public-spirited elite or technocracy who would successfully steer the economy, relying upon perseverance and reasoned argument. It was these people who had their hands on the economic rudder. It was not assumed that the technocracy was infallible but that it was flexible, able to adapt to different circumstances, problems and demands, willing to experiment and to learn from mistakes.

Since the economy was characterised by perpetual change, it was Keynes' view that it was essential for intervention to be discretionary. The idea of preset, inflexible, rule-following intervention was alien to Keynes. In his *Tract on Monetary Reform* (1923), he voiced his disapproval of using 'a precise, arithmetical formula' as the criterion for regulating the bank rate, government borrowing and trade advances. He favoured instead the use of 'a general judgment of the situation based on all the available data'.[72] He could not accept Irving Fisher's suggestion of a 'compensated dollar': 'I doubt the wisdom and practicability of a system so cut and dried. If we wait until a price movement is actually afoot before applying remedial measures, we may be too late.' Such a scheme, which involved automatic adjustment according to changes in a price index 'without any play of judgment or discretion', had no appeal to him. Economic control required research and understanding. It involved decisions on timing and method, both of which necessitated judgment, not the following of rules.

How was control to be achieved? Before the publication of the *General Theory* Keynes had established a reputation as a firm believer in monetary policy in effecting economic control. But the continuation of the depression undermined Keynes' support of monetary policy. In the final version of the book he announced that he was 'now somewhat sceptical' of the ability of variations in the interest alone to produce an optimal rate of investment. Fluctuations in the marginal efficiency of capital would be 'too great to be offset by any practicable changes in the rate of interest'.[73] Keynes believed that monetary policy *by itself* was an inadequate weapon with which to exercise economic control and, as such, the government, and not just the banking authorities, must assume responsibility for control. He believed also that monetary policy was ineffective in raising confidence and in overcoming a deep slump. But he did not believe, as has sometimes been assumed, that monetary policy was of little importance *in all situations*. In his opinion, the efficacy of monetary policy varied according to the economic climate.

Since economic management could not be left solely in the hands of the monetary authorities, it followed that the government would have to take a much more active role in economic affairs: 'The controls necessary to ensure full employment will ... involve a large extension of the traditional functions of government.'[74] What would this involve? First, the government would have to try to redistribute incomes so as to raise the propensity to consume. Second, as 'the duty of ordering the current volume of investment cannot safely be left in private hands', it was envisaged that 'a somewhat comprehensive socialisation of investment will prove the only means of securing an approximation to full employment'. Though the meaning of 'a somewhat comprehensive socialisation' is open to a variety of interpretations, it is clear that socialisation was not equated with socialism. For Keynes continued:

> But beyond this no obvious case is made out for a system of State Socialism which would embrace most of the economic life of the community. It is not the ownership of the instruments of production which it is important for the State to assume. If the State is able to determine the aggregate amount of resources devoted to augmenting the instruments and the basic rate of reward to those who own them, it will have accomplished all that is necessary.[75]

It would seem that what Keynes was suggesting was that public sector investment be used to raise aggregate expenditure to a level commensurate with a high rate of employment and that the ratio of public sector to private sector investment increase over time. Such a suggestion was in line with his repeated advocacy of public works expenditure as a means of restoring employment: a number of his most famous pamphlets, such as *Can Lloyd George Do It?* (1929; co-authored with H.D. Henderson) and *The Means to Prosperity* (1933), were written in an attempt to convince the government and the public of the efficacy of such expenditure. He was now arguing that public investment expenditure should be used not just as a temporary expedient (which suggested that it could be turned on and off at will), but that the level of public investment should grow continuously (though not necesarily rapidly) so as to provide a stabilising force in the system.

Perhaps Keynes' most significant contribution to the notion of economic control was his re-evaluation of the role of budgetary policy. Indeed, the phrase 'Keynesian Revolution' is now most commonly associated with the abandonment of balanced-budget principles and the acceptance of budget deficits or surpluses to regulate the level of economic activity. Keynes is attributed with having transformed the conception of the budget as a mere financial device governed by accounting principles to an effective instrument with which to exercise economic control. And yet the *General Theory* had nothing explicit to say about budgetary policy. Furthermore, his writings before 1939 cannot be described as being actively concerned with promoting a change in the public's attitude toward the role of the budget. Keynes did not argue against balanced budgets as such, but against the idea that expenditure should be reduced to maintain budgetary balance in the face of falling receipts. It was not really until World War II, in fact, that Keynes formulated in any detail his ideas on budgetary policy and that these ideas gained acceptance. In his 1940 pamphlet, *How to Pay for the War* (which originally appeared as a series of articles in *The Times* the previous year), Keynes showed how his aggregative framework could be used to analyse a situation opposite to that discussed in the *General Theory*. Moreover, he demonstrated how budgetary policy constituted a weapon for dealing with what is now known as demand-pull inflation. Keynes introduced the notion of the 'inflationary gap' and showed how the gap could be plugged. Relying upon the national accounting data then beginning to be assembled (a development directly stimulated by Keynes' approach), he estimated (on the basis of the existing price level) the extent to which aggregate demand was likely to exceed the supply of output. To overcome the inflationary consequences of excessive demand, Keynes recommended the introduction of a scheme of compulsory saving or deferred pay. This scheme had several potential advantages: it reduced the need for direct controls (such as rationing), which Keynes abhorred, and not only would it reduce inflation but it would provide a store of funds which could be released once the economy moved from boom to slump.

Keynes, then, provided a new perspective: his argument was in effect that what was at issue was not the balancing of the budget itself but the balancing of the economy as a whole. His contribution was to highlight the role of the budget in effecting a balance between aggregate demand and supply. Kingsley Wood's budget of 1941 was testimony to Keynes' influence: the budget marked a radical departure away from the conventional Treasury approach toward the Keynesian economic balance approach. The budget was incorporated into a macroeconomic vision.

The Keynesian and neoclassical models compared

We can now summarise the differences between the Keynesian and neoclassical models. The focus, the main area of interest, of the two models is different. The neoclassical model focuses on the determination of the value and distribution of a (usually) given output and the role of relative prices in the allocation of scarce resources. The focus of the Keynesian model is on the determination of output and employment and the role therein of effective demand.

The two models have different views on the significance of economic scarcity. Nicholas Kaldor provides a useful guide to these differences. The basic tenet of neoclassical economics, he argues,

> has been that production in general was confined by the scarcity of human and material resources; that human welfare can be improved only by 'economizing' in the use of scarce resources (whether of land, labour or capital) which means securing the best allocation of what is available. This meant that an 'economy' — a term which implied a community who satisfy their wants by mutual cooperation between their members — was necessarily constrained in its activities by its resource endowment: it was the poverty (or insufficiency) of resources which limited the satisfaction of wants.[76]

Keynes took a contrary approach: 'His main proposition was that in normal circumstances, production in general was limited by effective demand which determined *how much* of potential resources were effectively utilised.'[77]

Where the two models depart fundamentally is over their characterisation of the inherent tendencies of the unregulated system. The neoclassicist argues that the economic system tends toward (but, because of market imperfections, may not achieve) a full employment equilibrium. The Keynesian denies this, arguing that the tendency is toward an underemployment equilibrium. Further, where the neoclassicist sees equilibrium as stable, the Keynesian emphasises the volatility of the system — not only in terms of its cyclical fluctuations but in terms of the shifting nature of the long-term equilibrium to which it tends.

The Keynesian model points to the wayward expectational effects of uncertainty on investors and argues that this contributes to the volatility of the system through its effect on effective demand. While neoclassicists are well aware of the potent effect of expectations (moods of optimism and pessimism, shifts in confidence) and incorporate them into their analysis of short-period cyclical phenomena, there is a tendency in the neoclassical model to abstract from expectations (and indeed to assume perfect knowledge) in the analysis of value and distribution. This tendency reflects in part the habit of neoclassicists to separate monetary from real factors. There is no such separation in the Keynesian model. Money plays a critical role as 'a link between the present and the future'.

The models have different views on the equilibrating forces operating in the labour and capital markets. In the neoclassical model movements toward equilibrium are brought about by changes in relative prices (such as wages and interest rates), while in the Keynesian model equilibrium is restored by variations in the level of income and employment.

Given their different views on economic scarcity and the inherent tendencies at work in the unregulated system, it is not surprising that the two models differ in their attitude toward the nature, scale and need for governmental interference. Not all neoclassicists look upon governmental interference as negatively as did Robbins in the early 1930s. What they have in common, however, is a belief that the central aim of policy should be the establishment of a framework in which the efficacy of market forces is maximised and hence where resources can be allocated as efficiently as possible. Policies should therefore concentrate on improving the dissemination of information, improving the mobility of labour and other resources, discouraging restrictive practices and, to state the obvious, trying to encourage as competitive a system as possible. What neoclassicists have in common also is a belief that the source of capitalist drive, the inherent vitality of the capitalist system, resides in the private sector and that, as a corollary of this, the larger the public sector the less dynamic and the more constrained will be the private sector's entrepreneurial spirit. The Keynesian model looks upon governmental activity in a largely positive light. For it is only by governments' purposefully directing the system that full employment can be achieved and maintained and that inflation can be minimised. Again, ideas on what sort of methods the government should use to regulate the system vary from one Keynesian economist to another. The emphasis, however, is on the use of indirect methods of control, notably fiscal and monetary policy. While Keynes was anxious to avoid any direct interference with the exercise of individual initiative and choice, he believed that the growth of the public sector, or at least an increase in the relative importance of public sector investment, would provide an important stabilising force in the system. The assumption was that the public sector was somehow less prone to the degree of volatility which characterised the behaviour of investors in the private sector.

3
Australia adopts Keynesianism, 1930–45

IN tracing the changing nature of the Treasury line we need to establish not only a suitable conceptual framework but also the philosophical context out of which postwar Treasury thought emerged. In exploring this context one is struck by the extent of enthusiasm for Keynesianism. In contrast to the United States where the dominant mood was one of reservation, the outstanding feature of the Australian economics profession immediately before and particularly during World War II was the fact that Keynesian economics was so readily and widely accepted. H.C. ('Nugget') Coombs recalls in his recently published memoirs:

> The publication in 1936 of John Maynard Keynes' *General Theory of Employment, Interest and Money*, was for me and for many of my generation the most seminal intellectual event of our time. It was not an easy book. Many of the ideas on which it was based were then unfamiliar, and the book itself showed evidence of haste in composition so that its structure did not emerge sharply from initial reading. Nevertheless, it did not fail to generate excitement from first contact, and soon I had become convinced that in the Keynesian analysis lay the key to comprehension of the economic system.[1]

Such statements raise two questions. First, why was Keynesianism so readily accepted in Australia? Why did it generate such excitement? Second, just what did Keynesianism mean in the Australian context? In other words, did the acceptance of Keynesianism go beyond an acceptance simply of its policy aspects?

The financial orthodoxy of the 1930s

Throughout the 1930s the annual budget continued to be seen by most parliamentarians and certainly by the Treasury in terms of a mere financial statement rather than as an instrument of stabilisation. Crisp has commented in relation to Casey's 1938–39 budget: 'One gathered that the general level of economic activity had an effect on budget totals but hardly the reverse.'[2] This was a world concerned not with economic aggregates and their interaction but with independent, individual units. Before the Joint Select Committee on Public Accounts in 1932, the secretary to the Treasury, J.T. Heathershaw, was asked whether he thought the grand totals of the revenue and expenditure of the Consolidated Revenue Fund should be shown in the annual budget papers. He replied: 'I am inclined to question the value of a statement giving the total expenditure, as it appears to me to be almost meaningless.'[3]

Percy Spender has provided a first-hand account of the Treasury's approach to budgeting during the 1930s. He refers to the 'somewhat casual way' in which Stuart McFarlane ('Misery Mac'), the secretary to the Treasury, put the budget of September 1939 before him (Spender was then assistant treasurer):

> He presented me with a large foolscap piece of paper — I can see it now — on which he had worked out what I can only call his 'sums'. Our total expenditure for the different departments and services of government etc. would amount to so much. Revenue, at existing rates of taxes, direct and indirect, together with customs and excise, plus miscellaneous items, was estimated to amount to such and such. The difference between estimated expenditure and revenue would need to be bridged by increased taxation, customs and excise — different formulas being suggested for choice — and loans. There would be figures to suggest amounts thought capable of being raised by the latter method. It was for the government to make a choice between how much should be obtained by increased taxation, customs, excise, etc., and how much should be sought by way of loan.
>
> That, in substance, was the outline, and as such, stated the problem and how it might be dealt with in terms of mere money. There was nothing, however, to indicate a financial policy geared to war, or any statement of principle or planning as to how the economy of the nation was to be organised for war. It was, as I saw it, merely a statement on what money was called for by the various departments, and how it might be obtained.[4]

The budget, as Spender points out, was seen by the Treasury in terms of 'mere money', governed by accounting, balance-sheet, principles. Budgeting was simply a matter of estimating expenditure and then determining the ways in which the revenue to cover this expenditure could be raised. Balanced budgets were the inviolable ideal. That the budget could be used to mobilise real resources, that is, to channel and stimulate economic activity, was not envisaged. The Treasury's only concern was with 'sums', in particular with keeping these sums to a minimum.

J.A. Lyons, leader of the United Australia Party (UAP) and Prime Minister from December 1931 to 1939, agreed with the Treasury approach. Lyons was a disciple of the canons of sound finance and endorsed the principles of the premiers' plan. The Lyons government adopted a fatalistic approach to Australia's economic situation, arguing that all that could be done about the severe unemployment problem, apart from further reducing the costs of production (mainly by means of wage cuts), was simply to wait and pray for an improvement in the prices of Australia's export commodities. Eventually profits would reappear, but that day could not be rushed. Lyons' policies generally tended to dampen the course of economic recovery. In line with financial orthodoxy, the budget deficit became progressively smaller and strict control was exercised over the level of current public expenditure. Unemployment relief was paltry and hampered by a rigid adherence to the doctrine that public works spending should be on 'reproductive' items. In his budget speeches Lyons insisted that governments were extremely limited in their ability to provide full-time work for those currently unemployed. It was the private sector, not the public sector, which alone would ultimately absorb the bulk of the unemployed. He believed that relief schemes would not permanently ease unemployment, arguing that 'the work provided would be largely of an unproductive and temporary nature, and at the conclusion of it those who had been so employed would again be relegated to the ranks of the unemployed'.[5]

The Full Employment white paper

The attitude that governments were essentially impotent in their ability to deal with the problem of unemployment was to break down by the end of World War II. The outstanding symbol of the change in attitude occasioned by the war was the 1945 white paper, *Full Employment in Australia*.[6] The white paper opened with the declaration that the government considered full employment a 'fundamental aim'. Unemployment was branded an evil. The provision of 'the general framework of a full employment economy, within which the operation of individuals and businesses could be carried on' was deemed a responsibility and an obligation of commonwealth and state governments. This would involve, in very broad terms, the maintenance of expenditure on goods and services at a level commensurate with the preservation of full employment. In introducing the white paper to Parliament, J.J. Dedman, the Minister for Post war Reconstruction, argued that unemployment, by averaging more than 10 per cent for the twenty years from 1919 to 1939 (and peaking at more than 25 per cent in the worst years), was now considered a defining characteristic of capitalism. Given such a characteristic, the Labor government's full employment policy was a 'positive contribution to the security of the individual'. Dedman proudly declared that the white paper constituted 'a charter for a new social order'.[7]

For all its virtues as a statement of intention, the white paper had its faults. Butlin and Schedvin point to the dissatisfaction of those involved in its preparation: 'the economists most directly involved were the first to admit its glaring weaknesses: its high level of generality, lack of balance, reticence on wages policy and public finance, vague exhortation for improved efficiency, and lack of precision on how the transition problem was to be overcome.'[8] The question of just what purpose the white paper would serve was never satisfactorily solved, with the result that 'the outcome was an amalgam of ministerial statement and specialist report which served neither purpose adequately'. While the government made clear its intention to vary public sector expenditure so as to maintain full employment, a notable feature of the white paper was the scant attention given to the question of public finance. The government announced that as it intended keeping total expenditure high it would have to have the necessary finance. This should come mostly from taxation (presumably both direct and indirect). Though taxation was subject to limitations as a revenue source, it was believed that these limitations would incomes when the economy was operating at full employment to cover at least all current public expenditure (including maintenance) as well as to make a contribution to public capital expenditure. But the budgetary consequences of this were quite vague. All that the white paper contained were references to general principles such as avoiding tax rates that were 'too high', avoiding variations more than were 'inevitable' so as not to annoy the public, minimising the restrictive effects of taxation, and trying to achieve a higher degree of equity. Nevertheless, given the government's belief that taxation would not be able to provide all of the necessary revenue, it is clear that the likelihood of deficit financing was envisaged (though this was not mentioned explicitly). In line with this, it was noted that borrowing from either the public or the central bank could be used to provide necessary finance. The main problem with public borrowing, however, was that it entailed an interest burden. As for central-bank finance, though useful up to the point of full use of men and resources, if used beyond that point real incomes and the welfare of low-income groups would be at risk. Moreover, it could lead to instability of a kind strong enough to destroy full employment.

For all its weaknesses, the white paper was nevertheless a remarkable document. For it involved a fundamental break with the past. It involved looking at the economy differently. Output levels, rather than cost and price levels, were now the main source of attention. Linked with this, the importance of effective demand was recognised and emphasised. The attention given to output levels turned the government's attention to the economy as a whole and to seeing, at an aggregative level, its interrelatedness. Despite the haziness about just how the budget would be used, it was now appreciated that the budget affected, and was affected by, the rest of the economy. More importantly, the government was proposing a form of intervention in the economy previously considered unwise and improper. Expenditure levels were to be regulated by offsetting variations in public capital expenditure so as to maintain balance in total expenditure. And as a result, fluctuations in the economy were to be controlled, the instability to which the economy seemed inevitably prone was to be excised, and employment was to be maintained at continuously high levels. Such views represent the most remarkable aspect of the government's break with the past. Underlying the aim of full employment was the belief that the economy could and should be manipulated to achieve particular desired ends. Fatalism, the idea of subservience to the unregulated workings of the market economy, had been jettisoned. Even fluctuations caused by changes in export prices, previously accepted with resignation, were now thought to be capable of some sort of control. There was broad agreement among both government and opposition parties that some measure of active economic management was not only possible but necessary. Such management would be the saviour of the Australian capitalist system. It would be the exorcist of the insecurity caused by the depression.

It should be kept in mind, however, that in Australia the pre-Keynesian conception of the role of government in economic affairs was far removed from one of strict *laissez faire*. In fact Australian history has been characterised throughout by a dependence on governments and by a high level of government regulation. However, pre-Keynesian, pre-World War II, regulation was essentially piecemeal rather than integrated, microeconomic rather than macroeconomic. Only individual aspects of the economy and not movements of the whole economy were regulated. Regulation was exercised by a plethora of competing institutions including the federal government, the states, the Tariff Board, the Commonwealth Bank, the Commonwealth Arbitration Court, wages boards, and the Loan Council. A variety of marketing schemes operated also.

That prewar control was only piecemeal was recognised and criticised by Australia's leading economists. Roland Wilson, for example, pointed out at a conference held in 1934 on economic planning, that

> we are already planning in Australia and we have been doing so for a long time. We have planned, by means of tariffs and bounties, the course of the country's industrial development. We have desired, planned and achieved a greater extension of secondary industry than free development would have given us. We have planned our railway systems, we have attempted to plan our oversea shipping services, and we are even now attempting to plan the development of road transport. Afforestation and irrigation schemes are planned, and the elements of planning are beginning to creep into our monetary system.[9]

But Wilson continued by arguing: 'The examples I have cited are but scattered assaults on the objective. They are unco-ordinated, they have no integrating purpose, and they have produced no body of principles to be used as a criterion of success. We are muddled in our objectives and we get muddled results. We shall continue to do so until we take more thought for the morrow.' E.R. Walker suggested in 1943, in terms notably similar to those of Wilson, that the prewar economy was not only 'mixed' but 'muddled': 'Governments were never quite sure how far they should go along the path of control because they were surrounded by the clamour of sectional interests, some urging an extension of control in the directions profitable to themselves, and others arguing just as strongly for the removal of particular controls.'[10] Just as Wilson complained of a lack of any 'integrating purpose', Walker concluded that the key characteristic of prewar regulation was the absence of any 'dominant purpose'. By contrast, economic management as practised after World War II was a conscious attempt to manage the economy as a whole, to regulate aggregate demand so as to achieve and maintain high production levels throughout the economy and thereby ensure continuous full employment. With this aim in mind, much greater emphasis was placed on the need for improved coordination of policy weapons.

The Treasury Line

Explaining the acceptance of Keynesianism in Australia

How was it, then, that the Keynesian notion of economic management came to be accepted by the end of World War II? The discussion below considers three broad factors: the role of the wartime ALP government; the great depression's legacy of economic insecurity and the stark contrast of full employment during wartime; and the role of the small but relatively tight-knit Australian economics profession. Emphasis is placed on the last of these.

The Labor Party and Keynesianism

It has sometimes been suggested that the acceptance of the notion of economic management and Keynesianism in general was linked fundamentally with the fact that from 1941 onwards Australia was ruled by a Labor government. Emphasis has been placed in particular on the fact that J.B. Chifley, the Labor Treasurer and, from 1945, Prime Minister, was sympathetic to Keynesian ideas. In his biography of Chifley, L.F. Crisp points out that the Royal Commission on Money and Banking (1936–37), in which Chifley was a commissioner, happened to begin sitting in the same month that Keynes' *General Theory* was published. Crisp argues that from July of 1936 reference began to be made to the book by some of the economists giving evidence to the commission. Under the guidance of a fellow commissioner, Professor R.C. Mills of the University of Sydney, Chifley 'was perfectly placed to gain an early appreciation of the Keynesian "revolution" ... Chifley in a broad sense became a "Keynesian-of-the-first-hour"'. Crisp claims that this fact was 'of enormous significance for Australia in the years after 1941'.[11]

Crisp suggests also that 'experience and instinctive inclination had predisposed Labour men to Keynes' approach and central theses'. Though this is asserted rather than argued, it is true that the Labor Party had long been inclined toward interventionism. Perceiving the intransigence of bankers to be the fundamental cause of the depression, some members of the party suggested in the early 1930s that an 'inflationary' policy, entailing currency and credit expansion, be introduced. E.G. Theodore, Treasurer in the Scullin government, harped on the need for a fundamental change in attitudes and policies. He complained: 'Governments, no matter how valiantly they may have faced the problem [of unemployment] during election campaigns, are seldom able to deal effectively with it. It is the common and universal practice of Governments, almost without exception, to temporise with and palliate the evil when the crisis is at its worst, in the hope that an early revival in trade will bring at least a temporary relief to their troubles.'[12] Theodore believed that palliatives were not enough. Instead, active monetary policies, designed to inflate the economy and to enable governments to finance their budget deficits, should be introduced. These suggestions came to be known as the Theodore Plan. It could be argued that the Theodore Plan was in spirit, and in part in practice, a form of crude Keynesianism. But this does not necessarily justify Crisp's claim.

One must be careful to avoid labelling Theodore's ideas as being synonymous with those of the Labor Party caucus, especially given the hostility of the New South Wales members to the Theodore proposal. Moreover, the caucus, admittedly under intense pressure from Sir Robert Gibson and the Commonwealth Bank, was later to accept the balanced-budget proposals of the premiers' plan.

It has to be remembered also that a predisposition toward interventionism does not necessarily signify a predisposition toward Keynesianism. The point remains nevertheless that the Labor Party found it easy to accept that part of the Keynesian package which called for policies designed to produce a more equitable distribution of income and for the 'socialisation of investment' — as Keynes interpreted that term. And the popularity among ALP members of underconsumptionist ideas made the party receptive to proposals for increased spending as a solution to unemployment. It is also true that the Labor Party was particularly vocal during the war and particularly from 1942 onwards in declaring its belief that unemployment could be eradicated and in its insistence that it was the responsibility of federal and state governments to do so (though, again, such arguments do not by themselves indicate an acceptance of Keynesianism). In 1942 H.V. Evatt, then commonwealth Attorney-General, declared: 'With the lesson that it took the war to teach us, we can no longer assert that the problem of unemployment is insoluble, that men are out of work only because they are unfit or unwilling to work, that financial policy prevents their employment, that the task of maintaining full employment is not a responsibility of the national Government.'[13] Similar arguments were advanced with increasing vigour by Curtin and Chifley in parliamentary debates, radio broadcasts, newspaper articles and election speeches. Delegates of the Labor government preached the same message to overseas audiences and attempted valiantly to gain international acceptance of the need to ensure full employment.

The UAP government, by contrast, had been notably reluctant to commit itself publicly to a full employment policy. Nevertheless, an examination of the activities of a host of interdepartmental committees, various specialist committees and study groups formed in 1941 by the UAP government reveals quite clearly that a change in attitude toward employment and the notion of economic control predated Labor's electoral victory. As Butlin and Schedvin point out, 'the central concern of both re-establishment and economic committees was post-war employment prospects. With hundreds of thousands of men mobilised and unemployment not entirely eliminated, the vision of a return to mass unemployment after demobilisation was vivid; it was assumed that no government whatever its political complexion could avoid giving employment policy the highest priority'.[14] It would seem, then, that where the ALP differed from the preceding UAP government was not in accepting the need for and ability of governments to eradicate unemployment but in its willingness to make this commitment explicit. By 1942 even Menzies was openly supporting the notion of economic control (though, with the foundation of the Liberal Party in 1944, the preferred term was economic regulation).

In a radio address that year he made it clear that he believed that the choice facing Australia after the war was 'not between unrestricted capitalism and a universal socialism'. Menzies argued that 'we have learned a great deal about how to use private enterprise for our own social and national ends'. He was convinced that people had a deep-seated instinct to strive for progress and reward. This was the source of capitalist drive. But he was equally convinced that this drive should not be left untrammelled. Instead, we 'should seek to control and direct it in the interests of the people as a whole'.[15] By 1949 Harold Holt could declare, somewhat incongruously in the light of the excesses of opposition rhetoric during the 1944 and 1948 referenda campaigns, that 'I make no plea for catch-as-catch-can *laissez faire*... There is an important place for State planning in a modern community'.[16] Though such statements were perhaps politically opportunistic, they are nevertheless significant in that they reveal that a commitment to the maintenance of high employment and, underpinning this, an acceptance of the need for some sort of governmental economic management was not restricted to the Labor Party. This in turn suggests that there are more fundamental reasons than the election of the Labor government in 1941 which are needed to explain the acceptance in Australia of Keynesianism.

The legacy of insecurity

It would seem that the insecurity caused by the depression experience of the 1930s, one which affected Australia particularly severely, played an important part in the ready acceptance of the notion of economic control. A League of Nations report, published in 1943, referred to 'the helpless feeling of insecurity, the anxiety regarding the future of dependants, the frustration of idleness, [and] the sense of counting for nothing in the community' which the great depression had engendered.[17] Presenting the *Full Employment* white paper, Dedman offered a similar view: 'To the individual thrown into idleness by the failure of the economic system to provide employment, this failure meant poverty, frustration, disillusionment, and bitterness. Even those fortunate enough to remain in their jobs were threatened by a sense of insecurity.'[18] Reflecting this insecurity, pressure became intense for a governmental commitment to high employment. Australians wanted living standards raised and, above all, unemployment banished. As Herbert Burton put it in 1943, 'there is no question ... that among the great majority of people there is ... a strong and growing demand for freedom from the insecurity of slumps, from the anxiety of international rivalries and hostility, and for a more equal chance of a "good life" for all men — especially those within our own community'.[19] What was also important was the spectre of full employment occasioned by the war. Burton noted that 'one of the most widespread sentiments I have met in the last couple of years ... has been in effect as follows: "Now we are at war there is no unemployment, and the Government can find all it wants for war purposes. Why can't it find employment for all in peace-time?"'. This point was made again and again in wartime literature. L.F. Giblin, for example, declared in 1943: 'The demand for maintaining a high level of employment and a minimum standard of income is so strong and general that every Government here — and in many other countries — must adopt the corresponding policies as fundamental.'[20] Similarly, Roland Wilson argued in 1942 in a submission to a parliamentary committee that it was

> not likely that public opinion [after the end of the war] will tolerate the existence of widespread unemployment, especially when people have become used to heavy defence expenditure and its effects in reducing unemployment to negligible proportions. There will inevitably be a demand for a continuance of governmental expenditure, directed to peace time ends, in order to maintain employment at or near the maximum level.[11]

In short, the demand for high employment and, by implication, for the government to regulate the economy to achieve this end, became particularly potent during World War II and must be seen as highly significant in the acceptance of the Keynesian notion of economic management. More accurately, it should be seen as an essential precondition for the acceptance of a Keynesian stance. For it is not enough to want to achieve high employment. One has to have the expertise, the technical knowledge to achieve it. In this regard it would seem that the economists who joined the commonwealth public service during the war were of fundamental importance. For it was the economists who claimed to have the theoretical insights and technical skills to secure full employment and who were looked upon to provide guidance in managing the economy and in achieving the permanent abolition of unemployment so earnestly desired.

The economists

Because of the exigencies of war and because of an insufficiency of able administrators, many of the young graduates who joined the public service were able to bypass the established channels of promotion and assume relatively senior positions. An important lesson for these young economists provided by the war was that Keynes' theory seemed to have been vindicated. For the war was associated with unprecedented leaps in the level of government expenditure and also with a substantial decline in the level of unemployment. For those with economics training the causal connection between spending and employment became clearly established and the notion of economic control became a distinct possibility. It seems, however, that most of the economics recruits were sympathetic to Keynesian ideas even before they entered the service. Coombs notes that when he went to Sydney to join the Commonwealth Bank in the mid-1930s, 'I came into contact with a group of economists who shared my excitement over the *General Theory*'.[22] These included Leslie Melville, the Commonwealth Bank's Economist, and members of the Economics Department at the University of Sydney, such as R.C. Mills, Ronald Walker, Robert Madgwick, John La Nauze and Herman Black.

Coombs came into contact also with other economists in Sydney enamoured with Keynesian ideas such as Trevor Swan, J.G. Crawford and Jock Phillips. He points out that 'Mills arranged frequent staff seminars to discuss contemporary economic writing and at these my understanding of Keynes developed more fully'. There were also frequent informal discussions at local coffee shops with staff from the Commonwealth Bank, university staff and with some of the younger economists at the Bank of New South Wales, such as Leslie Bury, James Plimsoll, and Arthur Tange. Similarly, at the University of Melbourne Keynesian ideas were readily accepted. L.F. Giblin, Ritchie Professor of Economic Research, was 'deeply sympathetic to Keynesian thought'. Douglas Copland was also amenable to Keynes' ideas. And to the younger Melbourne economists, such as J.M. Garland, Gerald Firth and R.I. Downing, 'Keynesian theory made a prompt appeal'.

Possibly Coombs overstates his case. While in most instances they accepted his broad conclusions, not all of these economists warmed immediately to the way Keynes had presented his arguments. On his way to Britain in January 1937, Giblin was able to report on

> a leisurely reading in one piece of Keynes' *General Theory* — with not much more definite result than the need to read it again. In so many places I cannot get a convincing picture of things happening just so — there are so many alternatives and qualifications to be thought out. So much seems to require a careful statistical analysis and testing before one can feel that it is safely based, and Keynes is a bit offhand on that side.[23]

While Giblin, characteristically, worried about the empirical aspects of the argument, Leslie Melville questioned whether conceptually Keynes had broken entirely free from 'classical' analysis:

> Keynes has attempted to break away from the concepts of the 'classical' economists and has given us a brilliant start in formulating a theory suitable for a dynamic world. Nevertheless, he is often unable to shake off the earlier mode of thought. Throughout his book ... we can see him struggling to give expression to two conflicting ideas, the one static and the other dynamic. In his discussion of the principle of effective demand, savings and investment, the propensity to consume, the marginal efficiency of capital, and the general theory of interest, the dynamic approach is struggling for expression. It bursts out triumphantly in his discussion of expectations and employment. However, Keynes surrenders to the equilibrium [stationary state/static] viewpoint in formulating his statement of the general theory... Thus, despite the epoch-making nature of the whole book, it seems to me that Keynes's general theory fails to break away from the older concepts.[24]

Some of the younger economists, too, were critical of Keynes' mode of presentation. While in agreement with the thrust of Keynes' message, Ronald Walker complained that Keynes had been guilty of obfuscation and in particular of building 'a theory on concepts which cannot possibly be checked against concrete facts'.[25] He was referring here to the idea of aggregate demand and supply curves (as Keynes defined them) and to the idea that entrepreneurs will have an incentive to increase employment up to the point where expected proceeds equal the aggregate supply price. Walker complained: 'Mr Keynes's important practical conclusions could be reached without this laborious shadow sparring ... [His] discussion of fluctuations in investment would have the same bearing upon practical policy if he abandoned his concept of an aggregate supply function and concentrated upon a more realistic model of business behaviour.' Somewhat similarly to Melville, he added in a footnote: 'It is remarkable that so original a brain should be bound by the form of the theoretical schemes on which it was trained, even when challenging their practical conclusions.'

Nevertheless, these sorts of criticisms aside, it is noteworthy just how willing most Australian economists were to embrace the Keynesian message. Indeed in some cases, and Coombs would appear to be an example, the principal effect of the *General Theory* was not to produce neophytes but rather to act as a heart-warming and authoritative scripture for those who had been groping unsuccessfully for a theoretical structure to support what they already felt to be the truth.

A number of reasons can be put forward to explain why so many of Australia's rather small economics profession were willing to accept, at the very least consider carefully, Keynes' arguments. In the first place, there was something of a Cambridge connection. Giblin (like Keynes) was an old Kingsman, having joined the college in 1893. His acquaintance with Keynes dated from 1918 and was renewed not long after the publication of the *General Theory* when Giblin spent several months during 1937–38 in residence at Kings. Before his return, Giblin had corresponded with Keynes on *The Means to Prosperity* (1933) and reviewed it most favourably in the *Economic Record*.[26] Ronald Walker had studied at Cambridge, too, in the days of ferment — 1931–33 — when Keynes began drafting the *General Theory* and when his *Treatise on Money* was being criticised by the Cambridge 'Circus' (which included Richard Kahn and Joan Robinson). Another Cambridge connection was W.B. Reddaway, a former supervision pupil of Keynes and, in 1936–37, with the *General Theory* just published, research fellow in economics at the University of Melbourne. Reddaway reviewed the *General Theory* for the *Economic Record*. Fully appreciative of the significance of Keynes' insights, Reddaway expressed his strong support for the arguments presented. Yet another Cambridge connection was Colin Clark, who first worked with Keynes in 1930 on the Economic Advisory Council. On the recommendation of Keynes, who held his statistical work in high regard, Clark was appointed to a university lectureship in statistics at Cambridge, a post he held from 1932 to 1937. Clark soon established a reputation as one of the leading authorities on the calculation of national income. He returned to Australia in 1937 and set to work, with J.G. Crawford, on a statistical analysis of Australia's national income.[27] Keynes was later to urge Clark to return to Cambridge to organise the Department of Applied Economics (which the university was then considering establishing).

Clark's work on national income points to another factor which contributed to the acceptance of Keynes' framework among Australian economists: an interest in the aggregative approach. Referring to the nature of economic study in Australia in the 1920s, Douglas Copland could point in 1951 to 'the habit which Australian economists seemed to develop of seeing the economy as a whole, and of realizing the possibility of initiating centrally planned policy to counteract maladjustments within the economy'.[28] This may well be an exaggerated claim, influenced by hindsight. It is true, however, as Copland argues, that during the 1920s 'the national income was the focal point of discussion'. The main difference, he points out, was 'that whereas to-day we are mainly concerned with movements in some of the Keynesian variables which make up the national income and expenditure, the emphasis in the earlier period was on the national income itself, this being quite properly regarded as an index of economic welfare and thus a good starting point for economic enquiry'.

The appeal of the *General Theory* lay also, of course, and perhaps most importantly, in the fact that within the theoretical framework there was an implicit solution to the problem of unemployment. But the book offered not only a solution to unemployment but a solution which would not be a cause of social divisiveness. As Coombs puts it, 'it was one of the most attractive features of the Keynesian analysis that it seemed to by-pass the most divisive issues within our society. It seemed in everybody's interest that expenditure should be pitched at levels adequate to sustain business activity close to capacity and so to maintain high levels of employment'.[29] Another attraction was that Keynes' macroeconomic management promised to maintain high employment levels without direct regulation of microeconomic matters, that is without directly interfering with the exercise of individual choice and initiative. It promised also, and this was a message which Australian economists seized on, to restore vitality to the private sector. They, like Keynes, saw governmental initiative as an essential precondition for the restoration of confidence within the private sector and for the rehabilitation of entrepreneurial dynamism — an attitude influenced perhaps by a long tradition in Australia of public enterprise.

The experience of World War II confirmed for most Australian economists the veracity of the message. The remarkable increase in the relative size of the public sector during the war, and in particular the centralisation of financial strength in the commonwealth government following the introduction of uniform taxation in 1942, provided the necessary structural characteristics for Keynesianism to be tested. Robert Skidelsky, referring to wartime Britain, makes a point equally applicable to Australia: 'the problems of war finance provided the first opportunity to test out the new Keynesian techniques of measuring and regulating the levels of aggregate income and output. Keynes himself had doubted whether it would be politically possible "for a capitalistic democracy to organise expenditure on the scale necessary to make the grand experiment to prove my case — except in war conditions". The Second World War provided the necessary laboratory'.[30]

Another relevant consideration, as Skidelsky points out, is that periods of war can stimulate a willingness to experiment because they are associated with 'the large-scale replacement of official personnel' and/or an influx of '"new men" whose ideas, personalities and interests have previously disqualified them from "normal" politics'. Certainly in Australia, as was described in chapter 1, major personnel changes occurred in the commonwealth public service during the war. It was not so much a case, however, of official personnel being replaced as them simply being swamped by the large number of (at first) temporary recruitments. Most of the economists mentioned above were brought to Canberra during the war and were placed in strategic positions. For instance, Copland was appointed prices commissioner and economic consultant to the Prime Minister; Wilson, who had been commonwealth statistician since 1936, became secretary to the Department of Labour and National Service in 1940; Coombs was employed at first in Treasury and was later appointed director of rationing and, in 1943, became director of postwar reconstruction; Brigden was appointed secretary to the Department of Supply; Mills was chairman of the Commonwealth Grants Commission; Giblin was economic adviser to the Treasury; and, from 1942, Walker was deputy director-general of the Department of War Organisation of Industry.

Not only did these economists occupy powerful positions, but they were brought together into a single committee formally entitled 'The Financial and Economic Advisory Committee' but usually referred to simply as 'F & E'. This committee proved to be of fundamental importance in gaining acceptance of Keynesian ideas in Australia.

F & E was originally established in December 1938 by Lyons, with its chief role being to advise on the possible effects of a closure of trade routes by Japan. Membership was limited to Giblin (who was appointed chairman), Melville and Wilson. Following a suggestion by Roland Wilson in September 1939 the committee was reconstituted, to use Giblin's term, 'on a more formal basis'.[31] The membership was enlarged by the addition of Copland and J.B. Brigden and later of Mills, Coombs and Walker. The function of the committee was also enlarged and made more heterogeneous. Wilson's proposal was that the F & E should 'constitute a small central "thinking committee" to which all sorts of problems could be submitted for general advice'.[32] Its main task was 'to co-ordinate the basic economic policies of the various executive arms of the government'.

Writing in 1940, Wilson pointed out that F & E was 'entirely advisory in capacity, and is dependent in the main for its effectiveness on moral suasion and reasoned argument'.[33] Butlin notes that the views of the committee were disseminated by a variety of methods, such as 'uninhibited personal letters' by Giblin to senior administrators and by direct consultation with the Treasurer. Also of importance was the fact, as noted, that most members occupied influential positions throughout the public service, something which enabled the committee's views to be rapidly and widely disseminated.

The importance and direct influence of F & E declined sharply after 1941. (Even so, the individual members of the committee continued to have a powerful influence, something made possible in part by their strategic positions and in part by Chifley's renowned willingness to listen to, and seek advice from, his leading public servants.) The reasons for the decline of the committee's direct influence were implicit in its role, something of which Giblin was well aware:

> The first three years of the war were naturally the period of the Committee's greatest activity. In the earlier years the need was for the establishment of general principles for the war economy, a task suited to the interests and capacities of the members. And as the war progressed, the emphasis shifted to the need for efficient administration in harmony with the established principles and in this task no Committee can be of much use. In the process of time problems sorted themselves out and found a home in new departments or sections of departments where they could receive special attention on an adequate scale.[34]

Assessing the influence of the committee is a difficult task. Nevertheless, Butlin for one is convinced that for the first eighteen months it was of 'critical importance' and that its influence was 'powerful and pervasive'.[35] Its influence was such that 'many public servants and a minister or two came to adopt as their own, ideas and policies which had their genesis in the committee; even the phrasing of nominally decisive policy documents at times had an identifiable committee source with no reason to believe there had been any direct or immediate connection'. Coombs, too, has no doubts about the influence of the committee. He argues: 'It was the work of this committee which gave to the economic planning of the war an essentially Keynesian character.'[36] It seems essential, therefore, to investigate the ideas and attitudes of the individual members of F & E in order to understand in what sense their views can be described as Keynesian.

The philosophy of the F & E economists

What Keynes offered the F & E economists was a particular theoretical framework which encapsulated certain fundamental causal relationships and which thereby, especially when coupled with the national accounting estimates then beginning to be assembled, provided an intelligible and useful method of understanding the economy and of predicting its movements. As Coombs puts it:

> Keynes' achievement was to produce a simplified model of the system in which the enormous diversity of its components were grouped in a limited number of causally significant factors, and to express the relationship between these factors in language which was readily comprehensible. Given this model, it became possible by observation, by reasoning, and by intuitive judgement, to assess changes in the various factors and in the relationships between them in particular situations.[37]

It would seem, however, that when the F & E economists embraced the Keynesian model they embraced much more than even Coombs was aware of. What is notable about the F & E economists, in fact, is that they exhibited an outlook which encompassed all the features of the broadly defined Keynesian model described in chapter 2. As will be seen, their acceptance of Keynesianism was not simply an acceptance of the notion of economic management.

Australia adopts Keynesianism

In discussing the F & E economists, it seems appropriate to begin with Roland Wilson, given his dominant and lengthy influence on the Treasury in the postwar period. A valuable source of insight into Wilson's outlook is provided by a paper he delivered in 1934 to an Australian Institute of Political Science (AIPS) conference on national economic planning. Wilson was then 30, and the depression seems to have affected him considerably. Economic conditions between the wars had clearly demonstrated to Wilson the failure of the unregulated competitive system. The interwar world was a world of 'idle hands, rusting machines, rotting ships, and silent factories [; a world of] slums, ignorance, and empty bellies'.[38] (As will be seen, the one mental characteristic listed here, ignorance, was to Wilson the key evil.) Wilson was concerned, too, at the apparent inexorable tendency for recurrent depressions to grow ever more severe. This was a fact ignored by a community apparently resigned to the seeming inevitability of cyclical instability, a community which before the depression had not paid heed to the 'obvious clankings and groanings' of the economic machine — noises which, for those willing to listen, had been apparent even in periods of so-called normality. There had been a failure also to recognise, and here Wilson and Keynes were one, that the economy had always operated below maximum efficiency, even in those periods in which depression had been avoided.

Wilson acknowledged that the notion of a competitive market system was 'as true as any other short description' of the Australian economic system and he conceded that the philosophical justification of the system formed 'a theoretical conception of great beauty': 'It interprets the organization of the economic activities of man in part as a response to that universal harmony which pervaded the philosophy of its progenitors; and in part as a tribute to the divine genius of man in letting well alone. It represents that organization as a machine of amazing intricacy and infinite flexibility, automatic, all-embracing and all-sufficient.' But the competitive market system was indeed only a theoretical conception. It may have had explanatory value in understanding the economy of nineteenth-century England, but was now decidedly unrealistic: 'Neither in its operation nor in its results is the competitive system justifying the faith of its votaries.'

There were two main reasons why the competitive system had lost any relevance it once may have had. First, the economic environment had changed considerably over the previous twenty years. The economic machine had become more intricate, more complex, with the result that decision-making was increasingly more difficult and more prone to error and cumulative disruption. The economic system was also much more concentrated. 'The individual and compensatory decisions of a host of small producers have been largely replaced by the decisions of a handful of industrial chieftains, with the result that the field for the mutual cancellation of errors has been increasingly restricted.' In addition, the average standard of living had steadily increased, permitting much greater choice, and the pattern of income distribution, and hence social tastes and needs, had altered, thereby making it more difficult to forecast demand. Wilson denied the claim put forward by adherents of the

67

individualist philosophy that the economic system was inherently flexible. There was no such inherent tendency; in fact the system was becoming progressively less flexible.

Second, there were weaknesses 'inherent in the system itself'. For the competitive system to operate efficiently there were two key requirements: 'the economic actions of individuals must be rational and informed; and the control of the State in those matters which cannot be left to individual self-interest, must be equally rational and informed.' Wilson judged that neither requirement was adequately satisfied: 'In the individual we have had to reckon with ignorance and emotion. In the State, and more particularly in respect to the exercise of its control over purchasing power, we have had to reckon with ignorance, emotion, and sometimes with a sincere but misplaced conservatism.' Largely because of these behavioural deficiencies, the competitive capitalist system contained 'within itself the seeds of recurrent cycles of alternating prosperity and depression'.

Clearly, Wilson chose to blame ignorance and emotion as the fundamental sources of economic instability. People were not the rational, coolly calculating creatures which some economic texts seemed to suggest. The actions of the farming community were a good example. Wilson noted that prices in the primary industry had fallen to 'unprecedented levels', and commented: 'The farmer, ignoring the economic textbooks, has tried to catch up on falling prices by increasing supply. The two processes have tended to accentuate the disparity which produced them. What has become of the automatic adjustment?' Discussing some of the problems involved in economic planning, Wilson made clear his views on human nature:

> Man may be innately good, but he is not good enough. He may be capable of improvement, but the present must take him as it finds him. It finds him still a creature of emotions, ruled by instinct rather than reason. Under the stimulus of a fine ideal he can at times rise to noble heights, but in the ordinary course of everyday life he remains the imperfect social animal. His potentialities are great, but to an extent wider than the more enthusiastic planners care to admit, they remain potentialities... Impatience of authority, preoccupation with detail, the accumulated class resentment of the ages, ignorance, and the consequent domination of reason by emotion — all these are factors which limit the scope of planning.[39]

Again, emphasis was on the persistence of individual ignorance and emotion. Both had subverted the power of reason. Both had been a potent source of economic instability.

But despite such shortcomings in human behaviour, Wilson believed in social amelioration. Reason could replace instinct; a solution could be found to the current economic predicament. What was needed was the application of intelligence to what was essentially a man-made problem. The situation demanded 'conscious control and guidance of the economic process'. Wilson declared: 'Control, of a sort, we have. Control we are going to have. The choice is between wise and unwise control.' Just what was meant by 'control' was not made clear, but Wilson argued that planning was an essential element in wise control. And planning, in practical terms, required 'the establishment of some form of central "thinking agency", which will be better equipped than the existing political organization, to direct where direction is necessary and to withhold where intrusion would be harmful'. The sort of planning advocated by Wilson was not a form of socialistic or authoritarian planning. He was supporting what he referred to as 'the newer planning', or planning of the 'newer' school — an unfortunately vague concept. Such planning, he pointed out, was at this stage a feeling, 'an attitude of mind', rather than an articulated and carefully defined policy program. 'It impinges on social and political philosophy rather than on the technicalities of economics and finance. It urges us to seek the guidance of intelligence where hitherto we have relied on instinct.' It was a means of replacing individual emotion and ignorance by reason. In terms of practical implications, all that could be said at this stage was that planning sought to ensure 'that production will actually be undertaken and that the goods produced will be distributed — equitably, regularly, and in legitimate abundance'. Greater attention would be given to actual policies once the theoretical foundations were worked out fully.

In urging the adoption of planning, Wilson did not seek to replace capitalism but to repair it. In an earlier paper, written in 1932, he argued that to attempt to replace capitalism was 'something of a gamble', a gamble which he was not prepared to take. He had no admiration for present-day capitalism but believed its potential for improvement was considerable. The system needed to be given an opportunity 'to realise its full possibilities'.[40] Planning would provide such an opportunity, and it would do so without restricting individualism:

> The new social architects have propounded a system which they claim to be consistent with the retention of the existing framework of private enterprise. The profit motive will continue to be utilized as the most effective driving force for securing that provision of variety, and regulation of detail, which lies beyond the power of conscious direction. Competition will not be eliminated where it is required to hold self-interest in check.[41]

Nevertheless, the new planning would mean that private enterprise would be 'subject to more conscious supervision and will be afforded more adequate guidance than has hitherto been available'. Industry would be expected to exercise greater self-discipline. The state would have to cease its penchant for 'short-sighted economic policies'. Where automatic mechanisms did operate it was essential that the 'arbitrary and ill-conceived restraints' placed upon them by the state should be abolished. Above all, it was essential to implement 'a more vigorous and rational control of the machinery for creating and distributing purchasing power'. If it turned out that the necessary self-restraint required for effective planning failed to be forthcoming, it did not follow that planning should be abandoned. What would be needed was 'more, rather than less, planning'.

Wilson's outlook encapsulated in broad terms the views of the other members of the F & E Committee. They, like Wilson, had been profoundly affected by the depression experience. They were united in their distrust of unfettered market forces and were in agreement that such an unstable economic system could be, and needed to be, controlled. And all believed that they had the necessary wisdom and technical insight to advise on what form this control should take. Further, while they believed in the necessity of some form of control or management, they sought only to repair not to dispense with the capitalist system.

To Coombs, the pre-war world was 'a world where mass unemployment is a commonplace, where business are wrecked in the alternating boom and slump, and where the shock absorber for the vagaries of the economic system is the health, happiness, and lives of human beings'.[42] The system was in no sense self-regulating. The war, however, had clearly demonstrated the possibility of economic control: 'It did not take us long to discover that the workings of the economic system was something within our capacity to control... From the outset it was clear that governments were conscious that they could, by taking thought, bring into operation all the resources of manpower, equipment and materials which lay within our grasp.'[43] The fatalism of the interwar period had thus been abandoned. Such fatalism 'was the first casualty of the war'.

To Copland, the prewar world was 'a depressing picture of mass unemployment and depressed primary producers; monopoly and imperfect competition leading to an excessive inequality of wealth and incomes, and to a severe distortion of production from that most needed by society; unequal opportunities for health, education and occupation'.[44] He could not accept the neoclassical notion of an atomistic economy in which the pursuit of individual self-interest pushed the system toward an optimal level of output. Like Wilson, he claimed that because of 'ignorance, irrationality, uncertainty as to the future, and the economies of mass production, such a picture of society has never been true, and had recently become a horrible travesty of the truth'.

Copland had been making such comments since the mid-1930s. In an address to Harvard University in 1936 he declared:

> Capitalism under the control of the entrepreneur guided mainly by considerations of maximum profit is now completely discredited. It does not give economic security to the masses of the people; it does not provide the administrative machinery whereby increased technical efficiency is transformed easily into a generally higher standard of living. Countries have been able to absorb the shocks of depression and improved technique in inverse proportion to their dominance by the capitalistic entrepreneur.[45]

He concluded that the failure of capitalism under the control of the individual entrepreneur emphasised the imperative need for some form of state action, though he was willing to describe such action only in very general terms. The same point was made in a 1944 address, now reinforced by wartime experience:

> It is not practicable, and it would not be progressive, to seek a return to an individual economy. What we should seek to secure is that those aspects of the

productive economy which can no longer be individualist should not be in the control of private enterprise, because they give a dangerous and anti-social opportunity for exploitation, and for the perpetuation of insecurity. They should be in the control of the whole community, which is the only institution which is capable of administering them in the interests of the community as a whole.[46]

Copland agreed with the Keynesian and Wilsonian viewpoint that there was no inherent conflict between the exercise of economic control and the preservation of individualistic free choice. In fact, he insisted that some form of economic regulation was essential for the enhancement of choice and initiative:

> It is not socialism which *will* crush the individual. It is the economy of mass production which *has* crushed the individual. Only if we organise ourselves to control this Frankenstein monster of industrial production — and we can do so only through as far-reaching an institution as the State, representative of the whole community — can we hope to control mass production and monopoly, avoid unemployment, and regain *real* individual freedom.[47]

The regulation of private enterprise would not cramp or restrict the exercise of individual initiative and choice but would give it its first real opportunity to flourish, to be exercised without fear of insecurity. Conscious and purposive regulation of economic activity by the state which aimed at providing a secure economic environment would provide a basis for the intellectual, mental, political, moral and social freedom which Copland was convinced was lacking in the prewar world.

Melville agreed with Copland that ignorance and uncertainty were some of the key reasons why the neoclassical notion of a self-regulating economy was a 'horrible travesty' of the truth. Of the members of F & E Melville was possibly the one most concerned with the methodology of economics and in particular with the inadequacy of its behavioural assumptions. In his 1939 presidential address to section G of the ANZAAS conference Melville considered in detail the role of expectations in economic analysis. He was highly critical of conventional (neoclassical) analysis for its abstraction from uncertainty and, linked with this, its failure to pay adequate heed to expectations. Referring to writers such as Walras, Jevons, Edgeworth, Pareto and Marshall, he said:

> Most of them formulated their equations and conditions of equilibrium without any reference to the future or to rates of interest... In formulating their theories of equilibrium economists assumed, implicitly at least, that the future was known. In formulating their theories of interest they assumed that the present was known and proceeded to discuss interest almost as if its determination was independent of the general theory of value.[48]

The element of time had been largely ignored. Equilibrium analysis had come to be regarded as 'something which could be considered without reference to the future, to rates of interest, and to expectations'. Because of its static nature, Melville believed that neoclassical equilibrium analysis was of no use in explaining or examining trade cycles. Equilibrium analysis could not throw any light on why and when recovery turned to recession. 'The economic developments with which we are concerned are not developments from one position of equilibrium to another, for the postulated positions are never attained and are in fact unattainable. Neither is economic development a trend towards an equilibrium, and it is not a fluctuation about an equilibrium, with business activity alternatively over-shooting and falling short of the equilibrium state.' With some similarity to Keynes' shifting equilibrium model, Melville argued that 'even if a series of adjustments towards an equilibrium were commenced the adjustments themselves would so alter the data that the equilibrium would be disrupted'. To Melville, the key characteristic of the unregulated market economy was its cyclical tendencies. The point he was trying to make was that the economic system was essentially a dynamic one. Equilibrium analysis which ignored the effects of time and the role of expectations, equilibrium analysis which assumed hypothetical worlds such as stationary states, was of no use in understanding the real world.

Walker was less critical of equilibrium analysis than Melville and more equivocal than the other members of F & E about whether there was an inherent tendency toward full employment equilibrium. His view in 1943 was that empirical evidence indicated that equilibrium was a rare phenomenon. Elaborating on this, he noted:

> The weight of equilibrium theory suggests that failure to achieve equilibrium in practice *may* be due to continuous variation of the conditions of economic life; but it is equally conceivable a priori that there may be conditions which imply no tendency towards equilibrium. Since we are seeking a theory of economic development, such a possibility is not so distasteful as it may seem to the equilibrium theorist. If any set of conditions implies not equilibrium but continuous change — oscillatory or cumulative — there is no 'final' position for the dependent variables; every successive position is 'intermediate' to a subsequent one, and, though we may set out to construct a theory of market equilibrium, we finish up with a contribution (of sorts) to the theory of economic development.[49]

It is not exactly clear just what Walker wished to establish here — except for the fact that the system was subject to continuous change. The process being described, as with Melville, appears similar to Keynes' shifting equilibrium model in which the economic system is forever adjusting to new and unattainable equilibria. Certainly, however, there was no assumption that there was a tendency toward some sort of set of optimal conditions.

Though ideas on the meaning of economic control varied from member to member and over time, the F & E economists agreed that the notion of control should embrace action by the state designed to maintain outlay at a level sufficient to ensure continuous high levels of employment, to maintain business confidence, and to banish economic insecurity. The maintenance of outlay at full employment levels required planned, purposive action and, underpinning this, the use of an economically literate technocracy to advise on appropriate strategies.

Walker was the first of the F & E economists to embrace a Keynesian attitude to the role of the budget in dealing with economic instability. It would seem that his Cambridge days were critical here. As early as 1933 he was lamenting the fact that the idea of the government budgeting for a deficit during a depression had not gained wide acceptance.[50] By 1936, however, Walker had reached the view that the policy adopted in various countries, of spending on public works at the same time as preserving balanced budgets, was defensible in a context of unemployment. Such a policy was defensible because it was unlikely that public works spending would 'prime the pump' while people's confidence was shaken by the presence of unbalanced budgets. 'Such is the general state of knowledge that if a government wishes to enjoy public confidence it must either balance its budget or make a great show of effort in this direction.'[51] This was essentially the same approach adopted by Walker in 1936 in evidence before the Royal Commission on Money and Banking. If, he argued before the commission, one could abstract from the psychology of the business community and think purely in terms of the mechanical flow of money and purchasing power, an increase in the budget deficit was essentially the same as an expansion of loan expenditure, the names given to the two actions being the main difference. But the fact was that the reaction to the continuation and/or expansion of budget deficits was one of suspicion and lack of confidence. If this could be removed, if the general level of economic education could be raised, then the desirable policy to pursue would be to budget for deficits during depressions and for surpluses in booms. If the depression was protracted there was no sanctity in annual balancing or even balancing over a two- or three-year period. Nevertheless, Walker deemed it 'highly desirable' that ordinary current expenditure be balanced over a 'long period', that is, over the length of the cycle. This long-term balance was essential for the purpose of public finance administration. By 1939, however, he could argue that 'slavish adherence to budget balancing over *any* definite period may be inconsistent with the maintenance of full employment'.[52] Under cyclical budgeting the position would eventually be reached, as in annual budgeting, where there would be a need to choose between budget balance and full employment. To opt for full employment might necessitate abandoning even long-term budget balance.

From the start of the war the F & E Committee endorsed Walker's views and stressed the need for increased spending to ameliorate the employment situation. In defiance of the established fatalism, Giblin announced in 1939 in an F & E memorandum that 'the prevention and cure of unemployment is in a country's own hands'.[53] In October of that year Giblin discussed the views of the committee on the apparent increase in unemployment which had occurred in both the June and September quarters of 1939, and argued that unemployment was likely to become an 'acute embarrassment' to the government. There was only one solution: the Keynesian. 'The difficulty can only be met by spending — not planning, or commitment or raising loans, but spending; and spending for employment as much as and more than for defence.'[54] In December 1939 the F & E Committee recommended a departure from financial orthodoxy and advised Spender that, given the existence of a high level of unemployment, defence expenditure could for a time be increased without any need for a commensurate rise in taxation revenue. Later in the war, with real resources fully mobilised and inflation the key problem, the committee argued that taxation be increased and that a variety of direct regulatory measures be introduced as wartime expedients. When they were published in *The Times* in November 1939, Keynes' proposals on 'How to Pay for the War' generated immediate interest among committee members. From February to April 1940, seeking a solution to the problem of inflation, the committee considered Keynes' arguments in depth. Members quickly seized on the idea of an 'inflationary gap' and used it in formulating their policy recommendations.

Throughout the war frequent reference was made in the writings of the F & E economists to the fact that the wartime experience had demonstrated the importance of conscious action by the state to maintain an adequate level of demand. Writing in 1945, Giblin argued that a novel feature of economic thought as it had evolved up to the end of the war was 'the recognition that outlay will not maintain itself at the appropriate level [to ensure full employment] and that it is the duty of governments to take measures to ensure that it is so maintained'. Here again was the persistent theme of the economy's failure to be self-correcting. Giblin continued:

> Before the last war it was generally believed — and on quite reasonable evidence — that there was an automatic tendency in any economy to maintain outlay at something near the appropriate level [that is, at the full employment level]. It is only since then that experience under the between-war conditions, showed that the automatic adjustment was tragically insufficient to maintain outlay; and on that comparatively recent experience the need of Government action to maintain outlay has been recognized.[55]

The F & E economists, however, were keen to point out in their writings that keeping up a high level of outlay was a necessary but certainly not a sufficient condition for the achievement of full employment. What was required in addition, as Giblin put it in 1945, was 'something like a revolution in the canons of conduct of a large proportion of any people'. The members of F & E were adamant that the success of full employment policies would depend ultimately on the achievement of social consensus. They felt that greater self-discipline needed to be imposed and that a less selfish, more community-minded attitude be created. As we shall see, this raised important questions about the malleability of human nature.

The need for a change in community attitudes had been recognised and debated among a broad spectrum of Australian intellectuals since the early 1930s. As Tim Rowse points out, an important shift in the trend of philosophical discussion occurred in Australia in the 1930s, which was particularly evident among the members of the AIPS but also, as has been indicated, among leading Australian economists, and which involved the death of rational economic man and a recognition of the essential irrationality, imperfections and complexity of human nature and behaviour.[56] Linked with this change, and here Walker and Melville can be seen as being representative, were pleas for the adoption of a holistic social psychology to probe social life and, more fundamentally, to bring about a change in human consciousness and aspirations. As Rowse puts it, 'the intellectuals of the 1930s and 1940s, after recovering from the shock of finding that rationality was a dominant quality only in a restricted social enclave, began to emphasize the possibility of harnessing the manifest imperfections of social beings to ... [achieve] ... a common purpose'.[57]

The views of J.B. Brigden provide a useful insight into the trend of intellectual thought in the 1930s, and of the views of the members of F & E, on the malleability of human nature and on the possibility of social consensus. Writing in 1932 Brigden argued that it was time to realise, given an evident trend toward collectivism, that the question of 'social will' was of crucial importance:

> The twentieth century is forcing upon us a new collectivism. Whether it shall be of numerous rival groups, each individualistic to the core, or whether it shall be pervaded by a sense of social unity [which Brigden hoped it would], depends entirely on the individuals. 'Social Will' is not some mystic thing arising from the mass; it is the aggregate of individual Wills ... Social control ... can only come through a general growth of voluntary and co-operative *consideration*, one interest for another. And the moral leadership which may bring it forth is not likely to be a personal one. It must be widespread and pervasive.[58]

Brigden complained that those characteristics which seemed so essential to him for the individual to acquire voluntarily — unity, discipline, consideration, cooperation — were not being encouraged by economists. In fact, economists were responsible for diverting public attention away from the importance of 'social will'. Economics, unlike its parent discipline, moral philosophy, had 'grown hard, statistical, scientific, unmoral'. Economics had been insufficiently concerned with what ought to be, being preoccupied with what is.

Brigden was to take up these themes again in 1935 in his presidential address to section G of the ANZAAS conference. He began by describing the shift in thought which the depression had stimulated: 'The depression has brought out in dramatic fashion a general opinion already existing, and although we must discount the greater part of contemporary change, both in opinion and in practice, the trend of thought is an economic fact. Emphasis is passing from the alternative human desires for adventure to those for security, from progress to order, from freedom to discipline, and from competition to control.'[59] Brigden argued that if instability was to be overcome it was necessary to recognise that the profit motive was an inadequate and improper guide to, and rationale for, economic life. He had firm ideas on the sort of world he would like to see replace the existing one:

> Economists, being human, have their Utopia, too. Theirs is an economically-minded world in which the business community shall have acquired a sense of social responsibility, and where bankers at least will have become supermen, able to understand what to do when this Section shall have discussed some monetary problem. We should like to see a world where every large business gave an account of its stewardship in sufficient detail for it to be judged, and by a public interested

and wise enough to pass judgement. We should like to see a banking and investment system international enough, strong enough, and bold enough to say 'No' when booms threaten, and competent enough to know when to do it. We should like to see the difficulties of the problem appreciated.[60]

Brigden's ideal was a world dominated by the concepts of social responsibility and public accountability. There was also in Brigden's utopia an emphasis upon self-improvement and heightened intellectual capacity. What was required was an understanding of technical issues, interest and wisdom to pass judgments, competence to know when and what to do when a boom was apparent, and an appreciation of economic difficulties. All these behavioural characteristics had to be acquired; they were not inherent.

Somewhat pessimistically, Brigden appended to the passage above: 'But these are Utopian aspirations. Human nature is not yet built that way.' Other passages in his address, however, indicate that Brigden was not without hope. Of particular interest is the following:

> It required the Great Depression to start the idea of preventing the recurrence of depression. It always requires a great catastrophe to bring about a very radical reform. The powerful weapons of commercial propaganda may ... be used in the cause of general economic health. Central Banking is gaining great strategic power, and may be able to use it in a crisis with such a backing. It may lead to a real 'money power', inspired by a full-grown professional and scientific spirit, and able to maintain the confidence of both the investing public and the general public. Given such an authority there could develop all the discipline that is necessary and practicable for stability, economy, and progress. The machinery is relatively unimportant.
>
> This is the strategy for progress. It implies a recognition by business men that the profit motive is inadequate. That is to ask a great deal. It implies a recognition by others that political and legal force is as futile as physical force. That is to ask very much more. It implies co-operation and a new leadership. That is to ask for a miracle. Nevertheless the first may come from experience, the second from disillusion, and the third from necessity.[61]

Here again the hope was for cooperation, for self-imposed discipline (that which was externally forced being considered ultimately impotent), and for a lessening of the importance of pecuniary motives. There was also hope — and here Brigden seems to have some resemblance to Wilson's concept of a central thinking agency — for the establishment of a central banking authority embracing enough professionalism and technical expertise to inspire public confidence. Brigden's general conclusion was one of tightly restrained optimism that these hopes might eventually come to fruition and that popular ideas would one day advance 'out of their present infantile condition'.

If the 'great catastrophe' of depression had sown the seeds of 'a very radical reform', World War II saw these seeds take root and flourish. By 1944 Copland could argue that the war 'has done a good deal to restore unity of purpose among democratic peoples'.[62] He felt that there were strong grounds for confidence that an improved organisation of economic society could be achieved in the postwar period because, among other things, there existed 'a great mass of inarticulate opinion which could be brought into play, if properly organised and tutored, to support a constructive economic policy'. Copland warned, however, against over-enthusiasm about the possibility of such change occurring.

Likewise, even by the end of the war Giblin was a mixture of optimism and pessimism on the possibility of achieving the social consensus necessary for a successful full employment policy. Discussing the possible fate of attempts to secure full employment after the war, he argued in 1945 that 'the crux of the matter is the conduct of individuals. Most of us will need a new outlook. As of old, the Kingdom of God is within us'.[63] Giblin believed that 'people, in general, are reasonable enough, and as individuals mostly they can be counted on to play the full employment game'. But when individuals belonged to organised interests they acted quite differently: 'Organizations seem to collect all the vices and reject all the virtues of their members. Organized interests are in fact Satan's last and cleverest invention for the destruction of mankind.' There were also problems that were peculiarly Australian. Giblin was convinced that the British were 'more responsible and more realistic' than Australians. Australians were 'very given to romantic notions about everything concerned with production, and particularly about money'. Perhaps not surprisingly, Australians were also much less united: 'One would not expect much uniformity in public opinion with seven million people sprawled over three million square miles. Moreover they are segregated into States with most of their interests centred on the State capital. In peace-time the Commonwealth government and parliament are Sunday matters; for the working week it is the State administration that counts.'[64]

On the fate of Australia's attempts at a full employment policy, Giblin concluded that success was unlikely in the immediate future but would no doubt be achieved ultimately. Exercising his imagination, but with an underlying seriousness, Giblin concluded that the worst possible scenario was a situation in which a full employment policy was attempted but which was thwarted by the actions of avaricious groups blindly attempting to gain at the expense of others. In this scenario the cancer of self-interest and greed renders the economic corpus a near-fatal blow. But salvation comes through the education system. For in the midst of indiscipline, unemployment and economic stagnation a new generation has come into existence, a new generation raised on enlightened principles, instructed in the virtues of collective action, a new generation who can see all too clearly the faults of their parents and who are determined not to repeat past mistakes. Joining with their elders, who now too have seen the error of their ways and who, 'having good stuff in them at bottom', have acknowledged their foolishness and their material and moral bankruptcy, the new generation makes a fresh attempt (around 1965, Giblin ventured) to launch a full employment policy. This time it proves successful.[65] As with Brigden, social consensus arises ultimately from disillusion, experience and necessity. According to Giblin, people have faults, certainly, but they are malleable. With persistence and with the passage of time people can eventually be remoulded to embrace community-minded ideals. In this reformation education is the ultimate weapon. Effective leadership is also crucial.

Coombs, too, recognised the need for a change in social attitudes. Aware of some of the difficulties involved, he was nevertheless particularly optimistic about the possibility of achieving social consensus. With some similarity to Copland, he argued in 1944 that 'the war has created, at least at certain moments of its progress, a consciousness of social unity. That consciousness has not been sustained always at the same high level, but it is there, latent, and I believe ready to respond to calls upon it to achieve purposes sufficiently close to our national ideals'.[66] The war-weary population was 'anxious for change and willing to be inspired into social unity for a common purpose'. Coombs concluded that there were strong grounds for confidence that a full employment policy would succeed. The technical aspects of maintaining full employment would present no great difficulties.

In the 1944 Joseph Fisher lecture Coombs acknowledged that the maintenance of high employment levels could create problems both of excessive wage claims and of labour inefficiency. Increased bargaining power was held to be an inevitable corollary of a state of high employment. Coombs suggested that to induce wage earners not to use this heightened power as a lever to exact higher wages it was essential that they be convinced that their wages incorporated the fruits of increasing labour productivity. This could possibly be accomplished by having periodical reviews of changes in real production per head and having the basic wage altered accordingly. On the question of labour efficiency, Coombs recognised that problems such as reduced output, increased labour turnover and absenteeism would ensue once the fear of unemployment, which had once acted as a disciplinary force, had been removed. To overcome such problems it was essential that 'new attitudes and incentives' be built up:

> In the broadest community sense we can educate people to understand the relationship between efficiency and national income as a whole, and consequently its effects on wages, and on communal services, education, housing, public utilities, hospitals, clinics, etc. We can interest workers in figures of production, costs and efficiency for individual plants, and for production as a whole. We can educate them in the relationship between wages and profits on the one hand, and national income on the other ... We can build up a consciousness in the worker that his work is more significant to production as a whole, and a sense of participation in the total achievements of the economy'[67]

Again the emphasis, as with other members of the committee, was on the importance of education and tutoring from on high as the means of overcoming the debilitating effects of what the committee members judged to be the ignorance and myopia of their compatriots. Of course, underpinning Coombs' rather paternalistic faith in the possibility of educating people to understand economic relationships, of building up new attitudes, and of injecting a new consciousness, was the assumption that human nature is not fixed, that values and aspirations could be recast and that self-discipline could replace the discipline of the market. Coombs was confident that human malleability was such that the sort of social responsibility which Brigden had talked about in the mid-1930s could now be achieved.

If we are to take the members of the F & E Committee as a guide (all of them were, after all, among Australia's leading economists), Keynesianism had been fully accepted by the Australian economics profession by the end of World War II. The committee members agreed that purposive state action, backed by an appropriately qualified and well-informed bureaucracy, was essential for the operation of a more efficient, more productive, more equitable and more secure economic system. Such arguments flowed directly from the view that the unregulated economy could not look after itself: the state would be the *deus ex machina* which rescued an inherently faulty system. Fiscal policy was seen as the main tool of economic management, although most economists acknowledged (at least during the war and in the immediate postwar years) that there would be a need to continue to rely on some direct controls, such as price control. Particular importance was attached to the role of demand in determining employment and output levels. Coombs could announce in 1954 that the idea that production and employment levels were determined by the level of spending was the 'essence of the Keynesian analysis'.[68] All the F & E economists recognised also the importance of 'irrational' forces — those that sprang from ignorance and from uncertainty. The faith of this group of economists was that a governmental pledge to maintain aggregate expenditure at a level sufficient to ensure full employment would reduce uncertainty and instil a sense of optimism, thereby rendering expectations less volatile. But what is particularly interesting about the policy pronouncements of the F & E economists was their insistence that state action alone could not ensure the maintenance of full employment. There was general agreement that the essential prerequisite for successful economic management was a change in human values and attitudes. With varying degrees of optimism it was believed that social consensus, the adoption of a much more community-minded stance, needed to be and could be achieved, though perhaps only after considerable delay. Such a change could be brought about by an amalgam of experience, necessity and, perhaps most importantly, education.

II

The Treasury line, 1945–84

4

Keynesian theory converted into practice, 1945–55

A persistent concern of the Labor government throughout its postwar term was the possibility of a sudden and severe slump. It was assumed that at the end of the war there would be a short recession during the demobilisation phase which would then give way quickly to a powerful but short-lived boom. The boom would arise because of wartime arrears of demand and because Australia's primary producers would for a time enjoy high export prices due to temporary shortages of raw materials and foodstuffs in war-ravaged areas. Both sets of circumstances would lead to a rapid increase in aggregate demand. But the boom was expected to last perhaps two or three years before demand returned to a level which almost certainly would be insufficient to maintain full employment, indeed was likely, if left uncorrected, to produce a slump. This was a pervasive concern. John Stone notes: 'Everyone who, like myself, was completing his high school days just after the Second World War will recall the anxiety which prevailed generally at that time. Everyone feared that the war-time boom would be succeeded, perhaps after a few years "false prosperity" during the readjustment period, by the kind of post-war slump by which, throughout all history, wars had been succeeded.'[1]

But no such slump arrived. On the contrary, the boom continued and gathered force. Instead of unemployment the Australian economy was plagued with worsening labour shortages. The enduring problem became one of restraining a persistent, indeed accelerating, increase in the price level. The difficulty, then, for the Labor government and for the Treasury was not merely one of putting Keynesian principles into practice in a peacetime environment but coping with a situation quite the opposite to that to which the white paper had been addressed. This was a problem with which Labor, suffering from what Copland called 'depression psychology', never fully came to grips.[2] In the early Menzies years the Treasury came to recognise, and then tried to persuade the government, that there was a need for decisive and explicit fiscal action along Keynesian lines to deal with a badly overheated economy.

The Treasury line
Economic conditions, 1945–49

J.B. Chifley, Prime Minister and Treasurer, provided a neat summary in his 1945–46 budget speech of the difficulties likely to beset the economy during the transitional phase from war to peace. He noted that the excess of demand over supply was almost as great as at any time during the war and that excess spending power would be a dominant feature of the whole transition period. Moreover, the problem of excess demand would be reinforced by the 'great quantities' of savings which had accumulated during the war and which were held in highly liquid forms — in notes, in bank deposits, in war savings certificates and other securities. Reconversion woud be a gradual process: 'it will take considerable time to restore to civil production resources no longer needed for continuing war expenditure. Labour needs retraining and factories require new machines.' And there were likely to be delays in obtaining imports needed for reconstruction, either because of unavailability or because of foreign exchange difficulties. Chifley acknowledged that there were many things, notably housing, required urgently by the community. But, again, these needs could be satisfied only gradually. In short, there was a 'problem of potential inflation'.

By late 1946 the Prime Minister was able to announce that Australia had successfully passed through the first transitional stage. Most of Australia's war organisation had been dismantled. Employment was at record levels: factory employment was some 20 000 above the wartime peak. Chifley was convinced that Australia was 'developing a potential in secondary production capable not only of meeting a much wider home demand but also of supplying markets abroad'. Production overall was rising but was markedly insufficient in relation to demand, especially now that civilian employment was so much higher. And thus, not surprisingly, the danger of inflation continued and was in fact 'as formidable as ever'. Wool and wheat exports were enjoying high prices and the situation for Australia's exports of meat, dairy products and dried fruits was also generally favourable. The rapid rise in export income, however, had increased demand pressures still further and was making increasingly more difficult the government's attempts at price control.

A paper written late in 1947 by the government's Investment and Employment Committee (composed predominantly of officers from the Treasury, the Department of Postwar Reconstruction and the Commonwealth Bank) noted that the Australian economy was enjoying 'remarkable all-round prosperity' but warned that there were 'clearly some dangerous forces at work'. Since 1938–39 the size of the labour force had increased by almost 500 000. Half of these workers had been employed in the manufacturing sector. And yet nearly all secondary industries were looking for additional labour. Estimates of the Department of Labour and National Service showed that there were more than 100 000 unfilled vacancies, while unemployment was virtually non-existent. There was, therefore, little prospect in the immediate future of finding additional labour. Immigration could make no significant contribution until shipping improved. The committee noted that 'the drive to expand industry is tremendous' and that firms were 'doing their utmost to expand'. Poaching of labour was in evidence and had led to a serious increase in labour turnover. Of particular concern was the fact that basic industries were being starved of labour. This had had the effect of restricting output and pushing costs up. Industrial output was well behind the rate of increase of demand. Bottlenecks were being experienced because of shortages of labour, equipment and materials. Little relief could be expected from imports — a continued shortage of US dollars had necessitated that dollar imports be reduced. And it was envisaged that restrictions on dollar imports would soon have to be made more severe. It also seemed likely that prices would rise more quickly in the period ahead, mainly because of increases in wages. The committee concluded: 'We have now reached a stage at which, with all available labour employed, a huge demand for more labour remains unsatisfied. Meanwhile incomes continue to increase and this year will be boosted by record returns to the primary industries. Inflationary forces are therefore as strong as ever and since controls [on production, wages and materials] have been slackened off, these forces have a freer rein.'

An unfortunate consequence of the prolonged existence of inflationary forces, apart from the rise in costs and prices, was that it had encouraged 'the outcropping of many new and often small enterprises, all bent upon profiting by the current abnormal demand'. There had been a 'spreading of the industrial effort'; resources had been 'spread too thinly over too wide a field'. Productivity had suffered as a result.

The committee argued that it was desirable to maintain current taxation levels; indeed there was a strong case on purely economic grounds for increasing taxes (as had been done in the United Kingdom). The question of dealing with primary producers' incomes was considered particularly problematical. No satisfactory stabilisation schemes had been established and, it was argued, 'would now be very difficult to establish'. An attempt should be made, however, to encourage primary producers to reduce their debts and avoid 'lavish expenditure' on stock, land and equipment. Bank-advance policy had to be 'adapted to the times' but it had to be done selectively:

> There can be no case at all for an increase in total advances under present conditions. On the other hand, a contraction would do great harm if applied on an over-all basis. It would hit sound and unsound enterprises alike. The proper line is to be more selective, giving to sound and essential enterprises the finance they need but tightening up when over-expansion is showing itself or when enterprises are obviously of the mushroom variety.[3]

The possibility of returning to controls on the wartime pattern was clearly out of the question. Price control, however, could still play an important role. But the committee noted that 'without the support of wage-pegging and control of materials, price control must be allowed to register genuine increases in costs'.

Chifley noted in the 1948–49 budget speech, presented in September, that prices and costs had been rising at an increasing rate. Although the supply position was improving, key industries such as coal, iron and steel, and building materials were continuing to face grave difficulties in expanding output. The basic problem was their inability to compete satisfactorily with other industries to obtain labour, a problem compounded by the fact that the sort of employment they offered was heavy manual work. Workers had opted for 'more congenial occupations'. The government had come to the conclusion that immigration was the only salvation. Plans had been made which would bring to Australia more than 100 000 people a year. The Treasurer noted: 'Placement of migrant labour in basic industries, special housing schemes in key districts, and the provision of various amenities and services are direct means the Commonwealth is employing in a drive to get higher output in vital fields of production. So large and widespread are the benefits to be gained from success in this direction that no practicable effort can be spared.' The possibility of relying on imports to relieve supply shortages continued to be constrained by a shortage of US dollars. Although imports had begun to increase rapidly, the government had a continued responsibility to attempt to economise in the use of dollars. Accordingly, Chifley announced that it was planned in the forthcoming year to reduce the value of dollar imports below the level for 1948–49.

By mid-1949 three issues dominated the attention of the Investment and Employment Committee. The first was the fact that the rise in export and import prices had been halted by a mild recession in the United States. In the case of some exports (wool, wheat and lead) there had actually been a fall in prices (having increased by 17 per cent in 1946–47 and 24 per cent in 1947–48, the export index rose by 14.8 per cent in 1949–50). There was considerable concern that the recession would worsen and become a 'serious slump'. The second was the continuance of strong inflation in Australia: having risen by just over 4 per cent in 1947, the consumer price index rose by 10 per cent in 1948. Prices were expected to continue rising during the remainder of the year, though possibly at a slower pace (in fact the consumer price index rose by a further 10 per cent in 1949). The committee believed that there was a 'distinct possibility' that the inflationary trend would be reversed at some stage during 1950: 'Certainly there is no sign of a reversal in 1949, but the critical point could be reached in 1950, and when it is reached the change could occur very suddenly.' The notion of suddenness was stressed. It was important to realise that 'a recession is likely to occur with little warning'. Hence it was necessary to pay 'urgent attention' to possible countermeasures. In the meantime it was necessary to do everything possible to reduce inflation. For it was assumed that the higher the level of inflation, the more severe would be the economic downturn which followed it. The third issue was Australia's 'unbalanced development': industrial development was said to be 'top-heavy', in the sense that while manufacturing industries had undergone an 'extraordinary growth', basic industries and services had lagged seriously behind. The result had been power blackouts, persistent shortages of fuel, steel and other materials, housing shortages, transport interruptions, and restricted public utility services.

What was particularly disconcerting about Australia's unbalanced development was not only that it restricted the growth of domestic output and hence contributed to the continuance of inflationary pressures, but that it had left the Australian economy 'in a weak position to withstand any shock, such as might be occasioned by recession overseas and the ending of the inflationary movement at home'. The weakness arose in part because the postwar years had seen the rapid growth of industries producing plant and machinery for the private sector. The fate of these industries depended on the continued flow of new investment plans. 'Their level of activity is therefore highly vulnerable to any factor which disturbs business confidence, or otherwise limits the scope for further capital development of industry.' Another difficulty, the committee argued, was the fact that a number of manufacturing industries, such as those producing radios, refrigerators, vacuum cleaners, domestic electrical appliances, and footwear, had 'over-expanded in relation to prospective consumer demands'. The committee was convinced that 'when the present backlog demands and inflationary pressures come to an end many firms in these industries will be out of business, and many workers will lose their jobs'. There were additional difficulties: 'in nearly all industries there is a newly developed fringe of firms which are unlikely to survive when competitive selling returns. The resulting crop of failures and bankruptcies, and the over-expansion of plant capacity in certain directions, will also tend to weaken the flow of new investment demand.'

The committee acknowledged that the optimists might argue that there was great scope for further industrial development, particularly under the stimulus of large-scale immigration, and that a downturn in one sector (say in industrial plant and machinery) could be taken up by the expansion of another sector (say the building industry). But neither was likely to occur while the bottlenecks in basic industries and services persisted. And little comfort could be derived from the fact that one of the first effects of a recession was to reduce the influence of bottlenecks. For 'once a recession has begun, it tends to produce a cumulative decline of incomes, employment, and investment which might go well beyond the point at which all bottlenecks were eliminated by falling demand'. The committee concluded that the need was therefore imperative for prompt and determined governmental action to pursue deflationary measures and to encourage the expansion of basic industries and services.[4]

The Treasury and the role of fiscal policy

Before considering Labor's attempts to control inflation, attention needs to be drawn to the changes which occurred during World War II in the Treasury's attitude toward fiscal policy as a tool of economic management. Although the F & E Committee was transferred to the Treasury in September 1939, the Treasury did not openly embrace the committee's ideas on the role of the budget. In fact, during the early years of the war the committee's approach to economic policy was seen as being quite distinct from that of the Treasury. S.J. Butlin refers to 'Spender's willingness ... to seek advice and views from the Financial and Economic Committee, and his readiness to discuss issues with its chairman rather than to accept the traditional approach of Treasury officials'.[5] Spender confirms this in his autobiography. He acknowledges in particular the assistance of Giblin in formulating the revised budget of December 1939 (introduced to take account of the onset of war) and notes that 'in reaching my views I consulted advisers outside the Treasury; action hardly pleasing to the department'.[6] In his memoirs Coombs points out that at the beginning of the war, with unemployment running at about 10 per cent, F & E advised Spender that the increase in expenditure provided for in the revised December budget did not have to be matched by an increase in taxation. The Treasury, by contrast, believed an immediate rise in taxation was necessary.[7] Coombs, who had recently been appointed Treasury economist, declared his support for the F & E approach at a meeting convened late in 1939 by Spender and attended by Stuart McFarlane, secretary to the Treasury. McFarlane reacted to this angrily. As Coombs recounts: 'after we left Spender he told me I had no right to express opinions so inconsistent with the Treasury view (my first encounter with this concept) which it was his responsibility to determine'.

The Treasury's displeasure with Spender's actions in December 1939 was the result not just of damaged pride (by seeking outside advice Spender had violated the Treasury's conviction that on budget matters it was the highest authority), but because the views of the committee represented a threat to the conventional wisdom. Spender complained that the budget of September 1939 presented to him by McFarlane 'followed traditional patterns. It contained no statement of principle. It indicated no new financial doctrine or idea... This was a "business as usual" budget'.[8] Spender was proud of the fact that the revised December budget 'broke away from the orthodox'. The essential problem as he and the F & E Committee saw it was 'not in terms of money but in material and human resources'. Such a view, he acknowledges, 'was greeted with considerable doubt and criticism'.

Menzies summarised the Treasury's early wartime approach in a memorandum presented in March 1940. The Treasury's only concern was with financial matters. Its aim was 'to maintain investible funds so that public loans may be filled; to keep interest rates down; and to encourage the stability of industry so that taxation yields may be high'.[9] Paul Hasluck has also pointed to the Treasury's preoccupation with financial matters in the early years of the war, noting that the department's approach was thoroughly traditional: 'In the first year of the war its attitude was unimaginative and conservative and there are many stories to be heard from wartime administrators of senior Treasury officials who were still boggling at every thousand pounds of additional expenditure when war departments were talking in millions.'[10]

One must be careful, however, despite McFarlane's comment that he was responsible for formulating the Treasury view, not to assume that McFarlane, and the financial orthodoxy he embodied, was totally representative of Treasury attitudes. As described in chapter 1, World War II was a time of considerable flux for the Treasury. It was associated with the adoption of responsibility by the department for economic, as distinct from financial, management, by the recruitment of economics graduates, and by the establishment in 1943 of the GFEP section. It can be expected that the economic recruits were not always intellectually and temperamentally in accord with McFarlane and possibly on occasions sought to change his views. It can also be expected that given their age and given their economics training the steadily increasing stream of recruits would have been amenable to Keynesian ideas and to the approach of the F & E Committee. A passage from a Treasury memorandum written in mid-1941 (and with McFarlane's name attached to it) is relevant here:

> The fundamental aim of post-war society should be the maximisation of the community's social welfare. Opinions will differ as to what constitutes maximum social welfare but we can ... take it that the maximum possible real National Income. i.e. the maximum standard of living, is an essential pre-requisite.
>
> The minimum of unemployment is a necessary condition for a maximum Real National Income but it is by no means the only one. The nature of the output produced by an economic system in full employment may vary and it will be necessary to ensure that our post-war output does provide the basis for a maximum standard of living... If the making of roads which are at present unnecessary is the *only* means of providing employment for a section of the community, then it is desirable to make these roads. But if possible those men should be employed in the production of something which the community needs more urgently, say hospitals.[11]

Although the tone is guarded, the ideas expressed here show that there was a growing acceptance within the Treasury of the F & E line that the government could and should aim to achieve a high level of employment by maintaining output at a high enough level.

Although it is true that the Treasury (led by Frederick Wheeler, head of GFEP) engaged in a protracted dispute with the Department of Postwar Reconstruction over the contents of the 1945 white paper, the Treasury did accept fully the contents of the final draft and, in fact, had an important role in the final drafting. Apart from the white paper, the extent to which the Treasury's attitude had changed since 1939 can perhaps be best seen in the department's comment in a 1946 memorandum that:

> It is now fully accepted government policy that in framing the Budget, in scrutinising expenditure proposals and preparing revenue measures, the Treasury must be guided not only by narrow financial considerations but also by its assessment of the existing and prospective level of employment and National Income after taking into account the effect of the financial proposals under consideration. Banking and monetary policy must also be directed towards the same end by the Treasury. The Budget and monetary policy have become vital instruments of Government policy in relation to employment, the cost of living, wages and social justice.[12]

Here was evidence that the GFEP economists had come to grips with the need to look upon the budget differently, now that the department was responsible for both economic and financial management. The viewpoint was distinctly Keynesian.

Keynesianism by stealth

In the same spirit as the passage above, the Treasurer announced in the November budget of 1946 that

> works activity ... must be integrated with the general economic and employment situation. The Commonwealth Government, in co-operation with the State Governments through the Loan Council, is seeking methods by which to achieve an appropriate balance in the demands made upon our total and physical resources by private expenditures on the one hand and public expenditures, particularly works expenditures, on the other hand. Failure to achieve this balance can mean either falling incomes and unemployment or else that excessive competition for resources, with consequent pressure upon prices and costs, which is the real cause of inflation. Financial control, exercised through budgetary measures in the widest sense and the adjustment of loan works programmes, is the main instrument through which this balancing of expenditure can be accomplished.

As this suggests, the Labor government saw the budget as playing a major role not only in maintaining full employment but in the avoidance of inflation. Coombs confirms this. Writing in 1948, he noted that the government had contemplated that during the transition from war to peace, with the economy subject to an inflationary boom, 'the Budget would be deflationary in its effect. The institution of the Social Security Fund [National Welfare Fund] was designed to ensure that during periods of high employment substantial reserves would be built up — in effect, the Budget would provide for a substantial surplus'.[13]

It was also the govenment's intention, however, to disguise the extent of its surpluses. For it was faced with a war-weary population, tired of austerity, impatient with rationing and controls, anxious to spend its accumulated savings, and insistent that its heavy taxation burden be reduced. A public admission of a 'substantial surplus' was out of the question in such circumstances. To do so would only have made more vocal and widespread the demands for substantial tax cuts.

In this lay a real difficulty not only for Labor but for subsequent governments: the community's unwillingness to accept, perhaps its inability to comprehend, the need in certain circumstances for budget surpluses. Arndt complained in 1960:

> Throughout the post-war years, there has been a striking division between professional and lay opinion in Australia on the merits of fiscal policy for the control of inflation. Professional economists have been virtually unanimous in their acceptance of Keynesian principles of fiscal policy which imply that a policy of budgeting for surpluses is an appropriate and effective instrument for the control of demand inflation. Articulate lay opinion, as expressed in newspaper editorials, political, business and trade union circles, have [sic] been vigorously and almost equally unanimously opposed to fiscal policy principles and measures.[14]

Theory into practice

Arndt's description of the nature of 'articulate lay opinion' applied a fortiori to the immediate postwar years. Faced with such attitudes, the Chifley government had the choice of trying to educate the community in 'correct' economic principles (a strategy urged upon it by a number of economists) or of obfuscating its true budgetary position. It chose the latter, deciding to practise Keynesianism by stealth.

The Treasurer's budget statements were designed to avoid upsetting those who adhered to orthodox financial principles. Chifley was keen to portray himself as a cautious and conservative Treasurer, striving to achieve budget balance. In the 1948–49 budget speech, for instance, he proudly announced that the achievement of a small surplus in 1947–48 'meant that the huge war-time gap between revenue and expenditure had been eliminated and that Budget equilibrium, a prime condition of financial and economic stability in these times, had been attained'. He concluded his speech by noting that the crucial economic need was for 'greater all-round production'. The best way for the government to help in achieving this was 'by the wise use of its resources and a careful but progressive approach to economic and financial problems'.

In the 1948–49 budget speech Chifley explained the principles underpinning the government's taxation initiatives: 'security, in the largest sense, has all along been the key-note of the Government's financial and economic programme. We have aimed to reduce taxation and have done so, but not at any stage before financial conditions warranted the step. We have aimed to lift standards of social benefits and have done so, but, again, no measure has been adopted before the resources were in sight.' A similar line was presented in the 1949–50 budget speech: the guiding principle had been to refuse 'financial measures that were not clearly practicable and for which the resources were not in sight'.

Such statements, it can be noted, were quite in keeping with a Keynesian approach in that the message seemed to be that taxation changes had been made only when supply had improved to such an extent that it could cope with the extra demand pressures resulting from taxation reductions. On the other hand, such statements could easily be interpreted to mean that one of Chifley's main concerns was to weigh tax cuts against the resources available to the government. In other words, they suggested that a balanced-budget approach had been adopted: budgetary changes would only be made when the resources were available to do so.

A recurrent argument in Chifley's financial statements was the need to make provision in the present for possible future expenditure commitments. For instance, in a financial statement presented in February 1949 Chifley declared that conditions were such that there was 'a greater need than ever to conserve the resources presently available to the Government'. It was important that revenue should cover all expenditure commitments 'including provision for definite commitments still to be met'. In line with this, the government had balanced the budget and had built up reserves, including the National Welfare Fund and the War Gratuity Reserve, against future expenditures.[15] In the 1948–49 budget speech the Treasurer announced that it was imperative 'to create safeguards against any adverse turn in conditions, locally or abroad'. There were, therefore, 'strong reasons for making all possible provision now against commitments due to be met in later years'. Similarly, the Taxation Office noted in a 1948 publication that the establishment of funds to meet social service payments and other such expenditures 'were no more than wise precautions taken in a year when incomes were high against times when revenues may be more difficult to obtain'.[16]

The Prime Minister may well have genuinely believed that it was essential to build up large reserve funds to finance governmental expenditure in times of adversity. But it is difficult to avoid agreeing with Artis and Wallace's assessment that such statements were essentially 'plausibly sounding but spurious arguments' used by Chifley to disguise his true budgetary position and thereby alleviate the pressure for taxation reductions.[17]

The Labor government made much use of the Trust Fund account to obfuscate its true budgetary position. By virtue of section 5 (a) of the Surplus Revenue Act 1908, the commonwealth government could credit certain sums of expenditure to trust funds for subsequent use. These transfers, however, were often listed as current expenditure for a particular year even though they were not actually spent in that year. Through the use of the Trust Fund, particularly the National Welfare Fund which began operating at the beginning of July 1943, the Labor government managed to syphon some excess liquidity out of the system. Chifley claimed in both the 1948-49 and 1949-50 budget speeches that 'substantial' sums had been put aside in trust accounts, notably the National Welfare Fund and the War Gratuity Reserve (the latter being established in 1948). The balance in the National Welfare Fund, which at the end of June 1946 stood at $100 million, was over $260 million at the same date in 1950. This suggests that it made some, though an inadequate, contribution to reducing inflationary pressures.

The Chifley government also took advantage of the fact that accounting conventions deemed that the only expenditure which should be charged to the Consolidated Revenue Fund (CRF) was current expenditure, while capital expenditure should only be charged to the Loan Fund. This convention was important because the budgetary position, as described in the annual budget speeches, referred to the difference between expenditure from, and revenue paid into, the CRF. One way in which the government could disguise its true budgetary position was by breaking this convention and charging capital expenditure to Consolidated Revenue. This in fact became established Treasury practice during World War II and Chifley continued the practice into the postwar period.

Perhaps not surprisingly, the Labor government was criticised for its lack of candour, sometimes for being positively misleading, by those familiar with national accounting practices. The Institute of Public Affairs, for instance, complained in 1949 about 'the utterly confusing and reprehensible manner in which the public accounts are presented'.[18] Nevertheless, it concluded that the fact that the government had been able to reduce its short-term debt through the redemption of commonwealth Treasury bills suggested that budget surpluses had been obtained. A persistent critic was the *Sydney Morning Herald*. In his 1948–49 budget speech the Prime Minister announced that the estimated gap between revenue and expenditure was $36 million and that this would have to be paid for from the Loan Fund. The *Herald*, however, was quick to point out that some $76 million of capital expenditure had been charged to Consolidated Revenue, instead of Loan, and that had 'normal methods of accounting' been employed the Prime Minister would have had to confess to a prospective surplus of approximately $50 million.[19] Similar arguments were advanced in 1949: the *Herald* insisted that normal accounting standards had been violated and that the announced deficit was in fact a 'heavy surplus'.[20]

Economic management under Labor: success or failure?

How successful, then, was the Labor government in using the budget as an anti-inflationary device? It was the view of the government's economic advisers that the budget had been deflationary in its effect and had contributed, though only in a limited way, to the control of inflationary pressures. In a report presented early in 1949 on the state of the Australian economy, a committee of interdepartmental officers noted that the budget was exercising a 'mild deflationary influence' and supported this judgment by pointing to the fact that expenditure was being met from revenue.[21] In a paper written in June 1950 the Treasury noted that in assessing the impact of budgetary initiatives the overall cash result was more significant than the nominal budget result because 'it more nearly represents the net amount of spending power taken from or paid to the community as a result of public financial operations'. The department pointed out that using the cash-result approach, the postwar budgets of the Chifley government should be seen 'as being, in varying degrees, deflationary'. The most important component of the overall cash result was the value of Treasury bills issued or redeemed. On the figures provided by the Treasury, some $130 million of Treasury bills had been redeemed in 1946–47, $140 million in 1947–48, $130 million in 1948–49, and $30 million in 1949–50. No comments were offered on the significant drop in 1949–50. But the Treasury did add that a comparison of the overall cash results provided only 'a very broad indication of the economic impact of successive budgets'. What had to be taken into account also were the ways in which revenue was raised and public money was spent. For example, on the question of how the money was spent, the department noted that if the government were to increase heavily its expenditure on capital projects requiring scarce resources, the tendency would be to accentuate inflationary pressures.[22]

Account needs to be taken also of the scale and direction of both revenue and expenditure initiatives. Here the Labor government's actions appear in a generally unfavourable light, especially during its last two years in office. Labor reduced sales tax only once — in 1946 — and the relief given to companies was negligible. But reductions in personal income tax were announced in each of Labor's postwar budgets. The stimulatory effects of the income tax reductions were outweighed in the first two postwar budgets by significant reductions in defence expenditure. From 1947–48, however, commonwealth government expenditure began to increase and at an accelerating trend. Of particular importance were the changes which occurred in capital formation. Artis and Wallace point out that capital formation rose rapidly from 1948–49 and was sustained at a high rate for four years. They note that 'the expansion of the public sector over this period was quite dramatic and its inflationary effects could have been avoided only by greatly increased taxation rates. In quantitative terms this expansion was clearly the strongest discretionary fiscal action of the postwar period'.[23] Despite the strong increases in capital expenditure, personal income tax cuts averaging 16.6 per cent were announced in 1948, with further cuts averaging 23 per cent being announced in February 1949. The effect of these revenue measures was of course to compound the existing inflationary pressures.

What made these fiscal initiatives particularly inappropriate (at least from a purely financial point of view) was that they coincided with the cessation of price controls. It was Labor's firm conviction that direct controls were an indispensable supplement to purely financial (indirect) measures in dealing with conditions of excess demand. In his 1944–45 budget speech Chifley voiced his concern at what seemed to him to be 'a very dangerous tendency to assume that with the increasingly favorable turn of the war, these controls [price control, rationing and control of supplies] are less necessary and can be lightened'. He declared: 'There could not be a more dangerous state of mind or one more fatal to the stability of our economy.' In the *Full Employment* white paper and in the 1945–46 budget speech, direct controls were singled out as being crucial to a stable transition from war to peace. In the white paper it was argued that even after the transition period certain situations might make it 'necessary for governments to exercise some degree of direct control in order to avoid inflation'.[24] The problem for the Labor government, however, was that the power to control directly wages, prices, and capital issues was restricted to the jurisdiction of state governments. Twice in referenda, in 1944 and 1948, Labor attempted to have price and rent control incorporated in the constitution as a commonwealth power. It was defeated on both occasions. Following a series of High Court rulings on the use of the commonwealth's defence powers and with the failure of the 1948 referendum, the commonwealth's power to implement direct controls, with the exception of import controls, terminated. Financial measures, therefore, came to bear most of the burden of containing the mounting inflationary pressures, something which they were ill equipped to handle.

Despite apparent agreement that the budget had been slightly deflationary, the Treasury, the Commonwealth Bank and the Economic Division in the Prime Minister's Department were also in agreement that the Chifley government's anti-inflationary initiatives as a whole had to be judged a failure. An interdepartmental report presented in May 1950 noted that throughout the postwar period economic policy had sought to restrain inflation by a variety of measures. But it argued that while 'the position would have been worse without these measures, it cannot be claimed that they have achieved their purpose. The pressure of demand has proved too strong for them to cope with and, in addition, the measures have been progressively weakened by constitutional and other difficulties'.[25] In a report presented in the same month the Commonwealth Bank reached a similar conclusion:

> In practice governmental anti-inflationary policies and controls were progressively weakened [under the Chifley government]. It became increasingly difficult to limit public and private investment programmes; price and capital issues controls became more and more ineffective; the policy of building rural stabilisation funds had to be modified and ultimately abandoned because of political difficulties; and growing government expenditure and pressure for taxation relief reduced the deflationary effect of the budget. Whilst banking policy formally remained restrictive, it could make no substantial impact on the basic situation, but at best could merely prevent unwise banking policy making it worse. Finally, the difficulties of limiting the investment programme were intensified by the adoption of a heavy immigration programme.[26]

Coombs had come to the view as early as 1948 that Labor's anti-inflationary program was largely ineffective. In a paper presented while director-general of the Department of Postwar Reconstruction, Coombs announced that the aim of suppressing inflation had only been 'partly achieved' and that 'the longer the need to continue that suppression is maintained, the more difficult it becomes'.[27] A number of difficulties had been encountered: it had been politically impracticable to maintain 'significant' budget surpluses; farmers had generally been opposed to the extension of rural stabilisation schemes; and 'some inevitable price rises have led to pressure on wages, producing further increases in costs, and so still higher prices'. Coombs announced rather gloomily:

> Generally speaking, our experience does not support any great hope of being able to control future booms once the inflation itself has been established. The time to control the present boom would have been during the war, when the basic inflationary situation was being established. Since that was clearly not practicable, what follows now must be more or less unpleasant — it is a choice between controls or generally higher prices.[28]

Support for the use of offsetting variations in public capital expenditure, as described in the *Full Employment* white paper, was now dampened: 'Broadly, our practical experience has been such as to doubt the wisdom of emphasising too much the "compensating" character of anti-depression programmes... It is clear that Government investment programmes are much less flexible than we had hoped... Generally speaking, it would appear wise not to place too much emphasis on the flexibility of public investment programmes.' So too with rural stabilisation schemes: the operation of these schemes had raised doubts about 'the effectiveness of the "off-setting" principle which underlay a good deal of war-time thinking'. The basic problem was that primary producers were far more concerned with maintaining the current level of prices than with the long-term stability which the stabilisation schemes offered them.

Though decidedly less sanguine than a few years earlier, Coombs nevertheless remained convinced that the government could play a major role in stabilising the economic system: 'we are certainly better equipped than ever before to deal with economic flutuations. The difficulties are primarily political and social rather than economic and technical. While these factors will certainly limit the completeness of our success, they will not prevent partially [sic] and worthwhile achievement.' This was to become a popular theme among the economics profession — the idea that the essential problem in effective economic management was not so much the technicalities involved but the limitations imposed by the political environment (limitations which included trying to avoid that which was electorally unpopular and attempting to maintain effective control in a federal system) and those imposed by the social environment (in particular the attitude and degree of understanding of demand-management principles by the Australian public).

The risks of developmentalism: 1950–51

The rapid increase in the commonwealth government's capital expenditure from 1948–49 onwards was largely a reflection of Labor's commitment to a program of migration and development. The long-cherished developmental dreams of Australians were to be converted into reality. Labor had come to the view, as Chifley described it in 1949, that

> Progress in developmental works and immigration will open the way for the growth of private industry. Progress in these fields together will secure increasing markets for the products of industry, so that the whole economy can go forward. That in itself will afford the best assurance of steady full employment and rising living standards. It will also enlarge the foundations of our defensive strength which, in the troubled world conditions of to-day, must rank amongst our foremost national objectives.[29]

Chifley noted that the government had become engaged, or was contemplating involvement, in a whole range of undertakings in such fields as power development, water supply (the Snowy Mountains Scheme being the outstanding example), aviation, land transport, and the search for minerals. In addition, the government had set about 'tackling the population problem on a scale never attempted before'. It was expected that some 220 000 immigrants would arrive during 1949–50, with some 130 000 being able to join the workforce, and that thereafter the numbers would increase each year. The only foreseeable limits to the program were the availability of suitable people and the economy's capacity to absorb them. The Prime Minister claimed that 'already the benefits of immigration have appeared in a higher output of industries under-staffed and a faster rate of progress in building and other constructional projects. Key services such as hospitals have also gained relief from pressing shortages. Steadily the stream of new citizens and workers will broaden out to reach all branches of the economy'.

Theory into practice

The spirit of developmentalism was by no means unique to Labor. The Liberal-Country Party (LCP) government, which came to power late in 1949, was if anything even more enthusiastic about the program. While in opposition, Liberal and Country Party members had consistently argued that the problem of inflation arose because of supply-side difficulties. Governments needed to play an active role in stimulating and supporting the private sector and in providing the right framework within which the private sector could expand production. This implied not only a reduction in taxation (Robert Menzies, the new Prime Minister, and Arthur Fadden, his deputy, had long argued that taxation levels were too high and were destroying the incentive of the private sector) but also a considerable increase in government spending to meet the infrastructural requirements of a rapidly expanding economy.

Indeed it was the view of the Treasury and Commonwealth Bank that the LCP government was potentially more spendthrift than Labor and that their developmental plans (which included the aim of achieving a gross migrant intake of 200 000 annually) were potentially disastrous. The danger was that in the prevailing circumstances the increase in government expenditure entailed in such plans was bound to render the system highly unstable. The view of the Advisory Council of the Commonwealth Bank, as described by Frederick Wheeler, was that

> The new Government was placing considerably heavier emphasis on greater and more rapid development. If this development is achieved and hence the necessary transfers of resources in Australia made, concurrently with the development of an import surplus, the Australian economy will necessarily become highly vulnerable to any decline in activity overseas and if one believes that this decline overseas must come [then] a fairly severe depression in Australia becomes inevitable. In other words, there is a basic conflict between the rapid development of the present Government and the long term stability of the Australian economy.[30]

Unshakeable in their conviction that such a conflict existed and that the inevitable result would be a severe economic downturn, the story of the eighteen months or so from early 1950 was one of the Treasury and in particular the Commonwealth Bank doggedly persisting in their attempts to educate their political 'masters' about the need for effective deflationary measures and to rescue them from the economic insanity of overambitious developmental plans. The 1951–52 budget can be seen as the symbol of their eventual victory.

The basis of the Commonwealth Bank's opposition to an expansion of the developmental program was set out in a paper written in May 1950.[31] The Bank reasoned that an investment program, such as that proposed by the LCP government, which required more resources than were currently available (after consumption requirements had been met), could only be undertaken by obtaining more resources from overseas (assuming, that is, that it was not possible to reduce consumption standards below that which people currently wished to maintain). In other words, such a program was possible only by running an 'import surplus'. This raised two questions: how was the import surplus to be paid for and how would it be brought about? On the first of these, the Bank argued that the surplus could be financed for a limited time by running down international reserves, while in the long term the surplus would necessitate relying on overseas borrowing. The difficulties involved in obtaining dollar loans were not discussed. Instead, the Bank concentrated on the second question. It prefaced its discussion by arguing that many of the goods and services needed to fulfil the development program, notably engineering works and buildings, could only be produced locally. There was therefore a need for imports not only of materials and equipment but also of consumer goods. For such imports would enable physical resources and labour to be released from the consumer-goods industries and move to the expanding investment-goods industries. The Bank argued that an import surplus could and would not be achieved until it became profitable for Australian producers to import those particular goods and services required for the development program. The important point was that the substitution of imported for domestically produced goods would become profitable only when imported goods could be bought in Australia at a lower price than the equivalent Australian commodity. This meant, of course, that there would have to be a 'substantial' rise in Australian prices relative to those overseas.

If the development program proceeded, the relative rise in Australian prices would come about as follows. First, wage rates would be raised in the investment-goods industries so as to attract the labour needed to fulfil the development program. The increase in costs would lead in turn to an increase in the price of investment goods in Australia. Higher wage rates would then spread to the consumer-goods industries, leading eventually to rises also in the price of consumer goods. And so the process would continue. Australian prices would cease to rise only when the volume of imports, together with available Australian output, was large enough to meet consumption and investment demand and when enough resources had been released from the consumer-goods industries, victims of import competition, to make the investment program 'fully effective'. These changes would have a 'radical' effect on the Australian economy. Demand would have ceased to be excessive, because of the effect of higher prices and because of the increased flow of goods and services from overseas. And wage rates would be at a level where employers could afford no further increases, given the competitive pressure of imports.

The analysis had a strongly neoclassical flavour: relative price changes would operate deterministically to bring about a reallocation of resources and the establishment of a competitive equilibrium. Two points, however, were stressed. First, the adjustment process, in that it involved a rise in Australian prices even more rapid than had been experienced in the recent past, would necessarily conflict with the LCP government's electoral pledge to restore the purchasing power of the pound ('to put value back into the pound'). Second, 'once the changed price relationships had become effective in producing the desired import surplus and an appropriate pattern of Australian production, the Australian economy would be exceedingly vulnerable to adverse economic developments'. Three things would be needed for the economy to continue operating at a 'high level': the development and migration program would have to be kept stable (the meaning of which was left undefined); overseas borrowing would have to continue; and, though this was less important, overseas prices would have to remain relatively high. The Australian economy would find itself in a situation remarkably similar to the late 1920s. The Bank warned:

> If these conditions ceased to exist or were interrupted for a prolonged period, the task of readjustment would be acutely difficult. It would involve not merely the temporary financing of an import surplus without overseas borrowing and the maintenance of reasonable levels of employment by governmental action, but also a radical shift in the organisation of Australian production with widespread hardship and loss. There can be little doubt that in these circumstances Australia would experience a serious depression.

The government therefore had a choice in the sorts of policies it could pursue. On the one hand it could continue with a policy of trying to make effective an expanded development and migration plan and thereby be subject to all the sorts of difficulties outlined above. On the other hand it could choose a policy which aimed to achieve a rate of development which did not necessitate a radical change in the Australian pattern of production and hence one which offered a much greater chance of maintaining internal economic stability.

While the Treasury was in basic support of a development and migration program, it accepted the Bank's arguments on the consequences of attempting, to expand the program. Frederick Wheeler agreed that there was a basic conflict between the objective of attempting to increase population by more than 3 per cent per annum and the objective of maintaining price and cost stability. Like the Bank, he saw great risks in having a large import surplus financed by overseas loans. For there was no guarantee that borrowing could continue. If borrowing suddenly ceased, perhaps because of a recession in the United States, 'the impact on Australia could be disastrous'. Wheeler stressed the need for a package of deflationary measures. There was an urgent need to remove excess demand, for the inflation which it entailed bred inefficiency and disorganisation, and the stronger the inflation 'the more difficult [are] the adjustments required should a downturn occur and the greater the possibility of the extreme result, viz. a loss of confidence in the currency'. Wheeler suggested that a levy be imposed on wool and set aside in a fund to be disbursed to the industry when the problem of inflation had disappeared. Credit policy needed to be tightened 'substantially'. At the moment it was 'cautious but not seriously restrictive'. Present rates of taxation needed to be maintained, while new government expenditure commitments should be kept to a minimum. All low-priority works should be postponed. Tariffs should be reduced 'to encourage desirable imports and to discourage less important types of Australian production'. Wheeler stressed that all these policies needed to be adopted. To use only one or two 'would be quite inadequate'. Even if the package were adopted, inflationary pressures would not disappear but simply be contained. The price and cost rises, however, would not be 'too uncomfortable'.[32]

Unlike the Commonwealth Bank and the Economic Division in the Prime Minister's Department, the Treasury's package of deflationary measures did not include exchange rate appreciation — a measure which became a central source of debate among economists during 1950 and into 1951. In Wheeler's opinion, exchange rate appreciation was 'the most far reaching and most drastic instrument available' for dealing with excess demand. But a number of arguments were raised against a 'substantial' appreciation. There was, first, a possibility of the appreciation 'overshooting the mark', thereby destroying 'the expansionist mood of the Australian economy' and endangering the migration program. Further, it could cause balance-of-payments difficulties, making Australia reliant on the uncertain prospect of obtaining overseas loans. Appreciation had the additional drawback of being 'a general blunt instrument which hits without discrimination the strong and the weak, the desirable and the undesirable'. In addition, it was difficult to reverse quickly if this became necessary. An interim minor appreciation was opposed because 'in practice the exchange rate cannot be altered frequently'.

The Treasurer, Fadden, accepted his department's advice on the exchange rate question. The fact that Fadden was also leader of the Country Party no doubt made him even more sympathetic to the arguments raised against altering the exchange rate. Rural interests were strenuously opposed to any exchange rate appreciation, since it would lead to an increase in the price of Australian exports and therefore was likely to reduce sales.

The Korean War boom

Contrary to the expectations of the Investment and Employment Committee in mid-1949, there was no sudden reversal in the inflation rate in 1950; in fact during the second half of the year it began to accelerate. The overall result for 1950 showed a slight decline in the rate of increase in the consumer price index (9.2 compared with the 10.1 per cent rise in 1949). But in the twelve months to June 1951 the consumer price index rose by 19 per cent, while wholesale prices rose by 27 per cent. During the same period the basic wage leapt by 29.7 per cent.

Four factors in particular were responsible for these increases. First, there was the stimulus supplied by the 1949–50 budget. Despite the Treasury's assessment that the overall cash result was a small surplus, the 1949–50 budget must be seen as strongly stimulatory. Even on the Treasury's own figures, and keeping in mind the limitations of summary budget indicators, the surplus in 1949–50 was significantly less than in the previous year — suggesting that the budget was stimulatory. Auld's detailed analysis of postwar fiscal policy performance confirms this. Auld concentrates on the concept of 'fiscal leverage' which he defines as 'the net impact of income-creating and income-destroying components of the federal government's budget'. His calculations show that of the budgets introduced between 1948–49 and 1963–64, that of

1949–50 was the most strongly stimulatory.[33] Second, the Chifley government decided in September 1949 to emulate the British government and devalue against the United States dollar by 30.4 per cent and thereby maintain the existing parity with sterling. The decision drew harsh criticism from Australian economists. The result was obviously inflationary and provided a significant boost to the value of export receipts. In addition, by leaving the Australian pound undervalued, it gave rise to a large inflow of speculative capital during 1950 in anticipation of an appreciation. Menzies was eventually forced in October to make a public declaration that there would definitely be no alteration to the exchange rate. Third, the Arbitration Court decided in October 1950 to raise the basic wage for males by £1 per week and to increase the basic wage for females from 54 per cent to 75 per cent of the males' rate. Apart from this particular decision, Australia's system of quarterly wage indexation played a significant part in quickening the wage-price spiral. Finally, the announcement of war in Korea in June 1950 soon led to an inordinate rise in the demand for wool and other commodities. Having increased by 29.1 per cent in 1949–50, the export price index of wool rose by 111.7 per cent in 1950–51. The export price index of metals also rose rapidly. Export income increased dramatically, with exports of goods rising by 64.5 per cent in 1950–51.

Presenting the 1950–51 budget in October, Fadden pointed to the measures the government had taken to deal with the problem of excess demand. In the first place, various measures had been taken to increase supplies and productive effort: legislation had been introduced to deal with the Communist Party (members of whom, it was claimed, were responsible for a marked escalation in strike activity — the 1949 coal strike being held as the prime example); a number of controls, including petrol rationing, had been abolished; and a loan of $US100 million had successfully been negotiated with the International Monetary Fund. Measures were to be taken also to deal with the level of demand: an increase in sales tax (the first increase since the war), a rise in postal charges, and the introduction of a wool-deductions scheme. The last-mentioned initiative, which supplemented a levy of 7.5 per cent on the sale of wool introduced in August, required woolgrowers to pay a levy of 20 per cent on the value of their sales. This was then to be held as a credit against tax payments in 1951–52.

But what perhaps was the most striking feature of the 1950–51 budget was its ambiguity. On the one hand, it was designed to create the impression of being mildly deflationary. Fadden claimed that 'to meet expenditures from bank finance, and so add further to the volume of community spending power, would be wholly indefensible'. He went on to argue that revenue should be adequate to cover all expenditure. To avoid using Treasury bill finance was described as 'a prime objective of public finance under present inflationary conditions'. And yet, on the other hand, the Treasurer argued that 'the Government has been determined that migration and essential development shall go on, and, so far as possible, be accelerated'. And in his concluding comments Fadden referred again to 'the very large provision' which had been made for developmental works and immigration and other forms of expenditure.

The budget estimate was for a nominal surplus of $800 000. But as with Chifley's budgets, this figure was virtually useless as a guide to the impact of the budget. The Treasurer continued the practice of charging current expenditure to Loan, using the Trust Fund accounts, and altering estimated revenue from income tax to disguise his true budgetary position. On Auld's calculations the 1950–51 budget was in fact slightly expansionary, the strong rise in expenditure outweighing the deflationary effects of the revenue initiatives.[34]

The limitations of effective demand management

The unprecedented leap in prices and wages in 1950 and the apparent failure of the 1950–51 budget to deal with these increases fostered discussion of a topic which had been of concern to economists for most of the postwar period: the efficacy of demand-management to control and subdue an inflationary situation. The topic came under scrutiny at the ANZAAS conference held in May 1951, with both Douglas Copland and Gerald Firth discussing the question at length. It may be useful to consider their views so as to understand better the constraints facing the Treasury and the government and to get some idea of the extent to which economists saw the problems facing Australia in terms of weaknesses in human nature.

Copland pointed to the difficulties facing an Australian government in budgeting for a surplus. There were a number of problems involved, including the fact that 'the public has just not been educated to accept the idea of a budget surplus'.[35] Also, it seemed to be the case that there was 'a law of increasing government expenditure based on political and social factors, which both political parties find it impossible to reject in the interests of economic stability'. Under the sway of this 'law', governments found it increasingly more difficult to raise taxation to a level sufficient to ensure a budget surplus. Another problem was the nature of commonwealth-state financial relations. The existing system of divided taxing powers and taxation reimbursement grants was 'almost an invitation to the States to act irresponsibly'. Copland judged that throughout the postwar period the budget deficits of the states had offset the commonwealth's surpluses. The basic problem, however, Copland was to argue elsewhere, was that a full employment economy gave rise to 'forces which in the last resort can only be checked by the exercise of more restraint than has been customary by individuals and groups in a free society in buoyant times, a measure of restraint for which there is no precedent in the brief history of Australia'.[36]

Gerald Firth, professor of economics at the University of Tasmania and formerly an officer in the Department of Postwar Reconstruction, presented a penetrating analysis entitled 'Disinflation in Australia: A Democratic Dilemma'. Firth's aim was to explain the relative lack of success of federal governments to control the postwar boom. His arguments were in many ways an amplification of the points Coombs had made in his 1948 paper on the avoidance of booms and depressions. The key problem was said to lie in the political underpinnings of policy:

> most methods of control (including direct controls) necessarily operate by restricting expenditure, and consequently cut across the immediate economic interests of the groups adversely affected. In the post-war period, political resistance has been sufficient to confine disinflationary measures within the narrow limits set by 'practicability', which has prevented the introduction of any measures likely to offend the susceptibilities of influential interest groups.[37]

But not only had governments been overly concerned with the political practicalities of disinflationary measures; it was also the case that 'no important interest group has shown any willingness to make concessions in the interests of stability'. Firth was critical, too, of the tendency of the government's economic advisers to offer only that advice which they deemed politically acceptable to the relevant minister. The politicians themselves were guilty of 'assessing the practicability of economic measures in terms of political symbolism which is not necessarily based on rational analysis'. Interest groups were guilty of 'magnifying by their representations to ministers the apparent importance of adverse electoral repercussions'. Furthermore, there was a widespread ignorance of economic principles: people 'at all levels of politics' were unfamiliar with the 'purely technical requirements of a full employment economy'. Firth was critical also of the activities and preoccupations of economists during World War II:

> the 'reconstruction' opportunity for educating electorates and ministers in the means of preventing expansion from degenerating into boom and inflation was largely wasted in a spate of exaggerated propaganda for full employment as an end in itself... In the climate of opinion which prevailed from 1943 to 1946, the few economists who ventured to forecast the problem of excess demand failed to command the support (or even the attention) of a majority of their colleagues. The public documents and official statements of that time simply evaded the problem by careful draftsmanship.[38]

Another problem was the limitations imposed by federalism. The nature of the federal system was such that the commonwealth had to take the electoral brunt for unpopular taxation decisions and, despite uniform taxation, it could not regulate effective demand without state cooperation.

How, then, were these obstacles to the imposition of disinflationary policies to be overcome? Firth tentatively proposed two remedies: the establishment of an Economic Policy Tribunal, endowed with semi-judicial status, which would advise governments on how to achieve particular desired objectives and criticise decisions already taken, and the use of the 'educational' method, something which would involve persuading

> individual voters and interest group executives to accept (in general terms) the necessity of limiting private and public spending in ways which give an agreed measure of priority to 'developmental' forms of investment spending; and thus to encourage ministers to put forward combinations of disinflationary measures

which (provided that they have some claim to 'fairness' in their relative impact on various groups) will have some chance of winning them political approval instead of automatic unpopularity.[39]

Firth was far from optimistic, however, about the efficacy of the latter remedy. Outside of the public service he judged that there were 'perhaps only twenty or thirty people competent to translate economic technicalities into a form likely to influence public thinking'. The educational solution was likely to succeed only in the long term.

The road to the 'Horror Budget'

By early 1951, with inflation running at over 20 per cent, Fadden and his department had become deeply concerned about the state of the economy. In January the Treasurer informed his colleagues that 'the stage at which a "flight from the currency" could begin is now (and for the first time) within foreseeable distance, and it is one of our most urgent tasks to see that it gets no closer'.[40] What then could be done? Monetary policy had been progressively tightened since mid-1950, with calls being made to Special Accounts. In November the central bank issued a directive to the trading banks which aimed to instil a much more restrictive stance by requiring the banks to undertake only designated (essential) forms of lending. But there were quite clear limitations to the use of monetary policy as an anti-inflationary device — something indicated by the fact that advances continued to rise during 1950–51. One limitation was the ability of trading banks to borrow from the central bank against their Special Accounts funds. Another limitation arose from the government's determination to adhere to a 'cheap money' policy, a commitment which necessitated the central bank buying bonds to prevent a rise in their effective yield.

By February 1951 the Treasury had come to the conclusion that advance policy had 'probably been made as restrictive as is desirable' and suggested that further tightening might be achieved by making additional calls to Special Accounts and/or raising above 3.5 per cent the rate charged on loans by the trading banks from the central bank. It could see little point in raising interest rates: 'a Government decision deliberately to raise interest rates unless carried to very high levels could not be regarded as an important contribution to anti-inflationary policy.' But it believed that central-bank support of the bond market should be discontinued as it was clearly adding to liquidity. That this would entail a rise in interest rates was seen as being on the whole beneficial: 'if market forces produce a rising trend in interest rates the general effects of the rise would be in the right direction. Certainly the Government should not, in current circumstances, take special measures to prevent a rise in interest rates because such special measures would inevitably involve resort to the use of Central Bank credit.'[41]

Theory into practice

Given the limitations of monetary policy, what other measures were available? It was politically difficult to appreciate the pound, given the Prime Minister's declaration in October. Moreover, by early 1951 the Commonwealth Bank had swung around to the Treasury's viewpoint and opposed any alteration to the exchange rate.[42] The reimposition of direct controls was out of the question, given the LCP's longstanding denigration of such measures. Further, it was the view of the Treasury and the government that such controls did not strike at the root cause of the problem.

Perhaps by default, budgetary policy came to be seen as the key means of combating inflation. From early in 1951 the Treasury was urging upon Fadden and, through the Treasurer's memoranda and agenda, his cabinet colleagues, the need to introduce a budget surplus. In January 1951 Fadden announced: 'It is probably true that a budget surplus is one of the most effective weapons currently available to the Government — and also one which interferes as little as most with the freedom of the economy to shape its own course.'[43] Explanations were offered by the Treasury as to the cause of inflation and how a budget surplus could be used to stem the gap between demand and supply. Attention was drawn to the need to differentiate between the CRF result and the overall cash result and the need, if the budget was to be truly deflationary, for there to be not only a CRF but a cash surplus. The Treasury bolstered its case by pointing to the explicit use on occasions of budget surpluses in both the United States and Britain. It also drew attention to the fact, as the passage above indicates, that the attraction of budgetary policy was that it did not really restrict individual freedom — a point Keynes had stressed and one which the Treasury knew would have considerable appeal to the LCP government.

By July, three months after the LCP government had secured an electoral victory, the need seemed more acute than ever to take effective action. Fadden could announce: 'If there is one thing clear it is that the movement in prices and wages is accelerating at a rate which simply cannot be allowed to continue without disaster.'[44] Budgetary policy was now seen as the government's *only* real hope of preventing this disaster. Significantly, what had come to be appreciated was not just the need to budget for a surplus but that to effect a surplus, heavy reliance would need to be placed on the revenue side. Having argued yet again that the budget was 'by far the most potent direct instrument' available to the government, Fadden noted that 'in the practical circumstances of today reductions in expenditure are unlikely to make a substantial contribution [to achieving a surplus]. By far the greater contribution must clearly come from increases in taxation'. He continued: 'The rapid deterioration in our economic position makes it abundantly clear that we must achieve a very substantial Budget surplus in 1951/52. This will mean drastic increases in all kinds of taxation and perhaps even the exploitation of unorthodox forms of taxation.'

The budget which was eventually presented in September was an event of major significance in Australia's budgetary history. For the budget represented the first explicit use of fiscal policy for anticyclical purposes. The budget was Keynesian in practice, principle and spirit and openly so. And it was an attempt to meet the persistent criticisms that governments had failed in their attempts to educate the public in the principles of the 'new economics'.

Fadden began his budget speech by explaining the inflationary process and did so employing Keynesian gap analysis:

> The essential nature of inflation lies in a disproportion between money demand for goods and productive resources on the one hand and the supply of goods and resources on the other. This disparity began in Australia when the late war began and, though masked for a period by controls, it has been growing ever since... The post-war situation has at all times been an unstable one. The money demand for goods has continually risen in advance of the available supply of goods, both local and imported.

The cause suggested the cure: it was necessary to 'close the gap' between the demand for goods and services and the supply. The Treasurer was confident that 'a great deal' could be done to restrain both consumption and investment expenditure. He claimed that 'powerful measures' had already been undertaken to achieve this end through control of the volume of credit and the control of capital issues. But he insisted that budgetary policy was crucially important in regulating economic activity and he outlined, in straightforwardly Keynesian terms, the principles which he believed such a policy should follow:

> The Government believes firmly that under the present highly inflationary conditions total receipts should do more than cover total expenditure — they should be sufficient also to provide a substantial surplus. Modern thought on the relation of public finance to economic stability is quite clear on the point that in times of depressed trade and unemployment, governments may justifiably run into deficit and even finance some part of their needs with central bank credit, so raising the level of community spending power. It is a vital corollary of this view, however, that in times of excessive demand and scarcity of labour, governments should draw away from the public in taxation and loans more than they spend for current purposes... If ever there was such a situation which called for such a measure, it is surely the situation we now face in Australia.

Accordingly, increases were announced for a range of taxes, including income tax, company tax, sales tax and customs and excise duties. The nominal budget surplus was $229 million.

In most instances public reaction to the budget took the form of dismay and sometimes anger. It was nicknamed the 'Horror Budget' by the Labor opposition. To a few commentators, the budget was seen as a 'painful' but necessary purgative for Australia's bloated economic corpus. Other commentators were simply bewildered. The *Australian Financial Review* argued that the only people who seemed to be in agreement with the government's fiscal initiatives were academic economists. The *Sydney Morning Herald*, perhaps the budget's most vitriolic critic, at first blamed Copland for being the guiding force behind this piece of invidious economic strategy. Others blamed Coombs. Roland Wilson, who had become secretary to the Treasury in April 1951, eventually came to be labelled the villain of the piece.

Theory into practice

It is commonplace now to criticise the budget for being introduced too late and to note that the budget simply served to hasten and deepen a pre-existing downward trend. The budget, nevertheless, was very much a positive step: it was decisive; it showed a willingness to make greater use of the revenue side; it attempted to explain the causes of inflation and to show how the budget could and should be used to deal not only with a situation of economic stagnation but also with one of excess demand; and it did not try to hide the fact that what was being aimed at was a 'substantial surplus' — a brave admission for any Australian political party to make at that time.

Though the budget contributed to the onset of recession in Australia in 1952 it was by no means the initiating or chief cause. Rather, the recession was ushered in by a dramatic deterioration in Australia's balance-of-payments position, which in turn arose because of the collapse of wool prices from April 1951 (when the United States government withdrew from the market) and because of the arrival of a flood of imports during 1951–52. The latter was a reflection of the strength of the previous year's boom and of the tendency of Australian importers to overorder. As the Commonwealth Bank explained in 1951: 'Many of the orders for these goods had been awaiting fulfilment for twelve months or more, but owing to lack of shipping space, deliveries had been long delayed. With the contraction of other markets, overseas suppliers, with the assistance of costly, chartered tonnage, despatched these accumulated orders, and goods reached Australia in unprecedented volume.'[45] Both the fall in wool prices and the rush of imports were sharply deflationary — on the one hand because of the sharp drop in export income and on the other because of the serious decline in liquidity. Australia's international reserves were reduced by more than half (from $1593 million in 1950–51 to $699 million in 1951–52). In a desperate attempt to stop the flow of imports and halt the continued decline of reserves, import licensing was introduced in March 1952 on what was described as a temporary basis. The government announced that quotas were to be set so as to reduce imports in 1952–53 by about half their 1951–52 value — an aim which was largely achieved.

The recession of 1952–53 was neither particularly deep, certainly not by prewar standards, nor protracted. Unemployment peaked at just under 80 000 in January 1953. In percentage terms the increase was negligible (from 0.5 per cent of the workforce in 1951–52 to 1.7 per cent in 1952–53). More significant was the decline in output: there was an absolute decline of 0.2 per cent in GDP measured in constant prices in 1952–53. But 1953–54 saw a rapid recovery, with GDP growing in real terms by 6.4 per cent. The effect of the recession upon prices was not immediate — the CPI rising by 17 per cent in 1952 — but in 1953 retail prices rose by only 4.4 per cent and in the following year by a mere 0.8 per cent.

The recession could, however, have been considerably more serious if not for two factors: a marked improvement in Australia's external position which in turn was helped by good seasons and strengthening export prices; and the actions of the central bank to stave off a liquidity crisis by making large releases from Special Accounts, which were reduced from a peak of $1156 million in May 1951 to $314 million in November 1952, and which thereby enabled banks to increase their advances and help meet the needs of those forced to pay for imports. The 1952–53 budget was only mildly expansionary: company taxation was reduced; so too was sales tax; pensions were increased; and the 10 per cent levy on income tax introduced in the 1951–52 budget was abandoned. Fadden, and the Treasury, remained deeply concerned about the possibility of renewed inflation. Fadden explained to his colleagues in July 1952:

> For a number of good reasons I believe that we must reduce taxation, especially in those directions where increases were imposed last year as an emergency measure to curb inflation at its peak... But with a full sense of our responsibility as a Government we should squarely face the fact that such concessions can be made only if we are prepared either to embark upon the most ruthless cutting-down of expenditure in other directions or else to rely upon inflationary means of finance.[46]

Fadden was deeply embarrassed by the fact that although the CRF had shown a surplus of $197 million in 1951–52, there had in fact been an overall cash deficit of $90 million which had to be financed from Treasury bills. The estimates for the 1952–53 budget showed a considerably larger deficit: hence the need to slash government expenditure. And indeed public expenditure actually fell in real terms by 3.6 per cent in 1952–53 and by a further 5.5 per cent the following year. Even in December Fadden was arguing that inflation was the chief threat against which the government had to guard and that efforts would have to be made to stabilise aggregate spending:

> Many problems still remain; but, even with these, the prospects appear brighter provided we can hold fast to and consolidate the more stable position we have reached in the economic and financial field generally. Above all, we need to be on the closest guard from now on against the possible resurgence of inflationary pressures and we need to be ready to act promptly in the light of whatever develops. Further inflation could wipe out all the gains we have made and remove all chances of solving those various problems which still confront us.[47]

By 1953 the Treasurer was a considerably happier man. He was able to announce in the budget speech that 'it used to be axiomatic that every boom had to be followed by a slump. Yet the recent boom, one of the sharpest in our history, was brought under control without incurring anything that, by any stretch of the imagination, could be called a slump. That, I venture to claim, was a quite unprecedented achievement'. To Fadden, the efficacy of Keynesian demand-management principles had been established. They had been used to steer a course between inflation and unemployment, between boom and slump. Such was their success that much of the optimism surrounding the notion of economic control which had been in evidence in 1943–46 had been regained and the growing sense of disappointment and in some cases pessimism which pervaded the economics profession in 1948–51 had been halted.

It was not long, however, before political considerations acted to limit the extent to which policies were adapted in the face of changing economic trends. By 1954 it was evident that the pace of activity was quickening and that the economy, as the Treasury had feared, was heading toward boom conditions. Such was the strength of domestic demand that imports increased markedly and international reserves began to fall — by $259 million in 1954–55 and by a further $163 million in 1955–56. There was an obvious need for deflationary policies. But an election was due at the end of 1955 and the government chose to postpone the introduction of effective action. It resorted instead to moral suasion, stressing the need for community restraint in its spending habits. In September 1955 Menzies announced that import restrictions would be intensified and declared that the government had decided that equilibrium in the external-payments situation would be restored by 30 June 1956. But it was not until March 1956 (with the government having secured victory at the December elections) that effective action was taken to deal with the problem of excess demand.

The first half-dozen years of the postwar period were a time of transition for the Treasury. It saw a concern with unemployment replaced (permanently) by a concern with inflation. It saw the department learning to rely more or less solely on Keynesian techniques of demand-management and to forsake wartime controls. It saw the department coming to grips with the links between internal and external balance. While there was a continued concern with boom collapsing into severe slump, the period saw a growing realisation that the timing and severity of such a slump depended not simply on the state either of the United States or British economies but on the structural characteristics of the Australian economy and on the extent to which domestic demand pressures were permitted to expand.

It was a time of transition also in terms of Treasury personnel. Stuart McFarlane retired in 1948 and was succeeded by G.P.N. Watt, who had been first assistant secretary in charge of the Defence Division in Melbourne and an accountant by training. Watt, however, was the last of the old guard. He was succeeded in 1951 by Roland Wilson, who was a generation removed from Watt (being only 47 at the time of his appointment) and, more importantly, an economist/statistician by training. Wilson's association with the Treasury had begun in the 1930s. In 1932 Wilson left his post as lecturer in economics at the University of Tasmania to fill the newly created position of economist in the statistician's branch of the Treasury. In 1936 he was appointed Commonwealth Statistician. In the same year, in recognition of his importance within the department, he was given the additional title of economic adviser to the Treasury. He held both positions until 1940 and again from 1946 until his appointment as a secretary in 1951.[48] Before Wilson's appointment, Frederick Wheeler had dominated the department's approach to economic policy discussions and decisions. In the year following Wilson's appointment, Wheeler moved to a position with the International Labour Office. His successor was Richard Randall, who had been the department's principal research officer. Between them, Wilson and Randall were to be the chief architects of Treasury thought for the remainder of the 1950s and well into the 1960s.

Now headed by an economist, and with Postwar Reconstruction wound

The Treasury line

up and with PMC advising a Prime Minister largely uninterested in economic policy, the Treasury emerged as the dominant voice on economic policy — but with Coombs doing his utmost to let the government know the Commonwealth Bank's views. The Bank, we can note, had been placed in a potentially powerful position in 1945 by virtue of legislation enabling it to retain most of the central banking powers acquired during the war. Monetary and fiscal policies were to be coordinated and directed toward the goal of maintaining full employment. As we have seen, however, the Bank soon encountered a range of difficulties in implementing an effective monetary policy: as a result it was very much a case of monetary policy playing second fiddle to fiscal policy — the latter being, of course, the Treasury's preserve. Part of the difficulty for the Bank was the wariness, sometimes animosity, shown toward it by the trading banks, whose suspicions had been aroused by the attempted nationalisation of the banking system in 1947, and who resented the Commonwealth Bank acting both as a central bank and trading bank. It was not until 1959, with the separation of the Commonwealth Bank's activities and the creation of the Reserve Bank, that these concerns were completely allayed. And it was not until the early 1960s, as will see, that monetary policy became a truly active weapon of economic stabilisation, rivalling fiscal policy.

5
The problems of continuous growth, 1956–62

THROUGHOUT the first half-dozen years after the war, Australia's main economic problem was the persistence of excess pressure on domestic resources. Though dampened temporarily by the collapse of export prices, the rapid decline in international reserves and the severely deflationary action of 1951, domestic demand recovered quickly. By the mid-1950s both consumption and investment expenditure were of such strength in relation to available supplies that import levels were rising rapidly, the level of exportable goods was being reduced and, in consequence, international reserves were being depleted at an alarming rate. In addition, Australia was beset with inflationary difficulties. One must appreciate the contemporary significance of such events. Australia had avoided what past experience had deemed inevitable — collapse into depression following an intense but short-lived postwar boom. In stark contrast to what had been expected immediately after the war, the government's verdict early in 1956 was that the power and persistence of the postwar expansionary drive was such that it needed to be brought under control by a package of deflationary measures. These measures, introduced as a mini-budget in March 1956, served their purpose, this time without excessive disruption. But, significantly, once again they provided only a temporary check to the expansionary drive. By the end of 1960 the Menzies government had again come to the conclusion that stern action was needed to dampen boom conditions.

It was perhaps not surprising, then, that by the end of the 1950s it was beginning to be accepted in Australia that the disjunction between pre- and postwar economic performance was permanent and that a tendency toward excess pressure on available resources should be seen as the norm. To the Treasury, the chief threat to economic stability was clearly no longer one of insufficient demand leading to the underemployment of resources but one of excess demand leading to continuous and potentially virulent inflationary difficulties and to persistent balance of payments deficits. Australia was now faced with something quite different from the interwar experience: the problems of continuous growth. In the Treasury's view, such problems were ultimately problems of individual behaviour. Its underlying concern during this period and indeed after it was how to contain wage demands, how to avoid a tendency toward over-spending, in short, how to maintain a sense of economic responsibility in a situation of continuous full employment.

Economic conditions and policies, 1956–58

The aim of the mini-budget introduced in mid-March 1956 was to arrest the continued deterioration of Australia's external payments position by dampening domestic demand. The government's logic was that the rapid increase in imports since 1953–54 was 'the inevitable product of internal inflation'.[1] While import restrictions were a useful expedient, the only permanent solution to the drain on international reserves was to strike at the root cause. Accordingly, Menzies announced that public sector expenditure would be cut, company taxes increased, sales tax on cars raised from 16.6 per cent to 30 per cent and on commercial vehicles and motor cycles from 12.5 per cent to 16.6 per cent, and additional taxes levied on beer, spirits, tobacco, cigarettes and cigars. He announced also that arrangements had been made with the Commonwealth Bank to raise bank overdraft rates from 5 per cent to an average of 5.5 per cent (with 6 per cent being the maximum), and to increase fixed deposit rates by 1 per cent.

Anxious to avoid criticism that these measures would entail a jolt to economic prosperity, Menzies declared that prosperity had to be understood if it was to be preserved:

> Like so many other good things, it tends to generate forces which may turn out to be adverse to it... It should continually be emphasized that we are neither anticipating nor seeking to meet a depression, still less to make one. What we are trying to do is to prevent some elements in our prosperity from aggravating an inflation which could, if left alone, undermine our prosperity. That is why I say that all the adverse factors are manageable, provided that we are prepared to prefer a lasting prosperity to a temporary boom which, if uncontrolled, could lead to unhappy consequences.[2]

The message was that prosperity contained the seeds of its own unmaking, that it could not be left alone, and that it had to be controlled. The government's measures were deemed the essential prescription for the maintenance of prosperity.

Table 5.1 provides some indication of the nature of the Australian economy before and after the mini-budget. It can be seen that both private investment and consumption expenditure fell in 1955–56, while GNE increased by only 2.6 per cent. Such movements were only in part because of the March measures. Private sector expenditure had in fact been falling since mid-1955, and the mini-budget (as well as the credit restrictions introduced late in 1955) simply served to accelerate a pre-existing trend. The figures for

Table 5.1 Expenditure on gross domestic product at constant prices, 1954–55 to 1962–63

	Private final consumption expenditure	Private gross fixed capital expenditure	Public expenditure	Gross national expenditure	Exports of goods and services	Imports of goods and services	Gross domestic product
				per cent change at average 1959–60 prices			
1954–55	6.6	9.4	3.4	9.1	2.5	21.6	6.0
1955–56	3.2	5.5	1.9	2.6	8.6	-5.3	5.0
1956–57	0.9	1.2	-0.3	-2.4	12.7	-14.6	1.9
1957–58	3.3	5.2	2.2	5.4	-10.6	9.9	2.1
1958–59	3.1	2.3	8.5	5.7	14.5	2.9	7.4
1959–60	6.9	12.0	1.8	7.0	7.6	17.5	5.5
1960–61	1.8	8.1	2.4	4.5	5.2	13.0	3.4
1961–62	2.5	-4.1	6.1	-2.9	13.2	-14.4	1.2
1962–63	6.2	10.5	3.3	9.8	-2.2	17.4	6.9

Source: Adapted from Table 5.8b in NGB

The Treasury line

1956–57 indicate more clearly the deflationary force of the government's measures. GDP increased in constant terms by only 1.9 per cent in 1956–57 while GNE actually recorded a negative result. As a direct corollary of the economic downturn, unemployment began to rise (see Table 5.2). Standing at only 19 000 in 1955, it increased to 32 000 in 1956 and rose steadily thereafter, reaching a peak of 67 000 in 1958. Likewise, vacancies fell sharply from 48 000 in 1955 to 18 000 in 1957, reaching a low point of 16 000 in the following year. The downturn had a dampening effect also on wage rises. As Table 5.3 indicates, the rate of increase in average weekly earnings fell noticeably after 1955–56 and did not level out, as was the case with unemployment, until 1958. By contrast, the CPI actually increased in 1956–57 but, in line with other indicators, fell sharply thereafter (see Table 5.4).

Table 5.2 Unemployment and vacancies, 1954–62

	Seeking full-time work		Vacancies
	'000	rate, per cent	'000
1954	22	0.6	46
1955	19	0.5	48
1956	32	0.8	48
1957	52	1.3	18
1958	67	1.7	16
1959	66	1.7	20
1960	47	1.2	32
1961	112	2.6	12
1962	93	2.1	18

Source: Adapted from Table 4.15 in NGB

Table 5.3 Wage rates, 1954–55 to 1962–63

	Minimum weekly wage rates				Average weekly earnings	
	Adult males		Adult Females			
	$	per cent change	$	per cent change	$	per cent change
1954–55	28.73	2.5	20.02	0.7	34.30	4.9
1955–56	29.87	4.0	20.78	3.8	36.70	7.0
1956–57	31.27	4.7	21.74	4.6	38.40	4.6
1957–58	31.81	1.7	22.23	2.3	39.50	2.9
1958–59	32.42	1.9	22.94	3.2	40.70	3.0
1959–60	34.27	5.7	24.42	6.5	43.90	7.9
1960–61	35.51	3.6	25.22	3.3	46.00	4.6
1961–62	36.58	3.0	26.12	3.6	47.70	2.6
1962–63	36.76	0.5	26.22	0.4	49.00	2.7

Source: Adapted from Table 4.17 in NGB

Table 5.4 Consumer price index, 1954–55 to 1962–63

1954–55	0.7
1955–56	4.1
1956–57	5.8
1957–58	1.0
1958–59	1.6
1959–60	2.5
1960–61	4.1
1961–62	0.1
1962–63	0.2

Source: Adapted from Table 5.16b in NGB

In the 1956–57 budget speech, presented five months after the March measures, the Treasurer's judgment was that inflationary pressures had eased and that competition for resources was less intense. The economy, however, had not yet reached 'a fully balanced situation': demand continued to run ahead of supply. Costs and prices were deemed 'a crucial problem', average weekly earnings having increased in 1955–56 by 7 per cent, the CPI by 4.1 per cent. These rises were attributed partly to the delayed effect of the rapid increase in spending experienced over the previous two years and partly to the automatic wage adjustment practised in some states. Fadden was convinced that costs and prices were 'at the spiralling stage in which a cost or price increase affecting one commodity sets in train a series of cumulative cost and price increases, multiplying the original increase'. He was concerned also with the external situation, Australia's international reserves having fallen by a further $163 million in 1955–56 (after having declined by $259 million in 1954–55). It was not surprising, then, that the Treasurer argued that there was no valid reason to depart from existing policy: 'Whilst tension in the economy may have relaxed in some measure, there are signs enough that the pressures we have endeavoured to subdue could quickly revive and reassert themselves if restraint weakened. It may well be, indeed, that we are only now reaching the most difficult stage of the long struggle to control inflation. Certainly the recent behaviour of costs and prices suggests that strongly.'

In the 1957–58 budget speech the Treasurer announced that conditions had improved considerably over the preceding twelve months. The balance of payments had enjoyed a remarkable recovery. Export earnings achieved record levels in 1956–57, increasing in constant terms by 12.7 per cent. Largely because of the improvement in exports, international reserves were able to increase by $407 million in 1956–57. This represented a 65.4 per cent rise (see Table 5.5). Fadden was also pleased that the rate of increase in wages and prices had slowed down. The one negative feature of the economy was the rise in unemployment. But this was not considered a serious problem. It simply represented 'adjustments going on within particular industries and localities rather than ... any general weakness of labour demand'. Fadden's general verdict was that the economy had entered a situation of 'substantial balance, both internal and external, at a high level of trade and industrial activity'.

Table 5.5 Official reserve assets, 1954–55 to 1962–63

	Gold	Foreign exchange	Total		
	$ million	$ million	$ million	change	% to GDP
1954–55	125	653	785	−24.8	8.2
1955–56	146	469	622	−20.8	6.0
1956–57	103	918	1029	65.4	9.1
1957–58	131	813	952	−7.5	8.2
1958–59	120	788	929	−2.4	7.5
1959–60	133	812	1009	8.6	7.3
1960–61	138	867	1005	−0.4	6.9
1961–62	158	891	1115	10.9	7.4
1962–63	179	975	1243	11.5	7.7

Source: Adapted from Table 1.19 in NGB

By early 1958, however, sanguine attitudes gave way to anxiety. Afflicted by drought and overseas recession, rural production and export prices suffered an abrupt change of fortune. The export price index fell by 12.8 per cent in 1957–58, with wool and metals being the sectors most severely affected. Farm product fell in nominal terms by 20.3 per cent in 1957–58 (compared with a 12.6 per cent rise the previous year), while overall exports fell in constant terms by 10.6 per cent. It had long been held that the rural sector had a profound impact on the fortunes of the rest of the Australian economy. Accordingly, concern mounted in 1958 over the possible repercussions of the rural downturn. But after some initial doubts, occasioned by above-normal increases in the unemployment rate in January and February 1958, it became evident that the slump in the rural export sector would not lead to a more general business recession. In fact, Table 5.1 shows that GNE increased strongly in 1957–58 and continued to do so in 1958–59, while GDP managed to increase slightly in 1957–58 and then leapt by 7.4 per cent in 1958–59. In the 1958–59 budget speech, Fadden's last, the economy was described as having made 'notable progress', despite the fact that total farm income in 1957–58 was approximately one-third less than in the previous year.

Why was it that the rural downturn of 1957–58 had only a relatively minor effect on the rest of the economy? Fadden thought there were two main reasons. First, 'the expansionary forces which have operated in this country during recent years have great strength and have imparted a high degree of resilience to our economy'. The Treasurer was convinced that the power of internal expansionary forces, together with the greater diversification of the economy, meant that it was now in a much better position to resist 'external shocks'. Second, the maintenance of relatively buoyant conditions was the result of the government's 'timely and well-judged' fiscal and monetary measures. These had countered any depressive tendencies and had stimulated expansionary forces. Fadden cited the 'substantial' tax concessions and increased public expenditure in the 1957–58 budget, as well as the increased payments to the states in 1957–58, to bolster his argument. He announced that the government would continue to support the economy by budgeting in the 1958–59 for a nominal deficit of $220 million (£110 million).

Although the 1957–58 budget did indeed provide a degree of stimulus to the economy, the government's approach was essentially a cautious one. This caution was particularly evident in the Treasurer's comments on the government's taxation initiatives:

> We are in a position to give some taxation relief and we propose to give it. But we do not feel called upon to start undoing, step for step, the measures we undertook eighteen months ago for the very purpose of correcting an unbalanced situation and bringing about the kind of well-adjusted situation we now enjoy. Neither do we judge it necessary or desirable to give a wholesale boost to activity and expenditure.

The estimated cost to revenue in 1957–58 of the taxation concessions announced in the budget was $56 million. The taxation measures included an increase in the concessional allowances for maintenance of dependants and reductions in company tax, sales tax, payroll tax and estate duty. The most important initiative, which constituted nearly half of the full-year costs of the taxation concessions, was an increase in depreciation allowances. As Artis and Wallace point out, most of these concessions would have had only a minimal short-term effect. The changes in depreciation allowances would certainly have encouraged increased investment but invariably the response to such stimulus occurs only after a lag.

The 1958–59 budget, by contrast, was significantly more expansionary and the government was anxious that it be seen as such. 'We believe,' the Treasurer announced, 'that what we are doing will materially support business investment and consumer spending and so help to offset the effects of continued low export earnings.' Export earnings were expected to be $200 million less than in 1957–58. The dampening effect of this on the rest of the economy constituted 'the chief potential difficulty of the period ahead'. Using simple Keynesian logic, Fadden argued that such a threat necessitated an increase in expenditure sufficient to maintain activity at a level consistent with the full employment of resources. As noted, he announced that stimulus would be provided by budgeting in 1958–59 for a nominal deficit of $220 million.

The claim that the budget would be expansionary was greeted with considerable scepticism. Commentators pointed critically to the government's refusal to concede any taxation reductions or pension increases, and attention was drawn to the fact that some $70 million of the deficit was to be used to redeem maturing debt and therefore was best described as padding. More importantly, the deficit was said to be largely the result of the fact that, in contrast to postwar norms, total revenue in 1958–59 would be less than in the preceding year. Arndt's conclusion was that 'it is difficult to avoid the impression that the Treasury continues to be more concerned about the risks of a revival of inflationary pressures than about any dangers of recession and that, with rather more cunning than candour, it has played up the £110 million deficit as a sop to public clamour for an expansionary budget'.[3]

While it is true that the Treasury was worried about the risk of inflation, such scepticism about the expansionary effect of the budget was misplaced. Commonwealth government outlays increased strongly in 1958–59 — by 7.6 per cent which compared favourably with the 6.4 per cent rise in 1957–58. But whereas receipts rose by 6.5 per cent in 1957–58, they declined by 1 per cent in 1958–59. The commonwealth budget deficit, as a result, increased from $46 million to $271 million (or, in relative terms, from 0.4 to 2.2 per cent of GDP). The budget, then, was quite strongly stimulatory and helped contribute to the remarkable 7.4 per cent increase in GDP in 1958–59.

In its 1959 survey the Treasury rejected the argument that the diminished relative significance of the rural sector provided a sufficient explanation of the avoidance of general recession in 1958 and agreed with Fadden that the government's budgetary initiatives had played an important part in counteracting the cumulative effects of the loss of rural income. In 1950–51, at the height of the Korean War boom, farm product represented some 27 per cent of GDP. It declined rapidly after that, falling to 18.7 per cent in 1952–53, then to 14.7 per cent in 1956–57. In the following year it fell to 11.4 per cent — the lowest figure for the 1950s. The Treasury admitted that, given these structural changes, 'the effect of even a heavy fall in farm income is little more than marginal'. But it pointed out that the multiplier effects of a decline in rural income could nevertheless be considerable in the absence of counteracting forces.[4]

The department pointed also to the fact that Australia had benefited from a number of largely accidental factors. Australia was fortunate, for instance, that the rural sector had enjoyed such a propitious year in 1956–57. This had put rural industries in a much better position to withstand the difficulties of 1957–58. Australia was fortunate also that the drought of 1957 had been followed by a good season and that the persistence of depressed conditions was largely confined to the woollen industry. Several rural industries, such as wheat, barley, oats, meat and sugar, enjoyed a reasonably propitious year in 1958, thereby providing a psychological, as well as productive, boost to the rest of the economy. Australia was fortunate too, in part because of import restrictions imposed in 1955–57, that businesses had not been laden with excess stocks during the rural slump. There had been no need, therefore, to cut back production in order to liquidate stocks. The economy had been fortunate also that capital inflow had continued at high levels and that the United States recession had not proved persistent.

But over and above the contribution of anticyclical policies and a measure of good luck, the Treasury was convinced that the continued buoyancy of the Australian economy could be attributed mainly to the expansionary mood which pervaded the economy. As the Treasury put it, the prime reason why a widespread slump had not occurred in 1958 was because there had been 'a strong impetus to expansion in the economy and a fairly general determination in the business world to see the situation through'. Further, 'the spreading

Continuous growth: the Treasury's view

To the Treasury, the persistent strength of the postwar expansionary drive and the continuity of growth to which it gave rise were the most remarkable features of the postwar period. It seemed that there had been 'an altered balance of forces' since the war: 'there have been ... great differences in this period of rather more than a decade which mark it off from any earlier period and which suggest that new and powerful forces have been working in the economy, altering the nature of our economic problems, creating new problems and cancelling old ones. The instability we have experienced has been in some respects a different kind of instability.'[5] There had been booms but nothing that would have been called a slump by previous standards. There had been, and continued to be, tensions and pressures, but they were all 'one-way'. The department claimed that such an occurrence defied nearly all previous experience. Only in 'highly abnormal' periods such as the gold rushes and World Wars I and II (the long boom of 1861–90 was not considered) had there been comparable conditions of prolonged excessive pressure on resources. Thus, what was previously a self-evident and unquestioned rule about the course of economic activity — that economic activity took the form of bursts of progress followed invariably by prolonged periods of 'slackness and hesitation' — seemed applicable no longer. One-way tension and pressure, having persisted for more than a decade, had now become 'almost the usual state of things'.

The department's inaugural survey, that of 1956, dwelt at length on the fact that the postwar growth process differed from prewar experience in that it was 'deeper-seated, more determined and powerful'. The source of this new power was a fervent desire to progress materially and to increase Australia's population and to do both as quickly as possible. The force of the expansionary drive was such as to 'thrust aside obstacles and keep going in the face of events which, in other times, would have staggered the economy'. The aftermath of the Korean War boom provided a good example. At the end of the boom it seemed that Australia was in the midst of the 'classical conditions for a major industrial set-back'. In the event, some industries were affected detrimentally. But in the Treasury's view industry generally 'took the situation in its stride'. In a number of areas production increased 'almost as if nothing had happened'. Twelve months later the economy had returned to buoyant conditions.

This particular episode, as well as the economy's performance following the March 1956 measures and the rural downturn of 1957–58, provided the basis for the Treasury's belief that in the postwar period there had been an altered balance of forces. The lesson such events provided was that economic activity was no longer chained to an inexorable fluctuating pattern of boom and depression but could instead follow a more or less linear expansion path.

The problems of acquisitiveness

While the acquisitive drive shown in the postwar period had the important positive attribute of lessening the likelihood of intractable deep recessions occurring — stagnation could not occur if the flow of activity kept up its momentum — it also had a number of negative ramifications. The Treasury was convinced that the desire to progress materially had led to an overemphasis on consumption and an unfortunate neglect of the importance of savings. The central theme of the 1956 survey was that, both internally and externally, Australians had tried to spend beyond their means. The result had been excessive competition for domestic productive resources, particularly labour. This competition, to extend the chain of causation, had led to production losses, works interruptions, a continuous increase in costs and prices and a heightened demand for imports. The persistent upward trend in costs and prices since the war and the large fall in international reserves in 1954–55 and 1955–56 were taken to be measures of Australia's profligacy.

Australians were seen as having an insatiable thirst for goods and services and as being financially reckless. The devil in Keynes' system, the ethic of thrift, had vanished from the scene: 'we are like a family which has been spending not only the whole of its earnings but also the money it has in the bank — spending it partly to enlarge its house and acquire other durable possessions but partly also to have a general good time'.[6] The same point was made in 1957: 'A good many of us are prepared, if we can, to go beyond what we earn and borrow what other people have saved so that we may spend that too.'[7] Financial prudence had been sacrificed to the twin gods of acquisition and having a 'general good time'.

In the surveys of 1956–58 the Treasury attempted to draw attention not only to the problems associated with excessive consumption expenditure but also to the deleterious effects of an inadequate level of savings. An insufficient level of savings had two main effects. First, it starved both the public and private sectors of adequate funds for capital works and production. Lacking the capital to enlarge their future production capacity, industries would have to slow down or defer their plans. This could have harmful cumulative effects. Similarly, if public authorities had inadequate funds for works they would have to curtail their plans for expansion of future services. This would retard the provision of basic services and thereby retard progress in the private sector. Second, inadequate savings would lead to competition for the available funds. This would result almost certainly in higher interest rates which in turn would lead to higher costs throughout the economy.

A point emphasised by the Treasury was that the earnest desire in Australia for population growth, full employment and rising living standards could only be met if the output of goods and services increased continuously.

This, in turn, necessitated a steady enlargement of the capital structure. 'We have to build ahead of ourselves so that, as growth goes on, the basic services of the economy ... will meet the larger needs of the time.' What had been insufficiently appreciated was that the process of building ahead required 'a diversion of effort and resources toward meeting future rather than present needs'.[8] The need for such a diversion arose from the fact that the enlargement of capital facilities necessary to ensure future growth had somehow to be financed. The most appropriate source of finance was an increase in savings which meant, in turn, that present consumption levels would have to be reduced. To the Treasury, the fundamental conflict in a growing country was that between meeting both present needs and future requirements. Similarly, Fadden announced in the 1956–57 budget speech that 'underlying our whole economic problem has been the conflict between our efforts to enlarge our economy for the future and our effort to achieve higher levels of consumption in the present'. He referred to this as 'the central economic problem of the day'.

In addition to the fact that consumption was much more pleasurable than saving, this conflict arose largely as a by-product of the desire in Australia for rapid economic progress. The Treasury could note in 1956 that 'we look upon expansion as the natural and proper order of things and expect it to continue'. Businessmen were 'keen to make the utmost progress they can'.[9] Further, postwar Australia had been permeated by a widespread conviction that 'the economy ought to grow, had to grow, and should not be hindered from growing'.[10] The Treasury welcomed such an attitude but pointed repeatedly to the difficulties it could create if the mood of expansionism led to the abandonment of patience and prudence. Problems had arisen simply because Australians had attempted 'to do too much too soon in too many directions'.[11] In doing so they had put excessive pressure on available resources, leaving a legacy of high cost and price levels.

Convinced that there had been an overemphasis on the satisfaction of current needs to the neglect of future requirements, the Treasury insisted that the 'problem of financing expansion ... is unquestionably the core of the whole problem of growth'.[12] In 1958, in recognition of this, it devoted 24 pages of its annual economic survey to a discussion of the importance of having adequate funds to finance capital equipment and of how these funds might be obtained. The ideal situation, the Treasury argued, was one in which people and institutions voluntarily provided sufficient savings from their incomes to meet the economy's capital requirements. If this were to be insufficient, local savings could be augmented to a limited extent by overseas capital. The department noted that there was, however, a wide divergence between this 'ideal condition' and what in fact had happened in the postwar period. This divergence was expected to continue, but the department was not without hope. 'Far from accepting our level of savings as predetermined and unchangeable, we should search out and try to remove the influences which can be held to discourage savings and consider how best to increase them.'[13] The Treasury was rather vague, however, about just what could be done to increase savings. Its chief hope was that 'if output can be raised, making for a higher general standard of wealth, then it may also become easier to secure the necessary flow of resources to capital requirements. In other words, with higher real income people should be more able, and perhaps more disposed, to save from their incomes than they are to-day'.

The Treasury's hope, in other words, was that an increase in wealth would lead to a higher average propensity to save (alternatively, a lower average propensity to consume). But there were two problems with this. First, if an increase in the propensity to save was a function of a higher level of wealth, why had there been such a marked and continuing shortage of savings in the postwar period and why had the savings ratio fluctuated so much? Second, the Treasury's argument begged the question of how output and wealth could be increased. More particularly, it is not clear whether the Treasury view was that a sustained increase in output was only possible by first increasing the level of savings or whether it believed that increased investment and hence increased output made possible a higher level of savings. The difficulty in the surveys is that the Treasury alternated between suggesting, on the one hand, that the level of savings determined the level of investment and, on the other, that it was investment, by it effects on the level of output, which determined the level of savings. In other words, there was a confusing mixture of classical and Keynesian views on the relationship between savings and investment.

What was clear, however, was the Treasury's belief that a reduction in taxation was not the answer to the problem of insufficient savings. Indeed, it was the Treasury's view that so long as the level of domestic savings remained inadequate in relation to expenditure commitments, it might well be necessary to make up the shortfall by increasing the level of taxation. In other words, that which could not be achieved voluntarily would have to be achieved by force — by the use of 'compulsory savings'.

At this stage, then, the late 1950s, the main lesson drawn by the Treasury from the postwar experience was that it was essential that the growth process be a balanced one, in that aggregate demand had to keep in step with aggregate supply. The moral of the surveys was that, 'somewhat paradoxical though it may seem, [the] tendency to attempt too much in too many quarters is probably the chief danger against which we have to guard'.[14] Higher growth rates were dependent on 'appropriate restraint' on total expenditure and a 'proper relationship' between consumption expenditure and savings. They were dependent also on a 'proper relationship' between investment expenditure and savings. For it was not only consumption expenditure which had tended to be excessive. As the Treasury remarked in 1958: 'the levels of capital expenditure we have tried to achieve have, from time to time, risen far above anything we could have hoped to finance by sound methods, even had savings and capital inflow been much greater'.[15] Similarly, in introducing the mini-budget of March 1956 Menzies noted that it had been decided 'to impose a check upon investment spending which, although valuable, is at present in total beyond the capacity of either saving or borrowing to provide'.[16] As these comments suggest, balanced growth necessitated recognising limits and not exceeding them. Working within these limits would not restrict growth; on the contrary, more would be done and in a more efficient manner. As the department argued in 1957: 'We are likely to get more done and to do it better if we recognize the need to work within the limitations of our resources.'[17] The imperative need was for an increase in savings. In urging this, the Treasury was trying to kill two birds with one stone. On the one hand, to the extent that an increase in savings was the result of a decline in consumption expenditure, pressure on domestic supplies would be reduced, bringing with it decidedly beneficial effects. On the other hand, to the extent that an increase in savings enabled more investment to be undertaken, it would help to ensure the continuity of growth.

It should perhaps be noted at this point that the Treasury's concern for the establishment of individual and community restraint and discipline was to be an enduring one and was to be manifested in a variety of ways. It underpinned the department's complaints, made at various times throughout the postwar period, not only that people were spending beyond their means (and hence not saving enough) but that wages were increasing too rapidly. It was manifested also in the occasional implicit or explicit complaint that governments were spending excessively, were too willing to make extravagant promises and were 'crowding out' the private sector, and in claims that the economy was growing too quickly. In all cases there was a definite threshold beyond which it was imprudent to step. Whether the Treasury's outlook be predominantly Keynesian or predominantly neoclassical there has always been an insistence upon restraint, upon working within set limits. When these limits have been broken the questions have arisen: How can order be restored? Is exhortation enough? These were to be critical questions and ones on which the Treasury's view was to change over time.

The Treasury and the Australian economics profession

In the developmentalism fetish of the 1950s, which stressed the importance to Australia of rapid industrialisation, an active immigration program and high rates of economic growth, it was not surprising to find the Treasury's call for restraint being criticised, especially by those who had had intimate experience of the great depression. Sir Douglas Copland was prominent among these critics. Returning home in 1956 after an interlude overseas, it was not long before Copland launched into an attack on the Treasury viewpoint. He was rather incredulous that one of the major topics of current debate was whether the Australian economy was developing too quickly. 'How much better to be discussing this than to be worrying about the problems of devastating depression as we were just 25 years before!'[18] Copland marvelled at the strength of the expansionary mood, noting that it 'has survived all the obstacles and all the critics'. Among the obstacles was government policy. Copland was concerned that the Treasury's tendency to 'dwell too much upon the fears of inflation ... [was] likely to impede expansion by an over-emphasis upon measures designed ... to restrain total expenditure in a phase of growth'. In Copland's view, such restraint was unnecessary. He was convinced that the economic progress enjoyed since 1953 had been 'relatively sound and vigorous' and hence, by implication, was for now best left alone.

The Treasury disagreed. In its view, the postwar Australian economy had not become any more stable or sound; what was new was that it had become subject to a different form of instability characterised by inflationary and balance-of-payments difficulties. At the base of the department's outlook was the belief that 'when an economy like ours goes wrong, there is a big risk of it going completely wrong. Difficulties multiply difficulties and weaknesses create further weaknesses'.[19] The policy implications followed naturally. It was clearly important 'to check such tendencies at an early stage and prevent them becoming cumulative'. The system was non-correcting: 'it would be a grave mistake to suppose that our current economic troubles are due wholly to passing circumstances and are therefore likely to pass off or that this is the kind of situation which, if left alone, would correct itself'.

This basic distrust of the unregulated economy was shared by most Australian economists. Thus Arndt, for instance, in criticising Copland, argued in 1957 that

> without credit restraint, and all too belated fiscal action [in March 1956], price and cost inflation would certainly have continued for some time, very probably with increasing momentum. Such inflation ... would have steadily enlarged the evil legacy of higher costs, taxes and interest rates, smaller international reserves and tighter import restrictions which ... the 1954–6 boom has bequeathed to us. Moreover, each turn in the spiral of unrestrained inflation would have increased the risk of collapse of the currency, externally and internally.[20]

Arndt's comments point to another similarity between the Treasury and the Australian economics profession in general: a preoccupation with the inflation rate. Both were concerned not only to prevent a recurrence of the rapid inflation which had occurred during the Korean War boom but to eradicate the much more moderate but unceasing price rises which had occurred since then. Writing in 1956 in the first of the *Economic Record*'s biannual surveys of the Australian economy, the editor, R.I. Downing, bemoaned the fact that while an audience could always be found to discuss unemployment or the balance of payments, there was a general lack of interest in inflation. 'Equally, something — not necessarily the best thing — will always be done about unemployment, as a matter of political necessity, and about a balance of payments crisis, as a matter of financial necessity... But it is difficult to get anyone to do anything about inflation.' With the missionary's zeal, and perhaps aided by the fact that he was talking to the converted, he declared: 'It is the task of the economist to try to persuade us otherwise.'[21] Somewhat similarly, Coombs voiced his concern in 1959 at the apparent acceptance by the Australian public of 'creeping inflation' as a fact of everyday existence, a 'natural and inevitable' concomitant to the process of continuous growth. In explaining creeping inflation Coombs argued that it 'derives basically from attitudes of industrialists and traders, of wage earners and of consumers'.[22] What all had in common was a remarkable passivity toward rising prices and an insufficient appreciation of the harm such price rises, particularly when they became cumulative, could cause. Coombs' view, and it was shared by most Australian economists and certainly by the Treasury, was that there was an imperative need somehow to increase resistance to higher prices.

Such concern with inflation was indicative of the change in economic circumstances and policy priorities which had occurred since the war. Peter Karmel pointed to these changes in his presidential address to section G of the 1959 ANZAAS conference:

> Fifteen years ago it was believed that the leading problem of economic policy was the avoidance of mass unemployment. Governments made formal declarations that the maintenance of full employment was the prime objective of economic policy. The problems of price stability under a regime of full employment were recognized, but the full use of given resources was the preoccupation of public, politicians and economists alike. In the post-war advanced economy, whether it be Australia, the United Kingdom or the United States, mass unemployment seems as remote as famine. If the risk is still present, there is a general confidence that we have the knowledge and the weapons to prevent any spread of unemployment on a large scale.
>
> Indeed the fears of fifteen years ago have been quite reversed. Far from suffering from a deficiency of demand, we have suffered from an excess. It is the upper and not the lower end of the spectrum of economic activity, with which we have to concern ourselves. If full employment was the fetish of the forties, it is price stability which has become the fetish of the fifties.[23]

This concern with price stability was heightened by a widespread belief that the tendency toward excess demand was not transient but would prove to be persistent. In 1956 the Treasury referred to the problem of excess demand as 'continuing and deep-seated'.[24] Karmel could comment that the problem of trying

> to prevent the tempo of the economy from passing through full employment into inflation ... is not ... ephemeral, but is almost inevitably linked with the policy of rapid economic development which has, like full employment, become a tenet of faith of the Australian people since the war... This means that, although there may be ups and downs in economic activity from year to year, the underlying trend is towards inflationary conditions. Accordingly restraint in expenditure has been and is likely to continue to be a major problem of economic policy.[25]

Similarly, Trevor Swan noted in a 1955 ANZAAS address:

> Fears about the future, which are shared by many economists, arise from a suspicion that ... the will and/or means to the required policy action [to reconcile full employment with long-run external balance] are lacking, and that we are therefore faced with a persistent tendency towards over-spending, excessive wage costs, balance of payments deficits, and more or less permanent import restrictions with a consequent bias towards inflation and a 'distortion' (in some sense) of patterns of investment and production.[26]

The Treasury line

If excess demand was persistent, and if it had such deleterious effects, what could be done about it? Swan noted that there were at least two possible interpretations of the problem. One school of thought argued that the tendency to overspend was rooted in Australia's overambitious migration and development program. Hence, the problems associated with this tendency could only be overcome by scaling down or perhaps even abandoning the program. The second school was firmly opposed to any reduction in migration or any slowing down in the rate of economic development. As Swan described it, its view was that the tendency to over-spend 'springs from a spendthrift disposition of the body politic which makes us unwilling to set limits to our expenditure until we are faced with sufficiently hard facts in the form of labour shortages, dwindling international reserves, etc.'. If the problem derived from a behavioural characteristic, it followed that perhaps the only remedy was 'a programme of political and popular education' — the classic liberal response.

The Treasury's sympathies, it would seem, lay with the second school — this despite its comments in 1950–51 about an escalation of the development and migration program. Its comments in the 1958 survey made this clear. There were, it declared, 'the soundest practical reasons for endeavouring to keep expansion on the move'.[27] Further, 'from a national standpoint it is vital to us — and not on economic grounds alone — that expansion should be kept going at a good pace'. And the department voiced its strong support for the immigration program:

> Our main objective must be to keep expansion moving at a steady rate and this implies that we should keep up the flow of migrants, for there are now two things that can be said with confidence about immigration. One is that it gives to industry, and to the whole world of business, the assurance of steadily-expanding markets — an assurance which industry and business recognize and upon which they have come to base their forward plans. A second is that, although immigration at or about the recent rate does provide a fairly strong stimulus to both consumption and investment expenditure, it need not of itself give rise to unmanageable pressures on our economy provided its character and composition are adjusted to changing local conditions.

There was no inconsistency here. Contrary to what Copland thought, to disapprove of a tendency to do too much too soon was not necessarily to disapprove of a rapid rate of development. On the contrary, the Treasury's insistent pleas for expenditure restraint derived from a conviction, as noted, that such restraint was in fact the essential precondition for ensuring the continuity of economic development and for making possible an improvement in its rate.

The problem of external balance

In addition to the question of how to maintain price stability, economic policy debate in Australia in the second half of the 1950s was dominated by the question of how to maintain external balance. This was a question of the utmost importance to an economy as open as Australia's and plagued, as it was, by balance-of-payments deficits. Trevor Swan's 1955 ANZAAS address, mentioned above, and which bequeathed the now famous 'Swan diagram', proved influential in informing discussion of this topic. Swan's point was simple: internal and external balance were inextricably linked because both were primarily determined by two forces — the level of spending and the Australian relative cost situation. Swan's analysis made clear the policy implications for dealing with a situation characterised by overfull employment and a balance-of-payments deficit (this being zone four on Swan's diagram, the one which most closely fitted the postwar Australian situation). Two things were required: in the short run a reduction in real expenditure and over the long run an improvement in Australia's competitive position. The latter required real wages to keep in line with, and preferably to be lower than, movements in productivity and the terms of trade.

Swan was emphatic about the need for control of expenditure. He insisted that there was no point in discussing the scope of policies such as quantitative import restrictions, tariff policy or wages policy unless the level of real expenditure was first subject to 'proper control'. 'All can be good or bad, meaningful or nugatory, according to what steps are being taken to regulate expenditure.'[28] Such comments were directed at the government. It should be kept in mind that Swan's paper was delivered in August 1955 in the midst of the rapid decline in Australia's international reserves. His point was that the current situation required something much more positive than merely tightening import restrictions, which at that stage was all the government had done. He explained:

> if we try to use import restrictions as a substitute for cuts in expenditure ... then the fact that we are keeping out goods and keeping in liquidity means that the problems of excess demand are made more acute than ever, local costs are driven up, and we move still further away from equilibrium: with little prospect of ending the restrictions unless we not only mend our ways and make the expenditure cuts that we hoped to dodge, but also take steps to undo the damage done to the relative cost situation in the meantime.[29]

Although the government accepted such arguments, it procrastinated in implementing them. Eventually, however, they provided the rationale for the measures introduced in March 1956. In introducing these measures, Menzies made it clear that the government shared Swan's conviction that it could, and must, play an active role in regulating economic activity. Its faith, like Swan's, was that demand management could play a decisive role in bringing about not only internal but also external balance.

This confidence in the efficacy of demand-management was a reflection not only of the degree of technical understanding of the Australian economy which had been attained by the mid-1950s, but also of the growing belief that the problems which Australia faced were largely of domestic origin. The latter is nicely illustrated by Fadden's comments in the 1955–56 budget speech:

> In the very broadest sense we confront to-day, in yet another of its ever-varying forms, the problem of preserving stability in our economy. It is the economy of a young country, vast and rich but highly changeful, dependent to an extreme degree upon world trends which affect its trade, but influenced at least as much, and perhaps increasingly, by internal forces generated in the effort to build up its population, its defences and its industries at an urgent pace. Sometimes it is instability abroad that shakes our own stability. It is not so much that factor now, though it is not entirely absent. Our difficulties to-day are preponderantly of local origin and that is a vitally important fact.

The fact that instability was being generated primarily from domestic sources meant that, in principle at least, economic management was more efficacious. No longer could it be claimed that fluctuations in export income were the fundamental cause of Australia's instability and that therefore there was little that could be done to promote stable conditions. As the Treasury put it, 'it has repeatedly been emphasized that our troubles largely arise within Australia, from which it follows that they lie within the ambit of our own control'.[30]

This was a perfectly valid deduction, but it did little to assuage contemporary concern among academic economists about whether an effective economic policy was possible. Discussion of this topic, which grew in intensity in 1955–57, pointed to a range of obstacles which hindered policy-making. There were, for instance, the constitutional limitations imposed on the federal government, the federal system itself which enabled state governments to undertake expenditure on a scale quite contrary to the aims of national economic policy, and the independence of the CCAC which could sanction wage rises which were possibly prejudicial to the federal government's policy framework. There was broad agreement, however, that the main factors inhibiting policy did not belong to the institutional setting but were political. As Karmel put it in 1956:

> On the side of politicians there is too much readiness to compromise on matters of principle in order to placate various groups of influence in the community. There is too much weighing up of political consequences, too much fear that the Australian public cannot be made to see reason and will not follow a lead. Lack of courage on the part of the governments, combined with a three year parliament, leads to a hopeless situation as far as economic policy is concerned. For in the first year the government must honour its election promises, frequently made rashly and without thought to their consequences, and in the third year it must bear the forthcoming election in mind. This leaves only the middle year in which a rational policy can be pursued.[31]

But, as Karmel admitted, the attitudes of politicians were themselves 'only a reflection of the attitudes of the public generally'. Ultimately, then, so it was believed, an effective economic policy was dependent upon changing public attitudes, in particular increasing public acceptance: (and hence reducing the political risks) of deflationary policies in a situation of excess demand. Acceptance was a function of understanding and understanding was deemed a function of knowledge. Thus Karmel argued, and here he was reiterating arguments first put forward by the F & E economists during World War II, that 'the first stage towards making effective economic policy possible in Australia is to foster a greater sophistication in economic matters on the part of the general public'.[32] And the only way this could be achieved was by 'more open discussion of the issues involved'. Regular reports on the state of the economy were indispensable — hence the Treasury surveys were applauded by Karmel and others as an important contribution to informal debate of economic issues. So too were the *Treasury Information Bulletins*, which also began publication in 1956, for their role in providing statistical data on Australian economic trends. 'The more knowledge we have on our economy,' Karmel concluded, 'the more effectively will we be able to employ measures of policy to achieve our economic objectives.' Karmel's abiding faith, something which he shared with Keynes and other liberals, was in the ability to persuade through education. It was through education that the major obstacles in the way of effective economic policies — ignorance and myopia — could be overcome.

Economic conditions and policies 1959–62

It will be recalled that a more or less balanced situation prevailed in the Australian economy in 1957 and 1958. A marked upsurge in economic activity, however, began to become apparent in 1959, particularly in the second half of the year. Consumption expenditure began to increase rapidly from the June quarter of 1959. Private capital expenditure lagged behind the consumption boom by about a quarter (some commentators suggested half a year) but was clearly proceeding at a near-frantic pace by early 1960. A mood of buoyancy became apparent and gave rise to a speculative boom in property and shares.

The rapid rise in expenditure was associated with a progressive tightening of the labour market and the onset of labour shortages in some industries. In the twelve months to June 1960, registered unfilled vacancies increased from 20 000 to 32 000. And yet an interesting feature of Table 5.2 is that although unemployment declined from 1.7 per cent of the labour force in 1959 to 1.2 per cent in 1960, at no stage in 1960 was the labour market anywhere near as tight as in the mid-1950s when unemployment fell below 1 per cent for three consecutive years. Nevertheless, wages rose particularly rapidly in 1959–60. After having increased by 3 per cent in both 1957–58 and 1958–59, average weekly wages rose by 7.9 per cent in 1959–60. Somewhat similarly, minimum weekly wages for males rose by less than 2 per cent in 1957–58 and 1958–59, but then jumped by 5.7 per cent in 1959–60 (see Table 5.3).

These rises were only in part a reflection of the increased demand for labour. Two decisions of the CCAC contributed significantly to the wage escalation. In June 1959 the commission raised the basic wage by 15s. a week. Then, in December of the same year, it awarded an additional 21s. a week to the wage margins of metal-trades workers. This represented a rise of approximately 28 per cent. The award soon entered the wage structure of other industries, raising average margins by about 13s. a week.

The inevitable result of the metal-trades decision and of the subsequent flow-on adjustment to other employee groups was an increase in the pace of economic activity during the first half of 1960. The decision had a direct impact on personal consumption expenditure, which had already been stimulated by the rise in the basic wage in June and by a 5 per cent reduction in personal income tax in the August budget of 1959. As can be seen in Table 5.1, consumption expenditure rose in 1959–60 by 6.9 per cent. Though a large increase, it was in fact overshadowed by a 12 per cent rise in private investment. GNE surged forward by 7 per cent.

By the beginning of 1960 the Treasury had come to the conclusion that aggregate expenditure was rising more rapidly than aggregate output — demand overall was exceeding supply. The CPI provided evidence of this imbalance: having increased by 1.8 per cent in 1957 and 1.9 in 1958, it jumped by 4.5 per cent in 1959. The rise in prices and wages was a source of great concern to the Treasury. In the foreword to the 1960 survey, which appeared in May, the department announced that inflation had to be 'exorcised'. Echoing Coombs' comments of the year before, the Treasury remarked that what was necessary was 'a more general resolve to resist inflation as an evil in itself and a threat to the continuance of steady expansion'. Reviewing economic trends since 1957–58, the Treasury noted that

> whilst demand in general may not have been excessive over the period, demand for some products has been quite exuberant; and it is here that the link between cost and demand inflation is clearly established. Employers in those industries have agreed to higher wages because, in a time of rising sales, they have believed it paid them to do so. They either thought that, with the demand for their products high and rising, they could pass the wage increases on in increased prices without losing sales, or that they could absorb the higher wages in the profits that would flow from larger output and sales. By no means all employers have been in such a position, but those who have could set the pace.[33]

The Australian situation was such that wage increases were quickly and inexorably transmitted throughout the economy, especially given the concern of wage tribunals with the concept of 'comparative wage justice'. There was an imperative need, the Treasury argued, for 'decisive action' which would help build up resistance to this transmission process. New cost or price increases had to be prevented and an effort had to be made to ensure that those which had occurred were not passed on.

If there was a need to increase resistance to wage demands, how could this be done? One solution, used successfully by the government in February 1960, was to argue before the CCAC that no increase should be awarded in the basic wage and that automatic quarterly wage adjustments should not be reintroduced — both of these being in opposition to the proposals of the unions. Another solution was to use moral suasion, in other words to urge unions to exercise voluntary restraint in their wage demands. Menzies had tried this in 1955 and he resorted to it again in mid-1960, arguing that community effort was the only way to overcome community problems and that money gains provided only illusory benefits unless matched by productivity increases.

Yet another possible solution, and one which was debated in Australia at the end of the 1950s, was the trade-off solution. Interest in this was stimulated in part by the apparent trade-off between the increase in unemployment and the reduced rate of increase in wage rates during 1956–58, and in part by the visit to Australia in 1959 of Professor A.W. Phillips, the creator of the Phillips curve. Studying wages and unemployment in Australia from 1947 to 1958, Phillips concluded that an unemployment rate of between 3 and 4 per cent would be necessary to ensure that hourly wage earnings did not exceed productivity growth (the latter was assumed to be 2 per cent a year). In terms of actual numbers, the cost of price stability would be a rise in unemployment from 50 000 (the figure prevailing in 1959) to somewhere between 90 000 and 120 000. Commenting on this, A.H. Boxer argued that to deflate aggregate demand enough to raise unemployment to over 3 per cent and keep it there was 'politically impracticable and socially undesirable' and, perhaps more importantly, would have a detrimental effect upon economic growth.[34] Nevertheless, Boxer went on to argue that 'in order to keep price increases down to modest proportions ... the government might find it necessary from time to time to impose additional restraints on demand and force unemployment above the acceptable limit for a short while as a means of creating uncertainty about the future'. As will be seen, many commentators believed that this is precisely what the government had in mind when it introduced the measures of November 1960.

In addition to appearing before the CCAC, the government took two further initiatives in February 1960 to deal with the onset of boom conditions. First, virtually all import restrictions were abolished. The rationale provided was that in the long term resource allocation would be improved (because of the increased competition) and the growth process facilitated, while in the short term it would help drain off some of the economy's excess liquidity and help reduce the imbalance between supply and demand by permitting greater access to goods and services from overseas.

This strategy was quite different from that adopted in 1955–56 when conditions of excess demand were met by increasing the severity of import controls. In the earlier period, however, the economy had been subject to balance-of-payments difficulties, with reserves low and falling. At the beginning of 1960, by contrast, international reserves were in a particularly healthy state. Despite an increase in imports, exports rose strongly in the second half of 1959 (helped by a marked improvement in the terms of trade and in particular in wool prices). Furthermore, net capital inflow increased markedly in 1959–60, being nearly twice the annual average from 1955 to 1958.[35] Figures supplied by the Treasury in its survey of May 1960 indicated that Australia's holdings of gold and foreign exchange were well above $1000 million in early 1960. In addition, Australia's drawing rights with the International Monetary Fund provided a second-line reserve of over $400 million.[36] It was the Treasury's view that the time was right to complete the gradual relaxation of controls begun in 1957, despite the inevitable reduction in reserves which would occur.

The removal of import restrictions had long been an important aim of the Treasury. The department had made clear its attitude to restrictions in its 1957 survey, referring to their 'harmful nature' and pointing to 'the dangers that lie in a continuance of them'. It noted that 'there is nothing good to be said for import restrictions as such. They are damaging in their impact on local trade and industry, on the trade and industry of other countries, and on our relationships with those other countries. They cause dislocation to some local industries and give arbitrary protection to others, the result on both counts being to force costs up'.[37] Further, they caused all sorts of intractable administrative difficulties. The Treasury's opposition to import controls flowed also from its conviction that a satisfactory level of imported goods and services underpinned the continuation of Australia's economic growth. That which hindered the flow of imports was seen as necessarily damaging to the nation's future growth. As the Treasury explained in 1959:

> It has been apparent for some time that the success or failure of our plans for enlarging the Australian economy may well turn on whether we succeed or fail in getting access to larger resources from abroad — access, that is, to the larger imported supplies our economy will inevitably need. Failure in this regard could, plainly enough, be the rock on which our aspirations founder because there is nothing more certain than that, whatever we may do to enlarge local production, the general growth of the economy will require more imports — more imports for the purposes of industry, let alone consumption.[38]

Despite complaints that the decision to abandon import restrictions was too sudden and did not really seek to reduce demand (instead it operated solely on the supply side), the fact remains that the vast majority of Australian economists had been urging this very initiative for several years. When introduced in 1952, import restrictions were described as a temporary expedient. By the second half of the 1950s, with restrictions still in force, concern mounted at the possibility that they would become permanent. In 1958 both the Commonwealth Bank and the Tariff Board joined the chorus of those arguing against restrictions. The Tariff Board argued along lines similar to the Treasury and pointed to the need for an unhindered flow of imports, while the Commonwealth Bank complained about the detrimental effect upon resource allocation which the continuation of restrictions would have.[39]

The second of the government's initiatives was to support the Reserve Bank's efforts to bring under control the excess liquidity of the trading banks. The highly liquid conditions enjoyed by the banks in 1959–60 reflected partly the rapid increase in Australia's international reserves in the second half of 1959, partly the commonwealth government's decision to budget for deficits in 1958–59 and 1959–60, and partly the continued efforts of the Reserve Bank to support the bond market. Steps were first taken to reduce trading-bank liquidity in October and November 1959, with the central bank calling $70 million to Special Accounts. This was followed in December by a request to the trading banks that they alter their lending policies so as to achieve only a moderate overall expansion of advances during 1959–60. The Reserve Bank decided in February 1960 to supplement this request by increasing the SRD ratio by 1 per cent and, after agreement with the banks, raising the minimum LGS ratio from 14 to 16 per cent. This attempt at credit control, however, was to prove ineffective, largely because the central bank was committed to a policy of support for the bond market. As in the two other postwar booms, the central bank once again found itself in the invidious position of attempting to curb bank liquidity while at the same time taking action to ensure that interest rates did not rise.

It was obvious by mid-1960 that monetary policy was not working. Quite contrary to what the central bank had demanded in December 1959, advances rose by 11 per cent during 1959–60. From October 1959 to February 1960 seasonally adjusted advances rose by $46 million and then increased even more rapidly — by $76 million — between February and May. The Reserve Bank's response was to issue another directive to the banks, asking them in May that they achieve 'an early and significant reduction in the aggregate rate of new lending'.[40] But once again it seemed that it was wasting its breath. Three months later, in August, the central bank was forced to give the trading banks what it described as 'more specific directions' about the rate of new lending which it considered appropriate.[41]

Curiously, no fiscal action was taken to stem the boom until two-thirds of the way through the year. The Treasury was later to reveal that early in 1960 the government had considered and rejected budgetary action along the lines of that introduced in March 1956.[42] It was rejected for two main reasons. First, the external position obviated the need for severely deflationary action by providing an avenue for relief through the supply side. Second, the economy had only recently recovered from a period of economic downturn. The Treasury explained that

> psychologically, the situation [through most of 1960] was complex and unpredictable. Although, in the event, the speculative forces proved stronger than had been reckoned upon, there was reason to apprehend the effects more drastic types of action might have produced. Largely this was why the Government adopted a step-by-step approach and placed its reliance upon measures which could be expected to take effect gradually.

The 1960–61 budget, presented in August, was in line with the government's gradualist approach which sought to increase restraint slowly but surely. The Treasurer, Harold Holt, announced that the government was budgeting for a nominal cash surplus of $31 million, the budget result for 1959–60 having been a deficit of $58 million. Holt announced that the government, in order to achieve the surplus, was reducing the rate of increase in public expenditure below that achieved in 1959–60. Further, the 5 per cent rebate on personal income tax, introduced the previous year, was to be discontinued, while company tax was to be raised by 6d. in the pound. The taxation initiatives in the 1960–61 budget were indicative not only of the government's gradualist approach but of its continuing resolution to adopt measures which had a general rather than sectional effect. This was despite the fact that the boom was particularly pronounced in the motor vehicle and building industries. The government's motto for most of 1960 was 'gradual and general'.

This stance came to an abrupt end in November, when a package of measures was introduced designed to bring the boom to a sudden halt. Sales tax increases were introduced, restrictions were announced on the use of interest rate charges as a form of tax deduction, and the Reserve Bank belatedly decided to raise overdraft and fixed deposit rates, thereby squeezing further what had by then become a tight credit situation. The sales tax measures were designed specifically to affect the motor vehicle industry: the rate of tax on cars was raised from 30 per cent to 40 per cent, and on motor cycles and scooters from 16.7 per cent to 25 per cent.

In deciding upon these measures, the Menzies government was guided by two main considerations. First, monetary policy had clearly failed to bring about any significant reduction in the money supply or in its 'abnormally rapid' velocity of circulation. Second, imports rose more quickly after February than had been expected, while exports, which began to be afflicted by falling wool prices, failed to maintain the growth rate achieved in the second half of 1959. The result was a rapid decline in international reserves. From the end of June to the end of September reserves fell by $166 million and there seemed every indication that they would continue to fall unless corrective measures were taken.

The effect of the November measures on economic activity was abrupt and considerable, and ushered in a recession which persisted well into 1962. As can be seen in Table 5.1, GDP managed to increase by only 1.2 per cent in 1961–62, while both private capital expenditure and GNE suffered an absolute decline. The housing and motor vehicle industries were hit particularly badly. From a peak of 25 000 in the September quarter of 1960, the rate of new dwelling commencements fell to 20 000 by the March quarter of 1961. More significant was the decline in motor vehicle registrations. Having reached a peak of 31 865 in November 1960, registrations fell to 22 368 in December and to 16 254 in January 1961. The unemployment situation deteriorated throughout 1961, increasing rapidly from 71 115 in January to 89 367 in April. By December it had reached 116 000. It eventually peaked at the end of January 1962 at 131 500.

The Menzies government repealed the sales tax on non-commercial vehicles in February 1961. But no further action was taken until the August budget. Despite the government's claims that its chief concern was the rise in unemployment, the budget has been roundly criticised, at the time and since, for not being sufficiently stimulatory. The government refused to reduce either personal income tax or company tax. The only revenue initiative of any significance was a reduction in sales tax on household furniture, furnishings and appliances. The concessions granted were estimated to cost the government only $19 million in 1961–62.

The government's caution through 1961 reflected grossly inaccurate assumptions about the likelihood of an early recovery and of an upsurge in private capital expenditure. It reflected also a continuing concern with the possibility of stimulating renewed inflationary pressures. The Treasury concluded its 1961 survey by arguing that price stability had to be viewed as 'a central goal of policy'. In 1962, despite the rise in unemployment that had occurred, it informed readers that inflation 'is a grave social evil; it is also a pervasive economic malady and Australia has reached a point at which there can be no compromise with it... That prices and costs, the basic factor in our trading strength, should be kept stable has ... become a matter of almost fateful importance'.[43] Most commentators found this concern with inflation incredible, given the subdued state of economic activity. The Treasury was criticised for placing stability of prices and balance-of-payments equilibrium above that of full employment and economic growth.

Decisive action to rescue the economy from recession was not taken until February 1962. The government announced that the 5 per cent rebate on personal income tax would be restored, generous investment allowances would be introduced, and the sales tax on motor vehicles would be reduced from 30 to 22.5 per cent. The government also announced substantial increases in public sector expenditure and a rise in unemployment benefits.

The Treasury and linear progress

Despite claims that the 1961–62 recession was the deepest so far experienced in the postwar period, the Treasury felt no compulsion to revise its attitude toward linear progress. In 1957 the department had confidently declared:

> No one supposes that, having by 1962 or 1967 made certain headway, our economy will come to a halt... Probably for as far ahead as matters our economy will continue to grow in some directions if not in all and there will always be a problem, as there is now, of providing in the present for the larger needs of the future. Growth, in other words, is best regarded as a continuous process and the really important thing is the rate at which it proceeds.[44]

In 1961, however, the tone was slightly more guarded: 'No boom can go on indefinitely. Even if no official action is taken to curb it, forces inherent in the boom itself can be expected, sooner or later, to bring it to an end... The farther the boom has been allowed to go, the more violent the reaction is likely to be once the turning point is reached — possibly leading to widespread business failures and a great rise in unemployment.'[45] There is a distinctly Keynesian line here in the suggestion that the very forces producing a boom led eventually to its demise, the implication being that in an unregulated economy the transition from boom to slump was inherent and inevitable. It followed that anti-cyclical action such as that introduced in November 1960 was necessary, especially given the assumption that the more protracted the boom, the deeper and more widespread was the inevitable contraction.

The point remains, nevertheless, that the department's faith in continuous progress was dampened only marginally by the recession of 1961–62. In the surveys of the early 1960s the emphasis remained on the continuity of growth rather than on cyclical variation. For instance, the Treasury could declare in 1961: 'Since some of the forces that make for growth are intermittent, it must itself be somewhat intermittent, a matter of surge and pause, a burst of energy to-day and perhaps a degree of hesitancy to-morrow. These may be no more than undulations in a broad, strong flow of progress — such as we have had in Australia since the war — but their relative magnitudes can be highly important.'[46] The underlying image was essentially the same as in 1957. The economy, as depicted by the Treasury, was climbing a more or less linear growth path. The rate at which the economy moved along this path had been subject to considerable fluctuations. But the outstanding fact, and that which most impressed the Treasury, was that at all times (with 1952–53 being the only exception) it was climbing upwards.

In the terminology which began to be used with increasing regularity from the late 1950s onwards, it was the Treasury's view that the old trade cycle, with its severe peaks and troughs and which often involved an absolute contraction in output, had been replaced by a growth cycle in which the various phases of the cycle corresponded to either accelerations or decelerations in a process of continuous growth. Recession was the name given to a phase of deceleration, boom to a rate of expansion above the secular trend. Growth cycles, in other words, were simply variations in the rate at which economies continued inexorably along their linear growth paths.

Reactions to the recession

According to Waterman, the 1961–62 recession provoked a much more hostile public reaction than that which occurred during the downturn of 1952–53.[47] A very rough guide to this is the much greater volume and virulence of critical newspaper articles, editorials and letters in the latter period. A more satisfactory guide is the fact that in the federal elections of December 1961 the Menzies government came perilously close to defeat, its parliamentary majority being reduced from 32 to two (effectively one after the appointment of the speaker).

A number of factors can be suggested to account for the increased hostility. One reason is that 1960 marked the apogee of a boom in consumer durables and private houses that had been in progress throughout the 1950s. A key illustration of this boom was the proliferation of hire-purchase companies in the 1950s and the marked increase in the volume of their activities. Arndt points out that total outstanding advances of hire-purchase companies rose from $180 million in 1953 to $474 million in 1957, and by April 1960 had leapt to $824 million. He notes also that of the $520 million of new hire-purchase credit granted in 1959, two-thirds was used to purchase new and used cars, with most of the remainder being used to purchase household goods.[48] The increase in the relative importance of mortgage loans is indicated by the fact that by 1961 some 22 per cent of householders were purchasing their homes by instalments, compared with 15 per cent in 1954 and 8 per cent in 1947. The much greater use of mortgage arrangements and hire-purchase finance in 1960 compared with 1951 meant that many more Australians were affected directly by the credit 'squeeze' and the November fiscal measures. And more were affected by the reductions in overtime and normal earnings caused by the subsequent recession. The increase in debt caused by these measures, and the difficulties in meeting repayments, were bound to cause public hostility.

Also relevant here is that unlike the Korean War period it was not possible in 1961–62 to project the cause of the downturn largely on to external forces, such as the collapse of wool prices. Lydall expressed a common sentiment early in 1962 when he referred to the experience of the preceding twelve months as 'Australia's first independent slump',[49] by which he meant it had nothing to do with economic conditions prevailing abroad. It was widely believed that the blame for the downturn rested squarely on the shoulders of the government and its incompetent advisers.

But perhaps the most important consideration is that at the end of World War II, as we have already seen, it was commonly held that there would be a short and intense postwar boom followed inevitably by a slump, so that when the downturn came in 1952 it merely confirmed what had been widely expected. Moreover, to a generation which had clear memories of the 1930s the extent of unemployment and the duration of the slump of 1952–53 seemed negligible and led to a revised interpretation of the notion of economic downturn. 'Depression' became an obsolete phrase of use only in history texts; any downturn was now to be described as a 'recession'. The fact that there was a steady increase throughout the 1950s in the percentage of householders purchasing their homes and consumer durables by instalments was indicative of the growing confidence in Australia that the traditional trade cycle was largely a thing of the past. As Waterman puts it, 'the combination of job security and continually rising money earnings made instalment credit a sound and attractive method of increasing living standards — a poor man's hedge against inflation'.[50] The degree of confidence attained by the end of the decade was captured in a comment by Holt in the 1959–60 budget speech: 'Australia has succeeded in establishing improved industrial relations and a degree of economic, social and political stability unparalleled in our own national history and, taken in combination, not surpassed, I believe, by any country in the world today.' After 1952–53 the maintenance of unemployment a few decimal points either side of 1.5 per cent was taken for granted. In 1954 Karmel could claim that 'in Australia no government which tolerated any appreciable unemployment would survive an election'.[51] When in 1961 the official statistics showed that unemployment was above 2 per cent and when it continued as such for nearly twelve months (after reaching a peak of 3.1 per cent in January 1962, a postwar record), it was only to be expected that the result was deep disappointment and dissatisfaction.

Economic planning

The Australian economics profession shared this disappointment and dissatisfaction. As with the mini-budget of March 1956, one of the main complaints raised by economists about the government's November measures was their tardiness. In the earlier episode, commentators pointed to the fact that as early as June 1954 the Commonwealth Bank had drawn attention in its annual report to the need for measures of restraint to prevent the re-emergence of excess demand. There was very little in the 1954–55 budget, however, which could be described as anti-inflationary. In 1955 the Treasurer himself noted that by the end of the 1954–55 financial year 'we had all around us the unmistakable signs of active inflation' and went on to argue that 'our central pre-occupation in Australia should be the level of costs in our industries'. But again nothing was done to bring aggregate demand in line with supply. As has been described, it was not until March 1956, some two years after the boom had become clearly apparent, that effective action was finally taken. And it was not until then that central-bank support of the bond market was abandoned. But despite the complaints, and here was an important difference with the reception given to the initiatives of November 1960, the government's actions in March 1956 were welcomed. Downing thought that the policy measures 'will operate in the right direction and are of about the right magnitude'.[52] Professor Meade, visiting Australia from the London School of Economics, agreed but felt that the disinflationary process should in fact be carried still further.[53] And even in April 1957 Karmel was urging the government to ignore any calls for relaxation of its policy of restraint.[54]

The measures of November 1960, however, were deemed not only tardy but inappropriate. To deal with the first complaint, commentators pointed critically to the fact that although the government had come to the conclusion at the beginning of 1960 that demand was exceeding supply, very little was done to deal with excess demand. The removal of import restrictions was deemed a 'curious' solution in that it did not deal with the root cause of the problem. More importantly, it could work only slowly to moderate inflationary tendencies; in the meantime there was a risk of the country being flooded with imports. Commentators were particularly critical of the fact that no fiscal action, the most potent force for regulating demand, was taken until August. Even then, it was deemed insufficiently deflationary. And why, commentators asked, had the government continued to rely on monetary policy, even though it was clearly failing? When effective action was eventually taken, it was criticised for being too late to be of any benefit. In fact, what would have been appropriate several months earlier was now seen as quite inappropriate in that it served to hasten and exacerbate a pre-existing downward trend.

But the key distinguishing feature of criticism in 1960–62 was the attention drawn to the government's inability and apparent unwillingness to look beyond the short term. Moreover, complaints about the narrow horizon of government policies were coupled with increasingly more vocal demands for the introduction of some form of economic planning. Not surprisingly, the

Problems of continuous growth

radical fringe of the Australian economics profession, led by Professor E.L. Wheelwright of the University of Sydney, were particularly vocal in making these demands.[55] But it was not just the mavericks who demanded the introduction of planning. Wheelwright was joined by a wide array of academic economists, including Professor Cochrane of the University of Melbourne, Professor Arndt and Dr A.R. Hall of the ANU, as well as Sir Douglas Copland. Behind this broad agreement, admittedly, was a wide range of opinion on just what planning would and should involve and on who would be responsible for it. Wheelwright advocated a separate department of planning.[56] Hall suggested in 1962 that a planning section be established in the Prime Minister's Department.[57] Other economists, such as Arndt, believed that planning should be left to the Treasury.[58] All were united, however, in the conviction that government policies had to be framed within a long-term perspective and that there was a need for some sort of institution which would seek to improve the coordination of policy weapons.

This was a conviction widely held. In July 1962 Arndt could argue that

> everyone in Australia — except the Government and its official advisers — seems to be in favour of some form of long-term national economic planning. In recent months there have been demands for planning from business spokesmen, from within the Liberal Party, from the Labor Party, from economists of every shade of opinion, even from bankers... More and more thinking Australians are coming to the conclusion that the methods of economic policy making are not good enough and are attracted by the possibilities of some form of national planning.[59]

This same sort of enthusiasm for planning was apparent in Britain at this time, and arose largely because of Britain's relatively poor growth performance in comparison with her continental neighbours. Beginning in the late 1950s, it began to be claimed with increasing frequency that the French model could be adapted to the British situation and provide a basis for increased growth. The Conservative government of Harold Macmillan eventually came to sympathise with such arguments and established in 1962 the National Economic Development Council.

In Australia, however, pleas for the adoption of economic planning fell largely on deaf ears. The Menzies government went no further than offering two token responses to the prevailing dissatisfaction with existing techniques of economic management. One was to draw up the terms of reference, late in 1962, of a committee of economic enquiry. The other, again in 1962, was to establish a new branch in the Treasury, the Economic and Financial Surveys Branch. The branch was made responsible for developing programs of research into the following areas:

(a) Forward expenditure plans of public authorities in Australia and estimates of their expenditures for a period of years ahead, with an assessment of the implications of these estimates particularly for the Commonwealth Budget.
(b) Estimates of private expenditure for a period of years ahead;
(c) Estimates of gross national product, gross domestic expenditure, total market

supplies and total market expenditure (and the main elements thereof) for a period of years ahead, with an assessment of the implications for economic and financial policy;
(d) Trends in the Australian population and the growth of the work-force, both from natural increase and immigration;
(e) Forward estimates of the balance of payments for a period of years ahead.[60]

The branch was divided into two sections. Functions (a), (b) and (c) were the responsibility of the Expenditure Survey Section, while functions (d) and (e) were the responsibility of the Resources Section.

The establishment of the Economic and Financial Surveys Branch did not signal an acceptance within the Treasury of the need for economic planning. In fact, in the same year the branch was established, the Treasury argued strongly in its annual economic survey against any form of long-term planning. The Treasury articulated three key objections to planning. The first related to the target setting and forward calculations upon which the exercise depended. Serious doubts were held about whether targets for, say, five years could be constructed with sufficient accuracy for the purposes of economic planning. The need for central targets to be dependable was 'crucially important'. 'If they proved too high, it could bring on the familiar troubles of trying to do too much with too few resources. If they proved too low, it could produce frustration and loss on the part of those enterprises which found themselves capable of doing more than the targets provided for them.' Given the difficulty of estimating even short-term trends, it was highly likely that the targets would not be achieved. It was quite possible, therefore, that planning would ultimately be 'disruptive and discouraging'.

A second objection related to Australia's continued dependence on overseas trade. Just before the the publication of the 1962 survey, the secretary to the Treasury, Sir Roland Wilson, had noted that

> The Australian economy is more dependent than most on international trade, with exports and imports equivalent to about 13 per cent of the gross national product in recent years. Over 80 per cent of export receipts are still derived from wool, wheat and flour, meats and other primary products, the prices of which are determined by market conditions abroad whose production is subject to the vagaries of the seasons.[61]

Taking up this line, the Treasury argued in the survey that while the economy had showed greater resilience in the face of export fluctuations, unstable overseas earnings could still be 'highly disruptive'. The department expressed doubts about whether economic planning could be 'sufficiently protected' against such disruptions.

The third and main objection to planning was its potentially harmful effects on the notion of free enterprise. The Treasury was concerned that planning might limit individual initiative and stultify growing and enterprising firms by attempting to impose rigidity and certainty upon a system which was inherently unpredictable, uncertain and constantly changing. Moreover, the private sector, in which resided the source of capitalist drive, might be rendered impotent if planning resulted in the subordination of the judgment and aspirations of the individual beneath a collectively determined, but nevertheless fallible, formula.

In a critique of the Treasury view, Arndt argued that the weakness in the first and third objections was that it was being assumed that active measures would be taken to enforce the plan. But if instead a form of indicative planning were adopted, so that the plan was 'treated simply as a guide to business decisions, at most reinforced by various incentives designed to bring the firms' own interests closer to "the interests of the programme"', such objections lost much of their force. But he conceded that the question of stifled initiative (mentioned in the third objection) was a difficult one. Initiative, however, was largely a function of the degree of competition and there was no inherent reason why planning should preclude the potent force of foreign competitive pressures. Arndt found the second objection 'quite unconvincing' for the simple reason that the problem facing primary export industries was unstable prices and incomes, not that of determining output targets. And there was no reason why this problem would become any more difficult under a system of indicative planning.[62]

While critical of planning, the Treasury had also become more acutely aware of the difficulties in the way of effective demand-management. A point made repeatedly by the Treasury in 1960–62 was that there were distinct limits — constitutional, administrative, political — to the government's ability to control inflation. There were also a great many technical problems with demand-management. There were difficulties, for instance, in deciding when and to what degree corrective measures should be introduced: 'it is not always easy to judge what form action should take, how strong it should be or how long it should last.'[63] And economic forecasting was 'not a matter which lends itself to scientific accuracy'. There were also problems of 'understanding and attitude'.[64] Decisions about the timing and severity of policy measures were complicated by the fact that there was always a wide range of opinions on likely future trends. And there were likely to be many who 'will question the wisdom or desirability of, say, measures of restraint — even those of a rather gentle character — if they are designed to anticipate inflationary tendencies at a time when the economy seems to be merely enjoying exhilarating business conditions'.

The Treasury drew two main conclusions from this. First, it argued that there was a need for greater flexibility in the use of policy weapons — a line which had long been a favourite cry of academic economists — and a need for greater acceptance of the fact that on occasions abrupt changes in direction were unavoidable. Second, the task of controlling inflation had to be shared; it was not just the government's responsibility. The Treasury argued in 1961 that organised groups — whether they be sellers, buyers, producers or trade unionists — had the leading part in controlling inflation. More importantly, it argued that the cause of, and solution to, the problem of inflation lay ultimately in the hands of all those whose spending decisions went to make up aggregate demand. Government demand-management was an important weapon with which to control inflation but it was community cooperation, so the department argued, which underpinned its efficacy.

The events of 1956–62 illustrate nicely a fundamental difficulty in the Keynesian model: the problem of combining individualism and economic responsibility. The period highlights in particular the question of maintaining discipline in a social-democratic society subject to continuously high levels of employment. Keynes believed that the notion of economic control was in fact a policy of liberation. Governmental regulation of the economy would extend only to regulating aggregate demand. Now no longer shackled by the fear of mass unemployment, individuals would be left free to exercise choice and initiative:

> Whilst ... the enlargement of the functions of government, involved in the task of adjusting to one another the propensity to consume and the inducement to invest, would seem to a nineteenth-century publicist or to a contemporary American financier to be a terrific encroachment on individualism, I defend it, on the contrary, both as the only practicable means of avoiding the destruction of existing economic forms in their entirety and as the condition of the successful functioning of individual initiative.[65]

Keynes was convinced that despite the 'large extension' which he proposed in the traditional functions of government, 'there will still remain a wide field for the exercise of private initiative and responsibility. Within this field the traditional advantages of individualism with still hold good'.

Underpinning Keynes' mid-liberal stance was a belief, perhaps not in the perfectibility of people but in the possibility of gradual and continuous improvement. He was convinced that people, although heavily influenced by irrational forces, could still be persuaded to act reasonably, to solve problems collectively. Keynes, as noted in chapter 2, never abandoned his early meliorist stance. He was convinced that the irrational attitudes of people could be counterbalanced, possibly corrected, by the actions of the intellectually and theoretically superior technocracy overseeing the system.

Keynes did not consider in any detail, however, the possibility that governmental success in regulating the level of economic activity might jeopardise the concept of community consensus and cooperation. He insisted that 'the right remedy for the trade cycle is not to be found in abolishing booms and thus keeping us permanently in a quasi-slump; but in abolishing slumps and thus keeping us permanently in a quasi-boom.'[66] But, as the Treasury was well aware, the problem with an economy which is kept permanently in a quasi-boom is that there is always a risk of demand inflation and, perhaps more importantly, there is continuous pressure for wage increases and a risk that such pressures will become cumulative. Furthermore, such conditions are conducive to the passing on of cost increases by employers in the form of commodity price rises.

The faith of Keynes' followers, and here the F & E Committee provides a good example, was that there need be no conflict between individualism and economic responsibility in a situation of continuous high employment. To the extent that there was a conflict, the answer lay neither in increasing unemployment nor in restricting individualism. Rather, it lay in remoulding the ideas and attitudes of individuals so as to encourage greater self-discipline and the adoption of a broader, more community-minded stance.

After fifteen years of experience with continuous high levels of employment, the surveys of 1956–62 suggest that the Treasury still sympathised with this view. There is much in the surveys to indicate that the department believed that with reasoned arguments and with sustained exhortation, attitudes could be changed and there could be such a thing as 'an effective community stand against inflation'.[67] Each survey, after all, was an exercise in exhortation, an essay in persuasion. The Treasury's hope was that the surveys would lead to more informed debate of economic issues. In introducing the series, Menzies noted that they were written for the purposes of 'public information and guidance' and to help secure public cooperation. Cooperation, he argued, could only be achieved through understanding.[68] It was hoped that the surveys would play a vital role here.

But beneath a veneer of optimism there was tension in the Treasury's outlook. For while it talked of the importance of achieving 'an adequately informed common mind on the problems in which all have a share and towards the solution of which all must co-operate',[69] each of the surveys from 1956 to 1962 pointed to the failure to achieve this 'common mind'. In the surveys of the 1950s the description of economic agents was largely one of myopic creatures concerned only with the present and ignorant of future possibilities. They were concerned only with the gratification of their consumption needs and were oblivious to the collective results of such action. They had attempted to do too much too soon. They were reluctant to save; often they borrowed other people's savings so that they could spend that as well. And from 1959 onwards the surveys were full of arguments about trade unions persisting in attempts to gain higher wages and of employers acceding to these demands, and full of warnings about the pernicious consequences such behaviour would bequeath.

In short, reality seemed to betray the Treasury's ideals and made it question the degree to which human nature was malleable. Over time, as will be seen, the possibility of self-imposed economic responsibility became increasingly tenuous in the department's eyes. By the mid-1970s the notion of community cooperation had come to be considered naive. It was replaced by a belief that the most effective safeguard against excessive wage claims was to violate the sacrosanctity of full employment and create (or tolerate) a pool of unemployed sufficiently large to counteract avaricious tendencies.

6

Defence expenditure and efficient resource allocation, 1963–67

BY the second half of 1963 the Australian economy had broken free of the grip of recession and had entered a phase characterised by reasonably high growth rates, price stability and low unemployment. This phase of balanced growth, to use the Treasury's expression, persisted until the late 1960s when inflation re-emerged as a serious problem. While it is true that the economy had entered a phase of comparative stability, there were nevertheless a number of major policy problems during 1963–67. These problems were not imported, nor were they generated by the private sector. In effect they were created by the government's own actions, namely the marked increase after 1963 in governmental expenditure. Defence expenditure, in particular, rose quickly as a result of Australia's involvement in the Vietnam War. What made burgeoning public expenditure a problem was that it occurred in a situation in which for the most part resources were fully employed. Apart from the now all-too-familiar problem of having to attempt to keep aggregate demand in line with supply, the circumstances of the period conspired to highlight the scarcity constraint.

In these circumstances the Treasury's attention became increasingly directed toward the question of rational economic behaviour and the means by which decision-making techniques, particularly in the public sector, could be improved so as to make better use of available resources. The rapid rise in public sector expenditure provoked questions also about the desirable size of the public sector vis-a-vis the private. The Treasury emerged from the period convinced that some pruning of the public sector, at least in relative terms, was essential and that much greater efforts needed to be made to emulate the profit-maximising activities of private sector enterprises. Such changes were essential if resources were to be used more efficiently.

Efficient resource allocation

Treasury personnel

Before exploring the Treasury's growing interest in the question of resource allocation, it will be useful to note some of the staffing changes which had occurred in the department by 1967. Since the mid-1950s there had been remarkably little change in the upper Treasury echelons. Roland Wilson remained secretary from 1951 to 1966. Richard Randall, who had replaced Frederick Wheeler in 1952 as first assistant secretary in GFEP, became deputy secretary in 1957 and then secretary in 1966. Maurice O'Donnell replaced Randall as first assistant secretary in GFEP in 1957, and then in 1966 became deputy secretary. There was a noteworthy continuity, then, at the top of the Treasury ladder right through the 1950s and 1960s.

Both Randall and O'Donnell were in their twenties when the great depression reached its apogee; neither progressed straight from school to university; and both had been in employment for several years before undertaking university degrees. Thus, both experienced the depression first-hand and at a particularly impressionable age.

Randall was born in 1906 in Birkdale, near Brisbane. After only two years at Wynnum High School he entered Brisbane Technical College and studied woolclassing. By the age of eighteen he was woolsorting in Western Queensland and continued to do so for eight years. In 1932 he matriculated while working part-time in wool stores to support his private study. This achieved, Randall took a correspondence course in accountancy. He then enrolled in the Economics Department at the University of Sydney, headed by Professor R.C. Mills. When Randall graduated in 1936 he joined an 'elite' who had managed to obtain first-class honours under Mills (an elite which included J.G. Crawford, T.W. Swan, L.G. Melville and S.J. Butlin). In 1937 Randall was appointed Carnegie research scholar at the University of Sydney. He then joined the Premier's Office in Sydney as research officer, working as part of Sir Bertram Stevans' 'think tank'. In 1940 he moved to Canberra to join the Treasury. The following year, however, he enlisted in the AIF and spent most of the war in Western Australia. Randall did not resume his climb up the Treasury ranks until 1945. His rise thereafter, however, was rapid.[1]

O'Donnell was born in 1907, the year after Randall and three years after Roland Wilson. He attended Christian Brothers High School at Lewisham. In 1924 he joined the New South Wales Government Railways as a clerk in the stores branch. He remained at the railways for seventeen years. During World War II he joined the influx of temporary recruits enlisted by the commonwealth public service to help cope with the administrative strains imposed by the war. Upon joining the service, O'Donnell was placed in charge of the supply and shipping accounts section of the Ministry of Munitions, located in Sydney. This gave him the chance to complete a part-time degree in economics at the University of Sydney. He graduated with honours in 1942. In 1946 he became a senior research officer in the Treasury and in 1951 was placed in charge of the Commonwealth Sub-Treasury, Sydney. From 1953 to 1955 O'Donnell was assistant secretary in GFEP and from 1955 to 1957 was assistant secretary in charge of the Defence Division, Melbourne. As noted, when Randall became deputy secretary in 1957, O'Donnell was placed in charge of GFEP. He remained as such until 1965 when he left for a two-year stint as an executive director of the International Monetary Fund and the International Bank for Reconstruction and Development.[2]

For all the apparent stability and continuity at the top of the Treasury ladder, however, the early and mid-1960s saw the rise to power of a younger generation of Treasury economists. The outstanding figure is John Stone, who in 1962 was placed in charge of the new Economic and Financial Surveys Branch (see chapter 5). Stone was born in 1929. At the age of twelve he left his home town of Merredin, in outback Western Australia, and moved to Perth with his mother where he attended Perth Modern School. He soon established a reputation for academic brilliance. At the University of Western Australia he obtained first-class honours in mathematical physics and in 1951 won a Rhodes scholarship. For two terms at Oxford he studied nuclear physics and then switched to philosophy, politics and economics, again achieving first-class honours. In 1954 he joined the the commonwealth Treasury, working as assistant to the Treasury's senior London representative (and on secondment for a time to the British Treasury). He returned briefly to Australia in 1956 and then was appointed senior Treasury representative in London, a post he held from 1957 to 1961. When appointed to the assistant secretaryship in 1962 he was only thirty-three. He was to remain in charge of the Economic and Financial Surveys Branch until 1966, leaving for Washington in 1967 to become, like O'Donnell, an executive director of the International Monetary Fund and the International Bank for Reconstruction and Development.[3]

Stone was not the only relatively young officer appointed to the second division at this time. Roy Daniel, for example, was promoted to assistant secretary in 1961. Daniel graduated from the University of Melbourne in 1949 with honours in arts, majoring in economics. He joined the Treasury in February 1950, taking up a position in GFEP. In September 1955 he was appointed to senior finance officer, grade 2, in GFEP, his duties being to conduct and supervise research and investigation into the financial and economic policy aspects of trends in the Australian economy. In May 1956 he was promoted to chief finance officer, grade 1, and was placed in charged of the new Research and Information Section in GFEP. He occupied this post until his appointment as assistant secretary. Similarly, in 1963 Roy Cameron was appointed an assistant secretary in GFEP. Though Cameron was slightly older than Stone and Daniel, he too was a product of postwar university training. He lectured in economics at Canberra University College from 1949 to 1951, received an MEc from the University of Adelaide in 1951 (writing on standard hours and the basic wage), worked as an economist at the World Bank from 1954 to 1956, gained a doctorate in 1955 from Harvard (a study of inflation in Australia from 1945 to 1955), and eventually entered the Treasury in 1956, working in GFEP.

Likewise, by the mid-1960s the third division of GFEP was dominated by officers a generation younger than Wilson and Randall. An example was Bill Cole who was appointed a chief finance officer in the Financial and Economic Surveys Division in December 1962. Cole was born in 1926, graduated from the University of Melbourne with first-class honours in commerce, and entered the Treasury as a research officer in 1952.

One of the first tasks of Stone's Economic and Financial Surveys Branch was to prepare papers for the Vernon Committee on a range of topics: the balance of payments, overseas investment in Australia, the availability of credit, the growth of domestic savings and investment capital requirements, public borrowing overseas, the financing of public works and a projection of the workforce. Some of these papers were later published in revised form as supplements to the *Treasury Information Bulletin*. The supplements provide a valuable additional source of information on Treasury attitudes. They are of particular importance because the Treasury was able to explore specific topics in much more depth than space allowed in the annual surveys. The contents of the supplements will be analysed later in this chapter. We need first, however, to put the discussion into context by saying something about the changing nature of the Australian economy during 1963–67.

Economic conditions and policies, 1963–67

During 1963 and 1964 the Treasurer and his department waxed enthusiastic on the performance of the Australian economy. They were particularly delighted with the fact that inflation was virtually non-existent. What made the achievement of price stability all the more notable was that it was coterminous with the achievement of full employment and reasonably rapid economic growth. What had appeared conflicting objectives now enjoyed a seemingly happy coexistence. Such an achievement proved a source of great optimism. Stimulated further by a succession of mineral discoveries, which promised an end to Australia's persistent balance-of-payments problems and a diminution of her reliance on her traditional exports, the Treasury's confidence in Australia's future increased.

In introducing the 1963–64 budget, Harold Holt spoke in glowing terms of the year past, noting that it was not only a year of expansion but a year of stability, in which aggregate supply had broadly matched demand. Gross domestic product had grown in nominal terms by 8 per cent (6.9 per cent in constant terms) but the price of consumer goods and wages had increased only moderately. In fact, the CPI rose by only 0.2 per cent in 1962–63 (after having increased by only 0.4 per cent in 1961–62), while average weekly earnings rose by 2.7 per cent in 1962–63 (compared with a 2.6 per cent rise in the previous year). Here was proof, Holt concluded, of 'a great fact — one which the Government has consistently asserted — the fact that stability of costs and prices and economic growth can and do go together'. The achievement of wage restraint was singled out as probably the most important stimulus to growth. The Treasurer hastened to add, however, that stability (by which he seemed to mean the avoidance of inflation) was not the government's sole objective. It was, nevertheless, almost certainly the key requirement for sound economic growth.

The Treasury, too, voiced its approval in 1963 of the economy's newfound steadiness. Commenting on the course of recovery in 1962–63, it declared:

> Probably the outstanding feature of the period has been the steadiness of expansion. At times there has been talk of recovery hesitating or flattening out; but, when the facts have become available, they revealed little sign of this. Meanwhile, there has been little to indicate that, overall, the pace of expansion was likely to get too high. Speculation has not re-appeared in any significant degree and there is much to suggest that business at large prefers to keep to a steady rate of growth rather than attempt any spectacular thrust forward.[4]

The implicit suggestion was that the shock of recession had had decidedly beneficial consequences by putting an end to the reckless economic behaviour which prevailed through much of the 1950s and by imparting a more sober attitude within the business community.

Though pleased with the economy's steadiness, the Treasury was anxious to combat suggestions that the rate of growth was likely to falter during the 1960s. The onset of recession late in 1960 had given rise not only to attacks on government policy but in some cases to arguments that the economic growth enjoyed during the 1950s was simply a reflection of a particular set of temporary, and now expended, factors. Leslie Bury recalled in 1970 that the climate of economic discussion in the early 1960s was dominated by 'the doom-laden prophecies foretelling stagnation, the talk of a long-term chronic imbalance in the balance of payments'.[5] Typical of those who offered pessimistic prognostications was Maxwell Newton, managing editor of the *Australian Financial Review*. Newton asked at a conference convened early in 1962 to discuss Australia's economic growth whether there was any reason to be confident that 'we will be able to count on even that modest growth which distinguished our performance under stop-go in the fifties'. Newton thought there was cause for doubt. He pointed to the expansionary forces at work in the 1950s: the great increase in house building and non-dwelling construction in response to backlogs and annual incremental demand, the rapid industrial development, in particular in oil refining and in the manufacture of motor vehicles, household appliances and chemicals, and the high level of migration. He averred: 'Many of these groundswell movements are petering out. The great period of house building is over; the major work in motor vehicles, appliances and in major areas of chemicals is finished; the future migration problem may be to persuade people to come here.'[6]

Against this, the Treasury raised a number of arguments, though essentially it relied on articles of faith about the ability of industries to produce new varieties of goods and services and about the insatiability of consumer wants. It did offer, however, two substantive counter-arguments. First, the age distribution of the Australian population over the coming decade would act to stimulate demand, particularly for housing, and would provide a significant addition to the labour force. Second, Australia had greatly benefited from the discoveries during the 1950s, and in particular since the turn of the decade, of vast reserves of bauxite, copper, iron ore and oil. To the Treasury, the significance of these mineral discoveries could hardly be overstated, with the authors of the 1962 survey going so far as to claim that 'Australia has achieved the greatest breakthrough in point of resources since the crossing of the Blue Mountains a hundred and fifty years ago'. Such discoveries held the promise of converting Australia into 'a great industrial nation' capable of supporting a large population. The department declared: 'taken with resources already known, these new riches do, beyond doubt, lift the horizons of Australian growth quite incalculably'.[7]

A year later, reviewing economic developments in the 1964 survey, the Treasury could barely contain its ebullience. Here was a year 'scarcely without parallel in our history for broad and varied progress'.[8] Production had enjoyed a spectacular advance over the previous two years. But even more satisfying for the department was the fact that the economy could grow so quickly without disturbance to prices and without excessive importing or strains on labour and other resources. There were lessons to be learnt here about how to reconcile growth and stability:

> Seldom if ever have the two run together so completely and, be it noted, this happened in a period when the economy was largely free from direct controls. Maybe it was due in part to a chance balancing of forces — in all economic experience there is an element of that. But there had also been various policy measures and, along with these, a fairly strong community attitude which, though it wanted to see growth pushed on vigorously, equally did not want a renewal of inflation.

The message was that there had been nothing artificial about the economy's performance — it had not been the result of governmental controls but a reflection mostly of the attitudes of Australians. Certainly there had been an element of luck but more important was the fact that, unlike the 1950s, Australians had managed to act responsibly and with restraint. The behavioural ideals which permeated Treasury documents in the second half of the 1950s had now, apparently, been attained. And the department was hopeful that 'the fact that stability has been an established condition for some time, with speculation absent, could itself be a steadying influence on community attitudes and hence on the trend of demand'.

The Treasury was impressed also with Australia's strong balance-of-payments position and in particular with the performance of Australia's export industries. Though issuing its customary caveats, the department declared that it was 'tempting to believe that a lasting change for the better has occurred in our external situation generally'. It saw every chance for a further advance for Australian exports over the next few years. Such statements stood in stark contrast to the mood of pessimism in the 1950s and early 1960s which tended to dominate discussions of Australia's balance of payments. The idea became

The Treasury line

popular during the second half of the 1950s, especially after the dramatic decline in international reserves in 1954–56 and with the continuance of import controls, that Australia was fated to long-run balance-of-payments problems. During the 1960s, however, particularly as a result of a dramatic increase in mineral exports, there arose something of a reaction against what Corden calls the 'traditional pessimism'. The Treasury was in the vanguard of those who looked optimistically at Australia's balance of payments future. It was a measure of the extent to which this reaction had proceeded by the middle of the 1960s that when in 1965 the Vernon Committee produced a pessimistic projection of Australia's balance of payments it was subject to widespread, and often vitriolic, damnation.[9]

An air of exuberance was apparent also in the 1964–65 budget speech. The Treasurer enthused about the 'phenomenal results' of the year just finished. GNP had risen in nominal terms by 9 per cent (7.1 per cent in constant terms) and company income by 10 per cent. Exports had risen $618 million above the record result of 1962–63, thereby adding a powerful stimulatory force to aggregate demand. Table 6.1 shows that exports of goods and services at constant prices increased by 16.4 per cent in 1963–64, providing a strong boost to farm income. It can be seen also that private investment expenditure, too, increased markedly, rising 11.4 per cent in 1963–64 (after a strong increase of 10.5 per cent in the previous year). Consumption expenditure lagged behind but still managed to record a creditable 6.2 per cent rise. As in the previous year, Holt was keen to point out that such results had been achieved without any disruption to price stability. Despite a 9 per cent increase in wages and salaries and a 5.3 per cent rise in average weekly earnings, the CPI had increased only 1.7 per cent in the twelve months to June 1964 (according to NGB, 0.9 per cent).

How long such stability would continue, however, was a matter of doubt, especially given the sustained upsurge in demand. In its 1964 survey, issued in June, the Treasury noted that there was a distinct danger of renewed inflation. It was concerned in particular with the fact that the labour market for skilled and unskilled workers alike had become extremely tight, something evident in the fact that at the end of May registered unfilled vacancies had risen to 37 000 (compared with 16 000 at the same time the previous year) and in the marked increase in overtime working. Holt's verdict in August 1964 was that 1963–64 had seen a 'very formidable' growth in demand, one which was likely to continue and become excessive, especially given the large increases proposed in public expenditure, particularly in defence expenditure, at a time when Australia's resources were 'already fully committed'.

Accordingly, a variety of deflationary taxation measures were announced: a 5 per cent rebate on individual income tax, in operation since 1961, was discontinued; company tax rates were increased; so too were sales tax on motor vehicles and customs and excise duties on cigarettes and cigars. These fiscal measures were supported by a progressive tightening of monetary policy. Significantly, the Reserve Bank's actions in 1964 showed an acceptance of the need to operate not only on the availability of credit (the SRD ratio was

Table 6.1 Expenditure on gross domestic product at constant prices, 1963–64 to 1967–68 (per cent change at average 1966–67 prices)

	Private final consumption expenditure	Private gross fixed capital expenditure	Public expenditure	Gross national expenditure	Exports of goods and services	Imports of goods and services	Gross domestic product
1963–64	6.2	11.4	6.5	6.3	16.4	10.5	7.1
1964–65	4.6	13.5	11.3	10.2	−10.7	19.9	7.0
1965–66	3.0	5.0	10.4	2.3	1.9	2.8	2.1
1966–67	4.9	1.8	5.1	5.0	10.9	1.0	6.6
1967–68	5.6	6.2	8.7	4.9	6.0	11.6	4.0

Source: Adapted from NGB Table 5.8b

increased and attempts were made to restrict the availability of housing finance provided by savings banks) but also a need to operate on the price of credit by altering interest rates: overdraft rates, the yield on long-term bonds and a number of short-term rates were increased.

It was a mark of the government's concern with the possibility of a renewed bout of inflation that in March 1965 it intervened in the basic wage case and urged the CCAC not to award a wage rise. This was the first time the commonwealth had put such a recommendation since 1960. Counsel for the commonwealth argued that a rise in the basic wage of 10s. a week would add substantially to demand and would make more difficult the task of trying to keep the economy in balance.

But while moves were taken to dampen private sector expenditure, public sector expenditure grew seemingly without restraint. In the 1965–66 budget speech the Treasurer announced 'a greatly enlarged expenditure on defence, a substantial increase in payments to State governments, further growth in social welfare payments, increased international aid and increases in many other items encompassed in the Budget as a whole'. The result would be 'the largest expenditure increase for which a Commonwealth Budget has ever had to provide'. Although revenue would rise strongly it would be 'substantially short' of expenditure proposals. All this, however, was occurring at a time when 'the home economy has been and still is running at full pitch, with little if any current labour resources to spare'. In fact, aggregate demand had been exceeding supply for over twelve months, resulting in 'fairly strong and continuous' increases in costs and a large rise in imports. Wages and salaries leapt by 12.1 per cent in 1964–65, while average weekly earnings rose by 7.6 per cent. Imports rose even more rapidly, increasing in constant terms by 10.5 per cent in 1963–64 and by nearly 20 per cent in the following year. 'Clearly,' warned Holt, 'there are dangers in all this — serious dangers of disruption and instability'. The Treasurer was forced to announce further taxation rises. Personal income tax was increased by 2.5 per cent, while increases were introduced on customs and excise duties on petroleum products, beer, spirits and tobacco products.

Clearly, the private sector was being squeezed to make way for a rapid increase in public sector expenditure. Measured at constant prices, public sector expenditure rose from 19.3 per cent of GDP in 1963–64 to 22.4 per cent in 1967–68. The latter figure was the highest recorded since the early postwar days and it was not to be exceeded during the remainder of the 1960s and 1970s. Information on the growth rate of public sector expenditure is provided in Table 6.1. Another useful guide is Table 6.2 which shows what was happening to the commonwealth budget. It can be seen that budget outlays increased particularly rapidly in each year. Interestingly, in 1963–64 and 1964–65 receipts rose more quickly than outlays. After that, however, the opposite situation prevailed and the budget deficit grew progressively bigger. Table 6.3 shows the importance of defence expenditure in contributing to the rise in commonwealth outlays. It can be seen that defence expenditure doubled in the four years from 1964–65 to 1967–68. In relative terms, defence

Efficient resource allocation

Table 6.2 Outlays, receipts and deficit of commonwealth budget, 1963–64 to 1967–68

	Outlays per cent change	Receipts per cent change	Deficit $ million	Deficit per cent to GDP
1963–64	9.9	11.0	419	2.3
1964–65	9.3	16.8	183	0.9
1965–66	10.3	9.1	255	1.2
1966–67	12.1	6.5	552	2.4
1967–68	10.4	9.7	643	2.6

Source: Adapted from NGB Table 2.14

Table 6.3 Defence expenditure, 1964–65 to 1967–78

	$ million	per cent of total outlays of commonwealth budget
1964–65	583	12.9
1965–66	711	14.1
1966–67	912	16.2
1967–68	1065	17.1

Source: Adapted from NGB Table 2.15

expenditure rose quickly to constitute just over 17 per cent of total commonwealth outlays by 1967–68. It declined steadily thereafter, however, flattening out to around 9 per cent during the second half of the 1970s.

Despite the problems posed by such a rapid increase in government expenditure, the Treasury could note in 1966: 'We have had four years of strong continuous expansion but no general boom ... From the standpoint of economic management, the great fact about the period considered in this Survey is that the old sequence of boom, crisis and recession has been averted.'[10] How was this possible? The Treasury's explanation placed particular emphasis on the restraint shown in consumption expenditure and the rise in imports, both of which had served to keep aggregate demand roughly in line with aggregate supply. The phenomenal rise in imports from 1962–1963 to 1964–65 has been mentioned already. As for consumption expenditure, it can be seen in Table 6.1 that it began to slow down in 1964–65 and declined further in the following year. In relative terms, consumption expenditure fell steadily from 65 per cent of GDP in 1961–62 to 62.6 per cent in 1964–65, increased slightly the following year and then fell to 62.1 per cent in 1966–67. The restraint shown in consumption expenditure reflected in part the success of policy initiatives, particularly the taxation increases imposed in 1964 and 1965, designed to dampen such spending. Another dampening force was a severe drought, one of the worst in Australia's history, experienced in New South Wales and Queensland in 1965–66. The farm sector was afflicted also by a deterioration in the terms of trade after 1963–64. In addition, as the

Treasury pointed out in 1966, it seemed that there had been a notable degree of restraint shown by the buying public (alternatively, an increase in voluntary saving), this being partly a legacy of the debts incurred during the recession of 1961–62.

Some commentators have criticised government policy in 1965 for being overconcerned with the possibility of excess demand emerging. Perkins, for instance, argues that while defence expenditure rose sharply, much of it involved purchases from overseas and hence did not involve an addition to domestic demand. He suggests that the actual level of total spending in Australia in 1965 was such that a rebate rather than a surcharge of 2.5 per cent would have been appropriate. Possibly, he argues, 'the government felt that the creation of some slack in the economy was defensible to facilitate the necessary transfer of resources to the expanding defence sector and towards the mineral developments'.[11]

William McMahon succeeded Holt as Treasurer early in 1966 after the latter became Prime Minister. (And for the first time, incidentally, Australia had a Treasurer who had been formally trained in economics.) Bringing down his first budget in August, McMahon seems to have recognised that the government had gone too far in guarding against the possibility of excess demand. The Treasurer argued that an apparent decline in private capital expenditure (in fact, as can be seen in Table 6.1, private investment had slowed down considerably in 1965–66 and was to continue to do so the following year), combined with the lingering effects of the drought and the certainty that consumer spending would continue to fall, necessitated some stimulus be given to the economy. He declared: 'Within limits the Government wants the Budget to be expansionary. Indeed, if the Budget were not expansionary we would be taking other measures to ensure that expansion took place.' McMahon did not announce, however, any taxation reductions. The budget was to be stimulatory in the sense that outlays were to increase at a faster rate than in 1965–66, while revenue was to rise at a slower rate (for the actual results, see Table 6.2).

A year later, in apparent vindication of government policy, the Treasurer could report that over the previous twelve months aggregate supply and demand had been 'pretty much in balance'. But there were worrying signs. For while the CPI rose at an annual rate of just over 2 per cent in the first three quarters of 1966–67, the rise in the last quarter was equivalent to an annual rate of 5 per cent. And in the twelve months to June 1967 minimum weekly wage rates rose by 7 per cent (while average weekly earnings rose by 6.7 per cent). These were taken as signs of growing stress in the economy, signs that once again aggregate demand was increasing too rapidly. It was in part because of this fear of renewed inflation that in November 1967, after the announcement of the British Government that the pound sterling had been devalued, that the Holt government decided not to follow suit. Accepting Treasury advice, and ignoring the Department of Trade's protests, the parity value of the Australian dollar was changed from $2.50 to $2.149 = £stg 1.

Efficient resource allocation
Public/private sector balance

The escalation in defence spending and other forms of public sector expenditure between 1963 and 1967 was significant not only because of the problems its seeming inexorability raised for economic management but because it raised questions about the achievement of balance in the expenditure patterns of the public and private sectors. In the 1967–68 budget speech McMahon claimed that an imbalance had arisen between the two sectors. He said that there was a need 'to provide room for balanced expansion of the private sector'. This was not to argue that public sector expenditure should decrease in absolute terms. Indeed McMahon remarked that public sector expenditure 'grows inevitably year by year', that to a large degree the budget was 'pre-determined by past commitments', and that 'these necessities could not be denied and they are likely to increase'. But the clear suggestion was that the growth of the public sector had constrained the development of the private and that this necessarily was undesirable. The argument being advanced was that there was some sort of appropriate level of public sector expenditure which represented a balanced situation and that in order to achieve this situation a decline in public sector spending in relative terms was essential. Just what sort of division of GNE constituted a balanced situation was not mentioned, nor how one could determine the appropriate level. This was not surprising: such a division is necessarily arbitrary. McMahon was content to announce that the rate of increase in public sector spending in 1967–68 would be reduced to 9.5 per cent (the rate of increase in the previous year being 11 per cent).

Foreshadowing McMahon's comments in the 1967–68 budget speech, the Treasury made explicit in the 1967 survey, released in June, its views on resource allocation between the public and private sectors. The department conceded that 'there are large community needs not likely to be met adequately or at all if left to private initiative without support from the public authorities' and even argued that a 'gradual increase in the proportion of resources allocated to publicly-financed services can ... be expected as time goes on'. This said, the Treasury declared quite categorically: 'What the public sector takes the private sector cannot have.' Further, 'any reduction in the proportion of resources going to the private sector must to some degree tend to slow down the growth of its productive capacity'. And if the growth of its productive capacity was retarded then the rate of increase in its output must also be retarded which in turn 'must affect to some degree the community's capacity to devote additional resources to community services, national security and other public sector activities'.[12]

By the mid-1960s, then, the Treasury had become convinced that an increase in the relative proportion of public sector expenditure tended to have deleterious consequences in that it cramped the activities, initiatives and financial resources of businessmen. The lesson drawn was that public sector expenditure needed to be kept within strict limits. At the very least it was essential that more stringent efforts be made to calculate the benefits and costs of the resource use of proposals involving public sector expenditure — a point which will be explored shortly.

The Treasury and efficient resource allocation

The question of public/private sector imbalance was itself part of a broader problem highlighted in a dramatic way by the rapid rise in public sector expenditure, namely the problem of efficient resource allocation. In the 1966–67 budget speech McMahon argued that the rapid build-up in defence, since it was imposed on a fully employed economy, 'involved a substantial transfer of resources so that some activities had to be held back in order that others could go quickly ahead'. Consumption expenditure had been restrained by taxation increases 'in order to release resources for defence purposes and for other high priority uses'. The steep increases in defence spending raised 'profound issues of national priorities'. McMahon continued: 'with each successive rise in defence expenditure, we have become increasingly conscious of a developing conflict between major national purposes — between the requirements of defence and those of growth'. This conflict was 'real and substantial'. Accordingly, in framing the budget the government had been forced to make 'difficult choices'. In the 1967–68 budget speech, McMahon noted that the government was faced with 'the problem of choice and allocation': 'Pressed hard by competing claims, we had to decide what the broad allocation of resources should be.'

It could be argued of course that budgeting, by definition, has and always will involve 'hard choices' and allocative decisions and that McMahon's statements in 1966 and 1967 were therefore nothing particularly new. The evidence is clear, however, that the mid-1960s saw a heightened interest in the Treasury in the questions of choice and efficient resource allocation. Of particular relevance here are the spate of supplements to the *Treasury Information Bulletin* which appeared between 1964 and 1966. The supplements, as noted, were a product of the GFEP's Economic and Financial Surveys Branch, and they bore the mark of the head of that branch, John Stone. The supplements are of interest in that they provide a portent of the style of Treasury thought which was to emerge in the 1970s when Stone became deputy secretary (economic) and then secretary.

The Treasury's heightened concern with efficient resource allocation was particularly apparent in the 1966 supplement, *Investment Analysis*. It made its attitude clear in the opening paragraph:

> The pace and pattern of growth of an economy are greatly influenced not only by the *level* of capital investment undertaken but also by the *way* in which that capital is invested. In a fully employed economy capital, like labour, is a scarce commodity (i.e. can be put to a number of alternative uses) and it has to be put to the most effective use if economic growth is to be maximised.[13]

Previously, the line presented in the annual surveys was that the primary economic problem was one of attempting to ensure that an ever-expanding supply of goods and services match an ever-expanding level of demand. But here and in the other supplements the problem was seen to be not only how to secure a steadily rising level of inputs but how to use available inputs in the most efficient manner. This is not to suggest that the efficient use of resources had not previously been of interest to the Treasury. What is being argued is that by the mid-1960s the Treasury was urging a change in priorities, namely that efficient resource allocation should take precedence over the generation of additional resources as the nation's chief goal. The Treasury declared:

> The problem of capital tends to be seen in popular discussion as being one of obtaining enough of it. Certainly, it is a necessary condition of strong economic growth that a sizeable volume of new capital continues to become available. But it is not a sufficient condition: capital can be wasted by being uneconomically employed. If, by contrast, it is employed intelligently and efficiently, any problem of its availability lessens in importance, both because a lesser volume of capital is needed to achieve a given productive result and because experience seems to show that capital tends to be more readily forthcoming the more rigorous and dynamic the economy.[14]

The department's argument was that every society had multiple goals and that economic growth, though important, was only one such goal. But whatever the goal, 'in a country like Australia, where domestic capital accumulation is high, the problem of efficient allocation of capital might well be thought to take precedence over any question of further increasing the supply'. Re-evaluation of the relative importance of the two goals was clearly necessary: 'The need for a more equal balance between the two, at least, would appear to be undeniable.'

To note that the Treasury was urging a change in priorities is not to suggest that it had lost interest in the maintenance of high growth rates. On the contrary, a more efficient use of resources was seen as a means of improving growth rates. But in arguing for a change in priorities, it does appear that the Treasury did not share quite the same enthusiasm for rapid economic growth as did the community at large. In 1972, the Treasury pointed to the fact that

> ten years ago ... 'growthmanship' was all the rage. Economic objectives were almost invariably spoken of in terms of the innate desirability of achieving a faster economic growth; the rate of increase of the gross national product at constant prices was put to microscopic study, and the concept itself had become part of the stock-in-trade of all who wished to speak or write upon the topic. What was (and is) a very convenient tool of economic analysis had been elevated to something approaching the idolatrous.[15]

It is clear that by the early 1960s the Treasury for one had ceased to worship this idol. It had begun to worship instead economic efficiency.

Linked with the department's heightened interest in efficient resource allocation was a growing concern with the inadequacies of existing methods of economic decision-making. Again, *Investment Analysis* is of particular interest here. The supplement was essentially a plea for the adoption of a more rigorously calculative approach to decision-making in both the private and particularly the public sectors. It was in effect an exercise in teach-yourself economic rationality through the use of benefit-cost analysis.

The Treasury was convinced that investment appraisal techniques in the private sector were generally inadequate. It quoted with approval the view of Britain's National Economic Development Council, which maintained in 1965: 'There is much evidence that, although the management of most firms undoubtedly take their investment decisions only after careful consideration of the likely costs and benefits as they see them, these decisions are too often reached in ways which are unlikely to produce the pattern and/or level of investment most favourable to economic growth — or even most profitable to the firm.'[16] The Treasury, like the council, was critical of investment decisions based on criteria such as the pay-back period, the average rate of return on average capital, and the total return per dollar of outlay. All these techniques were unsatisfactory because they failed to make proper allowance for the effect of time. If the allocation of capital between various alternative uses was to be made more efficient not only would the time factor have to be removed but, linked with this, the risk and uncertainty involved in investment appraisal would have to be 'taken into account', 'assessed', 'weighed up'.

Despite the inadequacy of its techniques of investment evaluation, the Treasury considered decision-making in the private sector to be inherently more rational — in the sense that it produced more efficient results — than that in the public sector. In defending this claim, the department argued that the greater rationality of the private sector was linked to the fact that it employed discernible (if inadequate) criteria in decision-making. Further, the operation of market forces served to discipline decision-makers in the private sector. The Treasury was convinced, too, that 'in the private sector the incentive to maximize profits *tends* to direct capital to its most efficient uses'.[17] In the public sector, by contrast, there was a much greater possibility of investment occurring in unproductive projects. This was largely because, so the Treasury argued in an earlier supplement, 'it is difficult to apply the normal price mechanism to the products of such works, so that the criteria for judging their relative economic merits do not exist or exist only in rudimentary form'.[18] In addition, the public sector did not have to face the sort of disciplinary forces at work in the private sector; the public sector was not subject to the test of the market and there was no great incentive to maximise profits.

In order to avoid wasting resources, the argument continued, it was essential to employ techniques for assessing public investment decisions 'against proper economic criteria'. There was a danger that public capital be identified mistakenly as a sort of free good. Public capital investment was in fact just the same as private capital investment in that it made demands on scarce real resources. It was imperative therefore to attempt to allocate it as rationally as possible. This is where benefit-cost analysis was of great importance. The Treasury was confident that the adoption of benefit-cost analysis would ensure a greater degree of economic rationality in decision-making in the public sector, for it was a method of analysing an investment proposal by reference to certain specific criteria. Such a technique did not of itself provide new information, but it was an essential tool for assessing uncertainty and for deciding whether an investment was worthwhile.

Apart from the supplements, perhaps the best guide to the changed nature of Treasury thought by the mid-1960s was a special section appended to the 1967 survey, entitled 'Resources and their allocation'.[19] The section was written with the aim of redressing what was considered an undue and misleading emphasis on aggregate demand. Taking the existence of resource scarcity as an unquestioned fact, the department complained that concentration on the level of aggregate demand distracted attention from the question of how to put resources to their best use. The Treasury's discussion was a conscious effort to turn attention toward the supply side and it provided a simplistic outline of neoclassical economics, arguing that the problem of resource allocation was 'basically one of choice' involving opportunity costs. The fact that 80 per cent of GNE flowed from private decisions to spend meant that resource allocation was 'largely the result of innumerable private buying and selling deals in which prices are the chief regulator'. The point was raised, as had been done in the supplements, that the movement of relative prices tended to eliminate imbalances between supply and demand. But, adopting an 'imperfectionist' line, the Treasury acknowledged that insufficient competition in the economy hampered the allocative mechanism. Markets were not perfect and were influenced by such things as restrictive practices, taxes, subsidies, concessions and protective measures. Such phenomena modified the market's allocation of resources, often but not always in detrimental ways: 'So far as they impede the operation of the market mechanism they would generally, though not in all circumstances, tend to guide resources into relatively uneconomical or less efficient uses.'

As in the supplements, the Treasury again stressed that decisionmaking, particularly in the public sector, should be more rigorously calculative. It was essential that decision-makers 'consider whether, when the costs and benefits have been weighed up, some more economically productive use for the resources in question is not to be preferred'. Alternatives had to be taken into account. It was essential to try to count the opportunity cost of the use of particular resources, to try to calculate 'the economic return that would have obtained had the resources been put to their most productive alternative use'. Only then would it be possible to achieve some sort of efficiency in the allocation of resources.

Underpinning the Treasury's analysis, here and in the supplements, was a particular ideal-type: that rational economic agents are, or should be, calculating, deliberating creatures who take a rigorous approach to decision-making, in the sense that they consciously and systematically weigh up the costs and benefits of each particular situation, consider alternative uses (opportunity costs), make allowances for time-phasing (and thereby attempt to take into consideration risk and uncertainty), and aim always to maximise their gains.

This ideal-type had as its counterpart a vision of the Australian economy as being inherently flexible and adaptable. The moral which the Treasury sought to present was that the ability of the Australian economy to allocate resources efficiently was dependent on people exhibiting the characteristics listed above. The further people departed from this ideal, the further would the economy depart from allocative efficiency.

The key to economic efficiency in the public sector: benefit-cost analysis

The Treasury's interest in benefit-cost analysis needs to be put into perspective. The essence of the technique, as Russell Mathews points out,

> is that it extends the range of investment planning techniques and marginal analysis, which have been developed in private industry for purposes of evaluating investment proposals and deciding on operating policy respectively, into all those areas of the public sector where allocation decisions cannot be taken by reference to the price mechanism... Its distinguishing characteristic is its concern with the quantification and comparison of the costs and benefits of alternative courses of action.[20]

Proposals to use benefit-cost analysis go back to at least 1844, with the publication of a paper by the Frenchman, Dupuit, in which he proposed a framework for investigating the utility derived from public works. The method was relatively neglected, however, until the 1930s, when federal and state agencies in the United States used it in analysing water-development projects. The method began to be used extensively during the 1950s for an increasingly wide variety of problems. In both the United States and Britain it was used for analysing, among other things, defence and health expenditure. In 1961 a group of academic economists produced a report for the Kennedy administration which provided the first comprehensive review of benefit-cost analysis. In 1965 the *Economic Journal* published a detailed survey of the literature on benefit-cost analysis.[21] The authors of the survey noted that 'interest among economists in this technique has grown tremendously in the last few years'. They judged that the reasons for this included the growth of large investment projects and the growth of the public sector generally, in both absolute and relative terms. Both of these had made the explicit consideration of the consequences of investment decisions much more important and interesting than would have been the case 25 years before. Another factor was the rapid development of techniques such as operations research and systems analysis which had generated interest in matters of efficiency and investment appraisal.

Enthusiasm for benefit-cost analysis developed much more slowly in Australia. The Vernon Committee drew attention in 1965 in its report to benefit-cost analysis and noted that 'unfortunately, relatively little use appears to have been made to date in Australia of such analysis. Too often an analysis is undertaken, frequently as the result of doubts after a project has been commenced, instead of as a basic step in the planning process.'[22] In the following year the Treasury published its supplement on investment analysis.

Efficient resource allocation

In 1967 a detailed study of public investment in Australia was published under the auspices of the Committee for the Economic Development of Australia. The book was written by Russell Mathews and it discussed at length problems of resource allocation (including public-private sector balance) and pointed to the usefulness of benefit-cost analysis as a proxy in the public sector for marginal analysis.[23] Mathews discussed also the use which had so far been made in Australia of benefit-cost analysis, two notable examples being the evaluation of land-development proposals in the Queensland brigalow belt (a study undertaken by the Bureau of Agricultural Economics) and of the Ord River scheme (a report which was never published and one which, given the continued investment in the scheme, was apparently ignored). The technique grew steadily in popularity in Australia in the second half of the 1960s, with the commonwealth government taking the lead. But even by 1972 N.W. Fisher could complain that 'extension of the technique has been somewhat slower than might be wished, as neither the Commonwealth nor State Treasuries have required the general use of benefit-cost analysis. This attitude is somewhat at variance with government policy in other developed countries, e.g. Canada, France and Britain'.[24]

From the 1950s benefit-cost analysis became allied with the development of a new technique in budgeting: a technique usually referred to as planning, programming budgeting (PPB). Although nothing remotely resembling PPB was used in Australia in the period surveyed in this chapter, it nevertheless seems appropriate to offer here a few comments on the technique. The 'fundamental premise' of PPB, as James Cutt points out,

> is that policy and budgets are inseparable and that the relationship between the structure and implementation of budgets and the determination and achievement of policy objectives should be made explicit. PPB is thus a set of procedures designed to improve the basis for resource allocation decisions in both the public and private sectors and to secure a more efficient and more effective allocation of scarce resources. PPB is in effect a marriage between planning and the translation of planning objectives into programmes and in turn into projects, on the one hand, and budgeting procedures, on the other.[25]

Again, it was in the United States that this technique first grew in popularity. The RAND Corporation took the lead in developing the technique during the 1950s and it was eventually introduced into the US Defense Department in 1960–61. In 1965 President Johnson decreed that the technique be used by all federal agencies.

Consistent with its attitude toward benefit-cost analysis, Australia was much slower in accepting the technique, the only aspect of it which gained any interest in the 1960s being the use of forward estimates, which are one of the building blocks of PPB. Sir Frederick Wheeler points out that an informal project was begun in the Treasury in 1965 in which spending departments submitted three-year projections. He notes that 'this exercise was, however, limited in its status and scope — figures for expenditure trends under *existing* policies only were furnished by departments, on a non-commitment basis, and without any requirement of ministerial participation. They were processed in

Treasury by a few officers as a comparatively minor undertaking without any detailed scrutiny'.[26] In 1969 two Treasury officers (and an officer from the Public Service Board) undertook an investigation of the use of program budgeting in the United States, Canada and Britain. In 1970 the Department of Defence began to put into operation a five-year rolling program budget system. In the 1971–72 budget speech it was announced that henceforth all government departments would be required to submit expenditure estimates for a further two years beyond each budget year. And in the following year the Treasurer announced that the government intended to adopt a system of functional classification — another building block in PPB which aimed to show the total expenditure occurring under different headings (such as health, education, welfare, and so on). This classification system was first used in the presentation of the 1973–74 budget.

Even in 1976, however, Cutt could declare that 'the Treasury, the key department for the development of such an exercise in Australia, [does not] seem disposed to enter the field of forward planning, let alone PPB, with any enthusiasm'.[27] Given the Treasury's anxiety to improve the efficiency of resource allocation, how can this lack of enthusiasm for PPB be explained? Part of the reason lies with its awareness of the difficulties which were encountered in the United States after the full-scale implementation of the approach in 1965. As Sir Frederick Wheeler noted in 1973: 'it seems clear that the difficulties and disillusion associated with [the implementation of PPB] harmed the reputation of programme budgeting both in the United States and elsewhere overseas.'[28] Partly for that reason a much more cautious approach was taken in the United Kingdom, where the emphasis was simply on forward estimates. The Australian Treasury shared this caution. But what also made the Treasury wary of full-scale PPB was the planning element in the technique. The Treasury's wariness, and sometimes denigration of planning, was noted in the previous chapter. It is a topic to which we will return shortly.

Parallel philosophies: the Treasury and the Tariff Board

During the 1960s the Treasury and the Tariff Board moved on parallel philosophical paths. The Tariff Board became an important bureaucratic ally for the Treasury in its quest for greater allocative efficiency. As Glezer describes it, the second half of the 1960s saw a shift in the Tariff Board from a populist-corporatist stance to what he calls an economising approach to tariff-making. As it came to be practised by the Board, the economising orientation involved an emphasis on the 'careful calculation of costs and benefits as the primary criterion of tariff policy-making'.[29] By contrast, the central concerns of tariff-making for populists 'were the needs of Australian industrialists and workers in overcoming the cost disadvantages of local production', while corporatists 'dwelt less on the needs of an industry and more on the positive value of an industry to a country'. Not surprisingly, the

Efficient resource allocation

economising orientation differed from the populist-corporatist approach on the government's role:

> The economizing outlook pointed to the need for less government, less intervention and concern for the costs of protection on exporters and consumers. The corporatist orientation was focused on the need for government support, such as granting manufacturers a share of the market, and on the widespread benefits of industrial projects — propositions which populists rarely disputed.

A shift in the Tariff Board's approach became evident in 1967 when the board's chairman, G.A. Rattigan, began to denounce the ad hoc or tailor-made approach toward tariffs which involved the use of different criteria for different industries. Rattigan complained that there had been no attempt to look at the tariff structure as a whole and no attempt to consider its economic consequences. The traditional approach had had seriously deleterious effects on resource allocation by encouraging a movement of resources into the highly protected industries. What was needed was to determine how the effective (as distinct from the nominal) rate of protection was distributed and then, by the use of 'points of reference' which distinguished industries receiving high, medium and low protection, alter the tariff structure to redirect investment toward the less protected industries.

Apart from a heightened interest in resource allocation and an insistence on the need for careful cost-benefit analyses of economic decisions, there was another parallel in the development of Treasury and Tariff Board thought during the 1960s. For just as there was an upsurge of interest in the board in calculating the effective rate of protection so as to see more clearly the economic effects of the tariff structure, so too was there an upsurge of interest in the Treasury in calculating with more precision the effect of the annual budget on the economy. This involved essentially a greater recognition of the complexity of the ways the budget influenced the economy (quite apart from multiplier effects) and a growing dissatisfaction with summary indicators, in particular the change in the net increase in indebtedness. From the early 1960s, with defence expenditure rising, emphasis began to placed on the need to differentiate between public sector outlays occurring domestically and those occurring overseas. Increasingly more sophisticated analyses began to be presented of the initial impact of the budget on domestic demand. In 1963 the budget began to be presented in national accounting form. The revenue side of the budget in particular came to be analysed with much greater rigour. By 1967 the Treasury was able to provide an assessment of discretionary, induced and independent revenue changes.

Economic projections: the conflicting philosophies of the Treasury and the Vernon Committee

To return to the supplements to the *Treasury Information Bulletin*: a persistent and perhaps overstated theme in the supplements was the difficulty, and indeed sometimes the risks, of attempting measurement in the form of forecasts and projections. For instance, in a supplement on economic growth published in 1964 the Treasury declared:

> Since economic growth can be strongly influenced by changes in determining factors that are either unforseeable or beyond accurate prediction, forecasts of rates of growth, whether actual or potential, are necessarily subject to varying degrees of error... Not nearly enough can be known about the complex surrounding circumstances to permit anything better than a broad assessment of what growth might have been had all its potentialities been realised. Estimating the potentialities of the future will, of course, present still greater difficulties.[30]

Similarly, in a study in 1966 of the balance of payments the point was made clear at the outset that 'predictions of economic trends any significant way into the future are always hazardous'.[31] To attempt to anticipate now the long-term future of the balance of payments was a 'notoriously difficult' exercise and any result was liable to be misleading. In fact to try to do so 'would not only be pretentious but almost certainly harmful'. Projections were considered less hazardous than forecasts. But even with projections the practitioner 'soon learns humility and makes no particular claim as to the likely correspondence between his efforts to foresee the future and the outcome in reality'.[32] The undeniable truth was that in making projections, of the workforce for example, 'many of the crucial assumptions are essentially based on guesswork and this within a field in which guesses are notoriously prone to go awry'.

It has sometimes been suggested that the Treasury's denigration of the reliability of projections and particularly forecasts, and its implicit doubts about whether the usefulness of projections could possibly match the effort of preparing them, were linked with a desire to crush the report of the Vernon Committee. The Committee of Economic Enquiry, as it was formally known, was appointed early in 1963 partly in an attempt to take some of the sting out of the prevailing dissatisfaction with economic management. The committee was headed by Sir James Vernon and included Sir John Crawford (the former secretary to the Department of Trade and vice-chairman of the committee), Professor P.H. Karmel, D.G. Molesworth and K.B. Myer. There is a touch of irony in the fact that one of the recommendations of the committee was that an advisory council on economic growth be established, using as a model the Economic Council of Canada which had been set up in 1963. The committee, however, made it clear that it did not favour 'anything in the nature of a national economic plan involving individual industry targets for Australia, as this would require elaborate machinery and, in all probability, a considerably higher degree of government intervention in the economy than would be acceptable in this country'.[33] The functions of the council would be restricted to such things as preparing reviews of long-term growth prospects, reporting on topics referred to it, and acting as a consultative forum. Under the influence of the Treasury, which saw the proposed council as a threat to its economic authority, Menzies denounced the committee's proposal. Amid a string of barbed comments on the committee's recommendations, he said:

Efficient resource allocation

In the Australian democratic system of government based upon the consent of a free community, no government can hand over to bodies outside the government the choice of objectives and the means of attaining them in important fields of policy, particularly when such bodies would, through the power of publication, come to exercise what I described, I hoped not extravagantly, as a coercive influence upon governments.[34]

A major weapon in the Treasury's attack on the findings of the committee was its use of projections. Criticism was directed in particular at the arguments raised in the final chapter, which included the committee's policy recommendations, and Appendix N which was supposed to provide the supporting evidence for the conclusions drawn. The committee's method in the last chapter was to make projections of GNP, GNE, and imports and exports over the coming decade. The main conclusions drawn were that it would be difficult to maintain an annual growth rate of 5 per cent (the projected GNP figure); that by 1974–75 total expenditure would be more than GNP plus imports (aggregate demand would exceed supply); that there would be balance-of-payments problems because imports were likely to exceed exports; and that productivity would suffer because of a more rapid shift of labour into the tertiary sector. Despite its claim that forecasts of the state of the economy in ten or fifteen years time 'are extremely hazardous, can prove positively misleading, and are almost certain to be inaccurate', the committee could argue in the next breath that 'the projections contain important implications for the future of the economy'.[35] The committee argued that there would be a need for personal consumption expenditure to be reduced or, alternatively, for savings to increase (which would most probably have to take the form of forced savings by governments using budget surpluses); that investment would have to be increased (which would probably require more generous investment allowances); and that exports (especially of manufactures) would need to be increased and also perhaps imports would need to be reduced.

The Treasury argued that the committee had made several important errors in the formulation of its projections and criticised it for being unduly pessimistic. The Treasury pointed out, for instance, that the committee's figure of $3500 million for exports in 1974–75 implied an annual rise of only 2.5 per cent in rural exports. Since the early 1960s, however, the rate of increase had been 4.5 per cent. Further, the committee had been far too conservative in its estimation of the potential size of mineral exports. Also, it had miscalculated the amount of dividends and profits payable abroad, for it had relied on an estimated figure for 1964–65 of $424 million when in fact the actual figure was only $266 million.

The committee's use of projections and the methods by which it derived them was the subject of controversy, not only inside but outside parliament, with most commentators offering emotive (and perhaps unfair) condemnation. To a nation running high on optimism — this was 'the lucky country', as Donald Horne called his 1964 bestseller — it seemed that the committee had produced a series of unwarranted and unrealistically gloomy prognostications and a blueprint, so some claimed, for a siege economy.

The Treasury line

By discrediting the Vernon Committee the Treasury was able also to discredit indirectly the Department of Trade, whose viewpoint was seen to be closely tied to the committee through Sir John Crawford. Hence the dumping of the Vernon Report is often portrayed as an excellent illustration of the Treasury's power and its ruthlessness in dealing with existing and potential rivals. Some commentators, however, have maintained that the Treasury attack on the Vernon Report was more than simply an instance of departmental rivalry. Glezer, for instance, sees it as some sort of Treasury vendetta against Trade. He argues that the fact that Trade had successfully dissociated itself from the policy initiatives of 1960 'rankled in Treasury', with senior officers making no secret of their resentment. According to Glezer, Treasury saw the Vernon recommendations as 'a plot by Trade against them'. The demolition of the committee's proposals 'was the most notable episode in their retaliation'.[36]

While undoubtedly there was an important element of departmental rivalry and retaliation involved in the Treasury's discrediting of the Vernon Committee, it should be remembered that the Treasury was genuinely concerned about what it saw as a serious misuse of projections. What emerges clearly from Treasury publications before and after the publication of the Vernon Report is that the department's strictures on the use of projections flowed from a concern about undue and unnecessary commitment, an anxiety about the adverse effects of trying to fit the economy into a predetermined mould on the basis of something which was in effect a guess. The Vernon Committee had committed a serious error, so the Treasury believed, in using projections as the basis for making recommendations about current policy. Given the intrinsic difficulties associated with projections, the department felt there was simply no point in making policy decisions or commitments on the basis of a set of figures which were liable to be grossly inaccurate.

The reasons for the Treasury's opposition to the use of projections as a basis for prescriptive decisions can perhaps be better understood by considering the arguments put forward in the department's 1964 supplement on economic growth. The department's view was that 'particular rates of economic growth ... cannot be treated as ends in themselves'. The 'real question' which had to be asked was 'not how the growth rate compares internationally but whether, given the pattern of demand, the output required to meet that demand has failed to grow as fast as it might if all available resources had been used with the highest efficiency'.[37] Such arguments implied that the economy should be seen not as an ever-expanding mechanism needing to be thrust forward at the fastest possible growth rate, or needing to achieve a particular target growth figure, but simply as a device for satisfying an ever-changing variety of needs. Thus, if community demands were such that resources were used in a particular combination or pattern that yielded a lower rate of growth than another combination would have yielded, then so be it. What mattered was not growth rates as such but the satisfaction of ever-changing demands.

Such arguments are important in understanding the subsequent development of the Treasury line, for implicit in them was a disdain for purposive action, for governmental action designed to achieve particular goals. It was not difficult to take such arguments a step further and argue, along with Friedman, that what is supposedly natural is best. Following this line of reasoning it could easily be argued, for instance, that governments should not attempt to achieve an arbitrarily defined level or zone of socially acceptable unemployment; it should instead be left to seek its own inherently determined level.

Such arguments are important also in understanding the Treasury's opposition to economic planning. The Treasury's views can be contrasted with those of A.R. Hall, one of the leading proponents in Australia in the early 1960s for the introduction of economic planning. Hall could argue in 1961:

> if the Government had been prepared not only to take a long-term view, but also to do some thinking about the desirable rates of economic growth of investment and the composition of that investment, the misallocation of resources in 1960 — for instance, too much investment in housing and vehicles — may have been avoided ... Direction and guidance should ... be given on the pattern of investment which is required by the new circumstances... In short, the major problems facing the economy are really long-term ones. What is the desirable rate of growth? What is the level and composition of the investment needed to create that growth? What shifts in resources are necessary to bring the balance of payments into reasonable equilibrium?[38]

Hall and the Treasury were at philosophical loggerheads. The heart of the Treasury's opposition to economic planning sprang from a firm philosophical conviction, quite contrary to Hall's, that it simply was not the government's role to make pronouncements on what was the 'desirable rate' of investment and economic growth and the 'desirable composition' of investment. Such things did not require, nor should they be subject to, governmental 'direction and guidance'. The government could take action, certainly, to ensure the maintenance of a situation conducive to economic stability and growth, but it was the aggregated views of the individuals making up society, not the government, which alone could and should determine just what the rate of growth and composition of investment turned out to be. There was no place here for government fiat.

What needs to be recognised, then, when discussing the Treasury's 'demolition job' on the Vernon Report is that what concerned the department was not just the possibility of an institutional rival or a desire to seek revenge on what was perceived to be Trade's intransigence. It was worried just as much by the threat posed by an economic philosophy quite at odds with its own. The distinguishing characteristic of Treasury thought was a basic confidence in the speedy and efficient working of the market mechanism and, underpinning this, its unquestioned conviction concerning the responsiveness of economic agents to changes in relative prices. In 1966 the Treasury declared that 'the long-term future of the balance of payments is best safeguarded ... by working towards a flexible economy in which resources can flow to their most productive uses, and in which, as a result, producers can respond quickly and effectively to the new and changing opportunities that will arise'.[39] Such confidence in market processes implied a limited role for the government. There was simply no need for the government to take the initiative in trying to direct the pace and pattern of economic change; in fact it was likely to have deleterious effects if it did so. Those who wrote the Vernon Report, however, saw the world differently. In their view, businessmen often tended to be sluggish in their responses to relative price changes and, concerned with possible risks, were often anxious to avoid taking initiatives. It was perhaps not surprising therefore that the authors of the report came to quite different conclusions from the Treasury on the role of government. As E.A. Russell puts it,

> to change the structure of the economy, a key role will be played by non-market government forces which break through special hindrances to change. The Vernon report (and the enormous tradition that it reflects) finds the market a weak instrument for securing coherent, overall objectives. Well-informed administrators can nudge, encourage, entice, coerce the economy onto a better path... This is a view that extends naturally to making projections of the level and structure of output and demand, based on existing technical relationships, to announcing aggregate targets and government policy objectives which in total will provide a framework within which private enterprise will act confidently and vigorously and coherently.[40]

Glezer, somewhat similarly, has pointed to the philosophical differences which emerged during the 1960s between Treasury and the Department of Trade and Industry. Intensely committed to the expansion of local manufacturing, Trade advocated industry-specific policies which had as their aim the preservation and encouragement of a wide range of domestic industries. Its logic was that more industries meant more investment and hence more output. In its view increased output should take precedence over efficient resource allocation. The Treasury, by contrast, favoured economy-wide measures which aimed above all to improve efficiency and bring about an industrial structure which maximised comparative advantages.[41]

The Treasury and the neoclassical synthesis

Despite complaints that there was a tendency to dwell too much on the level of demand at the expense of considering resource allocation, the Treasury continued to argue that 'the level of demand is of prime importance'.[42] Indeed the Treasury acknowledged that one reason why resource allocation should now be given much greater emphasis was the fact that demand-management techniques could and had been used to ensure the full employment of resources. Since it could be taken for granted that they would be fully employed, the question now was how these resources could be used more efficiently. The point is, then, that the Treasury continued to see budgetary policy as having an indispensable role in balancing the economy. In fact, efficient resource allocation was held to depend upon proper economic management. The Treasury argued in the concluding paragraph of the 1967 survey:

Efficient resource allocation

In the Australian economy most choices affecting the allocation of resources are made through the mechanism of the market. To work effectively this mechanism needs to be as free as possible from obstructions to movement. Further than that, the aim must be to have the economy as a whole managed so as to preserve flexibility. Overall, this is in no small way a matter of keeping supply and demand in balance and avoiding the excesses and rigidities that hinder the response on the supply side to the changing pattern of demand.

Keynes would not have taken issue with such sentiments. The point remains, nevertheless, that the evidence in this chapter is that by the mid-1960s the Treasury's outlook could no longer be described as dominantly Keynesian. Its interest in efficient resource allocation, its Robbinsian talk of the choices faced by economic agents and the need to calculate opportunity costs, its depiction of the Australian economy as being inherently adaptable and flexible, and its claims that relative prices were of crucial significance in effecting change — all these indicated a growing attachment to neoclassical concerns and viewpoints.

This raises the question of whether something parallel had happened within the economics profession as a whole. What shifts had occurred in economic theory? A study of mainstream economic thought in the 1950s and 1960s indicates that from a *theoretical* perspective there was no Keynesian revolution. Instead, economics was dominated during this period by a hybrid model known variously as the 'neoclassical synthesis', 'bastard Keynesianism', 'neo-neoclassicism', and 'classical Keynesianism'. This hybrid was made up of elements from both the Keynesian and neoclassical models. More accurately, the synthesis represented a framework in which Keynes' insights were submerged within the neoclassical schema, something which could only be achieved by ignoring or misunderstanding, or pointing to logical flaws in, the basis of Keynes' fundamentally different vision of the economic system. It became standard to insist that Keynes' arguments required for their validation the assumption of wage rigidities. The 1950s and 1960s saw also, it should be noted, the mathematisation of economics, a switch in interest from partial to general equilibrium analysis and a pervasive desire in the profession to ensure that economics attained something of the status and exactness of the natural sciences by making it precise, objective, rigorously theoretical and amenable to mathematical insights.

The development of the neoclassical synthesis was associated with three names in particular: J.R. Hicks (some of whose ideas were discussed in chapter 2), Don Patinkin and Paul Samuelson. Hicks' contribution, which dates from 1937, was the formulation of the IS-LM (or SI-LL) diagram (a diagram which was also used by the American economist, Alvin Hansen — hence the diagram is often called the Hicks-Hansen framework). Hicks sought to use the diagram as a means of understanding Keynes' arguments and, more importantly, to show how Keynes' approach could be reconciled, with a few modifications, with 'classical' theory. With these modifications, Hicks announced, 'Mr. Keynes takes a big step to Marshallian orthodoxy and his theory becomes hard to distinguish from the revised and qualified Marshallian theories.'[43] The

IS-LM framework focused on the interaction between the commodities market and the money market and on the achievement of equilibrium in the two markets jointly and simultaneously. Equilibrium in the commodities market arose when saving equalled investment, in the money market when the demand for money (L) equalled the supply of money (M). Given that I, S and L were all a function of income and/or the rate of interest (while M was assumed to be determined exogenously by the banking authorities), Hicks argued that the IS and LM curves could be conjoined in a framework with the rate of interest on the vertical axis and income on the horizontal.

The IS-LM diagram became widely accepted and continues to be used as the standard expository device for introducing 'Keynesian' ideas. The popularity of the framework is readily understandable given its simplicity and, linked with this, its usefulness as a didactic device. In addition, it satisfies the manipulative longings of economists: the apparatus can be used to find out the effects of varying circumstances and assumptions and policies (with the shape and position of the curves moving accordingly). It is an ideal 'puzzle' for economists to play with.

If, as Trevithick has suggested, one is to distil the 384 pages of the *General Theory* into a single diagram, then the IS-LM apparatus is perhaps a useful device. Minsky argues that the framework has in its favour the fact that it makes 'explicit the interdependence of the commodity and money markets in Keynes's thought',[44] but, as is implicit in Trevithick's point, criticises it for failing to do justice to 'Keynes's subtle and sophisticated views'.[45] He notes that Hicks did not offer any explicit consideration of labour market conditions and that, partly because of this, the argument which Hicks presented is 'strangely truncated; it really says very little'. Minsky is particularly critical of the fact that the IS-LM framework offered 'an equilibrium rather than a process interpretation' of Keynes' arguments. Other commentators have argued that the main weakness of the diagram is that it is drawn on the basis of a given state of expectations. If, it is argued, expectations do change then it is likely, because of the interdependence of the curves, that not just one but both curves will shift and hence the final outcome becomes indeterminate and the diagram's heuristic value for policy decisions is undermined. Hicks has himself acknowledged recently that the IS-LM framework 'reduces the *General Theory* to equilibrium economics; it is not really in time'.[46] Still other commentators have criticised Hicks' article from another angle, that of mis-specifying the nature of 'classical' analysis.[47]

The IS-LM framework was an attempt to show that Keynes had exaggerated the extent to which he had departed from the 'classical' approach. Hicks's re-evaluation did not, in itself, constitute what was later to be called the 'neoclassical synthesis'; it was, rather, the first step toward it. The synthesis was achieved by modifying the IS-LM framework, adding to it a production function and an explicit consideration of the labour market, and introducing wealth and financial variables. The first economist to present the synthesis in a comprehensive and sophisticated manner was Don Patinkin, in his *Money, Interest and Prices*, first published in 1956 but submitted originally in 1947 as a doctoral dissertation at the University of Chicago. The analysis was placed within a Walrasian general equilibrium framework. The procedure Patinkin adopted need not concern us. It is necessary only to note his main conclusions. In the first place, Patinkin sought to show that neoclassical macroeconomics was theoretically consistent. Further, he tried to demonstrate that a Keynesian expenditure approach could be incorporated within a neoclassical framework. More importantly, he sought to show that the inclusion of such an approach did not violate the neoclassical notion of a self-correcting system.

In attempting to prove that the system was in fact self-correcting, Patinkin pointed to two equilibrating mechanisms: one known as the Keynes effect, the other called the Pigou (or, to use Patinkin's term, real-balance) effect. In both cases the mechanisms can only operate if there is wage and price flexibility. In the first case, it is argued that if the nominal money stock remains constant, then a reduction in prices will lead to an increase in the real quantity of money. Using an IS-LM diagram it can easily be demonstrated that in such circumstances the LM curve would shift to the right, a movement which will be associated with lower interest rates (provided, however, the economy is not in a liquidity trap). The reduction in interest rates should lead, in turn, to an increase in investment and hence in output and employment. Whether there would be a return to full employment depended, however, on the elasticity of investment which in turn depended on the expectational effects on investment of falling prices. Patinkin placed particular emphasis on the Pigou effect in demonstrating the existence, at least in theory, of self-correcting tendencies. The argument here is that a reduction in wages will be associated with a reduction in prices. As prices fall, individuals' real balances increase: in other words, the real value of people's monetary and financial assets increases and hence so too does the individual's purchasing power. The assumption is that a rise in the real level of wealth will stimulate expenditure (that is, will lead to an increased propensity to consume). In terms of the IS-LM diagram, the effect will be to move the IS curve to the right. As Minsky points out, 'the assumption which is fundamental to the neoclassical synthesis holds that an increase in paper wealth, as deflation takes place, is as potent as an increase in real wealth by accumulation in decreasing desired saving out of income'.[48] While there is no guarantee that the Keynes effect will be able to restore full employment, there is in theory no limit to how much real balances can increase provided prices continue to fall. The argument, then, is that the inducement to spend can be raised sufficiently to restore full employment through a process of price deflation. In this way the system must be deemed self-correcting.

The implication was that, as neoclassical theory had always maintained, persistent unemployment could only arise because of inflexibilities in the labour market, such as the existence of rigid wages. Patinkin readily conceded, however, that despite its theoretical importance, the real-balance effect was likely to be too weak and too slow to be of much practical consequence and that policy initiatives, the use of active monetary and fiscal policies, could and should be used to hasten a return to full-employment equilibrium. Denied the theoretical victory, Keynes' triumph was relegated to the policy sphere. His insights became relevant only in so far as it was necessary to expedite the process by which natural forces restored full employment.

The essence of what Paul Samuelson referred to as the 'neoclassical synthesis' (it was he who coined the term) was that once Keynesian demand-management techniques had been used to establish full employment, neoclassical theorising could come into its own. He first used the term in the 1955 edition of his highly successful text, *Economics*. The synthesis, as Samuelson defined it,

> combines the essentials of the theory of aggregative income determination with the older classical theories of relative prices and of microeconomics. In a well-running system, with monetary and fiscal policies operating to validate the high-employment assumption postulated by the classical theory, the classical theory comes back into its own and the economist feels he can state with renewed conviction the classic truths and principles of social life!⁴⁹

Given a state of full employment, interest could centre on resource allocation and the role of relative prices — the main neoclassical concerns. Cyclical fluctuations were recognised but abstracted from. For governments were assumed to have now the knowledge to prevent both inflation and unemployment (then taken to be largely independent phenomena). Given continuous full employment, Samuelson explicitly acknowledged, Keynesian economics would eventually become unimportant: 'if modern [Keynesian income determination] economics does its task well so that unemployment and inflation are substantially banished from democratic societies, *then its importance will wither away* and the traditional [neoclassical] economics ... will really come into its own — almost for the first time'.[50]

By the beginning of the 1960s Keynesianism had been meshed with the supposedly empirical phenomenon known as the Phillips curve. In an article published in *Economica* in 1958, A.W. Phillips said that empirical evidence (Phillips used British data stretching back for nearly a century) revealed a fairly close relationship between changes in money wages and the rate of unemployment.[51] He argued that the rate of change in money wages was greater as unemployment became lower. This relationship between wages and employment levels, plotted in diagrammatic form, became known as the Phillips curve. The curve became the basis of a massive research program: attempts were made to draw the curve for other countries, to test its validity, and to make it more sophisticated. In 1960 Samuelson and Solow modified the Phillips curve to show how the percentage change in the American unemployment rate had varied over the previous 25 years in relation to the percentage change in the annual inflation rate.[52] Samuelson and Solow concluded that to avoid inflation, unemployment would have to rise to about 5–6 per cent. A lower unemployment rate would necessarily entail inflation. For instance, an unemployment rate of 3 per cent would be associated with an annual inflation rate of 4.5 per cent. The implication of these findings was that there was a trade-off between inflation and unemployment. Samuelson and Solow were offering policy-makers a 'menu of choice': lower unemployment could only be purchased at the cost of higher inflation; policy-makers had to decide upon an appropriate mix.

The fact that keynesianism became widely associated with the Phillips curve indicated the extent to which a marked gulf had developed between what Leijonhufvud has termed the economics of Keynes and Keynesian economics.[53] The Phillips curve, with its law-like appearance, its guise of universality, its claim to have produced a precise diagnostic chart with which to guide the policy prescriptions of governments, was directly counter to Keynes' views on methodology. Keynes looked askance at attempts to turn economics into a 'pseudo-natural science'. Disagreeing with Robbins, he argued that economics was a moral science dealing with introspection and value judgments.[54] It dealt also with 'motives, expectations, psychological uncertainties'.[55] He stressed that economists had to be wary of treating the material under analysis as if it were homogeneous and constant. And he was convinced that 'the pseudo-analogy with the physical sciences leads directly counter to the habit of mind which is most important for an economist proper to acquire'. Keynes expressed similar sentiments about the mathematisation of economics. Quite apart from the methodological issues involved, Keynes would have considered the notion of a trade-off as something distasteful and defeatist. Weintraub puts the point well:

> Philosophically, Phillips curve addiction perpetrates a cruel hoax on Keynes in its invitation to abide *some* unemployment and *some* inflation; it has led some Keynesians to abdicate the promised land of full employment for the comfort of vague but possible price damping. It has led others to brush off inflation as unimportant. Keynes' entire intellectual commitment was to use reason to eradicate economic ailments rather than to 'trade-off' one ill for another malady.[56]

In Australia, as noted in the previous chapter, the publication of the original Phillips curve generated immediate interest, in part because it accorded with the movements which had occurred in wages and unemployment in the wake of the 1956 mini-budget. Interest was stimulated also by Phillips' visit to Australia in 1959. The idea that a trade-off existed became quickly and widely accepted. And it became a common criticism of the Treasury that it had relied on trade-off notions to maintain price stability. Such criticisms were offered following the 1960 credit squeeze and the taxation increases of 1964 and 1965: Peter Samuel, for instance, could maintain in 1965 that 'Treasury harbours a number of confirmed Paishs': a reference to Professor Paish who urged the British government during the 1960s to permit unemployment to rise and thereby eradicate the problem of inflation.[57] Similar criticisms were to be raised again in 1971 following the introduction of a deflationary budget by the McMahon government.

But while the Treasury's policy recommendations may have been informed by trade-off notions, the department has never been prepared, like some of those responsible for formulating and investigating the Phillips curve, to elevate economics to the status of mathematical exactness. Its questioning of projections and forecasts is obviously relevant here. And it has always, like

Keynes, emphasised the need for coupling economic insights with practical judgements based on accumulated experience. The essence of the department's approach was summed up in a comment by the Treasurer in 1970: 'if one peruses the learned [economic] journals ... both the abstractness of the arguments and the passion of the disputants recall to mind the theological controversies of long ago. All this adds up to is the recognition of judgment in so-called economic science, the acknowledgment of the subject as a coupled art and science, mutually dependent one upon the other.'[58]

The theoretical developments which constituted the 'neoclassical synthesis' — in particular the idea that the system could be shown to be self-correcting and that the 'classical truths' could come into their own now that full employment could be maintained — were of course a major influence on the evolution of the Treasury line. It was these sorts of ideas which recruits were being taught as undergraduates and which underpinned the theoretical tracts read by those Treasury economists seeking to keep abreast of developments within the discipline. It would be a mistake, however, to see the Treasury simply being swept along in the direction mainstream economics was following. As an explanation of the evolution of Treasury philosophy, this is not only far too simplistic, in that it portrays the department as being entirely passive and moving according to the dictates of economic fashion, but it also fails to explain sufficiently what it was that increasingly attracted the Treasury to a neoclassical viewpoint. Further, it pays insufficient attention to the fact that the Treasury's concerns are essentially pragmatic — its function is to provide advice on day-to-day policy issues — and that therefore any change in its attitude is going to be heavily influenced by the changing nature of the problems it faces.

On the last point, what emerges from this chapter is that undoubtedly the chief influence on Treasury attitudes during 1963–67 was the rapid rise in public sector expenditure, particularly on defence. This rise had the effect in part of keeping the department interested in Keynesian questions of economic management. For it raised questions of the inflationary consequences of aggregate demand exceeding aggregate supply and pointed to the need for active economic management. But just as important was the attention it drew to the traditional neoclassical questions of efficient resource allocation, the ranking and evaluation of alternative objectives, the calculation of opportunity costs, and the attainment of maximum economic welfare.

The rise in defence expenditure drew attention to these neoclassical questions in a number of ways. In the first place, the rapid increase in the relative importance of defence expenditure raised questions about whether some of this money could be better spent on such things as education, transfer payments, and so on. It raised questions, in other words, about how public sector expenditure should be distributed and how it might best contribute to maximising social welfare. Second, questions were raised about whether the money allocated to defence was being used to meet its stated ends as efficiently as possible. This question became increasingly pertinent after Menzies' rash announcement in October 1963 that his government had decided to purchase two squadrons of F-111 aircraft from the United States. Apart from the fact that the planes would not begin to be delivered until 1967 (a promise which, it soon became obvious, would not be fulfilled), the financial arrangements for the purchase of the aircraft can only be described as a fiasco: as one writer puts it, as far as escalating costs are concerned the F-111 was the military equivalent of the Sydney Opera House.[59] Third, the rise in defence expenditure and other forms of public expenditure led, as we have seen, to an increase in the relative size of the public sector. This raised questions about whether the public sector was absorbing too large a proportion of the nation's resources and whether the private sector was being hampered by this.

It was not surprising, then, that the Treasury was in the vanguard of those who pointed to the importance of efficient resource allocation. Furthermore, being responsible for financial management — in other words, having to consider the competing spending proposals of different departments (although it had no say in the defence vote), being responsible through the Loan Council for the competing demands of the states; and having to make recommendations about how to raise taxation to help meet the rise in expenditure — the Treasury could not help focusing on the sorts of questions noted above. Also, given its responsibility for financial management the Treasury was necessarily highly attuned to financial management techniques being developed overseas: techniques such as benefit–cost analysis and program budgeting.

The period 1962–67 saw not only a noticeable shift in the Treasury's interests but also, as we have seen, a growing rift between Treasury and the Department of Trade and Industry, a rift symbolised by the reaction to the Vernon Report. Underpinning this rift, and an expression of it, was a sharpening of the Treasury's identity vis-a-vis other departments. An ex-Treasury officer, who was in GFEP throughout the 1950s and 1960s, has suggested to the author that 'the crucial point in the emergence of the consciousness of the role of Treasury and GFEP was the 1960 economic measures, the 1961 near-election debacle of the Menzies Government, the subsequent Vernon Committee report and the response to it'. There persisted throughout the 1950s, the same officer argues, 'a heavy inverted snobbery in the Treasury': 'I recall very clearly the prevailing view in GFEP that it was inappropriate to call oneself an economist; we were in fact public servants doing economic work at times.' But in the post-Vernon period, he maintains, what had been only an 'emerging consciousness' of the department's role as an economic agency now gave way to a determined effort by the Treasury 'to assert its role as the pre-eminent and explicitly economic area of government'.

7

Heightened inflation and the abandonment of Keynesian meliorism, 1967–73

WELL before the downturn of 1974 the Treasury began to be plagued with gnawing doubts about the state of the Australian economy. The warning signs were apparent from the late 1960s and the Treasury was quick to take notice of them and to urge upon its political 'masters' the need for decisive counteraction. The key signs were, internally, a high and rising inflation rate which was in part a reflection of rapidly increasing wage rates; mounting industrial unrest; an intense and wildly reckless boom in mining shares in 1970–71 (the days of Poseidon, Narbarlek and Minsec); dollar difficulties (the Australian dollar was clearly undervalued); and a large increase in capital inflow (which had risen markedly since 1967–68 and which had a large speculative element). Externally, the early 1970s saw the breakdown of the Bretton Woods system: in 1971 the United States suspended convertibility of the US dollar into gold; from August to December, a time of turmoil in foreign currency markets, the major currencies floated relative to each other. Some semblance of order was temporarily restored in December with the signing of the Smithsonian Agreement. But this proved only a temporary pause before the Bretton Woods system finally collapsed.

It would be misleading, however, to suggest that the period surveyed in this chapter was all 'gloom and doom'. On the contrary, it was a feature of this period, particularly of the late 1960s, that there existed a pervasive air of confidence about Australia's long-term economic future. The Treasury began its 1970 survey by noting that 'expectations of growth in the seventies are everywhere running high'. It continued: 'The performance of the Australian economy in the inaugural year of the decade will not belie those hopes.'[1] All seemed set for the Australian economy to continue along its linear growth path, more than likely at an accelerated pace.

The sense of optimism which reigned supreme during the late 1960s–early

Heightened inflation

1970s was readily understandable given the changes which had occurred in the economy since World War II and particularly since the early 1960s. Writing in 1970, Sir Richard Randall argued that World War II was a watershed in Australia's path toward industrialisation. Before the war 'there had been little in the way of conscious determination to develop an economy capable of sustained growth'. Such was Australia's dependence on her rural sector that the 'fortunes of the farmers and those of the rest of the economy tended to move in parallel'. The war, however, provided a strong stimulus to widen the domestic industrial base and suggested a need for a larger population and a more skilled labour force. The postwar industrialisation process in Australia was such that by the end of the 1960s primary industries contributed only 9 per cent to GNP, whereas in the mid-1950s the figure was 15 per cent. Moreover, whereas manufactures made up only 5 per cent of exports at the beginning of the 1950s, they now made up 18 per cent. Together with the rise in the importance of mineral exports, such changes indicated that Australia was now much less dependent on her traditional exports. As Randall put it, 'the fortunes of the economy are no longer as closely tied as they once were to the vagaries of the seasons, or of overseas influences on the price of one or two commodities ... the country has now become sufficiently well diversified and developed to withstand temporary reversals in overseas trade'.[2]

Somewhat similarly, in 1969 the Treasury pointed with pride to the changes which had occurred in the Australian economy over the preceding decade: 'The economy has in many ways matured and at the same time has broadened its range of activities.' The capital market had become stronger and more diversified and had developed a much greater capacity to mobilise capital. The Treasury judged that 'the economic foundations are undoubtedly much stronger and wider than they were ten years back'.[3] Particular importance was attached to the discovery and exploitation during the 1960s of a range of mineral resources. Between 1960 and 1970 the compound growth rate of the output of the mining industry was approximately 14 per cent per annum. Representing some 1.8 per cent of GDP in 1964–65, mining output accounted for 3.8 per cent of GDP by 1971–72. But much more spectacular was the growth in mining exports. Accounting for only 6.6 per cent of total exports in 1960, exports of minerals grew remarkably rapidly during the 1960s to represent some 27 per cent of total exports by 1970. In 1971 the Treasury pointed out that as the 1960s progressed and as more mineral discoveries were made, 'it began to seem as though we might at long last have unlocked our perennial balance of payments problems'. An important barrier to rapid expansion seemed to have been broken: 'In earlier years it had been widely believed that our lack of resources such as these put severe limits on the scope for enlarging and diversifying industry in Australia and hence on our chances of carrying a really large population. Such doubts seemed now to have receded.' It was perhaps not surprising, then, given these changes, that 'a new sense of opportunity and new ideas of dimension took hold in Australia and spread widely abroad'.[4]

The story of this chapter is largely one of how this optimism began to be dented. To the Treasury, the main problem during 1968–73 and indeed thereafter was the rise in the inflation rate. The imperative need in fighting inflation, as far as the department was concerned, was to halt the rapid rise in wages and, as part of this, to subdue what it interpreted to be the heightened aggression and avarice of trade unions. In the face of what was seen as growing domestic disorder, the Treasury abandoned the remnants of Keynesian meliorism. As the 1970s progressed the Treasury moved ever closer to a purely neoclassical outlook. The benefits of market-imposed discipline, combined with a rise in the unemployment rate, became increasingly attractive to the department as a means of restoring order and efficiency and dampening an apparent tendency toward excessive wage demands.

Political developments and staffing changes in the Treasury

If 1968–73 witnessed growing economic disorder, it saw also, by postwar Australian standards, a degree of political instability. The Menzies era had come to an end in 1966. After seventeen consecutive years in command of the Liberal-Country Party coalition, Menzies decided to retire and Harold Holt was chosen to succeed him. The apparent political stability enjoyed under Menzies was soon replaced by a leadership battle within the Liberal Party which became particularly intense after Holt's death at the end of 1967. Holt's successor was John Gorton. His prime ministership lasted three turbulent years. Gorton soon attracted criticism for being irresponsible and indiscreet, for imposing a presidential style of leadership, for being unwilling to take advice, and for surrounding himself with only those who supported his ideas. A pertinent example of the last of these complaints was Gorton's decision in November 1969 to drop McMahon as Treasurer and replace him with Leslie Bury, previously minister for labour and national service and a former Treasury officer. It was McMahon, however, who was chosen to become Prime Minister in March 1971 after Gorton was deposed as leader. In one of his first initiatives, McMahon replaced Bury with Billy Snedden, a former lawyer who had acquired some economic expertise when in charge of the Department of Labour and National Service (1969–71).

McMahon was to face a series of major difficulties, most of which he was unable to tackle successfully. He proved ineffectual in uniting the party and bringing cohesion to the coalition. To the Australian electorate, he lacked charisma and confidence, particularly when contrasted with the Labor leader, Gough Whitlam. Moreover, McMahon presided at a time of rapidly rising costs and prices and of increasing unemployment. His position, and that of his government, became increasingly tenuous. At the end of 1972, after 23 years in opposition, the ALP gained victory in the federal elections. Whitlam became Prime Minister. Frank Crean, who had long been opposition spokesman on economic issues and who was well versed in offering criticism of Treasury policy, became Treasurer. He was to last two years.

Heightened inflation

Within the Treasury also, the late 1960s–early 1970s was a period notable for personnel changes. Two years were particularly important: 1969 and 1971. As described in chapter 1, 1969 saw the first major organisational overhaul of the department since the 1940s. The reorganisation resulted in the creation of three new divisions, a significant increase in the number of second and third division officers and, as part of this, the promotion of a number of sectional heads to assistant secretary status. In September 1969 the Treasury suffered a major loss when Maurice O'Donnell, deputy secretary, died following a heart attack. With O'Donnell's death, and unable to secure a third deputy secretaryship responsible for economic matters, Randall decided to assume personal oversight of GFEP and OER, leaving the other divisions under the two deputy secretaries, John Garrett and Don Craik.

The significance of 1971 lies in two key staffing changes which occurred in the second half of the year. The first was Randall's retirement following the presentation of the August budget. Randall's successor was Frederick Wheeler, whose role as head of GFEP from 1943 to 1952 was described in chapter 4. Wheeler left the Treasury in 1952 for a position with the International Labour Office in Geneva. He did not return to Canberra until 1960 when he became chairman of the Public Service Board, a post he held until his appointment as secretary to the Treasury.

The second major staffing change concerned John Stone. Having been in Washington since 1967, Stone returned to the Treasury in 1971 and was placed in charge of the Revenue, Loans and Investment Division. In November, Wheeler decided to appoint Stone to the new post of deputy secretary (economic). Stone thereby effectively took charge of economic policy. Frank Pryor, head of GFEP, and for many years Stone's senior, resigned in protest in what was a rare public demonstration of internal dissension. Pryor was replaced by Bill Cole, who had been director of the Bureau of Transport Economics since 1970 and whose acquaintance with Stone went back to their days in the early 1960s in the Economic and Financial Surveys Branch.

While it is true that Stone was to play a decisive role in the determination of Treasury economic policy advice throughout the 1970s — he was to remain deputy secretary until 1979 when he succeeded Wheeler to the secretaryship — one has to guard against the tendency to picture Stone as the sole source of Treasury opinion. Table 7.1 summarises the staffing changes which occurred in the upper echelons of GFEP during the 1970s. The table shows those officers listed in the various *Commonwealth Directories* between 1970 and 1979 who were either an assistant secretary or first assistant secretary in GFEP. It shows also their first degree, where obtained and date of graduation (where available).

As with Stone, what all the officers listed in the table had in common was long experience of, and hence outlooks coloured by, the sustained economic growth and prosperity which characterised the postwar period. All were witnesses, all could testify, to the growing resilience and maturing of the Australian economy. All had come to share an essentially positive interpretation of the economy's inherent proclivities and all were aware that the

The Treasury line

Table 7.1 GFEP second division officers, 1970–79

Officer	First degree	Date of graduation	University
A. H. Boxer	BA (Hons)[a]	1949	Melbourne
I. Castles	BCom	1956	Melbourne
R. W. Cole	BCom (Hons)	1951	Melbourne
H. F. Cruise[b]	BA (Hons)[a]	1951	Melbourne
B. W. Fraser	BA[a]	1960	UNE
C. I. Higgins	BEc (Hons)	1963	ANU
N. F. Hyden	BSc	1964	Melbourne
S. S. McBurney	BCom (Hons)	1949	Melbourne
J. V. Monaghan	BEc (Hons)	1951	Sydney
A. R. G. Prowse	BCom (Hons)	1952	Melbourne
F. C. Pryor	BA (Hons)[a]	1940	Sydney
C. R. Rye	BCom	1958	Melbourne
E. M. W. Visbord	BCom	1949	Melbourne

Sources: Who's Who in Australia; Treasury Submission to the RCAGA Attachment (c); information supplied by Treasury.
Notes: a signifies a major in economics.
b Cruise was designated assistant secretary (acting).

economy had become much less susceptible to destabilising forces orginating overseas.

But what perhaps stands out in Table 7.1 is that GFEP was dominated in the 1970s by graduates from the University of Melbourne: nine of the thirteen received their first degree from Melbourne (with six of them graduating between 1949 and 1952). It can be noted also that the two officers who were in charge of GFEP between 1972 and 1979 (Cole and Rye) were from Melbourne. By the end of the 1970s Rye was one of the department's two deputy secretaries, the other being Roy Daniel, who also was from Melbourne (another graduate of 1949). Boxer, Prowse and McBurney were members of staff in the Economics Department at Melbourne: Boxer was lecturer then reader, Prowse was lecturer (1958–62) and McBurney senior tutor (1950).

The dominance of Melbourne reflected in part perhaps a process of chain migration (Wheeler had a close relationship with the Commerce Faculty) and in part the attraction to the Treasury of having officers moulded in the Giblin-Copland tradition, that of practical, applied, empirically oriented economists. This said, it is nevertheless difficult to judge the influence of Melbourne on the course of Treasury thought. For while Giblin and Copland, and, after the war, Downing and others, were deeply sympathetic to Keynesian ideas (the *General Theory* continued to be listed as a prescribed text in Economics B as late as 1976), the commerce faculty was also long the home of Marshallian economics in Australia, with the *Principles* being a revered book. Giblin and Copland effectively severed their relations with the Melbourne commerce faculty at the outbreak of war in 1939. Giblin never returned to the university and Copland, though appointed to the new post of Truby Williams Professor of Economics in 1944, was occupied with wartime administration in Canberra and then with ambassadorial responsibilities in China, and relinquished the post in 1946. Wilfred Prest, who had arrived in Melbourne in 1938 to take up a senior lectureship, succeeded Copland to the position of Truby Williams Professor. He was to remain head of the Department of Economics until 1972 and during this time Marshallian economics exercised a decisive influence. Polglaze and Soper point out that Prest

> was always a true disciple of Marshall, believing that 'Economics is the study of mankind in the ordinary business of life', and that established doctrine is constantly in need of reconsideration in the light of changes in social conditions and institutions. His own copy of Marshall's *Principles* was famous. Lavishly interleaved with scraps of paper covered in tiny pencil script, it was commonly referred to as 'Prest's bible', and his students at one time pretended to believe that he was preparing the 9th edition. But they read their Marshall, and they read the modern works, and learned the importance of finding out the facts of the Australian economy.[5]

Each of the Melbourne graduates listed above were well versed in Marshallian economics: the second year of the Melbourne commerce course involved an intensive study of Marshall and Pigou, with both the *Principles* and *Economics of Welfare* being studied in depth. Keynes was introduced at the end of second year and was studied in detail in third year. Hicks was also considered in third year. Significantly, Keynes was not described as being at odds with Marshall; on the contrary, it was taken for granted that he was a Marshallian.[6] Clearly, then, it seems likely that the educational background of these senior GFEP officers played a part in the department's willingness to embrace a neoclassical viewpoint. But its significance should not be exaggerated. One of the Treasury officers who graduated from Melbourne in 1949 has pointed out to the author that 'the Commerce Faculty produced graduates designed in large measure for the business community and with a basically generalist sort of training. I think that we barely fitted the description "economists". We largely learned our economics on the job'. More significant in changing Treasury attitudes, there can be no doubt, were the economic problems which the department faced.

The cost problem, 1968–71

The topic which most concerned the officers listed above and which dominated the Treasury's annual surveys from 1968 onwards was what was referred to in the surveys as 'the cost problem'. To the Treasury, the 'cost problem' was essentially a 'wages problem', for the simple reason that wages were the main element in costs. The 'wages problem', in turn, referred essentially to the escalation in the rate of increase in wages apparent since the mid-1960s. In the decade to 1963–64 average weekly earnings grew on average by 4.4 per cent a year. From 1964–65 to 1967–68 the average annual rate rose to 6.15 per cent. An even faster rate of increase occurred thereafter, as can be seen in Table 7.2.

Table 7.2 Average weekly earnings, 1968–69 to 1972–73

	per cent change
1968–69	7.5
1969–70	8.4
1970–71	11.1
1971–72	10.1
1972–73	9.0

Source: Adapted from NGB Table 4.17

What particularly perturbed the Treasury was not the wage rises as such but the disruption to the 'historical' relationship between average annual wage increases and productivity increases. It warned in 1968 that 'the inevitable result of increasing money wages much ahead of gains in productivity will be a rise in prices; and the bigger the increase in money wages in relation to the gain in productivity, the greater the increase in prices'.[7] It was to repeat this point in each subsequent survey and to note with mounting anxiety that the differential between wage and productivity increases was widening. Discussing its 'rule' on the relationship between wage and productivity increases, the Treasury acknowledged that there were time lags involved, so that the change in prices did not necessarily occur immediately, and that the price increase might not necessarily be in exact proportion to the wage increase. It acknowledged also that measurements of productivity were only 'rough approximations'. But it was adamant that from a long-term perspective the relationship between money wage rises and price rises was clearly apparent. It noted for instance in its 1970 survey that over the ten years to 1968–69 weekly earnings rose at an annual average rate of 5.4 per cent while productivity rose by approximately 2.5 per cent a year. This left a gap of about 2.9 per cent. In apparent vindication of its rule, it noted that the average annual rate of increase in the CPI during this period was 2.4 per cent.

Clearly, the implication of the Treasury's argument was that ideally wages should not rise faster than the rate of increase in productivity. In taking this line, the Treasury was reiterating what had long been considered a sacred truth by many Australian economists. Writing in 1955, J.E. Isaac noted:

> It is now standard practice, whenever wage policy is discussed, to repeat with a clear and confident voice the principle that the general level of money wages should rise proportionately and no more than the increase in average product per unit of labour. The greatest threat to the objectives of full employment and price stability is the tendency for unions to push for wage increases which are out of step with productivity.[8]

Isaac described this principle as the 'modern iron law of wages'. Certainly in Australia it was a principle widely held. It was advocated regularly in the biannual economic surveys in the *Economic Record*, and it was a principle often put forward to the CCAC by economists and employers.

As Isaac pointed out in his 1955 paper, the underlying assumption of the

Heightened inflation

wages/productivity principle is that the wages/profits share of national income is more or less fixed, although it is recognised that short-term variations can and do occur either side of the long-term norm. Hence,

> an attempt to force a change in the distribution of income, it is assumed, will be defeated either by unemployment because profit margins are not high enough; or by higher prices where employers are able to pass on the wage increases. When, therefore, a plea is made to trade unions for a sense of restraint and responsibility in their wage demands, and for wages to be geared to productivity, it really amounts to saying that the existing share of wages is the highest possible. Any attempt to increase it will result in unemployment or inflation.[9]

This assumption rests in turn on the belief that employers will take whatever action is necessary to maintain a particular profit margin. The only way a rise in wages will not lead to a rise in unemployment is if market conditions are buoyant enough to enable employers to pass on cost increases in the form of price rises and thereby maintain their profit margin. On this reasoning, it would seem that for most of the postwar period conditions had been such as to enable cost increases to be passed on.

The Treasury fully endorsed the assumptions underlying the wages/productivity principle. It argued in its 1968 survey that 'if businesses are to attract capital for growth they must keep up the return on funds employed' and noted that their success in doing so could be seen by comparing the share in GNP at factor cost of wages, salaries and supplements with that of gross operating surpluses of trading enterprises. In the period 1953–54 to 1966–67 the share of wages had fluctuated from a high point of 57.8 per cent in 1957–58 to a low of 54.3 per cent in 1963–64. The Treasury noted:

> In most years the variation from the mean either way was small. This relative constancy of the proportions suggests that raising money wages faster than productivity can in fact increase the share of wages in gross national product very little and then only for a short time. Higher prices will help to restore the share of business profits and the result will be continuously rising costs and prices with all the difficulties that must make for export producers or others who cannot adjust their prices to higher costs.[10]

Table 7.3 shows the annual increase in the CPI from 1967–68 onwards. The upward trend evident in the table worried the Treasury considerably. It admonished readers of the 1971 survey that 'six per cent inflation is a serious

Table 7.3 Consumer price index, 1968–69 to 1972–73

	per cent change
1968–69	2.6
1969–70	3.2
1970–71	4.8
1971–72	6.8
1972–73	6.0

Source: Adapted from NGB Table 5.16b

matter' and pointed to the familiar arguments about the injustices of inflation and its deleterious effects on confidence:

> At that rate the real value of earnings and financial assets wilts too rapidly to be tolerated. It is viciously unjust to those unable to protect themselves against its inroads on their well-being — like people relying on small incomes or a store of savings. Worse — if unchecked, a six per cent inflation, by sapping confidence in money values, can quickly double its pace, as it has done recently in more than one major country abroad.[11]

But perhaps more important to the Treasury was the effect of a 6 per cent inflation rate on the allocation of resources and on Australia's competitiveness. As the department explained in 1972,

> such rates of price increase lead ... to increasing uncertainty across the whole field of endeavour. Whether on the part of businessmen seeking to plan future investment projects, governments seeking to assess the need for public expenditure in particular projects or areas, or in many other ways, misallocation of resources and the growth of inefficiencies abound under these conditions. Economic growth, both currently and in prospect, is eroded.[12]

The Treasury acknowledged that wages were not the sole determinant of costs, nor were costs the sole determinant of prices, but it was adamant that cost rises, and hence wage rises, were the main determinants of price increases. The department argued in 1972 that 'while prices for individual products will, from time to time, directly reflect demand conditions, empirical studies suggest that, in the aggregate, direct demand influences tend to be subordinate to cost influences... By far the major *direct* influences upon prices has been found to come from the cost influence, and particularly changes in unit labour costs'.[13]

What then determined wage rises? And in particular, why was there a marked increase in weekly earnings after 1968? Further, what could be done to alleviate the inflationary difficulties they bequeathed? (Perhaps, however, a more relevant question is why was it, given continuous full employment and given a governmental pledge to maintain full employment, that trade unions did not take advantage of their position earlier to push for higher wages?) Until 1971 the Treasury stressed the importance of conditions of excess demand for resources in general and labour in particular as the main determinant of wage rises. In such a situation the bargaining power of labour was increased while employers, faced with labour shortages and burgeoning demand for their products, were prepared to offer increasingly higher over-award payments to attract workers. Higher wages in turn gave rise to the continued growth of demand. And so the process fed on itself.

Such arguments were essentially a reiteration of a long-established Treasury line. Indeed discussing the context in which inflation had escalated at the end of the 1960s–early 1970s, the Treasury pointed in 1971 to the continuity with earlier experience:

> This cost-price problem has come rapidly to the fore-front over the past couple of years. Yet ... it was with us — though in a less conspicuous and insistent form — right through [the middle and late 1960s]. To an appreciable degree the forces

Heightened inflation

tending to generate inflation were held in check by fiscal and monetary restraints. From time to time also they were offset in part by the depressive effects of droughts and other adversities in the rural sector. But they were not extinguished and in the recent period they have made headway.

Basically, what has happened in our economy since the start of 1969 has been much the same pattern with what had gone before. There has been the same many-sided thrust for expansion, the same strong increase in demand for labour, materials and equipment, the same pressure for greater public outlays on facilities and services, the same mood of confidence and high expectations about the future.[15]

In its 1969 survey, released in July, the Treasury argued that the economy was showing symptoms of 'developing hypertension', a trend reflected in the tightening of the labour market since the start of the year. The number of unemployed (using CES data) fell rapidly from 65 000 in 1968 to 55 000 in 1969, while unfilled vacancies increased during the same period by 6000. In the August budget the Treasurer noted that demand was 'growing fast' and warned that 'there is a clear possibility that excess demand, helped by excess liquidity, could upset the balance of the economy'. After a brief respite from August to December 1969, in which 'demand and supply appeared to be rising pretty much together',[15] the labour market become progressively tighter during the first half of 1970. The Treasury could refer in its annual economic survey, released in July, to the 'worsening scarcities' of the labour market. The demand for labour was described as being 'excessively strong'. The marked rise in average weekly earnings and in particular the growth of wages or earnings drift — wages or earnings in excess of award rates — was held to be a reflection of the strong competition for labour.

The Treasury acknowledged of course that unsatisfied demand for labour was not the only cause of wage increases. It pointed to the importance also of wage-fixing bodies, notably the CCAC. It argued that an important reason why wages had begun to climb so rapidly from 1968 onwards was the 1967 metal-trades work-value decision, which became operative in two stages — in January and August 1968. The highest increase awarded in the metal-trades case was $10.05, while the standard 'tradesman' received $7.40. Although the decision was not intended to apply to other trades and industries, it was not long before claims were made to the commission for similar increases. The subsequent flow-on into other awards continued into 1969 and contributed to the overall escalation of wages rates.

But while the Treasury acknowledged the importance of the 'arbitral factor' and its role in spreading gains from one occupation or industry throughout the rest of the economy — irrespective of the existence of 'general pressure' — it nevertheless insisted on the primacy of demand factors. As it noted in 1971, 'a condition of strong and general demand for labour has usually provided the context in which other influences do most to raise the wage structure and that has certainly been true of recent years'.[16] It was not surprising, given the emphasis on the level of demand, that from 1968 onwards the Treasury stressed the need for deflationary policies. It was not always successful, however, in having its recommendations accepted.

The Treasury line

The 1968–69 budget was intended to be mildly deflationary. It was framed on the expectation that both private consumption expenditure and investment expenditure would increase strongly over the financial year and that GDP would grow more quickly than in the previous year (largely because the farm sector was now on a recovery path following a severe drought in 1967–68). The Treasurer announced that there was to be a reduction in the rate of increase of government expenditure (an estimated rise of 7.8 per cent compared with an actual increase of 10.4 per cent the previous year). In a statement attached to the budget speech, the Treasury warned that it was nevertheless the case that government expenditure would 'contribute substantially to the growth of demand and activity within the economy. With further strong growth in private spending in 1968–69, this could, in the absence of action to reduce the expansionary influence of the budget, lead to excessive pressures on available resources and on costs and prices and prevent improvement in the external current account'.[17] With this in mind, a range of taxation initiatives were announced, including increases in company tax and sales tax. It was estimated that, largely because of these changes, the overall result would be a reduction in the budget deficit from $644 million (the result for 1967–68) to $547 million.

The next budget, that of 1969–70, was in a number of ways a source of great disappointment for the Treasury. The budget was 'framed in the context of the economy moving, and being likely to continue to move, on a strong expansionary course'.[18] Given this context, the budget was, in one important respect, 'on the right track' in that the budget deficit was to be reduced substantially (from $385 million in 1968–69 to an estimated $30 million in 1969–70). The domestic surplus, described by the department in 1971 as 'exceptionally large', was expected to increase by $300 million. These changes were to be brought about by an increase in revenue about twice as high as the expected increase in Commonwealth expenditure. What was disappointing for the Treasury, however, was that government outlays were to rise at a faster rate than in the previous year (by 7.2 per cent compared with 6.8 per cent in 1968–69). More importantly, the rise in revenue was not to be achieved by any taxation increases. In fact, some minor concessions were announced. The Treasury had recommended, unsuccessfully, that there be substantial increases in sales tax. The department was unsuccessful also in opposing a proposal to relax the means test on pensions.

The Treasury's advice was rejected for two main reasons. First, 1969 was an election year and, as had been demonstrated often in the postwar period, governments are not predisposed in such circumstances to raise taxes — irrespective of economic conditions. Second, the Treasury faced Gorton's antipathy. The Prime Minister was inimical to the department, believing it to be obstructionist and 'conservatively sterile'.[19] It was a mark of his hostility toward the department, as noted in chapter 1, that Gorton acted to obtain an alternative source of economic advice.

But while the Treasury was unable to convince the Prime Minister of the need for a 'tough' budget in 1969, it was successful in securing acceptance of

Heightened inflation

the need to tighten monetary policy. In July the long-term bond rate on the commonwealth loan was raised; so too were the rates on short-term securities. The SRD ratio was increased in August and again in October. Also in August the maximum fixed deposit and overdraft rates of trading banks were raised. They were raised again in March 1970. A month later both the maximum savings bank deposit rate and maximum savings bank housing loan rate were increased. The extent of the credit squeeze was reflected in the much slower growth of M3: having increased by 9.1 per cent in 1969–70, M3 increased by only 6.2 per cent in 1970–71. Not all of this decline was attributable of course to the tightening of monetary policy; also significant was the achievement of a domestic budget surplus in 1969–70 of $500 million.

The 1970–71 budget, as described by the Treasurer, was intended to be precautionary but not repressive. Bury brought down a balanced budget: it was estimated that there would be a small overall surplus of $4 million (while the domestic surplus was expected to increase by about $50 million). Fairly minor increases in customs and excise duties, sales tax and company tax were announced. On the other hand, reductions were made in personal income tax. And it was estimated that expenditure would rise more quickly than in the previous year (by 11.2 per cent, compared with an increase of 7.9 per cent in 1969–70).

The actual budget results for 1970–71 suggest that the budget in fact was mildly stimulatory. The domestic surplus actually declined by some $60 million by comparison with the 1969–70 result. Further, again contrary to intention, outlays grew more quickly than receipts. Monetary policy, however, remained restrictive in 1970–71. M3 increased only moderately (6.8 per cent), this despite a rapid increase in international reserves.

The effect of the tight liquidity situation began to be reflected in the demand for labour during the second half of 1970. A sharp increase in unemployment occurred in the September quarter. At the end of April 1970 seasonally adjusted unemployment stood at 49 000. By the end of September it had increased to 63 000. During the same period vacancies fell from 55 800 to 48 000. Another sharp fall in vacancies occurred in February and March 1971, while unemployment increased slightly. The situation then stayed reasonably stable for the remainder of the financial year.

To the Treasury the changes in the unemployment situation were insignificant in comparison with the changes occurring in wages and prices. Writing in July 1971, the department noted that 'the relatively moderate rise in costs and prices, which had gone on through the earlier years of the big thrust for expansion in our economy, has given place to a trend which is much more formidable and disturbing'.[20] The Treasury noted with alarm the 'phenomenal rise' of 13 per cent in weekly earnings in the March quarter of 1971 (by comparison with the previous March quarter). It attributed a large part of this increase to the national wage judgment of 1970, in which the CCAC had awarded a 6 per cent wage rise. It continued to emphasise, however, the importance of demand conditions, this despite the fact that unemployment had increased in 1970–71. The department pointed to the urgent need for policies designed to dampen those sectors of the economy in which demand had been rising particularly quickly. Excessive demand 'was not only giving rise to cost increases but was providing the conditions under which these could be passed on in higher prices'. Making clear its views on what should be the aim of the August budget, the Treasury declared: 'It is to be expected, if only because of wage and cost increases which have already occurred, that there will be further price increases in the period ahead. Plainly, the policy of restraints on demand in various sectors will have to be carried further yet so that resistance to further cost increases may be stiffened and competition encouraged.'

The changed nature of trade union behaviour

What made the introduction of such policies all the more important to the Treasury was the department's conviction that a change in the attitude of trade unions had occurred in recent years. The Treasury was convinced that trade unions had become much more militant; they had become willing (and able) to use their power much more than previously to their own advantage:

> it is well to have in mind the attitudes which have latterly prevailed in the world of organised labour. These indicate a hardening disposition to obtain greater improvements in money wages and working conditions. There is amongst broad sectors of the work-force a greater readiness to press claims to the limit, less readiness to accept delay in the settlement of claims and a considerable speed-up in the cycle of claim, settlement and new claim. These new attitudes have found reflection in rising industrial unrest which, in terms of working days lost, has more than trebled in the three years to 1970.[21]

In the 1970–71 budget speech, Leslie Bury warned of the possibility that 'excessive demands for increases in money wages and other incomes — especially when pushed ruthlessly in conditions of full employment — could jeopardise prospects of balanced growth'. Likewise, Snedden made several references in the 1971–72 budget speech to changed trade union behaviour. Early in the speech he declared: 'In general, as we see the problem, there has been and still is a powerful upthrust of costs, stemming largely though not wholly from large wage claims relentlessly pursued.' He referred to 'the escalating level of industrial unrest', the 'rising tide of militancy', and the 'confrontations in industry [which] are often resolved only at the cost of grossly inflationary wage settlements'. As to the future, the Treasurer hoped that as a result of the budget there would be 'scope for a real lift in the standard of living which should be shared by many who would otherwise be the undefended victims of inflation and the self-seeking of stronger, more aggressive groups' — the last-mentioned being an obvious reference to trade unions.

Concepts such as 'militancy' and 'aggression' are not easily translated into figures. Nevertheless, there can be little doubt that the late 1960s saw the end of a long period of reasonably peaceful industrial relations and its replacement

Heightened inflation

Table 7.4 Industrial disputes, 1962–70

	Number of disputes	Working days lost ('000)
1962	1183	509
1963	1250	582
1964	1334	911
1965	1346	816
1966	1273	732
1967	1340	705
1968	1713	1080
1969	2014	1958
1970	2738	2394

Source: Adapted from Norton Table 4.1
Note: An industrial dispute is a dispute involving a stoppage of 10 workdays or more.

by a noticeable upsurge in industrial unrest, measured in terms both of number of disputes and working days lost (see Table 7.4). What is significant about the late 1960s is that not only did the number of disputes increase but so too did the average length of strikes and the number of workers involved in strike activity. What is interesting also is that the rise in strike activity involved to an increasing degree white-collar workers: a group traditionally seen as having a lower propensity to strike than blue-collar workers.

Australia was not alone of course in experiencing an upsurge in industrial unrest in the late 1960s. The same thing happened in most western countries, but in an even more virulent form. The worker-student uprising in France in 1968 is of course the most famous instance of this unrest. But strike waves crippled also Germany and Italy in 1969. In Britain there was nothing as dramatic as 'les événements de Mai' but it, too, was subject to increased strike activity. The number of days lost in strikes increased in Britain from 2.7 million in 1967 to 4.6 million in 1968, 6.8 million in 1969, and reached a massive 11 million in 1970, a level which had not been recorded since the general strike of 1926. Most of the strikes in Britain and elsewhere were settled by employers and/or governments agreeing to large wage increases. Such was the extent of these increases that Western Europe experienced a wages explosion in the late 1960s.

Against these domestic and international manifestations of worker unrest, the Treasury's prose, usually dry, became almost animated when describing trade union behaviour. Trade unions emerge from Treasury documents of 1970–72 as essentially avaricious institutions relentlessly pursuing higher and higher wages, leaving in their wake the unprotected to struggle against their inflationary legacy. To the Treasury, such behaviour could not be tolerated. Its message was that at the very least it was necessary to 'stiffen resistance' — to use its phrase. There was no point in attempting diplomacy. For the techniques of persuasion were impotent in the face of such avarice. There was no other remedy but the use of strongly deflationary policies.

The Treasury line
Incomes-prices policies

While the Treasury was content to continue to rely on fiscal-monetary policy packages to deal with excessive price and wage increase, suggestions began to be heard at the beginning of the 1970s, particularly after the presentation of the 1971–72 budget, about the need for alternative or supplementary techniques of economic management. A small number of Australian economists began to advocate the use of some form of incomes-prices policies. For instance, late in 1970 the editorial board of the Institute for Applied Economic and Social Research argued, without any elaboration, that 'there must be some direct action to restrain wage and price increases as well as restraint by monetary and fiscal policy'.[22] In the following year the institute expressed its disappointment that the 1971–72 budget failed to give stimulus to the economy and showed 'no sign of adopting an incomes and prices policy to combat incomes inflation'.[23] In the next issue of its journal the institute repeated its argument that it was the government's responsibility to implement an incomes policy which would act in coordination with monetary and fiscal policies.[24] But again it failed to explain at any length just what this would entail. Similarly, commenting on the state of the Australian economy in the light of the 1971–72 budget, Professor J.W. Nevile argued that 'in the current Australian situation the appropriate means to combat inflation is not a "tough" budget or a tight money policy but an incomes policy'.[25]

Very little, however, was to come of these suggestions. The LCP government remained largely indifferent to possible alternative measures. One reason for this lack of interest was that there was so little that was concrete about the suggested alternatives. As Nieuwenhuysen notes, the proponents of incomes-prices policies 'appeared more certain of the need for such policies than of the actual shape which they might take'.[26]

It seems appropriate to note here, however, that in 1973 and 1974, against a background of rapid wage increases and, from 1974, stagflation, there occurred a new burst of enthusiasm for incomes-prices policies. And this time it was much more broadly supported. Hagger points out that 'between [the middle of 1973] and the end of 1974 Australian economists appear to have reached an impressive consensus on prices and incomes policy. Practically all economists who discussed inflation in this period went on record as favouring the immediate introduction of a prices and incomes policy'.[27] Even the Liberal Party flirted for a while with incomes-prices policies. From April 1973 Billy Snedden, now leader of the opposition, began advocating an incomes-prices policy. A year later, during the 1974 election campaign, the opposition's economic policy document included as one of its main objectives 'the introduction of a prices and incomes policy (establishing a national conference to discuss the main issues, introducing guidelines for the growth of prices and incomes, abolishing the pace-setter role for the public service, and establishing the whole policy by voluntary co-operation or through the temporary reference of state powers to the Commonwealth).'[28] It was a measure of the extent of interest in such policies that a referendum was held at the end of 1973 on the

Heightened inflation

issue of transferring to the commonwealth power to control prices and incomes. The referendum failed.

In contrast to the general enthusiasm of the Australian economics profession, the Treasury remained distinctly cold toward the idea of introducing some form of prices-incomes policies. It tersely dismissed them in its 1971 survey, noting that 'such policies have been tried in certain countries, with little evidence as yet of lasting success. Most of the larger countries have rejected statutory price-incomes policy as either ineffective or undesirable in terms of longer-run resource allocation requirements'.[29]

A more detailed explanation of the basis of the Treasury's opposition to incomes-prices policies was provided in a speech delivered by Snedden in November 1971 and prepared in the Treasury. Unlike his pre- and post-treasurership stance, Snedden dwelt at length in the speech on the difficulties involved in implementing incomes-prices policies. A key point was that such policies could only work provided there was sufficient community consensus backing the policies. What had to be recognised was that the Australian economic system 'still functions principally on the pursuit of self-interest'. The problem was that so long as this was the chief motivating factor in economic behaviour, any apparent consensus was necessarily a fragile phenomenon:

> as in some other important aspects of our society, pursuit of self-interest, as seen by individuals and groups, leads to results which are not in the common national interest. It is not that these groups do not correctly perceive their self-interest and that therefore the whole problem can be solved simply by education. Experience alone shows many groups that, while money income gains are often illusory, there are sometimes real gains to be had by their actions. Of course, these gains are generally sustainable only in the short run and at the expense of others in the community. That very fact is the genesis of much of the problem — the fear of losing out, even in a relative sense, underlies many income claims which in the general economic context, are patently excessive.[30]

Snedden noted also that under an incomes policy the level of dissatisfaction with relative incomes would, over time, build up, leading eventually to an explosion of income claims. Another difficulty was associated with the fact that the criteria on which an incomes-prices policy operated would replace those established by market forces. There was a great risk, therefore, that resource allocation would be distorted. Further, controls were likely to beget more controls: 'Almost invariably, comprehensive price controls lead eventually to shortages and the need for extensive complementary controls (for example, over components and quality of products).' A system of price control would also have the serious practical problem of requiring 'an enormous administrative structure'. Snedden declared, and here his department made clear its philosophy:

> In saying that there are many problems in the full and comprehensive control of prices, I am not suggesting that the market now performs the allocative function ideally. I recognise that, for one reason or another — including, in many instances, a lack of real competition — a good proportion of decisions on prices are already

taken to some extent independently of market criteria. But as I see it, the approach to that problem should be to try to make the present system work better, rather than to throw it overboard in favour of complete public intervention in the pricing process.

The argument here was that the key to economic efficiency was not to increase governmental meddling with the market mechanism but, on the contrary, to allow market forces greater scope to operate. The Treasury, it would seem, could see no point in relying on remedies of the consensual type — a reaction, no doubt, to the rise in industrial militancy and the 'hardening disposition' of unions to obtain wage and other improvements. Such an 'artificial' panacea would only prolong the day of reckoning and ultimately exacerbate the inflationary problem.

Dealing with inflation: the 1971–72 budget

To recapitulate, it was the Treasury's view that the rapid rise in wage rates from the late 1960s reflected the onset of a tight labour market (which in turn was a reflection of excess demand for labour), the inappropriately generous decisions of wage-fixing bodies, and the increased aggressiveness of trade unions in their pursuit of wage claims. Of these, by far the greatest importance was attached to the first. For it was the first which in most cases was the essential precondition for the second and third. Consistent with this, in both 1971 and 1972 the Treasury rejected the idea that the heightened domestic inflation rate reflected overseas influences. The Treasury argued in its 1971 survey that 'the old notion of inflation being exported from one country to another through export or import price increases just does not fit the facts of this situation'.[31] Australians had largely themselves to blame for the current inflationary problems; it was excessive domestic demand and home-grown avarice that were at fault.

The question of imported inflation was dealt with at more length in the 1972 survey. But the conclusion was the same: 'while some of the momentum behind the recently intensified inflationary trend does seem to have originated overseas, much the greater part of it is left to be explained in terms of domestic influences.'[32] These sorts of arguments, however, were disputed both at the time and as a result of subsequent research. For instance, the Treasury view was challenged in 1973 by a Reserve Bank economist, Peter Jonson. On the basis of simulations carried out on the Bank's econometric model, Jonson concluded that 'Australia's current inflation [the period studied was from the second quarter of 1965 to the second quarter of 1973] owes considerably more to foreign influences than to "domestic cost pressures".[33] Three years later, two other researchers, again using the Reserve Bank model, came to a somewhat different conclusion: namely that while externally generated inflationary forces were of great and increasing significance in determining Australia's inflation rate in the period 1971–72 to 1973–74, they were only of marginal significance in 1969–70 and 1970–71.[34] By contrast, in the same year Nevile using his own econometric model, concluded that for the *entire* period analysed by Argy and Carmichael externally induced inflation had been relatively unimportant.[35]

The 1971–72 budget showed that the McMahon government fully accepted not only the Treasury view on the causes of inflation (and the primacy of domestic factors) but also its argument that a tough budget was the only appropriate response. Referring to the upsurge in costs and prices, Snedden announced that 'we are determined to combat this pernicious trend, slow it down and hobble it'. The budget included a range of deflationary policies: the levy on personal income tax was raised from 2.5 per cent to 5 per cent; company tax was increased; so too were customs and excise duties. It was estimated that the overall result would be a small deficit of $11 million (compared with an actual deficit of $75 million in 1970–71). The domestic surplus was estimated to rise by $170 million (to $630 million). Taking into account the government's decision to transfer payroll tax to the states, outlays were estimated to rise by 11.8 per cent (compared with a 14.9 per cent rise in 1970–71) and receipts by 12.8 per cent (compared with 12.9 per cent the previous year).

The logic underpinning the budget was straightforward:

> Undoubtedly, a significant part of the impetus [to cost and price inflation] has come from wage increases in various forms. These increases have reflected the level of demand and a willingness on the part of employers, under pressure, to pay more for labour. Apparently, it has been possible to pass on increased costs, wholly or partly, in higher prices ... [But] although cost increases and the price increases which follow them may be due, in the first instance, to increases in wages and other cost elements, they are without doubt stimulated and made possible by conditions of strong demand for resources. Hence, if resistance to such cost increases is to be stiffened, as it must be, there has to be a sufficient degree of restraint on potential demand for resources, particularly in those sectors where it is obviously running too high.

But not only would a deflationary budget stiffen employer resistance, it would also serve to slow down the rate at which wage increases introduced by institutional fiat (notably the national wage case) could pass through the system in the form of higher prices. Further, such a budget; by raising unemployment, would help dampen the militancy of trade unions — the implicit assumption being that trade union confidence and aggression was the product of the sustained strength of domestic demand. In other words, the Treasury's proposal in 1971, like that of November 1960, was that a policy designed to lower aggregate demand would usefully provide a jolt to labour by making job prospects less secure.

The aftermath of the 1971–72 budget

The 1971–72 budget was widely criticised by academic economists, financial journalists and some departmental rivals (including the Department of

Labour). What was criticised was not so much the logic of the Treasury's arguments but rather the premise upon which they were built: that demand was excessive and would, if not checked, continue to be so. In a statement attached to the budget speech the Treasury declared:

> Demand is expected to accelerate in 1971–72. In particular, a faster growth of consumer spending is likely, given a delayed impetus by the strong recent growth in money incomes and in savings. Gross private investment on dwellings should rise considerably faster than in 1970–71, and, despite moderating influences in some areas, other private investment should continue to grow overall. The financial position of the State sector will doubtless permit a very strong growth in expenditures to continue in that sector.[36]

McMahon himself noted in 1974 that the advice submitted to the government by the Treasury in 1971 was that demand would be rapid and 'demand inflation would then be superimposed on cost inflation'.[37] Most commentators, however, believed that demand had been slowing down for some time *before* the budget. Nevile, for instance, argued that 'in general ... there was a slackening of economic activity in the September quarter of 1970, and ... since then the level of activity has continued on a plateau, or if anything declined very slightly'.[38] The budget, on this view, would serve only to push the economy toward a recession. The aim of the budget, so the critics argued, should have been to supply a stimulus to economic activity, not dampen it.

Subsequent events would appear to vindicate the views of the critics. But the evidence is by no means unequivocal. If one were to consider only the GDP figures it would be difficult to detect any sign of a recession in 1971–72. What is notable in Table 7.5, however, is the marked decline in private investment expenditure in 1971–72 and its almost zero growth in the following year. Interestingly, however, consumption expenditure continued to rise, a reflection in part of the continued strong growth in wage rates. Paralleling the decline in investment expenditure was the rapid deterioration of the labour market. Seasonally adjusted unemployment rose from 1.3 per cent of the workforce in June 1971 to 1.9 per cent in June 1972 and peaked at 2.1 per cent in August 1972.

An important reason why the figures in Table 7.5 cannot easily be used to judge the significance of the 1971–72 budget is that the government's policy stance began to be reversed not long after the budget was presented. McMahon maintains that he came to the conclusion shortly after the budget was brought down that demand, as the critics claimed, was likely to flag, not soar. With the aim of stimulating expenditure, monetary policy was relaxed from October 1971, with interest rates being reduced and controls on lending removed. Then in December new grants were made to the states for the relief of unemployment in rural areas and for expenditure on schools. Additional grants to the states were announced in February 1972, following the premiers' conference. Also, contrary to Treasury advice, it was decided to restore the investment allowance for manufacturing plant and equipment (originally introduced in 1962) which had been removed early in 1971 as part of the anti-inflationary program.

Table 7.5 Expenditure on gross domestic product at constant prices, 1968–69 to 1972–73

	Private final consumption expenditure	Private gross fixed capital expenditure	Public expenditure	Gross national expenditure	Exports of goods and services	Imports of goods and services	Gross domestic product
			per cent change at average 1966–67 prices				
1968–69	5.5	9.7	0.5	8.3	7.2	3.2	9.0
1969–70	6.3	4.8	3.9	4.8	19.3	10.1	6.2
1970–71	4.2	6.4	2.5	3.6	8.5	3.1	4.6
1971–72	4.6	1.3	3.6	2.8	7.8	−2.1	4.5
1972–73	6.0	0.1	1.6	4.7	4.9	4.4	4.8

Source: Adapted from NGB Table 5.8b

The Treasury line

The government's turnaround is more readily understandable since 1972 was an election year. With unemployment at its highest for a decade, the government was anxious to be seen to be doing something to revitalise the economy. In April 1972 it was decided to reduce the personal income tax levy by 2.5 per cent and to increase pensions. Further stimulus was applied in the 1972–73 budget: pensions were raised further, transfer payments were increased, and substantial reductions in direct taxation were announced. Outlays were estimated to rise nearly twice as much as the rise in receipts.

Such stimulus was not in accord with Treasury advice. In its 1972 survey, released a month before the budget, the department made clear its opposition to any increase in the relative size of the public sector:

> while presently subdued conditions in the private sector might appear to promise ready opportunity for further public sector expansion, there would be dangers in pursuit of such a policy. Balanced development of the private and public sectors is needed to ensure growth prospects for the future... Any prescription for taking up slack in the economy through a major increase in public authority expenditures alone will distort the pattern of demand in a manner disadvantageous to the growth of the economy in the longer run.[39]

No attempt was made to support or explain these assertions, which is perhaps hardly surprising given the nature of the document. Nevertheless, the Treasury's comments are significant in that they reveal the department's philosphical bias against an enlargement of the public sector. This bias, then, was not a product of the actions of the Whitlam government. The Whitlam years simply confirmed a pre-existing stance on the desirability of maintaining 'balance' between the public and private sectors. Indeed, it has been shown in the previous chapter that such a concern had been expressed as early as the mid-1960s.

Exchange rate difficulties

While the Treasury was temporarily successful in gaining acceptance of its ideas on budgetary policy in 1971, it was much less so on the question of altering Australia's exchange rate. From 1967–68 Australia began to enjoy a string of balance-of-payments surpluses which served to push Australia's international reserves to record heights (see Table 7.6). This in turn gave rise to debate about the possible need to change Australia's exchange rate.

The rise in reserves was attributable to Australia's strong export performance and to a rapid increase in net capital inflow. Reflecting in particular the rapid increase in mining exports, overall export receipts rose in constant terms by 19.3 per cent in 1969–70 and by a further 8.5 per cent in 1970–71, considerably in excess of the rate of increase in imports (see Table 7.5). As can be seen in Table 7.7, capital inflow began its steep ascent in 1967–68. To a large degree the rise in capital inflow was a reflection of the mining boom which began in Australia in the mid-1960s. The mining industry proved

Heightened inflation

Table 7.6 Official reserve assets, 1968–69 to 1972–73

1968–69	$ million 1420
1969–70	1538
1970–71	2280
1971–72	3764
1972–73	4248

Source: Adapted from NGB Table 1.19

Table 7.7 Net apparent inflow of capital 1966–67 to 1972–73

1966–67	$ million 539
1967–68	1225
1968–69	1162
1969–70	757
1970–71	1402
1971–72	1834
1972–73	385

Source: Adapted from NGB Table 1.16

voracious in its desire for funds, whether from home or abroad, to help finance the very large capital expenditures associated with discovering and exploiting mineral resources. The rise in capital inflow was related also, however, to speculative movements in anticipation of the US dollar being devalued and, from the early 1970s, in anticipation of the Australian dollar being revalued.

Shortly before Christmas 1971 the LCP coalition was plunged into a bitter debate about Australia's exchange rate. The immediate cause of the debate was the Smithsonian Agreement of mid-December 1971 which saw, among other things, the US dollar devalued against gold by 7.9 per cent, the pound sterling effectively revalued against the US dollar by 8.6 per cent, and the Japanese yen revalued against the US dollar by 16.9 per cent. Since the Australian currency was fixed in terms of the pound sterling, it was widely thought that Australia, too, would revalue against the US dollar by 8.6 per cent so as to maintain parity. But this was something which the Country Party triumvirate of Doug Anthony, Ian Sinclair and Peter Nixon firmly opposed. They were keen to leave the exchange rate unaltered — a strategy much favoured by exporters and by domestic manufacturing firms competing with imports. Against this view, Snedden and his department insisted on the need for a full 8.6 revaluation. Anything less, so it was argued, would lead to retaliatory action by the United States and Japan and would have a seriously detrimental effect on the domestic inflation rate. Further, such a decision, by leaving the Australian dollar clearly undervalued, would lead to speculative capital pouring into the country. After a protracted and acrimonious series of cabinet meetings it was decided, first, to abandon the traditional link with sterling and henceforth to tie the Australian currency to the US dollar and, second, as a compromise, to revalue the Australian dollar against the US dollar by 6.3 per cent. This meant of course an effective devaluation against sterling. It meant also an overall devaluation of 1.75 per cent against Australia's main trading partners.

The three days of discussions highlighted the economic and philosophical differences between the coalition partners and revealed in particular the Country Party's narrow sectional interests. Much to McMahon's chagrin, he and Snedden were portrayed by the press as being weak-kneed in the face of Country Party bullying: much was made of the fact that the Country Party had threatened to walk out of the coalition if it did not get its way. But more important was the fact that the Country Party's dogmatism on the question of variations in the exchange rate put an effective end to any further discussions on the topic. This was despite the fact that Australia's international reserves continued to soar: they increased by a staggering $1544 million in 1971–72. With a revaluation out of the question, the LCP government attempted to reduce net capital inflow by the introduction in September 1972 of an embargo on overseas borrowings of two years or less. The overall effect on reserves, however, was minimal.

Effective action to deal with Australia's excessively high international reserves was not taken until after the Labor Party's victory in the December elections. In late December the new government announced that the Australian dollar had been revalued by 4.85 per cent against the US dollar. Less than two months later, in February 1973, the US dollar was devalued against gold. Australia did not follow suit, thereby effectively revaluing the Australian dollar once again — this time by 11.1 per cent. (In terms of Australia's main trading partners, the revaluations were 7.5 per cent and 4 per cent.) These exchange rate measures were supplemented by the introduction in December 1972 of what was called the variable deposit requirement (VDR) which obliged anyone borrowing overseas (with a maturity of more than two years) to deposit a portion of the amount borrowed, interest-free, with the Reserve Bank. Initially the VDR was set at 25 per cent. In October 1973 the VDR was increased to 33 per cent. Another key initiative was the decision of the Labor government in July 1973 to reduce tariffs across the board by 25 per cent. In terms of its impact on import prices, the tariff cut was equivalent to a revaluation of 2.5 per cent. Another effective revaluation occurred in September 1973, with the Australian dollar appreciating by 5 per cent against the US dollar.

It will be seen in the next chapter that these measures were not immediately effective in checking the growth of reserves. During 1972–73 reserves continued to rise rapidly, creating in Australia highly liquid conditions — conditions which were to contribute to an escalation in the rate of inflation.

Inflationary expectations and the abandonment of Keynesian meliorism

A novel feature of the Australian economy in 1971–72 was that, just as GNE slowed down and unemployment rose, inflation increased to nearly 7 per cent.

Heightened inflation

This was Australia's first taste of stagflation. The Phillips curve, not surprisingly, came under much greater scrutiny and doubts began to be expressed about its validity. How was it possible, it was asked, that rising inflation and rising unemployment could coexist?

One economist who had an answer was Milton Friedman. An event of great significance in the development of postwar economic thought was Friedman's presidential address to the American Economics Association in December 1967.[40] Friedman's address paid particular attention to two concepts: the so-called natural unemployment rate and inflationary expectations. Friedman's aim was to show, using these concepts, that the prognosis of the Phillips curve was faulty. To be more specific, his intention was to show that any trade-off between inflation and unemployment could only be short-term — a transitory phenomenon which lasted only as long as economic agents confused the money wage rate with the real wage rate. There could be no trade-off in the long term.

Since the department was to emphasise inflationary expectations throughout the 1970s, it is necessary to understand the nature of Friedman's arguments and to note his policy conclusions. It may be useful to deal first with the concept of natural unemployment. Friedman's analysis of unemployment involved a rehabilitation of classical doctrines in that he focused on the role of variations in real wages in bringing about equality of supply and demand in the labour market. The natural unemployment rate is, among other things, the level of unemployment at which the supply and demand of labour are brought into equilibrium. It was and is Friedman's contention that market forces will always operate, through changes in the real wage rate, to return unemployment to its natural rate (that is, to full employment equilibrium).

Much of Friedman's address was concerned with analysing the economic implications of governmental attempts to achieve arbitrarily selected unemployment levels. He sought to show in particular what would happen if the government proves *persistent* in its attempts to maintain unemployment below the natural rate. According to Friedman, the result would be not only an increase in the inflation rate but the onset of inflationary expectations: economic agents, now much more sensitive to price changes, will come to *expect* a certain inflation rate. Moreover, they will incorporate this expectation in all money-wage negotiations (adding say 3 per cent — if this is the expected inflation rate — to the base figure of their demands). But in doing so (assuming they are successful in their negotiations and therefore their actions lead to cost and hence price increases), they will in fact push the actual inflation rate above the expected rate. Expectations of inflation will, in such a situation, then be revised upwards. This will continue to happen each time it becomes clear that the actual rate of inflation has exceeded the excepted. Hence such expectations are described as adaptive or error-learning expectations. And so the process continues — *provided* the government persists in trying to maintain unemployment at a particular point below the natural rate — with inflation accelerating. The stable relationship between a particular rate of inflation and a particular rate of unemployment, as postulated by the Phillips curve, will soon vanish.

Whereas, say, a 3 per cent unemployment rate was associated with an inflation rate of 6 per cent, it will over time, because of inflationary expectations, become associated with an ever-higher inflation rate. A stable inflation rate can only occur if unemployment is at its natural rate. The natural rate, then, to provide another definition, is that level of unemployment where the expected and actual rate of inflation are the same (and hence where expectations do not need to be, and will not be, revised upward).

One implication of Friedman's analysis was that the ability of governments to alter real variables is strictly limited. For they can do so only as long as people misread economic signals: governments can only alter the real level of employment and output as long as economic agents continue to make systematic errors in their assessment of the expected inflation rate. The one positive and enduring contribution the government can make is to halt the rise in inflation. Just as it is the government's fault that inflation emerged in the first place, so too is it the case that the government can reduce and eventually eradicate inflation. The monetarist solution to inflation posited by Friedman has been neatly summarised by Trevithick:

> Since inflation is the result of past and present attempts by governments to over-utilize the productive capacity of the economy through the issue of new money, inflation can only be reduced by cutting the rate of monetary expansion. The objective of price stability can only be achieved by allowing the supply of money to grow at a rate equal to the rate of growth of real income. Nor will a policy of monetary restraint be without its painful side-effects for it implies a considerable period of *under-utilization* of capacity and high unemployment. Inflation can only be successfully tackled by reversing the direction of the policies which produced the inflation in the first place. A regime of strict monetary restraint will therefore be accompanied by unemployment rates in excess of the natural rate, for it is only thus that the necessary erosion of inflationary expectations can occur. If the government is determined to conquer inflation, it must be prepared to stomach the unpopular consequences implicit in a policy of monetary contraction. An inflationary binge will inevitably be followed by a deflationary hangover.'[41]

In short, Friedman's message was that governments have to stop attempting to reduce unemployment below its natural rate; the actual inflation rate has to be reduced below the expected inflation rate; in order to achieve this, governments have to bring about a progressive (but not sudden and drastic) reduction in expenditure by reducing the rate of growth of the money supply; and that inevitably, as part of this process, unemployment will rise. As Friedman remarks, high unemployment is 'a temporary side effect of curing inflation.'[42]

Before investigating the Treasury's growing interest in inflationary expectations, it seems appropriate to discuss here the ideas of another brand of monetarism, sometimes called Monetarism Mark II, but usually designated the rational expectations school. This school came into prominence, particularly in the United States, during the second half of the 1970s. Adherents to the school argue that, through long experience of inflation, economic agents can

Heightened inflation

readily differentiate between relative and absolute changes. But more importantly, they argue that economic agents have come to formulate for themselves the 'correct theory' of what determines price changes (and indeed the changes of any other variable). Invariably it is assumed that the theory which has been adopted is the monetarist: economic agents have come to realise that any action which increases the rate of growth of the money supply will inevitably lead to an increase in prices. And they have come to realise that money does not affect real variables. Further, it is argued that agents act more or less immediately upon the conclusions derived from their monetarist theory. They do not wait until the actual rate of inflation differs from the expected before deciding to act. Instead, they will immediately raise prices in response to any governmental action which leads to an increase in the growth of the money supply, making use of all the information available to determine with precision the effect of the government's actions.

Three of the implications of this theory should be noted. First, price adjustments occur so quickly that markets are always clear: the economy is always in Walrasian equilibrium (which in turn implies that any unemployment can only be voluntary). This contrasts with the Friedmanite version, which fits into the 'imperfectionist' category — the main obstacle to the establishment of equilibrium being the expectational errors of economic agents. The implication, however, is that, since these errors stem from inappropriate governmental action, the system will readily achieve stable equilibrium once governments desist from trying to reduce unemployment below its natural rate and pursue consistent policies. In rational expectations theory, by contrast, expectations do not constitute an imperfection. In fact, as Eatwell and Milgate put it, 'the rational expectations hypothesis removes the role of expectations as far as the determination of the long-run position of the economy is concerned; this is left to be characterised in terms of dominant behavioural relations which are specified independently of uncertainty'.[43] Second, government policy cannot affect real variables, even temporarily. In other words, Keynesian policies which attempt to regulate aggregate demand are ineffective. Indeed, as Hahn points out, if the world operates as the rational expectationists claim that it does, there is 'no need for Keynesian policies even if they could be used effectively. Nor is there an a priori ground for wanting the government to iron out the equilibrium fluctuations'.[44] Third, the cure for inflation need not be as 'painful' and as protracted as Monetarists Mark I would suggest. For provided the government makes clear its intention to bring about a progressive reduction in the rate of growth of the money supply, and provided that it can demonstrate that its intentions are genuine, appropriate changes in absolute prices will occur quickly.

The influence of the rational expectations school on Treasury thought will be discussed in the next chapter. For now, attention is drawn to the influence of inflationary expectations theory on the Treasury in the period up to 1972. Apparently, the Treasury immediately took notice of Friedman's message. The notion of inflationary expectations was first mentioned in the 1969 survey. The Treasury noted that:

The Treasury line

The danger, once costs and prices begin to climb faster, is that business and other calculations will be based on inflationary expectations. People will then be less disposed to hold money or invest in fixed interest securities. They will be quicker to spend ahead of expected price rises which the faster spending will help to bring about. The demand for funds to spend will build up and will not be much checked by higher borrowing costs.[45]

In a confidential paper on the national wage case of 1970 the Treasury complained that the decision would have a harmful effect on inflationary expectations.[46] In its 1971 survey it argued that the experience of overfull employment in a number of countries during the second half of the 1960s 'led to inflationary expectations being firmly implanted in business and labour attitudes'.[47] In the 1972 survey, with Australia experiencing stagflation, the notion of inflationary expectations was considered at length. The Treasury noted:

> What ... seem to have changed in recent years are the attitudes and expectations of the parties to wage negotiations. Expectations have probably always been a part of the wage bargaining process, tending to change with the ups and downs of the business cycle. In recent times, however, there may have been a change in expectations of a more far-reaching kind. In particular, expectations may now be reflecting the self-perpetuating and accelerating potentialities of quickened inflation... It may be, too, that both employers and unions have only recently begun to assess the full implications which a full employment economy holds for the bargaining process. With expectations changing in both these ways, both parties to wage negotiations may approach them in a different frame of mind than heretofore. In that sense, the present context is very different from that of the period from which the data leading to the early Phillips analysis were drawn.[48]

What were the policy implications of the onset of inflationary expectations? In its discussion of it in the 1969 survey the Treasury concluded by arguing that 'such psychological reactions can hinder the operation of counter-inflationary measures. The importance of timeliness in the dampening of inflationary trends should thus need no emphasis'.[49] In this the Treasury seemed to be suggesting that inflationary expectations could be prevented by general measures to dampen the inflationary process provided such measures were taken promptly enough. In its paper on the national wage case decision of 1970, however, the Treasury declared: 'although the objective elements in the situation must be the prime target of counter measures, it is important also to take steps of a kind which will counter the development of an inflationary psychology in Australia.'[50] The implication was that even if excess demand conditions were removed, and even if the measures were introduced promptly, it might be necessary to continue the policy of deflation in order to eradicate all remnants of an inflationary psychology. As the Treasury confided in the paper,

> the longer inflationary trends persist the more entrenched ... expectations become, and the more difficult they are to eradicate. As recent experience overseas has shown, it can require very strong measures indeed — *much stronger than would be needed to cope with the objective elements of inflation alone* — to make a substantial impact on the rate of increase in prices once such expectations become widely established.[51]

Heightened inflation

A somewhat similar argument was presented in the 1972 survey. In a discussion of whether the Phillips curve was dead, the Treasury noted that in a situation in which demand was high in relation to available resources and in which unemployment was low, high wage increases would almost certainly occur. It therefore followed 'that excess demand must be removed before policies *of any sort* can become effective in combatting the ensuing inflation'.[52] The department continued:

> the fact that, once an accelerating wage-price trend has become established, the removal of excess demand does not lead to an early significant slackening in the rate of wage and price increases does not imply that, in the absence of action to remove excess demand, the wage-price trend would not have gone on accelerating. The substitution of a high but relatively constant rate of inflation for such an accelerating trend will not be all that is desirable, but it will be a worthwhile advance in its own right.

Thus, as a corollary of the belief that inflation now required much stronger measures 'than would be needed to cope with the objective elements of inflation alone', the Treasury was arguing that deflationary policies should continue to be pursued even if the inflation rate appeared merely to stabilise rather than decline.

What can also be seen in the passage above is the acceptance of the Friedmanite notion that the reduction of inflation would necessarily involve the protracted use of deflationary policies. In the same vein, the Treasury declared at the conclusion of its 1972 survey: 'the prospects of an early return to the conditions of the 'sixties, when strong growth, exceptionally full employment and relative stability in the price level were all achieved with what seems in retrospect remarkable ease, seem remote'. This was to become an enduring Treasury theme (and undoubtedly a valid one): there are no quick and easy solutions anymore to the eradication of economic instability; the fight will necessarily take time.

There is always a risk of reading too much into Treasury documents by taking advantage of hindsight. Further, there is always a need for caution in making generalisations about Treasury attitudes, in that obviously not all Treasury officers will agree with the views presented in published departmental documents. Nevertheless, the views expressed in the 1972 survey suggest a pessimistic shift in the department's social philosophy, a shift seen also in the department's description of trade union behaviour and attitudes and in its denigration of the idea of the possibility of social consensus. There was now much less scope for reliance on trust and persuasion, on cooperation and the autonomous exercise of self-discipline. It would seem, then, that the early 1970s saw in the Treasury the breakdown of the optimistic, meliorist, (some would suggest naive) progressive view of human nature central to the Keynesian model. It saw also, though not explicitly, the disbandment by the Treasury of the notion that it was the government's responsibility to provide a safe, secure environment in which the maintenance of an arbitrarily defined level of full employment was guaranteed. Full employment and other protective pledges had created not only indiscipline but an environment in which inflationary expectations could fester. A stronger, more efficient and less inflation-ridden economy required that such pledges be done away with — a point which will be explored in more detail in the next chapter.

The Treasury, it might be added, can hardly be criticised for becoming wary of the notion of cooperation and voluntary restraint (and of the meliorist assumptions upon which it was based). There can be no doubt that by the end of the 1960s there had indeed occurred an attitudinal shift on the part of organised labour, a shift reflected in the interrelated upsurge in industrial unrest and rising wage demands. Such phenomena suggested unmistakably that the position of those who placed their faith entirely in the power of reasoned argument and the malleability of human nature was becoming increasingly tenuous. The question which Australia faced by the early 1970s was: given that there had been a shift in attitudes, one that had involved a growing determination and impatience to achieve absolute and relative wage rises, to restore a degree of wage restraint? The different answers to this question reflected not merely differing beliefs on the efficacy of market forces and on the desirability and effectiveness of direct government intervention. Fundamentally, the answer depended on different assessments of human nature and its capacity for change. While it is easy to condemn the Treasury for choosing to seek wage restraint through the use of what might appear to be punitive action (an active deflationary policy), the fact remains that the basis for believing in the main alternative — an incomes-prices policy — had become increasingly slim. By the beginning of the 1970s Australia was beginning to feel the full force of what Fred Hirsch, in his *Social Limits to Growth* (1977), has variously described as social scarcity and the paradox of affluence — the built-in frustration accompanying the growth process in advanced societies. Greater prosperity, together with improved communications, had the increasingly disruptive effect of simultaneously raising the expectations and aspirations of those lower on the social scale (increasing in particular their desire for 'positional goods and services' — such things as education to achieve prestigious jobs and housing in exclusive areas) while making increasingly difficult the fulfilment of these expectations (positional goods being by their very nature available only to a minority). As the problem of social scarcity became more evident, so too did its manifestations — higher inflation and increased frustration — and, gloomy that it may be, the more realistic did a Hobbesian model (of man versus man) become.

8

Economic instability and neoclassical resurgence, 1973–79

THE neoclassical synthesis, by definition, was a symbol of accord. It was heralded as a reconciliation of Keynesian and neoclassical analysis. Within this synthesised framework, its progenitors hoped, the economics profession would be largely free of dissension — at least over basics. The synthesis was a truce, a commonly accepted set of principles, 'truths', under which economists could pursue their scientific endeavours, produce hard facts, and avoid silly ideological differences. Samuelson proudly declared in 1955 when he unveiled the synthesis: 'In recent years 90 per cent of American economists have stopped being "Keynesian economists" or "anti-Keynesian economists". Instead they have worked toward a synthesis of whatever is valuable in older economics and in modern theories of income determination.' Samuelson claimed that the synthesis was 'accepted in its broad outlines by all but about 5 per cent of extreme left-wing and right-wing writers'.[1] Whether such claims could have been made about Australia is open to debate. But certainly surveying the literature it is difficult to find many instances of fundamental disagreement between academic economists before the mid-1960s. The publication from 1962 onwards of *Australian Economic Papers* could perhaps be seen as reflecting the emergence of an alternative body of opinion; but it really was not until the 1970s that it proved to be an important vehicle for Australian post-Keynesians to air their discordant views. As late as 1972 Nevile and Stammer could point to the broad agreement prevailing among members of the Australian economics profession. They argued that 'Australian economists ... are mostly confirmed Keynesians' — by which they meant that nearly all Australian economists believed firmly in the need for an active (discretionary) fiscal policy.[2]

In contrast to the apparent state of harmony among Australian economists, the neoclassical synthesis began to crumble in both the United States and

Britain from the mid-1960s. In part the dissolution of the synthesis was due to the battering from those more purely neoclassical — a battering often referred to as the 'monetarist counter-revolution' and led by Milton Friedman. The counter-revolutionaries sought not only to destroy Keynes' policy prescriptions but to rehabilitate the quantity theory of money and the deterministic and self-equilibrating view of the world which underpinned it. In part also, and it was this which proved particularly damaging, the dissolution of the synthesis was due to the onset of stagflation. This not only did wonders for Friedman's professional prestige, given his forewarnings in December 1967, but destroyed what had come to be a central element in the synthesis — the Phillips curve. By the mid-1970s the synthesis had disintegrated.

This is not to say that suddenly the profession was filled with disbelievers in the possibility of combining elements of the Keynesian model with the neoclassical. Rather, it is to say that those whose understanding of the economy and whose policy prescriptions were based on trade-off notions, those who took for granted that unemployment could be dealt with by increasing expenditure and budgeting for deficits, were thrown into disarray. Some doggedly maintained their faith, some were left unsure what to believe, some turned to Monetarism Mark I or Mark II, others turned to balanced-budget principles and argued that the economy had been the victim of a gargantuan public sector, a plethora of regulations and a greedy trade union movement. In the main, however, while Keynesian policy ideas were subject to serious questioning, it continued to be generally acknowledged that aggregate demand was an important determinant of the level of economic activity.

Reviewing the Australian situation in the 1970s, Hagger distinguishes three phases in the discussion of fiscal policy and its role in combating inflation and thereby provides a guide to the disintegration of the synthesis. The first was the trade-off phase (continuing on from the 1960s), during which it was taken for granted that fiscal policy could readily be used to exploit a short-term trade-off between inflation and unemployment. Sometime in 1973, however, this phase gave way to an incomes-policy phase — a phase referred to in the previous chapter and one which lasted until the end of 1974. Hagger argues that during this phase 'fiscal policy was seen in a new light as a device for bolstering wage and price restraint — a way of *improving* the short-run trade-off between inflation and unemployment, rather than *exploiting* that trade-off'.[3] He suggests that the change in emphasis reflected the view that to bring about any significant reduction in the inflation rate would necessarily have entailed unemployment rising to a socially unacceptable level. Apparently, however, Australian economists were continuing to assume that some sort of trade-off existed. The third phase was an expectations phase, in which fiscal policy was seen as contributing to the task of reducing the *expected* inflation rate and hence the actual rate. This change in attitude, Hagger argues, reflected the growing influence of the rational expectations school, whose belief that there is no trade-off was noted in the previous chapter.

While it is important to be aware of these three phases, perhaps the more significant feature of the 1970s was the extent of disagreement which arose. It was here that the dissolution of the synthesis was most apparent. By the end of the 1970s, as Nevile points out, some economists had come to the conclusion that fiscal policy was dead. Most, however, continued to accord fiscal policy a valuable role in macroeconomic management. But just what form this role should take was a source of great debate:

> The trouble is that different groups give diametrically opposed advice about appropriate fiscal policy to combat stagflation. On the one hand it is argued that fiscal policy should aim to balance the budget (or at least to reduce the deficit as much as possible) either in order to reduce inflationary expectations and restore confidence or in order to reduce interest rates. An opposing view is that fiscal policy should fight inflation by cutting taxes either to reduce costs or to increase productivity. Another view is that fiscal policy should be used to increase output, at least moderately, with the strategy to reduce inflation built around prices and incomes policies.[4]

What path did Treasury thought take in the 1970s? In terms of Hagger's three phases, the answer is that the Treasury bypassed the second phase and moved directly from the first to the third. In terms of Nevile's competing groups, it saw the Treasury take the lead in arguing that the role of fiscal policy was to reduce inflationary expectations and restore confidence by moving toward budget equilibrium. In terms of the models outlined in chapter 2, the period saw the Treasury move ever closer toward a purely neoclassical viewpoint. The department came to the view that the rise in unemployment from 1974 onwards was largely a reflection of inappropriately high real wages. In such circumstances, the Treasury reasoned, expansionary policies would not relieve unemployment; they would serve only to increase it. The prevailing assumption was that there was no trade-off between inflation and unemployment; instead, more inflation simply led to more unemployment.

Economic conditions and policies: the Whitlam years

By early 1973 the Australian economy was enjoying buoyant conditions. Demand was rising strongly. The growth in demand was stimulated in part by the highly liquid conditions prevailing, a reflection in turn of the continued rise of international reserves (during 1972–73 Australia's reserves increased by a further $1079 million) and the progressive relaxation of monetary policy from late in 1971. Both of these factors permitted a great increase in bank lending: having risen by $278 million in 1971–72, trading bank advances increased by $1238 million in 1972–73. Demand was stimulated also by a powerful international commodity boom in 1972 and 1973. Australia's export price index rose by nearly 29 per cent in 1972–73 (with the wool index rising by 148.6 per cent and meat by 21.1 per cent). For the first time since 1956–57, Australia managed to record a surplus on its current account (a creditable $691 million). For Australia's exporters this meant, of course, a very substantial increase in income. Demand was stimulated also by further wage rises:

although the rise was slower than in the previous two years, average weekly earnings still rose by a relatively high 9 per cent in 1972–73.

Another factor contributing to the buoyancy of the Australian economy in 1973 was the strong growth of government expenditure. Mention has been made already of the overgenerous pre-election budget of 1972. The new Labor government proved even more spendthrift. After 23 years in opposition, bristling with ideas about how to improve Australian society by legislative initiative, and committed to a greatly expanded role for the public sector, Labor found it difficult to exercise expenditure restraint. Commonwealth government outlays increased by 12.6 per cent in 1972–73 and then, as can be seen in Table 8.1, leapt by 19.4 per cent in 1973–74.

Table 8.1 Commonwealth government outlays, receipts and deficit, 1973–74 to 1979–80

	Outlays	Receipts	Deficit	
	% change	% change	$ million	% to GDP
1973–74	19.4	25.6	293	0.6
1974–75	45.9	28.0	2566	4.2
1975–76	22.5	19.7	3585	4.9
1976–77	10.3	17.0	2740	3.3
1977–78	10.8	9.5	3333	3.7
1978–79	8.5	9.1	3478	3.4
1979–80	9.1	16.0	2034	1.8

Source: Adapted from Norton *Deterioration of Economic Performance* Table 4A.2

The extent to which the fiscal actions of the Whitlam government stimulated the economy during 1973–74 has been a source of considerable debate. For while outlays increased rapidly, receipts rose even more quickly, with the result that the budget deficit was reduced to under $300 million. There was in fact a domestic budget surplus. The increase in receipts was not due, however, to an increase in income tax: Labor was constrained by an election promise not to alter income tax. The rise in receipts was a reflection instead of inflation and the remarkable increase in wages which occurred during 1973–74, both of which will be discussed shortly.

Even if Labor's fiscal actions during 1973–74 are deemed largely neutral, as Barry Hughes claims,[5] the fact remains that the situation called for neither expansion nor neutrality but for a restrictive stance. For Australia found itself by the second half of the year in the midst of a powerful boom. Demand rose much more quickly than available supplies, something reflected in the fact that while GNE rose by 9.6 per cent in 1973–74, GDP rose by only 4.2 per cent (see Table 8.2). Fred Gruen argues that 'the demand pressures operating during the 1973–74 boom were of a greater intensity than Australia had experienced for at least fifteen years and perhaps greater than we had experienced since World War II'.[6] Clearly, the imperative need in this sort of inflationary situation was for measures of restraint.

Table 8.2 Expenditure and production at constant prices, 1973–74 to 1979–80

	Private final consumption expenditure	Private gross fixed capital expenditure	Public expenditure	Gross national expenditure	Exports of goods and services	Imports of goods and services	Gross domestic product
				per cent change at average 1966–67 prices			
1973–74	5.2	3.4	4.4	9.6	−5.5	27.3	4.2
1974–75	3.0	−10.8	9.7	1.0	6.9	2.7	1.6
1975–76	3.1	4.4	5.4	0.7	4.2	5.1	2.4
1976–77	2.4	2.7	1.0	3.2	7.7	9.9	2.8
1977–78	1.4	−2.2	3.8	−0.4	2.4	4.5	0.9
1978–79	3.2	10.0	1.4	5.1	5.8	8.8	4.6
1979–80	1.9	1.1	0.2	−0.3	7.8	1.1	1.3

Source: Adapted from Norton *Deterioration of Economic Performance* Table 4A.12

In its 1973 survey, released in August, the Treasury noted that the demand for labour was 'booming' and that the labour market was becoming increasingly tighter. Perhaps the best indicator of this was the fact that at the end of June registered unfilled vacancies were, in seasonally adjusted terms, at their highest level since 1954. As early as April overtime working by factory employees had reached a level equal to the highest recorded.

And yet a curious thing happened in 1973–74. Throughout the postwar period it had always been the case that the higher unfilled vacancies went, the lower were the number registered as unemployed. But as the Treasury pointed out in its 1973 survey, although unemployment dropped sharply between August 1972 and February 1973, it had remained 'virtually unchanged' since then. While vacancies continued to rise during the first half of 1974, unemployment declined only marginally. Barry Hughes argues that such was the level of unfilled vacancies in mid-1974 that, if one were to use past results as a guide, the number registered as unemployed should have been approximately 25 000 to 30 000. Instead, the actual level of unemployment was around 80 000.[7] Similarly, the Treasury recognised in its 1973 survey that 'a very strong demand for labour is associated with a higher level of unemployment than has been customary in the past in otherwise similar circumstances'.[8] In explaining why this had happened, the Treasury admitted that the reasons were 'not entirely clear'. But it was convinced that there was 'undoubtedly an element of structural imbalance involved. Certain categories of labour are no longer required in the same locations as before'. But this only begs the question: why was it that certain employees were now no longer required? No answer was provided. Another relevant consideration, the department noted, was that the evidence of overseas experience indicated that 'an important factor causing "hard core" unemployment to rise is the effect of rising wages on employers' calculations of their requirements of labour, particularly unskilled labour'. But exactly how employers' calculations had changed and how this might affect the demand for labour was not explained.

Two other factors which have been put forward to explain the changed relationship between unfilled vacancies and the number of unemployed are the substantially higher level of unemployment benefits granted by the Whitlam government and the sharp reduction in the migrant intake in the early 1970s. In February 1972 the McMahon government increased unemployment benefits by 70 per cent for adults and by 83 per cent for those in 18–20 years age group. Unemployment benefits continued to rise relatively rapidly under Labor. Perhaps more significant though was the Whitlam government's decision in March 1973 to abolish separate unemployment rates for those in the 16–17 and 18–20 years age groups and to institute a single rate for all those qualifying for unemployment benefits. It may have been the case that these changes encouraged young people either to opt for unemployment benefits instead of seeking employment or to prolong their search for a suitable job. But the significance of the increase in benefits remains shrouded in doubt. Certainly, however, it must be judged a negligible factor in the period after 1974 since this period saw a marked slowing down in the rate of increase in benefits, the abandonment from November 1975 of indexation of benefits for those aged 16–17 years, and the taxation of benefits from 1976.

There can be little doubt, however, about the importance of the reduced migrant intake in 1972 and 1973. The Treasury noted in its 1973 survey that there had been a 'dramatic' decline in net migration. From a figure of 123 000 in 1970, net migration fell to 85 000 in 1971 and had then collapsed to only 28 000 in 1972.[9] The fall in net migration was a major contributor to the appearance of labour shortages. Those industries which had come to rely heavily on migrants as a source of labour — notably the vehicle, iron and steel and building industries — were placed in great difficulty.

Not only were there critical labour shortages during the 1973–74 boom but also severe shortages of materials. The problem arose largely as a result of difficulties in obtaining goods and services from overseas (which in turn was related to the boom in international trade and the disturbances to shipping in the wake of the quadrupling of oil prices late in 1973). It was also due to the high level of industrial stoppages in Australia. Working days lost more than doubled between 1972–73 and 1973–74, rising from 2573 million to 5426 million — a record level. Faced with these shortages, producers began to overorder on a substantial scale — a development which was later to create severe difficulties.

In these circumstances, it was perhaps not surprising that prices and wages accelerated sharply. In 1973–74 the consumer price index rose by 13 per cent while the implicit price deflator for GDP increased by nearly 15 per cent (see Table 8.3 for the CPI figures). The change in both indicators was a reflection of the force of the boom and the extent of excess demand. During 1973 the rise in the CPI was a reflection also, however, of a rapid increase in the price of foodstuffs. And both indicators were influenced by the rise in the price of imports (a reflection in turn of booming conditions in a number of major economies and of OPEC's oil price decision in December 1973). In addition, the increases were a delayed response to earlier wage rises.

More significant than the rise in prices was the rise in wages which occurred in 1974. Australia was subject to a wages explosion: having increased by 14.8 per cent in 1973, average weekly earnings leapt in seasonally adjusted terms by 28 per cent in 1974 (see also Table 8.4). The wages explosion was a

Table 8.3 Consumer price index, 1973–74 to 1979–80

	per cent change
1973–74	12.9
1974–75	16.7
1975–76	13.0
1976–77	13.8
1977–78	9.5
1978–79	8.2
1979–80	10.2

Source: Adapted from Norton *Deterioration in Economic Performance* Table 4A.13

Table 8.4 Wages, 1973–74 to 1979–80

	Award wages		Average weekly earnings, males
	Adult females	Adult males	
1973–74	25.3	18.2	16.2
1974–75	39.7	30.5	25.4
1975–76	20.1	14.9	14.4
1976–77	13.8	12.9	12.4
1977–78	9.3	9.2	9.9
1978–79	5.8	6.5	7.7
1979–80	7.4	8.7	9.9

Source: Adapted from Norton *Deterioration in Economic Performance* Table 4A.10

reflection of a whole range of interrelated factors: the tight labour market conditions; the desire of workers to raise wages above the existing and expected inflation rate and to seek protection against a remarkable increase in interest rates; the improved bargaining power of trade unions and their successful use of increased strike activity; the official encouragement of wage rises by the Whitlam government and in particular its determination to achieve the implementation of equal pay as rapidly as possible; and the willingness of certain industries — notably vehicles, iron and steel and transport — to offer sufficiently high wages to overcome desperate labour shortages and buy industrial peace.

In dealing with this inflationary situation, Labor looked to non-fiscal measures to supply restraint. During most of 1973 Labor's key anti-inflationary initiatives were the external measures noted in the previous chapter: the exchange rate appreciations of December 1972 and February and September 1973; the use of the variable deposit ratio (which was raised to 33 per cent in October 1973); and the 25 per cent cut in tariffs in July. Most of these measures were designed primarily to prevent the continued rise in Australia's international reserves. They were anti-inflationary, however, in that a reduction in reserves would reduce liquidity and in that they would reduce the imbalance between demand and supply by encouraging a higher level of imports. Also, the reduction in import prices would have the effect of increasing competitive pressures on Australian producers. None of these measures, however, could be expected to have an immediate effect on the inflationary situation. All tended to operate rather slowly. And none acted to reduce demand directly. As anti-inflationary measures they were subject to the same sorts of criticisms as those levelled at the removal of import quotas in 1960.

Apart from these external measures the Whitlam government introduced a rather novel anti-inflationary device in 1973: the Prices Justification Tribunal (PJT). The PJT came into operation in August 1973. Those companies coming within its jurisdiction were required to notify the tribunal of impending price rises and then to justify them publicly. Just how successful the PJT was in restraining price rises has been much debated. Neville Norman has concluded that the actions of the PJT reduced inflation by somewhere between one and two percentage points. He notes also, however, that to the extent that the PJT was successful in reducing price rises in the face of rapidly increasing costs, it had the effect of squeezing the profits of a number of industries.

The weapon which Labor came to place the heaviest reliance on was monetary policy. The Treasury noted in August 1973 that financial conditions were 'generally easy', this despite the fact that a call had been made to statutory reserve deposits in April. Another call, however, had been made in July, to become effective in August. The Treasury declared: 'Other things being equal, a harder monetary policy permits an easier fiscal policy, and vice versa. Obviously higher interest rates, which tend to accompany a hardening monetary policy, bring with them costs; on the other hand, by shifting private sector preferences from spending on real assets to spending on financial assets, higher interest rates can make room for an increased level of public sector spending.'[10] The message was designed to appeal to the Whitlam government: if fiscal policy was not going to be used to apply restraint then the only alternative was to implement a much tighter monetary policy. The message was accepted and from September 1973 interest rates began to rise sharply, while in the same month the Australian dollar was revalued once again. By mid-1974 interest rates had reached unprecedented heights. Compounded by a reversal in Australia's balance-of-payments position (which saw international reserves decline by $384 million after six years of continuous growth), the economy was subject to a particularly severe credit squeeze in the second and third quarters of 1974. The extent of the squeeze is evident even in the annual figures. As can be seen in Table 8.5, M3 rose by 14.5 cent in 1973–74 (compared with 25.7 per cent in 1972–73) and M1 increased by only 2.3 per cent (compared with 26.3 per cent the previous year).

The credit squeeze must be judged a major cause of the recession which developed in mid-1974. But it was by no means the sole cause. Gruen notes: 'The speed of the upswing [in 1973–74] had been so great, the shortages of materials so widespread and the consequent over-ordering so substantial both locally and overseas that a major recession was probably inevitable by the time

Table 8.5 Money supply, 1972–73 to 1979–80

	Per cent change	
	M1	M3
1972–73	26.3	25.7
1973–74	2.3	14.5
1974–75	12.6	15.4
1975–76	14.1	14.4
1976–77	8.4	11.0
1977–78	8.6	8.0
1978–79	16.7	11.8
1979–80	12.9	12.3

Source: Adapted from NGB, Table 3.3

Labor was re-elected in May 1974 (though this was not foreseen at the time).'[11] The extent to which business stocks accumulated in 1974 was unprecedented. Gruen notes also that the stock build-up was some 35 per cent greater than the previous peak — recorded in the mid-1960s. In explaining its scale, he suggests that during the first half of the year it 'was probably a conscious scramble to build up stocks and for the second half a dire necessity which took many traders to the brink of insolvency and beyond'. An additional factor responsible for the recession was the profits squeeze which occurred during 1974. While the wages explosion was clearly the dominant factor contributing to the profits squeeze, what was significant also was the environment in which the explosion occurred: the sudden appearance of weak markets (which made it difficult to convert cost increases into price rises), the restraints imposed by the PJT, the great difficulties in obtaining finance, and the much more severe competition provided by imports. The sudden economic downturn in most of the industrialised west in 1974 did not, it would seem, contribute significantly to the onset of recession in Australia. The international recession proved to be more significant in prolonging rather than initiating Australia's economic difficulties.

The recession was soon reflected in the unemployment rate. In the March quarter of 1974 registered unemployment stood at 85 000, declined to 82 000 in the June quarter, then jumped to 123 000 in the September quarter, and by the December quarter had climbed to 214 000. It was to climb higher. Here was a turning-point in Australia's postwar economic history. Although unemployment during the second half of the 1970s did not reach anywhere near the sorts of peaks which occurred during the interwar years, the mid-1970s did see a sharp departure from what the experience of three decades had suggested were 'normal' levels of unemployment.

Labor and the Treasury

From its election in December 1972, relations between the Treasury and the Labor government moved between mutual suspicion and outright hostility — attitudes which were reflected in the government's determination to seek alternative sources of advice. The decision to cut tariffs across the board in July 1973 was the first of a series of initiatives at odds with Treasury advice and an example of the Whitlam government's use of 'outside' advisers. The decision arose from the deliberations of a small committee, chaired by G. A. Rattigan, and without Treasury representation. The Treasury warned that the cut would make it difficult to have another revaluation (which it considered a superior weapon), would cause uncertainty, and might be seen as unjust. The department was ignored. The following month Frank Crean, the Labor Treasurer, announced that the government would be budgeting for a domestic deficit of $162 million; Treasury had stressed the need for a surplus. The Treasury was successful, however, in its recommendations that monetary policy be tightened. Later it was to be criticised for not having drawn the government's attention to the severity of the credit squeeze and the unemployment it would entail.

The department was to lose out again in mid-1974 when it urged the Whitlam government, which had just secured an electoral victory, to inflict upon the economy a sharp deflationary package — a package now somewhat infamously referred to as the 'short, sharp shock' strategy. The Treasury's proposal entailed the introduction of a mini-budget which would include increases in income tax, a 10 per cent rise in petrol excise, an increase in tobacco and spirits excise, higher company taxes and increased charges for postal and telephone services. The strategy represented an anxious attempt to re-establish wage restraint and dampen inflationary expectations. These aims were to be achieved through a slow and determined process: the initial shock may have been short and sharp but, clearly, to rid the system of inflationary expectations would necessarily be a protracted process. The essence of the strategy was, so some would describe it, to beat wayward elements into submission. In less polemical terms, the aim was to raise and maintain unemployment at a level sufficient to engender a sense of economic responsibility. Though at first supported by Whitlam, the strategy was rejected by the Labor caucus. Persistent, the Treasury again recommended in August 1974 that strong deflationary measures be introduced and again it was ignored. Indeed there were claims that the department had acted subversively, at the very least misleadingly, in the way it presented its budgetary proposals. Relations between Treasury and Labor progressively worsened, reaching their nadir at the end of 1974, the time of the so-called 'loans affair', in which the government attempted to bypass established Treasury channels and authorised a proposal to raise a loan up to a maximum of US$4000 million, supposedly for temporary purposes. As will be seen, it was not until the middle of 1975, with the appointment of Bill Hayden as Treasurer, that a degree of reconciliation was achieved between the government and the Treasury.

Labor's response to the downturn

In presenting the 1973–74 budget, Crean had announced that the budget was 'not simply an economic document' but was 'an important instrument whereby we give effect to our goals and aspirations'. In the 1974–75 budget Labor's 'goals and aspirations' came very much to the fore and the economic considerations were largely ignored or dismissed. The Treasurer announced that 'the conventional response to inflation has relied almost entirely on the creation of mass unemployment. Those who advocate such a course in present conditions are unable to say what level of unemployment would markedly reduce inflation. The Government is not prepared deliberately to create a level of 4 or 5 per cent, or perhaps even higher unemployment.' But as Barry Hughes notes, while Labor was certain that the Treasury line was reprehensible it was unclear what to put in its place. Little attention was given to the problem of inflation, bar a vague reference to negotiations about a cooperative approach

The Treasury line

to wage movements. The government's main aim was to get on with the job of implementing its program of social reform and in the process 'take up the slack emerging in the private sector'. Crean declared:

> Crucial as the fight against inflation is, it cannot be made the sole objective of Government policy. This Government is committed to the program of social reform to improve the position of the less privileged groups in our society and to maintain employment opportunities... The Government's overriding objective is to get on with our various initiatives in the fields of education, health, social welfare and urban improvement. The relatively subdued conditions in prospect in the private sector provide the first real opportunity we have had to transfer resources to the public sector.

Outlays were estimated to rise by 32.4 per cent, while receipts were to increase by 30.8 per cent. It was estimated that the overall result would leave the government with a small domestic surplus, though one that was some $189 million less than the 1973–74 result.

The government's policy stance was to be revised several times over the next few months. A week after the budget had been brought down the Australian dollar was devalued by 12 per cent. Treasury had opposed the decision, arguing quite correctly that it was inflationary. In November a mini-budget was introduced, again contrary to Treasury advice. The mini-budget was predicated on the need to stimulate the private sector. Personal income tax and company tax were reduced and credit restrictions eased. In December additional measures were taken to improve the liquidity position of companies, while import quotas were introduced on a range of textile products. In January the capital gains tax, introduced in August, was abolished. In February it was announced that additional funding would be provided to the states. The result of all these changes, together with the increase in expenditure caused by the growth in unemployment, was a quite remarkable rise of 46 per cent in federal government outlays in 1974–75. As can be seen Table 8.1, receipts grew much less quickly. The result was a dramatic, and historically unprecedented, growth in the budget deficit.

The Labor government's expansionist phase came to an end, in principle if not entirely in practice, after Bill Hayden became Treasurer in June 1975. Hayden had opposed the budgetary largesse of 1974. And after becoming Treasurer he was to be strongly influenced by the arguments put forward to him by his departmental officers. The figures for the 1975–76 budget perhaps belie the extent to which the government's ideas had shifted toward the Treasury line, and indeed John Stone argues that it is too often forgotten that this, too, was a 'big-spending' budget.[12] The budget estimate, it is true, was for a further increase in the deficit of $232 million. Nevertheless, the rate of increase in outlays was to be reduced by half and was to be lower than the increase in receipts. More importantly, the budget rhetoric was radically different. Expansion of the public sector was to be restrained; the private sector was to be given more room to develop. To have increased the budget any more than was now being aimed at was deemed 'a prescription for accelerating inflation'. To have attempted to offset a large budget deficit by a tough monetary policy — the line the Treasury had presented in 1973 — was now rejected as 'an unacceptable option'. These were new times with new problems needing new approaches: 'We are no longer operating in that simple Keynesian world in which some reduction in unemployment could, apparently, always be purchased at the cost of some more inflation. Today, it is inflation itself which is the central policy problem. More inflation simply leads to more unemployment.'

The simple proposition in the last sentence was to become the keystone of the Treasury's approach to economic policy during the second half of the 1970s. Whatever doubts the Treasury may have had at the beginning of the 1970s were now erased: the department was convinced that the Phillips curve was indeed dead. The notion of a trade-off between inflation and unemployment was now patently erroneous. The department argued in 1975: 'Unlike the foregoing policy paradigm — in which some reduction in unemployment could always be purchased at the cost of some more inflation — it seemed clear that if inflation took off from its present high base it would almost certainly lead before long to even greater unemployment.'[13] From this premise the department derived its policy prescription: 'Fight Inflation First'. In 1977 it argued that 'control of inflation is fundamental to the achievement of other economic policy objectives'.[14] The other major problem, that of unemployment, had to stand in line behind inflation and could not be attended to until prices and wages had been brought into order. That the twin problems of inflation and unemployment could not be dealt with simultaneously and that the unemployment situation might in fact deteriorate in the meantime, was taken to be an unfortunate but unavoidable fact of life, yet another of the Treasury's 'economic realities' that the community had to bear with patient acceptance. Top priority was given to the restoration of business confidence. This required a marked improvement in the profitability of business activities and the restoration of some sort of normalcy in the historical relationship between wage and profit shares.

Economic conditions, 1975–79

The Australian economy was to remain in a depressed state, at least by postwar standards, for the remainder of the 1970s. As can be seen in Table 8.2, output levels rose in both 1975–76 and 1976–77 but then collapsed, with GDP rising in real terms by a mere 0.9 per cent in 1977–78. A sharp improvement in output followed, succeeded by an almost equally sharp decline in 1979–80. The record with inflation was slightly better (see Table 8.3). After peaking at 16.7 per cent in 1974–75, the CPI hovered around 13 per cent during the next two years. It then fell quickly and by 1978–79 was just over 8 per cent. In the following year, however, it crept back over the 10 per cent mark. Perhaps the most distressing aspect of Australia's economic experience in the second half of the 1970s was the rise in unemployment. As can be seen in

Table 8.6 Unemployment, 1973–79

	per cent of labour force
August	
1973	1.8
1974	2.4
1975	4.6
1976	4.7
1977	5.7
1978	6.2
1979	5.8

Source: Adapted from Norton *Deterioration in Economic Performance* Table 4A.9

Table 8.6, unemployment rose continuously from 1973, eventually peaking at 6.2 per cent of the labour force in 1978, and then declining marginally.

Real wages and unemployment

How can such high levels of unemployment be explained? Throughout the second half of the 1970s the Treasury consistently argued that the fundamental cause of the increase in Australia's unemployment rate was the persistence of excessively high real wages. It noted in 1976, for instance, that 'the rapid increase in the relative cost of labour which gave rise to severe retrenchments in 1974–75 has been largely maintained in an excessive level of real wages which, until rectified, will continue to maintain unemployment at high levels'.[15] The Treasury continued by arguing that the real wage increases which occurred in the early 1970s, in particular during 1974, were an 'integral part of Australia's high inflation-high unemployment economic environment'. There had been a dislocation of so-called 'normal relationships', in particular the relationship between real wages and productivity, which in turn had distorted factor shares. Excessive real wages, it was stressed, had contributed both to the onset of recession and its prolongation. In 1977 the Treasury judged that the imbalance between real wages and productivity was persisting and was in fact 'clearly large'.[16] John Stone asserted that the 'real wage problem', as he called it, 'was the central and most difficult problem facing the Australian economy'.[17] In 1978 there was little apparent improvement. The fact that employment growth had been sluggish was said to be largely a reflection of the fact that the labour market was still adjusting to the rise in real wages which occurred during the first half of the 1970s.[18]

In emphasising the importance of real wages in determining the level of employment and unemployment, the Treasury was not arguing that the price of labour was the sole determinant of the demand for labour. The other major determinant was the level of output. Indeed it was the Treasury's view that 'if neither the state of technology nor the relative costs of inputs change, the demand for labour will vary with output'.[19] Its emphasis on the relative cost of labour sprang from a conviction that the rise in unemployment during the second half of the 1970s was much greater than one would expect to have arisen simply from the decline in output. Reiterating the views of the OECD, the department argued in 1978 that although the fall in production in the mid-1970s was not as severe as in the recessions of 1951–52 and 1960–61, the level of unemployment was considerably higher.[20] The conclusion drawn was that 'the severity and duration of unemployment in this recession cannot be explained by the reduction in aggregate demand'.[21] Indeed the department was convinced that 'the severe distortions to fundamental economic relationships that arose in 1974 would have adversely affected employment whatever their effects on output'.

How was it, then, that the rise in real wages had led not only to the onset but also to the prolongation of unemployment? Surprisingly, the Treasury did not provide during 1976–79 a detailed explanation of the link between real wages and unemployment in any of its budget statements. In 1976 it argued that the effect of higher real wages had been to encourage employers to make 'more intensive use of existing labour, including overtime'.[22] In 1977 it argued, without supporting evidence, that excessive real wages had led to 'a heightened tendency to substitute capital for labour' and claimed that such substitution was 'now seemingly occurring at an advanced rate'.[23] A somewhat similar view was put forward in the following year: 'Firms have naturally sought to offset this rise in costs by economising on labour input and substituting capital for labour.'[24] The same claim was made in 1979.

A slightly more satisfying explanation of the real wage-unemployment nexus, one which rose above mere assertions, was supplied in the department's 1978 study of labour markets. The analysis was purely neoclassical and based on marginal analysis. The Treasury postulated that 'unless the cost of extra labour is less than the value of the resulting output, it will be unprofitable for an employer to take on more employees'.[25] To look at this another way, 'as long as the value of each worker's output rises, then real wages can rise. For the economy as a whole, employment will tend to be sustained as long as the growth in labour costs does not exceed the growth of productivity'. Where labour costs exceeded productivity growth, unemployment could be expected to follow. The department argued that this was precisely what happened in 1974 when the real labour cost explosion occurred. The explosion, the Treasury explained in another publication,

> had the effect of driving a wedge between the value of output produced by the least productive workers employed by firms and the wage that had to be paid to them. Businesses found themselves in the position of having to pay wages to some workers which exceeded the value of their contribution to production and naturally economised by reducing the number of such workers they employed, including through the introduction of labour-saving innovations.[26]

The labour market was considered to be fundamentally the same as any other market and subject to the same forces, the same 'economic realities', as the rest of the economy. Therefore, the golden rule of neoclassical economics continued to apply: 'Wages are, after all, prices, and a basic tenet of economics is that when a price rises (and other conditions remain constant), the quantity demanded falls.'[27]

The Treasury argued that the real labour cost imbalance contributed to unemployment in three main ways. First, the rapid rise in wages was the main cause of the significant rise in the inflation rate which occurred during the 1970s and this 'in turn depressed consumer spending, business investment and net exports, and thereby contributed to the overall reduction in the level of output, which in turn led to a reduction in the demand for labour'.[28] Second, the fact that wages rose more rapidly than prices led to 'serious declines' in the profit levels of businesses. This had several consequences. In the first place, 'it was only to be expected that business would be looking for opportunities to scale down operations that had become unprofitable, and to reduce their demand for labour, which in most cases constitutes their greatest single cost factor'. The wages explosion also made investment in additional capacity a less desirable proposition and a riskier one, and it had led to a revision of expectations concerning future profit levels. This in turn had acted to dampen the overall level of investment and hence aggregate demand and had created a bias toward short-term, low-risk investment. Third, real wages increased relatively more rapidly than other productive inputs, thereby increasing the attractiveness of capital substitution. 'Where there is scope for choice between different technological processes which produce a similar output,' the Treasury explained, 'higher labour costs will induce business to choose more capital-intensive methods.'

Such arguments inevitably raise a host of questions. For example, was such substitution a 'natural reaction' — are businessmen always economically rational especially when the economic resource to be displaced is labour? And was it the case that the labour market operated like all other markets? Much of the Treasury's argument appeared to be simply an inference based on its view of how economic agents behaved: because employers act rationally (in that they are cost minimisers), then labour substitution *must* have been occurring. But what empirical evidence could the Treasury offer? There was in the first place the anecdotal evidence of business journals. But more satisfactory to the department was the evidence of the available investment statistics up to 1978. These showed that despite recessed conditions there had been an increase in private investment in plant and equipment in 1976–77 and 1977–78 (rising from 7.5 per cent of non-farm GDP in 1975–76 to 7.7 per cent in 1977–78). This fact, together with the sluggishness of employment during the period despite a slight improvement in output, provided the basis of the department's 'evidence' that substitution had been taking place.[29]

But there are of course problems with making such inferences. One problem, as the Treasury itself admitted, was that 'it is impossible in practice to separate those investments that have been made or planned solely in response to the change in relative factor costs from those that have been made in the normal course of activity'. Further, if capital-labour substitution had been occurring 'on a significant scale', why was it that productivity levels had fallen instead of rising? Another question raised about the Treasury's inferences, one which cast doubt on the rationality postulate, was why was it that the level of female employment had grown more strongly than males, given the much more rapid increase in female wages?

Another consideration, one which the Treasury was well aware of but did not discuss at any length in its budget papers, is that if one is to talk about the rationality of capital-labour substitution then one needs to show not only that the absolute price of labour has increased but also its price relative to capital. The relationship is complicated because the rise in wages, by reducing profitability, will in itself raise the user cost of capital. The effect, as Chris Higgins of the Treasury points out, will be to moderate the initiating change in relative factor prices.[30] On the Treasury's evidence the real unit cost of labour moved in line with the real unit cost of capital from 1959 to 1971; thereafter labour costs moved well ahead of capital costs, the differential being greatest in 1976. After 1976, however, labour costs had fallen and capital costs had accelerated, thereby reducing but not eliminating the disparity: by 1977 labour costs were still well above the trend level.

The difficulty, however, is to find satisfactory measures of capital costs and labour costs. The Treasury admitted that measures of the cost of capital 'are still experimental and cannot be used with great authority'.[31] The particular measure which the Treasury used for the conclusions noted above were based on the approach adopted in 1976 by a Treasury research team led by Chris Higgins.[32] In 1978, however, another Treasury team, led by Neil Johnston (who was a member of the 1976 team) used a different approach and came to somewhat different conclusions on the question of when capital became price-competitive in relation to labour:

> the development of the real wage/productivity gap is more than matched by a rise in the cost of capital over the course of 1974 and 1975 . . . It is not until late in 1975, and thereafter, with the steadying in interest rates and the recovery in the stock market, that the price competitiveness of capital is re-asserted. The introduction of the 40 per cent investment allowance from January 1976 also contributed to that turnaround; the co-incidence of the investment allowance and the double depreciation provisions in the first half of 1976 led to a sizeable reduction in the cost of capital during that half-year.[33]

But despite differences over timing, the broad thrust of the argument was nevertheless consistent with other Treasury documents: 'relative factor movements have resulted in a sizeable amount of substitution of capital for labour.'[34]

As for the question of measuring real wage costs, this became a matter of earnest debate in the second half of the 1970s — a debate sparked off by the Treasury's emphasis on the real wage imbalance or 'overhang'. The question arose: what is the best way to measure the extent to which real wages have risen above productivity levels? Gruen noted in 1979 that 'the empirical issues separating the various proponents revolve around the best base period for such comparisons, the appropriate sector of the economy for productivity estimates (i.e. whether it should be the non-farm *market* sector or the non-farm sector of the economy), whether actual or trend productivity should be used and, if the latter, whether trend productivity has changed significantly in recent years'.[35] By 1980, however, Sheehan and Stricker could note that some consensus had emerged on the question of the overhang's measurement, with general agreement being reached that the most appropriate measure was the Treasury's 1978 formulation of a market sector hourly measure (which largely eliminated the question of whether to use trend or actual productivity). But they noted that such data was only available annually and (at that stage) only up to 1976–77. It was in part because of this that while most Australian economists agreed that the rise in real wages relative to productivity (the overhang) and the profits squeeze were important causes of the the rise in unemployment in 1974–75 (and possibly, Sheehan and Stricker added, in 1975–76), there was still much debate by the end of the 1970s over the significance of the overhang in explaining the changes in the level of unemployment which had occurred since 1977.[36]

Whatever disputes there were about measuring real wage costs, the Treasury was convinced that the answer to the problem of unemployment lay primarily with a reduction in real wages. As the department argued in 1976:

> Unless and until the real wage is brought down relative to productivity in the process of winding inflation rates back, it will not be possible to restore fully the level of economic activity and to provide sufficient new job opportunities to reduce unemployment significantly. In the circumstances that prevail, those who argue for the increase or maintenance of real wages (or those who take decisions intended to increase or maintain them) are in effect, unwittingly or not, contributing to the maintenance of unemployment at present high levels.[37]

In 1978 the department again claimed that the only way the burden for the market adjustment of real wages to productivity levels could be shifted from the unemployed 'is for some of it to be borne by those, more fortunate, who are employed — that is, for there to be a reduction in real wages'.[38] At the very least it was essential that there be restraint in money wage claims. The Treasury admitted in 1978 that the evidence since 1976 suggested that the exercise of such restraint might have only a marginal effect on the real wage level. But it argued: 'Whether or not money wage restraint gave rise to real wage reductions — and it might well not — it must be judged the most efficacious way in which sustainable recovery could be more speedily achieved.'

The question is, then, just how were real wages to be reduced, since this was the key to a reduction in the level of unemployment. Some commentators insisted that the Treasury did not really know how to reduce real labour costs, bar vague suggestions about the need for a more decentralised wage-fixing system. While it is possible to sympathise with such criticisms, it needs to be remembered that the Treasury was arguing for a reduction in real wages *relative to productivity*. As Chris Higgins has argued, 'there are non-trivial differences between that formulation and absolute reductions in the real wage'. He noted also that a persistent theme in Treasury analysis had been that the economy is, given the actual movements in money wages, adjusting *slowly* in the inevitable direction of reducing the real wage overhang, with high unemployment in the interim. A slower increase in administered money wages would *accelerate* that adjustment process and lower the rate of unemployment over the adjustment period. In the course of doing that it would probably lead to a higher integral of total real incomes, perhaps even of the real incomes of those *presently* employed.[39]

To the Treasury it was not enough simply for real wages to fall and for the 'historical' relationship between wages and profits shares to be restored. Neil Johnston, an assistant secretary in GFEP, argued in 1979 that 'the effects of the [real wage] overhang could well linger on [after it has been largely erased] as the stigma attaching to labour — that it is overpriced — could well take some time to wear off. There may also be a case for *overcorrection* of the overhang to redress the loss of business profits and boost firm's [sic] confidence in the market and in the prospect for satisfactory returns from future investments'.[40] The suggestion, emphasised by Johnston himself, was that it was not enough to return to some supposed normal relationship between wages and productivity. Instead, the balance had to tip in favour of productivity and hence profits. A similar compensatory mentality could be seen in John Stone's comment in 1977 that

> until the profit share gets back at least to where it used to be we will not see recovery to anything like the kind of 'full employment' world to which we now look back nostalgically. And having used a comparison of 'where we used to be' I would also go further to say that my own personal view is that the profit share will need to rise, at least for some time, above 'where it used to be' if we are to get a sustained rise in private fixed investment.[41]

The suggestion was that recovery was dependent not just on the profit share increasing but, more importantly, on it rising *above* the level it had maintained during, presumably, the 1960s. In both cases the idea was akin to the Friedmanite notion that to rid the system of inflationary expectations, unemployment would have to rise above the natural rate. An indefinite period of overcorrection was the necessary price to pay for past excesses.

In keeping with the neoclassical vision, the Treasury was quick to point to institutional barriers to wage flexibility and label them as responsible for maintaining unemployment higher than it otherwise would have been. An institution which came to be treated with considerable scorn by the Treasury was the Commonwealth Conciliation and Arbitration Commission, a body staffed in the main by non-economists making decisions of profound economic importance and, to the Treasury, pernicious consequence. John Stone was all too willing to denounce the commission. Speaking in 1979 he complained that its decisions 'are not notable as models of economic, or indeed even logical clarity, and therefore it is usually difficult to identify from within them the factors influencing that body'.[42] The commission's decision in April 1975 to reintroduce semi-automatic quarterly wage indexation was seen as a perfect example of an unwillingness or inability to accept economic realities. In light of its conviction that real wages had to decline, it was perhaps not surprising that the Treasury was highly critical of the decision. Since at the time of its introduction real wages were at an excessive level, wage indexation 'tended to perpetuate those excessive real wage levels longer than a less fettered system would have done'.[43] The Treasury was convinced that indexation 'prolonged the duration of the recession and intensified its impact'.[44] The wage indexation system, however, was soon modified — most decisions involved only partial indexation. The Treasury welcomed this move but remained critical of the system and the body responsible for its prolongation.

Perhaps the most interesting aspect of the Treasury's analysis of the real wages/unemployment issue was the clues it offered of the way the department saw the operation of the economic system. There was to the Treasury a sense of natural order about the economy, something suggested by its continual references to 'normal', 'usual' and 'fundamental' relationships and its use of the word 'distortions' to describe what happened to these relationships in the 1970s. This sense of natural order provided the basis for a deeply felt conviction about the determinism, the inexorability, of economic processes. The department remained steadfast in its view that the natural order would, indeed had to, prevail: distortions would not remain but would, perhaps only after much delay, be corrected. This aspect of Treasury thought was particularly evident in its insistence that the real labour cost imbalance or overhang would eventually be corrected by market forces. In 1977 it argued that 'clearly, if the wage settlement processes do not serve to further reduce the share of labour in the national income, market forces will operate to reduce employment or at least the rate of growth of employment, and the same end will be attained — but more slowly and much more painfully'.[45] In 1978 it claimed that 'the market's adjustment to correct for the persisting real wage overhang is, one way or another, inevitable'.[46] Similarly, in 1979 it insisted that 'one way or another [basic economic realities] will effect their influence; the question of course is how long that will take, and what otherwise unnecessary costs will be incurred along the way'.[47] It will be seen shortly that this sense of natural order, this belief in an inherent correcting mechanism, informed the Treasury's viewpoint on a range of topics. In all cases the message was that 'economic realities' had to be recognised for what they were. Given the inevitability of adjustments to distortions, the most rational response was to take whatever action was necessary to facilitate these adjustments.

The government's restricted role

If a reduction in real wages was the key to an improvement in the employment situation and if there was a need to facilitate market adjustments, what was the role of government? Before 1975 the Treasury seemed to embrace an essentially Keynesian line in its public statements on government policies. In 1973 it continued to endorse what was then a well-established Treasury tenet, that given the uncertainty of economic events it was essential that government policy be flexible. In a statement attached to the budget speech of 1973–74 it argued: 'Any assessment of economic prospects in 1973–74 must ... be subject to a degree of uncertainty and, for this reason, policies must be readily adaptable to changing economic circumstances.' In 1974, in one of its taxation papers, the Treasury rejected the concept of automatic adjustment of taxation for inflation and strongly supported discretionary taxation policies. 'It would be fair to say,' it asserted 'that the consensus of opinion supports a need for discretionary action.' It continued: 'Indeed the alternative view is a counsel of despair — it implies that governments are more likely to be wrong than right in judging the need for stabilisation policy action.'[48]

During the second half of the 1970s, however, the Treasury was to grow wary of flexible or discretionary policies. Although it continued to believe in the need for stabilisation policies, it moved a long way from the 1961 argument that 'sharp changes' in the direction of policy were sometimes necessary to deal with an ever-fluctuating economic system. Perhaps more importantly, the Treasury grew increasingly sceptical of just what governments, using stabilisation policies, could achieve. By 1979 the department could advance the view that the experience of the 1950s and 1960s had been misleading. What now had to be recognised was that governments, even if they wanted to, could not guarantee full employment:

> So far as the effectiveness of instruments is concerned, there is probably still, as a legacy from the sustained period of good economic performance in the 1950s and 1960s, an unwarranted belief in the controllability of the economy and in the precision of use of policy instruments — that is to say, in the possibilities for 'fine-tuning' offered by macroeconomic policy... That is, to be sure, a continuing area of controversy, but the experience of the 1970s throughout the industrialised world suggests that policy advisers are hardly being myopic if they argue that the degree of policy effectiveness is severely limited, that 'controllability' is circumscribed.[49]

From the mid-1970s the Treasury argued consistently against the use of an expansionary policy (in the form of larger budget deficits) as a means of reducing unemployment. In its view such policies simply did not work anymore; indeed, they were positively harmful. In 1976, for example, the department maintained that the large budget deficits and substantial absolute increases in public expenditure which occurred under the Whitlam government 'proved ineffective and the upturn in activity in the first half of 1975 that they had sought to foster proved to be unsustainable'. The Treasury argued that the 'the massive stimuli of 1974–75 carried within themselves the seeds of their own undoing'.[50] In 1978 Keynesian ideas were rejected outright: 'The degree of unemployment and under-utilisation of capacity that now exists is not primarily the product of deficient demand in the private sector of a kind that can be lastingly boosted to any desired degree by conventional fiscal/monetary stimulus.'[51]

The basis of the Treasury's opposition to the use of larger deficits was summarised in a statement attached to the 1976–77 budget speech. To have budgeted for a larger deficit in the forthcoming year, the department said, would have had a whole series of deleterious effects:

Inflationary expectations and inflation would have been exacerbated, not only because such an outcome would have been seen as failure by the Government to control its own activities, but also because of the massive infusion of liquidity into the economy implied by such a deficit. Such a set back to the quelling of inflationary expectations, and to confidence more generally, would have further depressed private consumption and private investment spending... With inflationary expectations reinforced and renewed uncertainty engendered, business would not have willingly built up its stock levels. Again, with no further inroads to be expected in the rate of inflation, Australia's competitive position vis-a-vis our major trading partners would have deteriorated further; the inevitable strengthening of import flows which would have resulted would also have dampened domestic production.[52]

John Stone expanded upon these arguments in 1979 in a paper given to a seminar on the significance of the budget deficit. One significant feature of Stone's paper was his anxiety to acknowledge that a policy of expanding the budget deficit did indeed have Keynesian effects: 'The argument does not involve a rejection of the standard multiplier analysis which traces the effects on final demand of changes in budget outlays, budget receipts and transfer payments.'[53] Further, 'I do re-emphasise ... that there is no suggestion that so-called income and expenditure effects of budget expenditures, transfers and receipts are unimportant — they are of course extremely important'. Stone's point, however, was that these Keynesian effects were not the only effects of larger budget deficits. There were a whole range of other effects: 'the monetary effects of the deficit, effects on the balance of payments, effects on wage determination, and the effects — both direct and through these channels — of the budget deficit on confidence and expectations in the economy at large'. It was Stone's view that this latter group of effects 'more than offset' the stimulus that might come through income and expenditure effects.

What was significant also about Stone's paper was his view that economic agents were particularly sensitive to price changes and, more importantly, anticipated the effect of government actions — just as the rational expectations school argued. Stone was convinced that 'expectations now adjust rapidly to changing economic circumstances and find their rapid reflection in actual economic behaviour'. Pursuing this line, he argued that the expansionary policies of the Whitlam government failed essentially because of their adverse effects on expectations. Memories of this period lingered on and therefore any increase in the budget deficit arising from an increase in expenditure would be interpreted 'as a step back towards "big government" spending, associated as that was with the turmoil of the the mid-70s', and would thereby alarm economic agents, making them more cautious. Stone dismissed the suggestion that what was necessary was a campaign of 'public education' to overcome such 'irrational' responses to larger deficits:

> Personally, I do not believe that a 'brainwashing' approach of that kind would be in any way effective, for the very good reason that ... the concerns in question are in fact very rational indeed. In short, in such circumstances consumers and/or businesses actually do have good grounds for expecting the economic outlook to

deteriorate. If, as would be likely, this were reflected in their own spending decisions, the 'expectations' effect would bring forward that 'real' deterioration.[54]

Stone went on to reiterate this point, offering his support of the arguments of the rational expectations school:

> I can only say that my very clear judgment is that in present circumstances the result [of an expansion in the budget deficit] is likely to be adverse — and considerably so. This judgment is reinforced by my conviction that the attitude which it attributes to the private sector (i.e. that an increased budget deficit and the tendency that involves towards higher inflation are fundamentally disruptive to economic stability) is basically correct. This, in the formation of 'rational expectations', can only serve to bring the adverse consequences closer in time so that there may not even be the appeal of short-run positive activity and employment consequences flowing from fiscal stimulus.[55]

In the Treasury's view, the government could only establish (and should be content to do so) what it referred to as the 'pre-conditions' for recovery or, more generally, for the conduct of economic affairs. It could only establish a favourable 'environment' which would encourage the private sector, in which resided the true source of capitalist drive and vitality, to restore the economy to full activity. Such an environment was one which increased the scope for market forces to operate, helped to remove distortions surrounding price signals (oil parity pricing was thus welcomed), facilitated change and encouraged mobility and flexibility, and provided a flow of reliable and up-to-date information for the formation of rational expectations. In an attempt to do this, a broad, non specific, policy approach should be adopted.

The Treasury maintained that the government needed to set a good example. Larger budget deficits could be expected to have detrimental effects because they would be 'seen as a failure by the government to control its own activities';[56] they would 'be taken as looser belts all round'.[57] It was in part for this reason that the Treasury rejected the idea of the government attempting to control inflation by tightening monetary policy but attempting to deal simultaneously with unemployment by increasing the budget deficit — the strategy known as the 'policy-mix' solution. If the government were to do this, the Treasury declared, 'there will be effects on perceptions in the private sector and in centralised wage setting of the following kind: "the government says it's pursuing an anti-inflation policy yet it can't even get its own house in order; look, it's resorting to still larger Budget deficits; we do not believe it"'.[58]

Given the importance of expectations it was essential that the government's policy aims be credible. And credibility entailed the government having to exercise the same restraint it believed the rest of the community should exercise. It was not enough to preach; practice was crucial. The government had to show that it was genuine in its attempts at restraint. It had to convince economic agents of its intentions and its trustworthiness. It was unclear, however, whether the Treasury believed, as did the rational expectationists, that once the government had established its trustworthiness in this respect, prices would quickly fall.

The Treasury line

The Treasury argued that another useful role the government could play was the establishment of monetary targets or ranges. Unlike Friedman, the Treasury stressed that it was in favour of 'conditional projections' rather than 'precise and rigid' M3 targets. But it believed that the announcement of projections could provide a greater degree of certainty and predictability for decision-makers:

> The announcement in each of the last two Budget Speeches (and initially in March 1976) of a successively lower projected range for M3 growth in the financial year has contributed substantially to a return to stability and greater certainty in financial markets. The projections have effectively fulfilled their intention of indicating the Government's expectations for the appropriate monetary environment consistent with progress towards its economic objectives. Given the outcomes, it must be judged that these policies have made an important contribution to the success of anti-inflation policy.[59]

As with the repeated declarations that the government was aiming to achieve and maintain budget balance, monetary projections were 'a manifest [sic] to seek stability' in the midst of 'a still highly uncertain and inflation-ridden world'. More specifically, the announcement of monetary projection ranges had three main aims. First, to 'demonstrate that the aims of monetary policy fit within a coherent overall policy'. Second, and again the Treasury departed from Friedman with its reference to the need for some discretion, to 'indicate that greater medium-term "steadiness" in monetary management is to be pursued but without abandoning an appropriate measure of discretionary responsiveness'. Finally, and perhaps most important to the Treasury, 'by providing a "peg" of stability, attempt to exert a direct influence upon public expectations, which in present-day conditions are central to the inflationary process'.[60]

In short, by the mid-1970s (and increasingly afterwards) the Treasury had become sympathetic to the neoclassical line that intervention should aim to provide a stable, orderly environment for economic activity by setting rules and establishing a clearly defined framework. Such a framework did not of course preclude changes in policy. But the Treasury insisted that changes should occur only gradually, should be clearly articulated, and should be understood by all. The discretionary element had to be exercised with extreme caution.

The Treasury and the Fraser government: 1975–79

In terms of budget rhetoric, the Liberal–National Country Party government which came to power late in 1975 was a close adherent to the Treasury line. Not long after being appointed Treasurer, Phillip Lynch made clear the government's philosophy:

> To some, cutting back on government spending and the deficit seems paradoxical; we hear it argued that that will not contribute to economic recovery but, on the

contrary, will simply serve to depress activity still further. In today's world that orthodox 'keynesianism', in my judgement and in the judgement of the Government, is no longer appropriate; on the contrary, it is hopelessly outdated.[61]

The point was repeated in the 1976–77 budget speech. Whatever the virtues 'pump-priming' policies may have had in earlier days of economic stability, they were now 'clearly inappropriate'. Any possible virtues had now 'entirely evaporated under conditions of high inflation, high unemployment and a public sector already bloated beyond belief'. The correct approach was 'to achieve a balanced budget, though not overnight, and to ensure that all policies — fiscal, monetary, wages and external — be directed to the same end', that they be 'a unified and coherent whole'. These became the standard arguments used in budget speeches for the rest of the decade.

Rhetoric was not always translated into practice. As can be seen in Table 8.1, the Fraser government was still a long way from budget equilibrium in 1979–80. Though the path was by no means direct, the government was nevertheless able to reduce the *domestic* deficit from $2258 million in 1978–79 to $567 million in 1979–80. Further, the government was able to reduce significantly the size of the deficit in relation to GDP. The reduction occurred in part because of the exercise of expenditure restraint but more importantly because of increases in revenue.

Relations between the Fraser government and the Treasury were less than harmonious; the decision to split the department in November 1976 was eloquent testimony to this. The split was precipitated by heated debates between the Treasury and Fraser in 1976 on the questions of tax indexation and exchange rate devaluation. In the middle of the year Treasury fought strenuously against Fraser's suggestion that tax indexation for individuals and stock valuation adjustments for companies be introduced immediately rather than be phased in over three years. It was adamant that the move would result in a severe decline in revenue and thereby lead to a much larger deficit than it considered desirable. The department was not able, however, to convince the Prime Minister, and in May the introduction of immediate indexation and stock valuation was announced.

The dispute over devaluation occurred at the end of 1976. With capital moving out of the country and with Australia's international reserves having declined by $1053 million in 1975–76, Fraser became convinced that the Australian dollar was overvalued. The Treasury believed, however, that any exchange rate decision should be postponed and insisted that it was preferable simply to pursue the prevailing policy of expenditure restraint and to maintain tight monetary conditions. According to Barry Hughes, the Treasury 'did not contest the view that the dollar was overvalued. It maintained rather that restriction on the external front would complement the inflation first strategy elsewhere, and that the dollar could be defended against speculators by major international borrowing'.[62] Fraser, however, decided to exercise what Hughes calls his 'Prime Ministerial Prerogative'. Late in November 1976 it was announced that the Australian dollar had been devalued by 17.5 per cent.

The Treasury line

Commentators have argued that the tenacity and doggedness with which Treasury pursued its line in both these instances, and in particular its supposed leaking of information to *The Age* about the devaluation issue, left the Prime Minister convinced that the department wielded a disproportionate degree of power on economic policy matters within the public service. It was partly as a result of this conviction that it was decided to split the department. The justification offered was that it had become too difficult for a single minister to be responsible for both economic and financial matters. Therefore it seemed desirable to have two separate departments and two separate ministers. There was the additional advantage that the Department of Finance would be able to concentrate on the task of reducing public sector expenditure, something which the Fraser government had told the electorate it was keen to achieve.

The Treasury and the market

When discussing the nature of Treasury thought in the second half of the 1970s, there is perhaps a tendency to concentrate too much on the Treasury's analysis of inflation and unemployment and its policy prescriptions. What is not appreciated enough is that this particular aspect of the Treasury line was but one part of a broader view of the functioning of market economies and of the role of governments in such economies.

The Treasury's view of the functioning of market economies emerged clearly in its contribution to what has been called the growth debate. During the late 1960s to early 1970s the notion of economic growth came under attack from environmentalists warning of ecological disaster and from doomsday predictionists claiming imminent resource exhaustion. Responding to this attack in a Treasury economic paper published in 1973, the department waxed eloquent on the order, harmony and responsiveness of the market mechanism. A central theme of the paper was that those who attacked growth were foolishly attacking the wrong subject. For growth was not an independent phenomenon but a reaction to, a result of, aggregated individual decisions and demands. The Treasury was convinced that problems commonly attributed to growth were in fact manifestations of a failure to allow market forces to operate. Such problems were not intrinsic to the growth process at all. Excessive environmental pollution could be used to demonstrate this. The department argued that pollution problems arose because no charge was usually imposed on the use of environmental resources such as air, rivers, lakes, oceans and landscapes. It declared: 'Any resource will be grossly over-used if its use is unrestricted and no charge is made for it.'[63] The solution was obvious: it was not to restrain the rate of growth but to equate the private costs of a particular decision with the social costs, 'to change the conditions under which producers and consumers are allowed free and unrestricted use of the "shared resources" of the environment'.[64] The best way to do this, following Pigou, was to alter the price structure, and hence the signals provided to economic agents, by levying taxes or imposing licences. The 'polluter pays' principle was considered preferable to the 'public pays' principle.

What was particularly noticeable about the Treasury's analysis was its confidence in the efficient operation of the market mechanism, its unbounded faith in the economy's capacity for adaptability and for continuous technological advance. The Treasury could declare that 'in a real sense, technical progress "creates" resources, so that the faster and further growth continues, the greater the availability of resources (at a given real cost) will be'.[65] Further, 'it is of the very essence of technological change that alternative methods or substitute products are invariably available in the longer term ... This process of substitution and expansion in the range of alternate materials, sources and processes is going on all the time'. Hence, fears of imminent resource exhaustion were misplaced:

> It is difficult to forecast what the consequences of exhausting particular resources would be. For any particular mineral it would happen only gradually, by a process which involved a steady rise in price. Presumably patterns of production and consumption would gradually adapt towards what they would have been had the mineral never existed in the first place. Moreover, developments in substitute minerals and processes and in the pattern of demand can mean that an 'indispensable' mineral at one time might become redundant at another.[66]

The department's faith in the essential adaptability and flexibility of the Australian economy was if anything to strengthen as the 1970s progressed. Its basic confidence in the market mechanism underpinned each of the TEPs published in 1978–79, which covered a range of topics including structural adjustment, job markets, energy markets and technological change. (The discussion of the last two topics was prepared in the Treasury's Resource Allocation and Development Division. Established in 1978, the division was responsible for providing advice on questions relating to the efficient use of Australian resources, aspects of taxation policy and industry assistance.) The Treasury's confidence in the operation of market forces could be seen, for instance, in its stance on the question of structural adjustment. It was common practice by the mid-1970s to talk of 'the crisis of manufacturing' and to point with grave concern to the fact that manufacturing's share of GDP at constant prices had slipped from 25.4 per cent in 1972–73 to 22.4 per cent in 1977–78 and that its share of total employment had fallen from 24.7 per cent in 1971 to 19.8 per cent in 1978. Indicative of the concern which this caused was the establishment of two committees in the second half of the 1970s (the Jackson and Crawford Committees), both of which investigated the malaise in manufacturing, and the publication in 1977 of a governmental *White Paper on Manufacturing Industry*. The Treasury's response to the 'crisis' was simply to argue, in line with views put forward in the 1960s, that 'there can be no rational justification for aiming at any pre-determined economic structure, or seeking to defend the existing economic structure'.[67] Changes in the economic structure were considered 'only the means through which the economy keeps pace with the changing demands the community makes of it'. 'Particular economic structures or directions for change,' therefore, 'cannot sensibly be advanced as ends in themselves'. Moreover, the Treasury believed there was no need to fear the employment consequences of structural or technological change. Such fears were misplaced because they ignored the fact that the complex linkages, interrelationships and interdependencies between economic agents were such that the economic system was able to cope with any endogenous or exogenous disturbances. The department could argue, for instance, that 'market economies embody complex linkages across markets, such that the very process of decline in some industries signals the opportunities for expansion in others'. In the Treasury's view, it was the essence of technological change that it not only imposed costs but also provided opportunities.[68] There was no reason why economic difficulties should become cumulative: 'In a flexible, continually adjusting economy, along with specific employment losses there can be expected to be employment gains. Just as activity in some industries is necessarily deterred by the expansion of others, so job displacement in a particular industry can bring cost savings elsewhere in the economy with the consequent potential for new and additional demands and new employment opportunities'. Further, it had to be kept in mind that 'the fortunes of individuals (or even some firms) seldom depend solely on the fate of a single industry. Most employees are capable of performing work in a variety of industries, displaced funds are mobile, and displaced capital equipment can often be put to new uses'.

Such a view of the nature of structural change gave rise to a particular set of policy prescriptions. Some observers, such as the Jackson Committee, believed that the government should take a lead in counteracting the apparent decline of manufacturing by the use of policies such as depreciation and other investment allowances, research grants, relocation grants, export incentives, retraining schemes and aid to particular industries. The Treasury line was that governments should not attempt to mould the nature of economic change or to question the desirability of the direction of change. To do so would be to question that which had been ordained by the decisions of each individual member of the community. In the Treasury's eyes such action was irrational: the collective results of individual decision-making were considered largely sacrosanct. The department also supported phased reductions in protection levels, arguing that 'their major strength is the continuous, *automatic* pressure they put on the affected industries to slough off their least efficient components and consolidate their most efficient firms, processes and products'.[69]

Underpinning the Treasury's arguments on the nature of structural change was the idea that the economy was self-correcting. In fact the department adopted an explicitly Walrasian point of view and insisted that 'there exists a broad tendency towards general equilibrium across all markets'.[70] That the adjustment mechanism was only a tendency was emphasised. Adopting an 'imperfectionist' viewpoint, the Treasury stressed that this did not necessarily mean 'that the general equating of supply and demand in all markets is ever fully achieved'. It remained convinced, nevertheless, that 'economies tend to move towards the elimination of imbalances in supply or demand'. It maintained that 'even within a highly ossified framework, market forces are still operative in seeking to offset the consequences of that ossification'.[71] Those who argued for a much more direct form of government intervention in dealing with structural change were criticised for making 'insufficient allowance for the operation of prices and markets and the continuum of economic adjustments that tend to bring about the equality of supply and demand'.[72] To assume that the economy's inherent adjustment mechanisms could somehow be aborted was dismissed as 'unrealistic'.

The essence of the Treasury's vision as it had evolved by the end of the 1970s was captured in a passage in the concluding section of TEP no. 3:

> The Australian economy, with the bulk of its production responsive to market forces, signals emerging excess demands for, or supplies of, particular commodities through market prices. The best predictions of future industry prospects are made at a decentralised level by businessmen, workers and consumers as they respond to such changing market opportunities. The very process of decline in some industries changes relative prices in a way which opens up new opportunities for investment, employment, and more highly valued types of output. Future full employment will not depend on governments finding things for private enterprise to do.[73]

How can the department's faith in the adaptability and efficiency of the market economy be explained? Ultimately, so the arguments in TEP no. 2 would suggest, it derived from its view of human nature, in particular its belief that people wanted to make 'right' decisions, these being those which 'give them what they want'. In the Treasury's view, 'the desire of each individual person, firm or group to get the best results from any situation allows the market to play its part'.[74] The department was convinced that economic agents were essentially rational, in the sense that they were carefully calculative. Decisions were made on the basis of probable costs and returns. Expanding on this, the Treasury said:

> The returns may, of course, be of many kinds and may include altruistic considerations as well as [a] range of other non-material values... Decisions may also be influenced by the circumstance — increasingly present in the case of the well-to-do — of not having to weigh up too carefully the pros and cons, especially on minor matters. Even those on modest incomes make many decisions, out of habit or otherwise, with little or no conscious consideration of how to get the most for their money. Nevertheless, the process involved in reaching any rational decision is essentially a benefit/cost calculus; and although the reasoning process is expressed in many different ways, it tends to become increasingly conscious and articulated as decisions become more important.[75]

The Treasury stressed that the efficiency of the market system derived not only from the maximising behaviour of individuals but from the discipline imposed by market forces. The Treasury believed that one of the great benefits of the market system was that it instilled the discipline which economic agents were unwilling or unable voluntarily to impose on themselves. Discipline was built in to the market:

> Since predictions of industry profitability inevitably carry a component of judgement and a possibility of error, it is critical that society retain the flexibility to discard investments premised on forecasts which turn out to be faulty. This flexibility is built into the market system of profits and losses which disciplines investors and holds them accountable for their forecasts. Bad private investments are not perpetuated; good ones are expanded.[76]

That which tended to hinder or obstruct mobility and flexibility was viewed with disdain. So too was that which distorted price signals. Thus, advocates of schemes to set Australia's energy prices at below-parity levels incurred the Treasury's wrath. To set prices at such levels 'simply confer[red] an unnecessary subsidy on energy users and their customers and induce[d] them to make economically inefficient decisions about consumption of and investment in energy-using products and processes'.[77] Inflation, similarly, was seen as a fundamental evil because it distorted the signals upon which economic decision-makers acted.

Likewise, that which substituted dependence for discipline was looked at askance. On this point, it should be noted that the Treasury's dislike of budget deficits was not just because of their supposed harmful effects on inflation and inflationary expectations but, as with protection policies, because such deficits necessarily entailed a dependency relationship. As it argued in 1979, 'the deficit arises fundamentally from the high level of public expenditure. That in itself, and particularly when public expenditure increases rapidly, can impair the vitality of the private sector even if it is fully met by taxation. Dependencies are created; entrepreneurship and individual effort are weakened'.[78] For the same reasons, the Treasury warned of the difficulties inherent in tariff protection:

> Experience with protection shows that public or government forecasts of the prospects of individual industries are not subject to the same sort of review [as occurs in the market system of profits and losses]. Once a government assumes political responsibility for an industry's future, two things happen; the government cannot allow that industry to fail, and its managers and workers are consequently spared the discipline of selling their products on its merits. The outcome is a highly inefficient economy and a reduced level of national economic welfare.[79]

Such arguments were entirely in accord with the sorts of views put forward by Lionel Robbins in the early 1930s. There was in such comments an implicit ideal, one which Robbins made clear, which involved decision-makers having to stand on their own feet, having to suffer fully the results of miscalculations and misjudgments, and being forced to plan and to calculate more carefully and with increasing sophistication. Such an ideal could not tolerate soft options, protective devices, safety valves. Also like Robbins, governmental interference was seen essentially in a negative light — in so far, at least, as it weakened the capitalist spirit of enterprise.

During the second half of the 1970s the Treasury moved closer to a purely neoclassical stance. But while it emphasised the importance of real wages and pushed the neoclassical line that workers had priced themselves out of a job, it did not take the extreme neoclassical view that the rise in unemployment could be wholly attributed to the rise in real wages. It continued to acknowledge the importance of output and aggregate demand levels. And although the Treasury came to the conclusion that governments were essentially impotent in their ability to reduce unemployment directly and although it began to point to the economic virtues of balanced budgets and stressed the need to keep government expenditure to a minimum, it continued to acknowledge that there were such things as income and expenditure effects. It hastened to add, however, that such effects were swamped by negative expectation effects. There was also, interestingly, something of a Keynesian emphasis on the uncertainty and capriciousness of investment decisions and a stress on the need to gear economic policies to maintaining business confidence. Yet the emphasis throughout was on the economic rationality of economic agents. Moreover, unlike Keynes, the outstanding feature of Treasury thought was its faith, its certainty, that market forces operated always to move toward the equilibration of supply and demand in all markets and hence toward the full use of capital and labour. The system was depicted in true neoclassical fashion as being inherently mobile, flexible and adaptable, the main blemishes, the main reason for the present lack of flexibility, being institutional arrangements blind to 'economic realities'. Quite apart from whether or not it be detrimental, there was on this view very little need for active government intervention.

9

The ascendancy of the market-based approach, 1980–84

THE first four years of the 1980s saw in Australia remarkable changes in the mood of the community and in economic performance. The period opened in a burst of optimism, with Prime Minister Malcolm Fraser suggesting that Australia was on a threshold of a resources boom that would ensure the continued economic strength of the nation for at least the remainder of the decade. In 1980–81 the non-farm sector grew faster than at any stage since the early 1970s, a result which suggested to some of the sceptics that Fraser had not exaggerated. In 1981–82, however, wages increased rapidly (a reflection in part of the anxiety to enjoy the fruits of the resources boom), inflation continued on an upward path and the rate of growth faltered. In the following year the economy collapsed into a deep recession. For the first time since 1952–53 a negative rate of growth was recorded. Unemployment increased dramatically in 1982 to reach its highest level since the 1930s. The grand vision of a resource-led recovery began to be dismissed as a mirage. After half a dozen years of rhetoric on the need for budgetary restraint, after having finally achieved a more or less balanced budget in 1980–81 and 1981–82, and faced with the prospect of having to hold an election sometime in 1983, the Fraser government resorted to budgetary largesse in 1982 — suggesting to some commentators that the government had 'lost its nerve'. A growing sense of community pessimism was averted in 1983–84 by an unexpected turnaround in the Australian economy. Coincidental with the success of the ALP under Bob Hawke at the 1983 federal elections, the economy grew strongly and employment increased rapidly.

The Hawke government came to power preaching the need for, and efficacy of, consensus and 'national reconciliation'. Somewhat reminiscent of the rhetoric of the postwar reconstruction phase, emphasis was placed on the power of reasoned arguments and active consultation between governments,

The market-based approach

business and the union movement as the means to a stronger and more stable economy. This attitude was given some substance by the holding of a National Economic Summit in April 1983 and by the introduction of a prices and incomes accord between the government and the Australian Council of Trade Unions (ACTU). In apparent vindication of the accord there was a notable slowing-down in inflation and wage rises in 1983–84. While much was made of the need for consensus, the Hawke government continued to use much of the rhetoric of its predecessors, pointing for instance to the need for budgetary restraint and the evils of large budget deficits. And, surprisingly, the new government was not only willing to question some of the ALP's sacred economic nostrums and to entertain the idea that there might be some virtue in deregulating the financial sector, but was prepared, unlike the Fraser government, to convert words into action: the outstanding example being the decision in December 1983 to float the Australian dollar.

Faced with sudden changes in most of the major economic variables, and faced with a change of government, the Treasury felt no great compulsion to change its basic philosophy: it continued to see the world in essentially the same way as outlined in the previous chapter. It remained steadfast in its view that there was a need to eradicate the distortions which plagued the economy, in particular the problem of inflation. The Treasury could see in the events of 1980–84 only a vindication of its pre-existing causal assumptions about how the economy worked and what was needed to ensure sustained economic recovery. In its analysis of the economic instability of the period and in its recommendations on how this instability might be overcome, the Treasury was, in most instances, more vocal than ever in its support for market-based approaches and in its condemnation of governmental interference.

In part, perhaps, the consistency in Treasury thought was a reflection of John Stone's continuing presence. To the surprise of many commentators, Stone was retained as Treasury secretary after the ALP's electoral victory. It was Stone in fact who took the initiative, pre-empting any possibility of being forced from his position by announcing his resignation in August 1984. The announcement came just before the handing down of the budget and was given maximum publicity, as was Stone's vitriolic Shann memorial lecture, delivered during his last days as secretary. Stone's resignation was in part a public statement of dissatisfaction with the forthcoming budget. But more fundamental in making up his mind, it would seem, was a growing sense of isolation and impotence. Commentators have made much of the fact that the new Treasurer, Paul Keating, increasingly tended to bypass Stone after the decision to float the dollar and to seek instead the advice of the department's other senior officers, such as Bernie Fraser, who was chosen as Stone's successor. For Stone, however, such treatment was merely a continuation of that practised by the Liberal treasurer, John Howard. Relations between Howard and Stone (and in fact the Treasury in general) deteriorated markedly after the 1980 election. Several factors were responsible: the leaking of material written by Stone and embarrassing to Fraser and Howard; Howard's censuring of Stone after the latter's appearance before a Senate committee in March

1981 at which, so the press reported, Stone seemed to support a resources rent tax; and Howard's preference for seeking advice from the Reserve Bank. Stone's growing sense of dissatisfaction with the LNCP government was compounded by the 1982–83 budget. This budget symbolised the extent to which, depending on the political circumstances, the Fraser government was prepared to depart from the Treasury line.

Economic conditions and policies, 1979–81

In 1979–80 and in particular in 1980–81 there was a strengthening in the process of economic recovery. In 1979–80 for example, the rate of increase in average total employment was the highest recorded since 1973–74. Employment increased at an even faster rate in 1980–81: by 2.6 per cent. Stone could argue early in 1981 that 'the labour market has changed beyond recognition from what it was even eighteen months ago'. There had been, he noted, 'a marked and continuing — one might almost say dramatic — lift in the growth of total employment'.[1] Another indicator of the economy's strength was the fact that despite an increase in the participation rate, there was a decline in unemployment in both 1979–80 and 1980–81 — thereby reversing a six-year upward trend. In 1980–81 the rate of growth of the non-farm economy was the fastest recorded (using the expenditure-based measure) since the early 1970s, this despite a depressed international economy reeling from the sharp increases in oil prices in 1979–80. By far the greatest contribution to output growth in 1980–81 came from a sharp rise in private sector expenditure. Private investment expenditure, in particular, grew by over 21 per cent. Non-dwelling construction leapt by nearly 30 per cent. While the increase in private capital expenditure was broadly based, the strongest growth was in resource-related sectors. The Treasury noted with pleasure in 1981 that private investment expenditure as a proportion of GDP had returned close to the level which had prevailed during the 1960s and early 1970s — a return, presumably, to something approaching 'normality'.

In explaining the strengthening of private sector activity in 1979–80 and 1980–81, the Treasury judged that it could

> be attributed in no small way to the general anti-inflationary thrust of the policies which have brought about [a lowering of the inflation rate and an improvement in profitability] and have helped, in so doing, to create a more favourable economic and investment climate. Changes in relative energy prices, which have favoured development of resources with which Australia is generously endowed, have also contributed to this economic recovery. These latter changes are in some respects fortuitous but the speed and vigour with which investors have moved to take advantage of Australia's increased comparative advantage in the energy-related resource sector owes a good deal to steps having been taken earlier to re-establish the pre-conditions for a high level of investment, in resource and non-resource areas alike.[2]

In its reference to relative energy prices the Treasury was acknowledging the

The market-based approach

significance of the second oil price shock — the 140 per cent increase in oil prices in 1979–80 — and the comparative advantage which it bestowed on Australia's rich supply of non-oil energy resources. But the point remains that it disagreed with those who insisted that the decisions of OPEC were the primary reason for Australia's investment boom and new-found economic strength. What had instead been of major significance was the existence of a favourable environment within which investment could occur. And this environment had largely been provided by governments. For what governments had done was to move toward balanced budgets and to make 'room' for the private sector. With an 'I-told-you-so' tone, John Stone triumphantly declared in 1981:

> It is fashionable in some quarters to put our current relatively fortunate position down to good luck and the machinations of the oil sheiks. But the truth is that the strong growth in business investment that is under way is related not simply to the energy pricing policies of OPEC. Not only is the investment upsurge much more widely spread than that, but even in the energy or energy-related area it can also be said that those developments alone would not have been sufficient to stimulate investment if the more general climate for investment had not improved so markedly. There are many countries with rich resource endowments that are not displaying the strength of the Australian economy at present. The U.S. economy today is one such country and the Australian economy earlier in the 1970s was another.
>
> Inconvenient though the conclusion is to those who still hanker after 'big government' spending programs, the increasingly inescapable truth is that the current attractiveness of business investment in Australia is closely related to the drive against such policies which, with some fits and starts as always, has been evident since the mid-1970s. In this respect I point particularly to the Budgets of 1978–79 and 1979–80, which most importantly involved tight expenditure restraint and also, particularly in 1979–80, a significant reduction in the deficit. These Budgets, which were greeted with cries of dismay from many quarters, were associated with a further strengthening in output growth.[3]

In 1980 the Treasury confidently remarked that 'it is clear that we are facing potential growth prospects which, in the next few years at least, are different in kind and in magnitude from the experience of much of the 1970s. The mainspring of that growth is, of course, resource-based investment'.[4] In the following year the Treasury announced that the surge in investment under way provided Australia with 'the opportunity to reap the benefits of a period of sustained economic growth'. But this was on the proviso 'that increases in wages and prices can be contained and reduced'. Emphasising this last point the Treasury noted that while there were obvious similarities with the late 1960s — in the opportunities which the resource boom presented — it nevertheless had to be kept in mind that 'one contrast — the importance of which it is almost impossible to overstate — is that the underlying rate of inflation is now about three times what it was then'.[5] Concerned as ever with the rate of inflation, the Treasury noted with displeasure in 1980 that, as in 1978–79, there had been a reversal in 1979–80 of the previous downward trend in prices and that wages and earnings had accelerated. There was a further increase in 1980–81 in the inflation rate and a sharp rise in average weekly earnings — the latter reflecting the operation of the wage indexation system, increases awarded under 'work-value' judgments, and increases in over-award payments. The greatest danger to the economy, the department warned in 1980, was 'that the prospective surge in private business investment and the (in some cases associated) increase in public sector infrastructure investment could result in straining the existing capacity of the economy, leading to an upsurge of wage increases and an acceleration in cost and price inflation'.[6] This is precisely what happened.

The implications of the resources boom

Amid what proved to be exaggerated claims about the prospective magnitude of the resources investment boom — with Fraser arguing that during the 1980s mining and related resource development was likely to be of the order of $29 billion, the ANZ Bank citing $38 billion, and the Australian Industries Development Association suggesting a figure of $80 billion — a debate occurred in the late 1970s and early 1980s on the economy-wide effects the boom was likely to have. Central to this discussion was a consideration of the so-called 'Gregory thesis' — a reference to the arguments advanced in a 1976 article by the ANU economist, Bob Gregory.[7] The 'Gregory thesis' is the antipodean equivalent of the 'Dutch disease' and British 'deindustrialisation'. It refers to the effect on other sectors of the economy which are likely to arise from the rapid development of an individual sector which is heavily export-oriented: in Australia's case the mining sector, in the Netherlands' natural gas, and in Britain's North Sea oil. The argument begins by noting that the balance-of-payments effect of the growth of the export-oriented sector is likely to be one of large surpluses. These will occur mainly because of the increase in exports but also possibly because of an increased reliance on capital inflow to help finance the development of the sector in question. While offsetting forces are acknowledged (there is, for instance, likely to be an increase in imports — reflecting the 'new' sector's need for capital goods and the growth of income of those employed directly or indirectly by the new sector — as well as an increase in overseas payments), the assumption is that persistent and possibly even chronic balance-of-payments surpluses will occur. In Australia's case the evidence of the mining boom of the late 1960s–early 1970s suggested that this was a valid assumption. The next stage of the argument is to point to the method by which the economy might adjust to the balance-of-payments surpluses. In a situation of freely floating exchange rates the surpluses would tend to be corrected by the appreciation of the domestic currency in relation to foreign currencies. Under a fixed exchange rate system the same end could be achieved, but only of course by a deliberate decision by the authorities to revalue the currency in line with the result which the market would have dictated. If, however, an attempt is made to maintain an undervalued nominal exchange rate the same end will still be achieved — because of an inevitable increase in inflation — through the real exchange rate. Whichever way adjustment occurs, the argument continues, the pre-existing export sectors and those sectors, notably manufacturing, which compete with imports will be adversely affected. They will suffer because of the reduction in demand caused by the exchange rate appreciation and, if the adjustment is brought about by an increase in inflation, by the gradual reduction in competitiveness and profitability. A simple point emerges: a resources boom has both benefits and costs, with the main beneficiaries being the new export industries and the traditional sectors the main losers.

But how great were the losses likely to be? This was the question which Gregory sought to answer in his 1976 article. He attempted to quantify, in a very broad way, the effect the mining boom of the late 1960s–early 1970s had had on other sectors of the Australian economy. He used as the standard of measurement the notion of 'tariff equivalents'. Gregory claimed that the effect of the mining boom on the rural exporting industries was equivalent to a doubling of the tariff level. The effect on the import-competing sector was held to be roughly equal to setting the average tariff at zero and imposing an import subsidy. Here, clearly, was a major reason for the present malaise of manufacturing. Both rural export industries and manufacturing firms, Gregory argued, had suffered much more from the balance-of-payments effect of the boom in mineral exports than from the 25 per cent cut in tariffs imposed in 1973.

With these sorts of pessimistic arguments in mind, amid a growing list of counterarguments and with a powerful resource boom in prospect, John Stone presented late in 1979 a widely publicised and, in most cases, highly acclaimed analysis of the implications of the imminent boom.[8] Stone's starting point was to note that during the 1980s Australia would continue to be a net importer of capital. To put this differently, the necessity of having to rely on foreign capital as a supplement to domestic saving would give rise to persistent capital account surpluses. He argued next that 'in the decade ahead there seems to be every reason to believe that we are going to be very successful at exporting', for almost certainly there would be a strong growth of mineral exports. The combination of net capital inflow and rapid export growth implied, in the absence of any substantive change in imports, chronic balance-of-payments surpluses — as in the 'Gregory thesis'. Stone's argument was that the maintenance of balance-of-payments equilibrium necessarily meant that Australia would have to sustain a deficit on the current account of the balance of payments, something which could only be achieved by increasing imports. The inescapable conclusion, therefore, was that 'the more successful, in the decade ahead, we prove to be at exporting, the more successful *we are also going to have to be* at importing'. There was 'no alternative'. For the propositions being advanced were but a 'mere logical deduction' from the national accounting identity that domestic investment equalled domestic saving *plus* the deficit on the current account of the balance of payments. Such propositions were, therefore, 'unchallengeable'.

This raised the question of the manner in which the increase in imports would occur. Stone argued that there were two options: 'either we can act positively to ensure that import growth substitutes for our own least efficient producers, or we can allow the economic forces involved to produce the required current account readjustment by affecting our efficient producers (exporters as well as our more efficient import-competing industries) as well as our inefficient ones.' The first option, which Stone strongly supported, implied gradually reducing import protection as export income grew. Stone did not support, however, an 'across-the-board' tariff cut, such as occurred in 1973. For the imperative need was to reduce first 'the protection of the things we do worst', that is to concentrate initially on the most highly protected (and hence least efficient) industries. In the absence of a reduction in protection, and with a continued rise in exports, international reserves would increase and, as in the 'Gregory thesis', readjustment would occur through the paths of inflation and/or exchange rate appreciation. The inflation alternative was deemed clearly unacceptable, with Stone arguing that 'I take it utterly for granted that without the maintenance in this country of policies designed to root out inflation there is unlikely to be any real future for Australia in the 1980s'. The only reasonable alternative was exchange rate appreciation. But in Stone's view this could only be described as a 'half-sensible' solution. The first option, that of reducing import barriers, was considered clearly superior to exchange rate appreciation: 'whereas the latter strikes at our efficient (exporting) industries as well as (indiscriminately) at our import-competing industries, the former is designed to let the readjustment occur to a greater degree at the expense of our inefficient (most highly protected) import-competing sectors.'

In his 1979 address and in particular in a speech delivered late in 1981, Stone considered the question of whether there was any way Australia could reduce her reliance on foreign capital. The significance of this question lay in part in the fact that to some Australians the idea of persistent and possibly increasingly larger capital account surpluses seemed to imply, worrisomely, an increasing degree of foreign ownership of Australian companies and resources. The Treasury did not share this concern. The department had long had a reputation for being a strong supporter of foreign investment. John Gorton complained in 1971, not long after being deposed as Prime Minister, that the Treasury had 'an almost pathetic dog-like gratitude for foreign investment'.[9] The department's support for foreign investment was based on the fact that, despite a notably high propensity to save by any international standard, there had been and would continue to be in Australia a persistent deficiency of domestic saving in relation to investment demands. Foreign capital, the Treasury concluded correctly, could therefore only be seen as an indispensable supplement to domestic saving. The Treasury continued to adhere to this view throughout the 1960s and 1970s. There occurred, however, a gradual change in the department's ideas on the dangers inherent in an overly selective approach to the type of capital inflow considered permissible. In the early 1960s the Treasury's approach was to emphasise the risks of selectivity:

The market-based approach

> If Australia is to grow fast, it must have some inflow of capital from abroad — and probably a substantial inflow. Such inflow is desirable, in part to bring the know-how which some forms of enterprise require. The fact that it comes in and remains under foreign ownership and control creates problems, some of them political rather than economic. It may also come in at times and in forms we do not particularly want or in amounts greater than we want.
>
> But while something might be done to regulate the flow and encourage some classes of investment rather than others, it has to be remembered that the decision to invest or not to invest here rests with people elsewhere, largely if not entirely beyond our influence. Anything done to discourage forms of investment having no particular value is apt to involve the risk of discouraging other investments, some of which we may very much need.[10]

By 1972, however, a change had occurred in the department's attitude. The context of this change was a surge of nationalistic fervour about the extent of foreign participation in the mining boom — a fervour exploited in the late 1960s by Gorton and the Country Party leader, McEwen, and captured in the latter's catchcry, 'Buy back the farm'. The Treasury announced:

> Ten years ago ... it was possible to argue, with some force, that any hesitancy in Australia's welcome to capital from overseas in any form would have far-reaching effects in frightening away other potential investors. Today, this 'startled fawn' approach to the matter is widely recognised as no longer tenable. Similarly, whereas ten years ago arguments on this question could be largely conducted in terms of the contribution of foreign capital to Australia's economic growth, today such arguments may be regarded as only part of the picture.[11]

The Treasury also acknowledged that capital inflow, in some of its forms, could seriously aggravate the task of domestic economic management. The department was rather oblique, however, in its discussion of how capital inflow might be regulated and what could be done to minimise the instability which speculative foreign investment might cause.

Being guilty of obliqueness was not a criticism which could be applied to Stone's 1979 and 1981 speeches. He did not discuss the pros and cons of foreign investment but did make clear that the only way Australia could lessen her reliance on capital inflow was by reducing domestic investment and/or increasing domestic saving. Analysing these alternatives, Stone argued that there was little point in attempting to hold back business investment and little possibility of increasing domestic saving (the latter being, in any case, an undesirable objective in that it meant a lower level of consumption expenditure). He emphasised, however, that an obvious way to reduce reliance on the savings of foreigners was to use domestic saving with greater efficiency. Government was singled out as being the party chiefly responsible for squandering scarce savings in various uneconomical public projects. Stone cited as examples the 'over-extravagant Opera House' and such 'fantasies' as the Ord River scheme. He acknowledged, however, that even within the private sector the growth of monopolistic power had substantially reduced the efficiency of the marketplace and encouraged on occasions the same sort of waste of capital as occurred in the public sector. But he remained convinced that 'in the private sector ... the profit and loss account provides at one level a constraint over such waste of capital. Evaluation of proposals can, on average, be expected to be more rigorous and, with costs borne by investors themselves rather than the general community and bureaucratic/political reputations not so paramount, bad investments are more likely to be admitted and even terminated'.[12] Similar sorts of arguments, we have seen, had first been advanced in the mid-1960s by Stone and his fellow authors in the various supplements to the *Treasury Information Bulletin*.

The Treasury used similar reasoning in 1981 to argue that infrastructure should be provided wherever possible by the private sector rather than the public sector. The basis for this argument was 'the belief that it is the private users who are in the best position to evaluate the requirements for certain kinds of infrastructure and, given those requirements, to assess the cost effectiveness of alternative projects'. A greater reliance on the private sector to provide infrastructure would mean considerable gains in efficiency and would mean that projects were 'tested by the discipline of the market'. Repeating what was a popular Treasury theme, the department noted that 'in the public sector, such discipline either does not apply at all, or if it does, applies only in a much vitiated form. Yet it is by concentrating on the most cost-effective projects that the community stands to reap the maximum gains in real income from its limited resources of labour and capital'.[13]

Quite apart from a belief in the greater efficiency of private sector activities and the virtues of market discipline, the Treasury's arguments in 1981 reflected a more immediate concern about the inflationary dangers inherent in the LNCP's overly ambitious infrastructural program, undertaken in anticipation of the resources boom. The Treasury had been aghast at Fraser's decision at the 1980 Premiers' Conference to accept, indeed to encourage, a greatly enlarged borrowing program. The department could see several dangers in this, notably an increased strain on the financial sector, leading to higher interest rates, and the encouragement of accelerating wage demands. These fears proved to be well-founded.

Economic conditions and policies, 1981–84

The rate of growth of the non-farm sector slowed suddenly in the second half of 1981–82. In the following year the economy sank into a deep recession: in 1982–83, for only the second time since the war, a negative rate of growth was recorded. The situation was compounded by the depressed state of the international economy and by the misfortunes of the rural sector. Much of eastern and southern Australia was afflicted in1982–83 by the worst drought on record. The Treasury's estimates showed that farm incomes fell in 1982–83 by over 50 per cent, easily the largest fall recorded during the previous 30 years. Private consumption expenditure slowed in 1982–83 and private investment expenditure collapsed. The extent of the recession could be seen in the sudden jump in unemployment which occurred in 1982–83. Unemployment rose rapidly from 6.2 per cent in 1981–82 to reach 9 per cent in

The market-based approach

1982–83. It peaked at 10.4 per cent in the September quarter of 1983, the highest figure for 50 years. The deterioration in the labour market was also reflected in the sudden halt in employment growth in 1982–83, with the total number of people in civilian employment actually declining by 1.4 per cent, the largest fall for 30 years.

As 1982 progressed, the prospect of a resources investment boom seemed increasingly unlikely. The Treasury noted in August 1982 that 'some of the more marginal resource investment proposals have been abandoned and others rescheduled or deferred indefinitely'. It stressed, however, that these developments had to be placed in perspective and it counselled against the increasingly popular view that the resources boom had come to an abrupt halt: 'Just as the succession of announcements of various development proposals in 1980 and the first half of 1981 may have built up exaggerated perceptions about the likely size of the resource investment surge, so the subsequent deferral or cancellation of some of them may have engendered exaggerated impressions of the magnitude of the downturn, at least in the short-term.'[14] But the department admitted that 'the seriousness for the medium-term prospect of the recent change in the climate for *new* investment decision-making should not be underestimated'.

In talking of a 'recent change in the climate' for investment the Treasury was referring to the sharp increases which had occurred in wages and other labour costs and in interest rates in 1981–82, both of which had squeezed profits and made new investment increasingly unattractive. In the Treasury's view there was a direct link, as in 1974–75, between the increase in wages and the spiralling unemployment. But it acknowledged that while there were parallels with the events of 1974–75, the recent increase in labour costs had not been as great as in the earlier period (the rise in average weekly earnings being in the order of 15 per cent in 1981–82). The depressive effects of loss of competitiveness and reduced profitability had been heightened by the fact that the acceleration in labour costs 'occurred in a situation where profits had not fully recovered from the earlier squeeze, where real interest costs were much higher and where the lessons learned from the earlier experience worked to encourage faster adjustment reponses'.[15] It was for this reason that the labour market had deteriorated so markedly.

In an attempt to moderate wage rises a 'wages pause' was adopted in December 1982. The wages pause was the brainchild of the Prime Minister. The scheme was made possible by first convincing each of the premiers of the desirability of the pause and then securing acceptance of the pause in the relevant state and commonwealth arbitral tribunals. The scheme was accepted by the various arbitral tribunals on 23 December. It was agreed that there would be a pause in wages and conditions until at least 30 June 1983. In some cases the scheme was supplemented by the introduction of legislation freezing the wages of public sector employees.

The depressed state of the labour market, together with the wages pause, led to a marked slowing down in the rate of increase in wages in 1982–83. The pause ended in October 1983. In the meantime, however, the Fraser government was defeated and another wages experiment — the prices and incomes accord between the new Labor government and the ACTU — had begun. The accord, too, recognised the need for wage restraint and sought to achieve it, in something which to Stone defied economic logic, through a centralised system of full wage indexation. In the year to May 1984 wages rose by 8.9 per cent, being almost exactly the rises granted in the two national wage increases (of October 1983 and April 1984). The Treasury was pleased to announce in 1984 that the real wage overhang, which had jumped in the early 1980s, had now narrowed: there had been a 'sizeable' fall in real unit labour costs. There had also been an improvement in the profit share. Both in fact had returned to levels typical of the late 1960s and early 1970s. 'It is clear,' the Treasury noted, 'that an important amelioration of the factor price imbalances which plagued the Australian economy for much of the 1970s and early 1980s did take place in 1983–84.' The Treasury was also pleased to announce that there had been a significant reduction in the inflation rate. After rising by 11.5 per cent in 1982–83 — twice the level of Australia's major trading partners — prices slowed sharply in 1983–84, with the CPI rising by 6.9 per cent. In the second half of 1983–84 prices rose by only 1.8 per cent.

The Australian economy enjoyed a rapid recovery in 1983–84, a reflection of the improvement in Australia's competitive position, the breaking of the drought, the recovery in the international economy and the stimulus provided by the 1982–83 budget. Employment increased by 4.1 per cent from its trough in April 1983 to June 1984, easily the strongest increase of any other 'recovery' period since the early 1970s. Significantly, however, while economic activity expanded strongly in 1983–84, the main stimulus to aggregate demand had been provided by additions to non-farm stocks, a remarkable increase in farm product, and a sharp rise in public sector expenditure. Private investment expenditure remained sluggish and was a source of concern.

The other main worry for the government during 1983 was the pressure placed on the exchange rate by speculative flows of capital. Early in the year there were substantial capital outflows in anticipation of a fall in the value of the Australian dollar. The Labor government responded decisively, announcing a 10 per cent devaluation on 8 March. At the end of the year the opposite problem occurred — substantial inflows of speculative capital. Believing the alternatives to be undesirable — a revaluation (which would serve only to provide quick profits for speculators) and the imposition of capital inflow controls (which would penalise those who genuinely needed to borrow overseas) — the government announced on 9 December that the existing administered exchange rate system had been terminated and that henceforth the value of the Australian dollar would be determined by the forces of supply and demand: the dollar, in other words, was to be floated.[17]

The Treasury and the Campbell Committee

The float was not the only step taken in December by the Labor government toward deregulating the financial sector. In addition, and just as importantly, it

The market-based approach

removed virtually all foreign exchange controls. Soon after, in January 1984, the government announced that it had accepted the principle that there would be advantages to the Australian economy if a limited number of foreign banks were allowed entry. Additional steps were taken in April 1984, with the government announcing that the number of foreign exchange dealers would be increased by authorising suitably qualified non-bank financial institutions to deal in foreign exchange. (The applications of forty such institutions were accepted two months later.) Also in April, Australian stock exchanges were deregulated.

Even if the government's options were limited and floating was the only sensible course left open to it, it nevertheless remains true that the decision was of considerable historical importance. Some would view it, admittedly, simply in terms of Labor's anxiety to be seen as an economically responsible government, a symbol, in the government's apparent desire to forge a strong bond with the financial sector, of its rejection of Labor traditions. From the point of view of economic and political rhetoric, however, the decision stands as a symbol of the degree to which interventionism had grown in disrepute while deregulation and market-based approaches had gained in acceptance and popularity. That said, the point remains that in very few areas outside the financial sector were words converted into action.

Surprising as they were, since they were Labor initiatives (and at odds with the party's election statements), the float and the concomitant moves to deregulate the financial sector were not taken in a vacuum. The idea of deregulating the financial sector had been a major topic of debate since the end of the 1970s. Instrumental in this respect, and providing a focus for the discussion, were the activities of the Campbell Committee. The Committee of Inquiry into the Australian Financial System, as it was formally entitled, was appointed in January 1979 and included Sir Keith Campbell, the chief general manager of the Hooker Corporation, who was appointed chairman, and J.S. Mallyon, the chief manager of the Reserve Bank. The inquiry was the first to be held since the 1936–37 Royal Commission on Money and Banking. It provided, in the submissions to the inquiry, the written responses, interviews and commissioned studies, and in its two lengthy reports — an interim report presented in 1980 and the final report presented in 1981 — a wealth of information on the operation of the financial sector and an invaluable guide to the economic philosophy of a wide variety of groups and individuals.

The committee made clear from the first sentence of the final report the faith which underpinned its investigations and recommendations:

> The Committee starts from the view that the most efficient way to organise economic activity is through a competitive market system which is subject to a minimum of regulation and government intervention. The Committee is conscious that unregulated financial markets do not always work perfectly: they may not be sufficiently competitive and information may be costly or difficult to obtain. As well, free markets might not ensure stability and confidence — essential pre-requisites of an effective financial system. It nevertheless holds firmly to the view that the discipline of the market remains the most economically efficient

basis for allocating funds and resources from the viewpoint of the community as a whole.[18]

The committee's conviction that the only route to financial efficiency was to minimise intervention implied, as Peter Sheehan puts it, 'that the central problems of the current system arise from present levels of government intervention'.[19] Consistent with these philosophical preconceptions, the committee recommended (to list but a few of some 300 specific findings and recommendations): removal of the remaining ceilings on interest rates; that approval be given to the entry of foreign banks; abolition of captive market regulations; relaxation of exchange controls and movement to a free exchange rate; and privatisation of government-owned financial intermediaries.[20]

It is a notable irony that the Treasury, which had been in the vanguard of those who advocated market-based approaches, opposed many of the committee's major recommendations. While the Treasury warned of the distortions which most forms of government intervention could cause, it had long viewed regulation of the financial sector as an exception. Usually sympathetic to most aspects of the Treasury line, Michael Porter could complain in 1978 about 'the *techniques* of monetary control that Treasury has appeared to suggest and support', techniques which included the suppression of markets for foreign exchange, the periodic manipulation of capital controls, complex exchange control rules, 'rigid but jumpy' interest rate policies, and the exclusion of foreign banks from the Australian capital market. 'While it is undoubtedly true,' Porter continued, 'that policy makers often find their preferred policies rejected, such that they are forced to suggest less attractive alternatives, to the best of my knowledge free capital and exchange markets have *never* been endorsed by Treasury or the Reserve Bank; so far as I know they have never been suggested to the Treasurer, the Prime Minister, or Cabinet as desirable means of facilitating monetary stability.'[21]

By the early 1980s, however, an increasing number of Treasury officers had begun to have doubts about the efficacy and desirability of some of the techniques listed above. The department was divided in particular over the question of whether to float the dollar. That Stone strongly opposed the decision taken in December 1983 was well known. But it was also known that a number of other senior officers, including Bernie Fraser, were in favour of it (as was, incidentally, the Reserve Bank). By 1984, however, Stone had been persuaded of the virtues of the float and departmental unity had apparently been restored. In a surprise revelation in the Shann memorial lecture, Stone announced that he was convinced that the Labor government's decision 'will stand as its greatest achievement when all else has been forgotten'. He pointed out that in May 1984 he had informed the OECD's Economic Development and Review Committee that he believed that the floating of the dollar and the abolition of exchange controls constituted 'the most important single step in economic policy to be taken by an Australian Government in the post-War period'. 'There is no doubt in my mind,' Stone told the committee, 'that, over time, they will work very much to the end of "locking" Australia into the wider world, with all the benefits — and no doubt problems also — which that will entail. Moreover ... the decision to float the Australian dollar will ... enhance the authorities' ability to control the money supply and hence — if the will is there to do so — inflation.'[22]

Despite this recantation, and despite Bernie Fraser's recent praise of the moves to deregulate the financial sector, describing them as a 'first-best' solution (something which will be explained later), it would seem remiss not to consider some of the arguments presented by the Treasury to the Campbell Committee. The Treasury fully accepted the proposition that a market-based system produced the most efficient allocation of financial resources. Further, it acknowledged that 'the inherent responsiveness of financial demand and supply is to some extent stifled both by regulation and macroeconomic distortions'. But the fact remained that banks were not just profit-making institutions but were centrally important in the maintenance of public confidence in the financial system. They were the institutions which provided 'the basic payments mechanism for the economy as a whole'. Hence, there was a strong case for some degree of control. 'There will be a continuing need,' the Treasury declared, 'for some measure of regulation to provide adequate information to guide investors' decisions, to prevent abuses ... and sustain macroeconomic stability'.[23] The Treasury also argued that direct controls might occasionally be needed as a necessary supplement to market-oriented instruments for the purposes of monetary policy. The department's argument was effectively that while controls necessarily reduced the efficiency of the financial sector, an even greater threat to efficiency was the existence of macroeconomic distortions such as inflation. If controls successfully helped remove these distortions, then their deleterious effect on the efficiency of the financial sector was a price worth paying:

> Macroeconomic policies are seeking to reduce the costs inherent in fundamental distortions in capital markets and in the economy generally, and in the poor economic performance to which those distortions lead. If successful, such reductions in costs could be expected to outweigh considerably the increased allocative and equity costs associated with the application of supplementary direct controls.[24]

The aspect of the Treasury's submission to the Campbell Committee which received the most publicity was its rejection of suggestions that the Australian dollar should be floated and its support, instead, for the existing exchange rate arrangements. We need to be clear about what these arrangements were. It will be remembered that in November 1971 the traditional link with sterling was terminated and the Australian currency was tied instead to the US dollar. In September 1974 further changes were made, the fixed link with the US dollar being discontinued and the exchange rate linked to a 'basket' of currencies weighted to reflect their trading significance to Australia. In November 1976 additional changes were made, the Australian dollar now having a variable link to a trade-weighted 'basket' of currencies and its value changing daily against all currencies. The system, it should be noted, still

The Treasury line

involved an element of discretion: the level of the exchange rate was monitored by four senior officials and the aim was to make the changes small and frequent. This was not, as is sometimes claimed, a managed float. While the changes in November 1976, the Treasury explained, 'resulted in the rate responding to short-term external developments to a greater extent than in the past, the present ... system continues to provide considerable scope for Australian governments to influence the rate in the short term and to insulate the Australian economy and financial system, to some extent, from overseas financial markets and overseas economies'.[25]

In arguing for the status quo the Treasury based its case not so much on the satisfactory performance of the existing arrangements but on the difficulties which could and had occurred with more market-oriented arrangements. It pointed to the fact that the exchange rate impinged on the entire economy:

> The exchange rate is one of the most important prices in an economy because it affects international transactions and, less directly but pervasively, many domestic transactions. As such, it impinges not only on the state of the balance of payments but on the whole gamut of a country's economic structure and performance. The level of the rate, and the arrangements by which the level may vary, are therefore of considerable importance to that structure and performance.[26]

Given the importance of the exchange rate for the entire economy, and given that a move to a more market-oriented system would almost certainly lead to wider fluctuations in the exchange rate, a departure from the present 'administered system' would mean a more unstable economy, one in which prices fluctuated more sharply and in which capital inflow would be more variable. The Treasury pointed also to the growing dissatisfaction of governments with more market-oriented systems. These had 'not proven particularly successful'. There was increasing recognition, it claimed, 'that exchange rate movements can have a major impact upon domestic cost and price levels (or factor shares), and that the burdens thrown upon the international trading sector of the economy (both businesses and those employed by them) by erratic swings in their competitive price and cost levels are both difficult to justify and likely to be counter-productive in terms of the policy strains they set in train'.[27] The Treasury sealed its case by noting that while the exchange rate's primary role was to achieve external balance, under the present system it could also be used as an additional weapon in achieving domestic policy objectives. It was necessarily the case, then, that 'a change to a more "market-oriented" system would place the whole burden of maintaining domestic economic stability on the domestic instruments of policy.'[28]

Against this, it could be argued that, under a floating system in which the Reserve Bank is no longer a participant in the foreign exchange market, the money supply is likely to be less volatile and hence so too are interest rates. It may well be, then, that it is easier for the monetary authorities to stabilise domestic interest rates because the exchange rate now bears the brunt of movement of funds in and out of Australia. Moreover, if the primary aim of the policy adviser is to unleash disciplinary forces on a recalcitrant economy, then a more freely floating exchange rate is likely to be attractive. This in fact seems to be the chief virtue to Stone of the decision to float the dollar. In his view, the depreciation of the Australian dollar, which has occurred since the float, has had a beneficial effect on the competitiveness of Australian industry. It has also reduced real wages — another virtue to Stone. But the main advantages of the float is that foreign exchange markets can and will provide the disciplinary pressure on the economy which governments might otherwise choose not to impose.

The role of government: the need for consistency and expenditure restraint

Several interrelated themes stand out in the Treasury's analysis of government policy during 1980–84. There was first of all the argument that there was an inverse relationship between the 'health' of the economy and the size of the public sector — whether the latter be measured by the size of the budget deficit or the size of the public sector borrowing requirement (PSBR). Thus the Treasury argued in 1980, for instance, that an important reason why there had been an improvement in the economy in 1979–80 was because of a 'significant reduction' in the commonwealth sector borrowing requirement and because of the remarkably small contribution of public sector expenditure (a mere 0.2 per cent) to product growth. Similarly, in 1981 the Treasury noted that the strong recovery of the previous two years had been associated with a 'substantial reduction' in the commonwealth budget deficit. It followed, of course, that if the economy was to continue to recover there would be a need for a further reduction in the relative size of the public sector. 'The total public sector's expenditure on goods and services,' the Treasury explained in 1981, 'has declined slightly as a proportion of GDP since the mid-1970s — almost entirely because of a declining Commonwealth share — but that proportion remains well above what it was in the 1960s and early 1970s, when private sector activity was last expanding strongly and when in any case the subsequent march of events may suggest, with hindsight, that the proportion was already too great to be sustainable over the longer term.'[29] There was 'no escape', it continued, from the need to reduce public sector demands on real and financial resources so as to make more 'room' for private sector activities.

Another theme in Treasury documents, one that was a logical corollary of the first, was that there could be no justification for departing from the strategy which had been employed throughout the second half of the 1970s. In 1980 it dismissed the suggestion that, with the economy improving, there might be a case for a more 'relaxed' approach. In the following year it argued that there was a continuing need for 'bearing down hard upon inflation at home' and pointed out that the progress made in recent years was a 'good reason for persisting with the same basic strategy in the years immediately ahead'. In 1982, with the economy now deep in recession, the Treasury was adamant that while economic conditions had changed the underlying problems had not. 'The curtailing of inflation,' it announced, 'and the correction of other fundamental imbalances in the economy are still the necessary pre-requisites for re-establishing economic stability and sustainable growth.'[30] There was no justification, therefore, for changing the thrust of the present policy stance. In supporting its argument that there was a need for sticking with the existing relatively restrictive stance, the Treasury used as an additional justification the critical role of expectations and uncertainty. 'The pervasiveness of uncertainty and the intractability and volatility of expectations in recent times,' the department pointed out in its submission to the Campbell Committee, 'has led to the advocacy of the *steady* pursuit of simple and well understood policies as being preferable to the former paradigm of "fine-tuning".' The essential ingredients in a suitable macroeconomic policy framework, it believed, were stability, predictability and workability.

With unemployment rising dramatically, and aware that it would have to fight an election sometime in 1983, the Fraser government brought down a strongly stimulatory budget in 1982. The budget estimate was for a deficit of $1674 million (which compared with an actual result of $549 million in 1981–82). The Treasury had argued for a deficit of no more than $500 million, which implied, given the downturn in the economy, an increase in the deflationary impact of budget policy. John Howard, the Treasurer, and Professor John Hewson, his personal adviser, advocated a $1000 million deficit, which would be what was necessary, they believed, to maintain the existing degree of tightness. The Prime Minister's Department, however, advocated a stimulatory budget, suggesting that the deficit rise to $1900 million. As it turned out, the Prime Minister's Department largely got its way. The Treasury suffered a major defeat.[31]

The actual budget results for 1982–83 saw commonwealth budget outlays rise by 6.3 per cent in real terms, the largest budget rise since 1974–75 and considerably above the average increase of 2 per cent during the previous seven years. Budget outlays as a proportion of GDP rose to record levels while the PSBR nearly doubled. In the following year, 1983, the new government brought down a budget with a much larger deficit — estimated at $8361 million. The actual deficit turned out in fact to be slightly smaller than expected. But the point still remained that there had been a continuing departure from the previous stance of fiscal restraint — something indicated by the fact that the deficit in 1983–84 was equivalent to 4.3 per cent of GDP, compared with 2.7 per cent in 1982–83 and only 0.4 per cent in 1981–82. The Labor government blamed its predecessors for the size of the deficit, making much of the fact that Stone had informed Howard late in February 1983, a week before the election, that the projected deficit for 1983–84 was approximately $9000 million. A slightly more restrictive stance was adopted in 1984, the government bringing down a budget with an estimated deficit of $6745 million. Stone was highly critical of the budget, arguing that the deficit could have been reduced without much difficulty to only $4400 million.[32]

The Treasury was aghast at the changes which had occurred in the budget

The market-based approach

since 1982. The inevitable result, it believed, would be tremendous pressure on financial and real resources, leading to a surge in interest rates and increased inflation and inflationary expectations, all of which would dampen expenditure. The rise in interest rates would lead also to increased capital inflow which in turn would put upward pressure on the exchange rate. 'The consequent decline in expenditure on Australian goods and services,' it argued, 'provides another offset — in some circumstances perhaps more directly important than the interest rate effects — to the direct expenditure-creating effects of the budget deficit.'[33] There were also quantity risks: 'If interest rate pressures approach the unacceptable, or if expectations develop that they are likely to do so, excess money can build up very quickly — and with equal speed spill across the exchanges via haemorrhage on the capital account of the balance of payments.'[34]

Implicit in these comments was another popular theme of Treasury documents: the inability of governments to promote, for anything longer than the short term, increased economic activity and lower unemployment by using stimulatory policies. The experience of 1974–75, in the Treasury's view, demonstrated that such policies ultimately 'did nothing to restore the private sector' and left only a legacy of inflation. Indeed, the Treasury went further, insisting that such policies were likely to exacerbate the situation because of, among other things, the effect on expectations. But there was an additional consideration: unemployment might result not only because of capacity underuse but because of structural rigidities. To the extent that unemployment was caused by the latter, the Treasury's view was, again, that governments could do very little about it by using macroeconomic weapons. If, however, the government adopted a more appropriate form of microeconomic intervention by removing some of the legislative shackles which needlessly hampered the private sector, the situation could be considerably improved. It is worth quoting at length here the arguments put forward by the department in 1984:

> It is worth recalling ... that even in the 1950s and 1960s, when macroeconomic policies were conducted considerably more successfully than in the 1970s and, to date, the 1980s, Australia's economic growth rates generally lagged behind the OECD average.
> At the risk of some over-simplification, it can be said that, in the main, this was the result of inappropriate microeconomic policies — excessive regulation (including, needless to say, in the financial sector) and protection in its many guises.
> In the end, no amount of manipulation of the instruments of macroeconomic control can transform a non-competitive, inflexible and sluggish economy into one which can generate strong economic growth. The dynamics of growth spring from the ability to adjust to changing circumstances. Regulation and protection can impair that ability. The short-term benefits from increased protection and other forms of assistance distract from more substantial adverse effects over the longer term... As is evident in parts of Australian manufacturing industry, even high and increasing levels of protection cannot guarantee jobs. In the ultimate structural change cannot be avoided; either an industry makes the necessary changes and becomes competitive or it eventually shrinks to insignificance. Attempts to resist

the inevitable put at risk the beneficial effects that can and do flow from structural adjustment.³⁵

The views offered here on microeconomic policy were closely allied with those of the department on macroeconomic policy. For the argument was, again, that there was an inverse relationship between the general vitality and efficiency of the economy and the degree of interference by the government — whether this interference be in an expenditure sense (with an excessively large public sector impinging on the real and financial resources of the private sector) or in a regulatory sense (with the government placing too many legislative hurdles in the way of economic agents in the private sector).

The Treasury and the saving ratio

The first half of the 1970s saw a remarkable increase in the household saving ratio, the ratio of household saving to household disposable income. Averaging around 8–9 per cent during the 1960s, the saving ratio climbed dramatically to reach a peak of 17.3 per cent in 1974–75. It declined slowly thereafter. In 1979–80 it stood at 12.6 per cent, still well above the average for the 1960s. The behaviour of the saving ratio in the period 1980–84 was testimony to the volatility of the economy. For the ratio rose in 1980–81 and 1981–82, fell in 1982–83, and then rose sharply (by 1.2 per cent) in 1983–84, being tentatively measured at 13.6 per cent.³⁶ However, a slightly different picture of household saving behaviour in the first half of the 1980s emerges using what the Treasury calls the 'adjusted' household saving ratio. This is derived from the ratio of private consumption to adjusted household disposable income, in which farm income is replaced by its sixteen-quarter moving ratio. The Treasury notes that the adjusted ratio 'seeks to abstract from the volatility in farm income which tends not to be reflected to nearly the same degree in farm consumption'. Making these changes we find that the adjusted ratio moved in the same direction as the standard ratio, with the exception of 1982–83. Whereas the standard ratio fell in that year the adjusted ratio continued to rise.

The economic significance of the saving ratio lies in the fact that an increase in it necessarily means that the proportion of disposable income devoted to consumption has declined and hence so too has (potential) aggregate demand. The behaviour of the ratio perplexed the Australian economics profession. Nothing comparable had occurred since the early 1950s when, with the soaring inflation of the Korean War boom, the saving ratio increased suddenly. The experience of the 1970s differed from this, however, in that the ratio rose higher and refused, unlike in the aftermath of the Korean War boom, to return to 'normal' levels. The behaviour of the ratio was all the more perplexing because it was not a uniform international phenomenon. For Australian economists, the rise in the ratio added to the growing disillusionment with mainstream economics. For it had become the accepted wisdom that during a recession, with unemployment rising and with overtime payments reduced, households would attempt to maintain previous consumption standards, with the result that the saving ratio would fall. It was part of this same wisdom that inflation would have a similar effect. For the reduction in the real value of liquid assets would encourage a switch from saving to the purchase of physical assets more likely to hold their value.[37] But in 1974–75, with Australia facing a situation of both high inflation and, by postwar standards, high unemployment, the saving ratio increased rapidly to unprecedented heights. How could this be explained?

In the mid-1970s the Treasury line was that the change in the behaviour of the saving ratio was a reflection of the onset of pervasive uncertainty. It argued in 1976:

> Contrary to the view that purchases of goods and services should be the best hedge against their effects, inflation and inflationary expectations, by creating uncertainty in respect of future prices and incomes and by eroding the real value of accumulated savings, caused consumers to save more, and spend less, of current incomes... It was not until well into 1975, as the rate of inflation appeared to stabilise and unemployment stopped rising so sharply, that consumers began to adjust their spending to the large real income increases that had occurred previously.[38]

The Treasury was to continue to emphasise for the remainder of the 1970s the link between the uncertainty engendered by inflation and the high level of the saving ratio. This explanation was used to support the 'fight inflation first' strategy. Given the argument that stimulatory policies would exacerbate inflation, the Treasury could claim that any stimulus would not lead to a rise in the propensity to consume but would instead simply increase the saving ratio.

In explaining the rise in the adjusted ratio in 1980–81 and 1981–82, the Treasury pointed to 'the usual lags in the response by households to real income growth' (habit persistence, as economists are fond of calling it) but pointed also, consistent with its usual explanation, to the 'loss of consumer confidence and increased uncertainty in the face of increased inflationary pressures and a weakening labour market'. The reference to 'a weakening labour market' was given more prominence in the next year, 1983, as an explanation of the continued rise in the adjusted ratio. With the economy having experienced a deep recession in 1982–83 and with inflation falling in 1983, the department continued to emphasise the importance of uncertainty in affecting saving behaviour but now argued that 'rising unemployment and deteriorating economic conditions' should be seen as the main causes of uncertainty. In 1984, however, the Treasury's explanation was almost entirely in terms of habit persistence, with the department arguing that the main influence on the ratio was the size of personal income growth in 1983–84: 'There is typically a lag, perhaps averaging of the order of a year, in the response of consumption to sharp movements in income growth, and consumer spending propensities are probably relatively low in respect of some of the incomes which recorded rapid growth in 1983–84.' Some commentators have argued that the Treasury's acknowledgment in 1983 of the importance of unemployment as a cause of uncertainty suggests that the department had come to the view that it was now necessary and possible to fight inflation and unemployment simultaneously. But as we have seen, any change in the department's viewpoint was marginal. There had been no lessening of the department's conviction that the removal of inflation was the chief priority. There could be no reduction in unemployment without continued adherence to the strategy of 'bearing down hard' on inflation.

Achieving wage restraint: decentralisation versus the accord

It was the Treasury's view, as we have seen, that a major reason for the downturn in activity in 1982 was the rise in wages and other labour costs which had occurred since 1980 and in particular in 1981–82. The increase in wages had reduced the competitiveness of Australian exports and increased the difficulties of those competing with imports. Difficulties then began to spread:

> The slowing in output of the traded goods industries (and hence in demand for associated inputs of goods and services) contributed to a more general easing in domestic demand which limited the ability of firms in areas more sheltered from international competition to pass on increases in their labour costs in output prices. Squeezed between a sharp rise in labour costs and constraints upon their ability to raise prices, firms' profits fell sharply and they were increasingly forced to cut production, economise on inventories, close marginal plant and prune their labour forces.[39]

Not only were there these sorts of direct effects but the Treasury was convinced that the acceleration in labour costs had led to a downward revision of investment plans by reducing assessments of competitiveness and profitability, by generating inflationary expectations and, 'by reviving memories of 1974–75, created damaging uncertainty about future cost and price behaviour and the outlook for the economy more generally'.

The Treasury acknowledged that a range of factors were responsible for the sharp increase in wages. It pointed, for instance, in what was a scarcely concealed criticism of Malcolm Fraser and his much-heralded $29 billion resource boom, to the fact that exaggerated assessments of the likely magnitude of the boom had led to the formulation of wage claims 'in anticipation of benefits which had not, in fact, yet begun to flow'. But the department attached primary responsibility for the wages surge, as in its explanation of the 1974–75 period, to the institutional framework within which wage rises were negotiated: the short-sighted policies of the Conciliation and Arbitration Commission and the exercise of monopolistic powers by trade unions. The Treasury was particularly critical of the CCAC. In surveying the economic outlook for 1980–81 the Treasury announced that it expected average weekly earnings to rise by 12 per cent, after having risen by 9.5 per cent and 7.75 per cent in the preceding two years. 'While this projected acceleration in wages must be viewed with concern,' it noted, 'a lower forecast could only be derived from an assumption that the Conciliation and Arbitration Commission will bring down more economically rational awards than it has in the past.' 'Experience suggests,' it added acidly, 'that such an assumption would be unrealistic.'[40] In the Treasury's view the only sensible thing which the commission had done was its decision in July 1981, taken in a situation of growing wages drift and escalating industrial unrest, to abandon wage indexation. There can be no doubt that the Treasury hoped that the commission would also abandon its 'work value' judgments. The department complained in 1980 that 'the current so-called "work value" round — which, notwithstanding what it purports to be, is in the process of spreading a wage increase of a fairly uniform magnitude through most of the workforce — is an indication not only of the momentum that this flow-on process can gather but also of its basic economic irrationality'. The Treasury went on to dismiss 'work value' decisions as being, 'for the most part, nothing of the kind'.[41]

In John Stone's opinion, the sudden leaps in unemployment in 1974–75 and in 1982–83 had been inflicted upon Australia 'by a few particular greedy and ignorant trade union leaders, abetted in some degree by some of their business counterparts and, not least, by the arbitral tribunals'. Stone pointed in particular, in explaining the rise in unemployment in 1982, to the role of the Amalgamated Metals, Foundry and Shipwrights' Union (AMFSU):

> Towards the end of 1981 we experienced in Australia a more than unusually notorious example of centralised wage-fixing between certain metals industries trade union leaders and a limited number of Metal Trades Industries Association employers and leading to an increase in hourly wages costs approaching 25 per cent. During the course of 1982 the results of that master-stroke were seen in the loss of jobs by roughly 30,000 or so metals trades workers and the bankruptcy of a great many metals trades firms. During 1983, that process continued further. Meanwhile the leaders of the AMFSU moralised even more vocally about the need for governments to restore full employment.[42]

It was not contractionary policies, Stone argued, which had caused the rise in unemployment in 1974–75 and 1982–83. It was in fact the actions of cartel elements in the labour market, pushing for and winning large increases in wages, which were to blame. There had been an unwillingness in Australia, Stone lamented, 'to view the workings of labour markets like other markets — in terms of supply, demand and price'. 'Yet employment, unemployment and wages — the things which do attract attention and concern — are nothing more than the labour market reflections of the operation of supply, demand and price.' The undeniable truth was that the only way unemployment could be reduced was by a reduction in real wages.

Given the deleterious effects of rapid and generalised wage rises, how was the restoration of wage restraint possible? One way, the most 'painful' and protracted way, was to rely on what the Treasury called the economy's 'natural' forces, that is to rely on the inevitable increase in unemployment accompanying excessive real wage rises. Eventually the rise in unemployment would lead to a weakening of the bargaining power of trade unions and to some slowing in the pace of wages growth. Another solution was to rely on 'artificial' constraints, such as the 'wages pause'. The difficulty here was that there was a possibility of a wages explosion once the pause ended. Another difficulty was that the pause could last only as long as state governments supported it, the federal government having no constitutional power to implement a national incomes policy.

An alternative solution, the prices and incomes accord, was an attempt to achieve wage restraint by establishing and maintaining a consensual relationship between the government and the union movement: a consensus, in this case, achieved only by the government agreeing to index wages. The Treasury, as we have seen, had long been sceptical of approaches of the consensual type, looking dubiously at the possibility of self-interested organisations being persuaded to act reasonably. In the year before the accord began, the Treasury made it clear that it had not changed its mind:

> The experience of recent years both in Australia and abroad indicates the enormous difficulties involved in seeking to obtain a non-inflationary agreement at the national level that will be adhered to by all the diverse parties involved. The Government cannot itself control wages and the collapse of two centralised systems of wage regulation over the past decade demonstrates the extreme difficulty of achieving restraint by voluntary consensus alone.[43]

In a revealing comment on the collective harm which the actions of trade unions could cause, the Treasury pointed to the institutional arrangements and behavioural characteristics which prevented 'restraint by voluntary consensus alone':

> While trade unions were originally established to serve social purposes, their ability within a highly industrialised economy to negotiate wage rates across whole sectors of industry and to seek to have them adopted as legally enforceable minima poses basic difficulties for the efficient functioning of labour markets and hence for the restoration of price stability and full employment. It requires a good deal of intelligent understanding and self-restraint if these powers are not to be abused, but rather directed towards serving the longer term interests of both those of their members who are in work and those other members of the work-force (and potential work-force) who are unemployed and who will be condemned to remain so at the 'non-market-clearing' wage rates which trade union negotiators have 'succeeded' in forcing upon employers.[44]

In the Treasury's view the only way the wage-fixing process could be made more rational was by moving toward a more decentralised approach to wage determination. The great advantage of such a system was that it would bring

> the focus of responsibility for bargaining outcomes closer to the work-face and to the fortunes of the individual firm involved and its employees... This would be the more so to the extent that it encouraged both sides of the bargaining table, management and employees alike, to take into account the inescapable economic interrelationships between wage levels, price competitiveness, profitability and employment — not in abstract terms, but in direct relation to the immediate problems and circumstances facing their particular firm and hence their own independent livelihoods.[45]

The problem, however, was how to achieve such a system. The results of the collective bargaining practised in the metal trades industry late in 1981

The market-based approach

demonstrated beyond doubt that wage moderation would not necessarily follow simply from the adoption of a non-arbitral framework. If trade unions were the villains of the piece, what could be done to police them? The CCAC could perhaps be altered or possibly even disbanded, but how was it possible to break the power of, say, the AMFSU? These are questions to which we will return shortly.

The Treasury and the real world

In a recent editorial in the *Australian Financial Review*, the editorial writer claimed that Australia was saved from being an 'economic basket case', such as Argentina, by her resistance 'to the attractions of ideologies of mindless nationalism and self-sufficiency, fear of the rest of the world, and balance of payments pessimism'.[46] Australia had been guilty, however, of adhering to a policy of importing-substituting industrialisation. In the writers view this policy was the main reason why the economy had performed so much below its potential in the two decades from 1950. Commenting on these arguments in a letter to the present author, a former senior office in the Treasury wrote:

> During those two decades, the Department of Trade was the bureaucratic stronghold of those ideologies, and the Treasury was the centre of opposition to them. The ironic result was that Treasury operated as the Department *for* trade (e.g. in persuading the Government to abolish import licensing in 1960) and Trade as the Department *against* trade (e.g. in conceiving and winning support for local content plans). I would argue that, if Treasury had been less influential, Australia might have clung to import licensing and 'a quiet life of profitable incompetence' for its manufacturers, as New Zealand did; and that, if Trade had been less influential, Australia might have participated more fully in the great expansion of trade between the industralised countries which occurred in the 1950–70 period — thereby experiencing a more rapid growth in living standards and faster progress toward a more adaptable and resilient economy.

The same officer, commenting on the reference in chapter 8 to the Treasury's 'unbounded faith' in the market (a phrase which seemed to him to imply that that faith was unjustified), remarked that 'my own view is that it is those who showed unbounded faith in policies which defied the market who have been shown to have been naive'. Somewhat similarly, one of the main themes of Stone's Shann lecture was the folly of trying to override market forces and the harm to living standards which had been caused by the governmental tendency to control 'everything that moves'. Similar themes, as we have seen, pervaded nearly all Treasury documents during 1980–84.

Such statements raise the question: what sort of world did the Treasury want to create? If it was naive to have faith in policies which defied market forces, did this imply that Australia could and should attempt to create (or recreate) some sort of free-market economy? The discussion of the Treasury's contribution to the Campbell Committee would clearly suggest that the answer was no. But its comments, and those of Stone, on wage fixing and the role of trade unions have led some commentators to answer unequivocally in the affirmative. Paul Kelly, for example, argues that the Treasury's call in 1982 for a more decentralised wage determination system implied that 'the traditional craft-union structure in Australia would need to be disbanded'. Kelly believes that 'this would amount to social engineering. It would mean negotiations company by company — one of the most radical social changes in Australian history'.[47]

Bernie Fraser, however, strongly denies any suggestion that the department is advocating radical changes. It is taken as 'given' in the department, he argues, that Australia is and will remain a mixed economy 'in which governments (at all levels) are important players along with market forces'. While there is scope for debate about the appropriate extent of government involvement, for the most part 'that debate in Australia is about changes at the margin — and probably fairly gradual changes at that'. In Fraser's opinion, 'this situation renders arguments in favour of general "market" or "interventionist" approaches pretty sterile'. To describe the Treasury as 'free market'-oriented is to caricature it:

> It is one thing to appreciate the benefits that could flow from an unfettered market system *if* the conditions necessary for the establishment of such a system could be statisfied: it is another thing to believe that those conditions can be established and sustained on a wide front. A better characterisation of the Treasury is to see it as a force for 'economic rationalism'. In our mixed economy market forces do play a major role. To ignore them, or to intervene in ways which fly in the face of them, is apt to produce policies which do not contribute as they should to sustained improvements in living standards.[48]

Fraser also rejected the common criticism that the Treasury offered advice 'as though we lived in a perfect world', choosing only the best option and 'apparently oblivious to the practical constraints'. The 'second-best' option, Fraser argued, could be defined as the best available one *if* certain constraints were taken as given or immutable. In offering advice, the Treasury was well aware of the constraints and well aware that some of them were immutable. It did offer, at times, second-best options. But it had also been the department's practice, Fraser argued, to question the immutability of the constraints, to ask whether perhaps they could be 'broken down and removed'. The best example of this, the adoption of a 'first-best' solution, was the present deregulation of financial markets. 'Not too many years ago,' Fraser noted, 'the constraints (the regulations) were seen as being too much a part of our "accepted" system for their removal to be widely advocated. This example illustrates both the mutability of constraints and the kinds of processes of inquiry and education that are likely to be necessary to bring about desirable change.'[49]

It was with a similar frame of mind, that of questioning what were perceived to be immutable constraints, that Stone was led to argue for fundamental changes in Australia's wage-fixing system. Stone was contemptuous of those who attached to the present system (a word which he always preferred to place in quotation marks) an element of 'sacred bovinity'. The fact that the system had been in existence since early in the century and that 'its

The market-based approach

mechanisms are inextricably intertwined with the power structure, indeed the very ethos, of the Australian trade union movement' was in itself no reason for not questioning it and for labelling as 'unrealistic' any suggestion that it be changed or abandoned. 'Have we come to this,' he asked late in 1984, 'that in Australia today "reality" is to be equated in this — and other — areas with the posture of the ostrich. If so, we may well abandon hope for the future of our country, because in that case nothing will be more certain than that it will not have one.'[50]

Behind Stone's complaints about the deleterious consequences of the narrow-minded exercise of monopolistic power was a call for a greater awareness of the effect of wage rises by those who negotiated them. As noted, questions can certainly be raised about the likelihood of a non-arbitral framework necessarily resulting in greater wage moderation than the present system. The speed with which wage rises spread through the labour force would almost certainly be reduced (an important benefit in the Treasury's opinion) but such a framework would not in itself weaken the monopolistic elements which exist in the labour market and which are capable (as was shown in 1981) of exacting large wage rises. That said, surely Stone and the Treasury are nevertheless to be praised for asking questions about what is one of the fundamental problems facing an advanced capitalist democracy such as Australia. More particularly, surely Stone was entitled to be contemptuous of those who resisted calls for change simply by dismissing such calls as unrealistic. And surely the Treasury has been performing a valuable service in questioning what have often assumed to be immutable constraints. Whether the Treasury's alternatives be deemed unpalatable, unachievable or unworkable, it would seem to be self-evident that there is considerable value in questioning existing arrangements and in not bestowing upon them an aura of 'sacred bovinity'.

The Treasury's questioning, as we have seen, has been directed not only at the labour market but at the activities of governments and business. Its guiding assumption, and again this would seem unchallengeable, has been that a reasonably flexible society is desirable (and that to avoid it would be fairly disastrous in the long run). The question is: how do we go about getting it? Unlike many of its critics, the Treasury, with its emphasis on responding to societal needs broadly defined in the market, does at least proffer an answer. Some might see in its answer nothing more than an excessive faith in the efficacy of market forces. But others, and they have a good case, might instead see the Treasury as seeking to maintain the principles of liberal democracy against the forces of corporate power (with corporate broadly defined).

10

Explaining the transition

THE story of the preceding chapters has been described in terms of a gradual shift in the Treasury's outlook from a predominantly Keynesian model to a predominantly neoclassical model. This shift involved primarily a move from seeing the Australian economy as an inherently unstable system (one in which full employment occurred only by chance and then fleetingly) to seeing it as a self-righting system (though one which, for a variety of reasons relating to rigidities and other market distortions, might not always be operating at full employment). Such a shift in vision, it has been shown, was associated with a change in the department's attitude toward the role of government: the latter vision contrasts with the former by suggesting a much more restricted role, and much less need, for active government intervention.

However, what is noteworthy about the Treasury line as it had evolved by the mid-1970s is that the department went much further than simply suggesting the appropriateness of a less interventionist stance. The Treasury came to believe that even if governments wanted to attempt to reduce unemployment they could do so only *indirectly* — by providing the right framework in which the private sector could lift itself out of recession and exercise unimpeded its inherent vitality. The message was that gone were the days when governments could hope to honour a pledge to maintain full employment. Furthermore, the Treasury came to see the actions of governments as often being not the solution to the problems of unemployment and inflation but as a major *source* of them: by the very pledges of governments to maintain full employment (which gave rise to false expectations and which encouraged a tendency to insist on accelerating wage rises by those who believed that they could take for granted that a job was always available); by their 'crowding-out' of the private sector (in both commodity and financial markets); by their budget deficits (which not only contributed to 'crowding-out' but also increased the money supply and hence inflation); and by their creation of dependency relationships (which weakened the vitality of the private sector and which encouraged the socially unproductive habit of seeking maximum protection and assistance).

The story of the preceding chapters was also one of a shift in the Treasury's priorities. In the immediate postwar years the maintenance of full employment was accorded top priority. From the early 1950s onwards, however, inflation was increasingly seen as something almost as evil as unemployment. By the mid-1970s the containment of inflation had taken priority over attempts to reduce a high and increasing unemployment rate. Accompanying the change in the department's priorities was a change in its interpretation of the relationship between unemployment and inflation. Before the 1970s the two were viewed either as largely independent phenomena or, and increasingly this was the case, as connected but exchangeable, in the sense that an increase in one could be traded off for a decrease in the other. By the mid-1970s unemployment and inflation were seen not only as connected but unidirectionally related: higher inflation was the cause of higher unemployment. (Whether there was still some sort of reverse trade-off, in that higher unemployment might contribute to a reduction in inflation, was a point generally omitted from discussion.)

The postwar period saw also a growing interest in the Treasury in efficient resource allocation and a determination to secure a framework which improved allocative efficiency. Associated with this change was an increasing concern with institutional arrangements, such as the decisions and practices of the CCAC, the changed nature of trade union behaviour, and the governmental system of protection and assistance, which hampered the mobility of the factors of production and the flexibility of price (and especially wage) adjustments.

The story has also been, it must be added, one of significant continuities in Treasury attitudes: for instance, the persistent stress on the exercise of restraint (in spending habits, wage demands, and so on) as a key to the maintenance of economic stability. Also, the conviction that although Australia was very much a dependent nation her problems were to a large extent of internal origin and hence, by implication, could be solved or at least alleviated by domestic action, whether it be through governmental policies or simply by Australians acting differently (by being more innovative, by trying to maximise comparative advantage, by being more reasonable in their demands for wage rises, and so on).

The shift in the department's philosophy was of course not unique: in very broad terms something parallel occurred within the economics profession, in Australia and abroad. Attention has been drawn to the muting of Keynes' theoretical heresies from 1936 onwards and to the submergence, in the 1950s and 1960s, of an expurgated brand of Keynesianism within a neoclassical framework (the neoclassical synthesis). Attention has been drawn also to the monetarist counter-revolution, which began in the late 1960s, and to the rise of the rational expectations school, both of which pointed to an even more explicit neoclassical resurgence within the economics discipline.

To state the obvious, the Treasury could hardly escape being influenced by the changes occurring in the nature of economic theory and by the research programs which occupied the profession. But it would be entirely inadequate to suggest that the shift in the Treasury's outlook was *simply* a case of the department following broader philosophical trends. As noted in chapter 6, to rely on such an 'explanation' would be to present an overly simplistic picture of the Treasury as a passive follower of economic fashion. Moreover, it would be to ignore the fact that in Australia the Treasury took the lead in the 1970s in propagating the neoclassical faith. Standing aloof from those who sought a solution to economic instability by the adoption of a prices-incomes policy, that 'particular piece of witch-craft' as John Stone called it, the Treasury insisted on the need to give greater scope to market forces, to 'fight inflation first', to forsake expansionary policies and move toward budget balance, and to take inflationary and rational expectational responses into account. That these sorts of ideas were often summed up by the epithet 'Stone Age' is testimony, despite its denigratory flavour, to the Treasury's role in Australia as a leader rather than a follower of economic fashion.

The significance of the 1970s

How, then, can the shift in the Treasury's outlook be explained? There can be no doubt that the economic experience of the 1970s, especially the events of 1973–75, was of critical importance in the transition in the Treasury line. For the 1970s represented a sudden, then increasingly protracted, departure from what had come to be considered 'normality'. The 1970s saw the dissolution of a whole host of what were thought to be 'usual' or 'traditional' relationships. It saw, for instance, the coexistence of inflation and unemployment. It saw the maintenance of relatively high levels of unemployment in 1973 despite the existence of excess demand. Likewise, it saw unemployment continuing to rise despite the economic upturns of 1976 and 1978. It saw a remarkable increase in the saving ratio and a sustained fall in the ratio of business fixed investment to GDP. It saw a sudden increase in the wages share, and hence a diminution of the profits share, and the maintenance of this new relationship through the second half of the decade. It saw the onset of a real wage 'overhang' — a distortion, as the Treasury described it, of what was thought to be the normal relationship between real wages and productivity. It saw also reversals in sequential relationships. As a team of Treasury researchers noted in 1976:

> The share of business profits in total income tends to vary with the business cycle; as activity expands the increased sales are spread over relatively fixed costs leading to greater profit margins. In previous recessions the business profit share moved coincidentally with overall capacity utilisation. It is noteworthy that in the most recent experience, the profit share started to fall, and sharply so, *two* quarters before the overall cycle turned down.[1]

Similarly, Chris Higgins of the Treasury could point in 1979 to what he considered an outstanding feature of the mid-1970s, namely that real wages had risen sharply and the profit share had fallen in advance of the downturn in aggregate activity. Higgins argued: 'That combination of timing is unprecedented in post-war Australian experience.' He added: 'So, too, is the size of those movements.'[2]

Explaining the transition

Higgins' last sentence points to another way in which the 1970s provided such a marked contrast with what had been considered 'normality'. For such was the size of the movement in a number of key economic variables, especially in the first half of the decade, that they provided something of a 'scale shock'. Unemployment was on a scale and of a duration unprecedented in the postwar period. The rate at which prices and wages increased in 1973–74 had not been experienced since the early 1950s: it was not surprising that the term 'wages explosion' came into vogue to describe what had happened. Industrial disputation rose markedly to reach record levels. The rate of increase in public sector outlays and receipts and, in particular, the scale of the budget deficit were, again, unprecedented in the postwar period. So too was the size of the public sector borrowing requirement. Tariffs were suddenly cut in 1973 by 25 per cent. In the early 1970s official reserve assets leapt dramatically to reach record levels and in 1972–73 M3 rose by almost 26 per cent. There were also marked fluctuations in the exchange rate and sudden rises in interest rates.

But how did the dissolution of 'normal' relationships and the remarkable change in the magnitude of many key economic variables contribute to the transition in the Treasury's outlook? In particular, how did they make the department increasingly sympathetic to the neoclassical viewpoint? In the first place, attention was drawn irresistibly to the importance of relative price movements, in particular the role of real wages, as a determinant of economic change. Chris Higgins noted in 1979 that three 'stylised' aggregate facts had 'dominated Australian macro-economic discussion of the labour market, and perhaps of the economy generally: (a) the sharp increase in the unemployment rate during 1974–75 and its continued high level; (b) the sharp increase in (average) real unit labour cost in 1973–74 and its continued high level; and (c) the occurrence of (a) with a short lag of around 12 months after (b)'. Higgins argued that 'the coincidence in the stylised facts is compelling and since it, in turn, coincides with the theory of economic text books, it is treated [by many others, including himself] as more than coincidental, it is regarded as causal'. The significance of the real wage explosion lay in particular in the reduction which it caused in profitability. As described in other chapters, the Treasury view was that this had led to factor substitution and also, as Higgins put it, 'to investment *contraction* of a size which accounted for a signigicant part of the slowing in aggregate demand'. In this way relative price changes had acted to reduce unemployment both directly and (via the effect on aggregate demand) indirectly. In Higgins' view, it was 'hard to ignore the factor price-output link. This was not just a nominal inflation phenomenon ... but, above all for investment, a relative price phenomenon. That being the case, the ... observation that output appears to be the prime determinant of employment is a superficial observation in the analysis of the 1974–75 period'.[3]

Real wages were, of course, not the only relative price to alter dramatically in the 1970s. The other major change in relative prices was the sudden upsurge in energy costs: the quadrupling of crude oil prices by OPEC in 1973–74 and their doubling in 1979–80. The Australian economy was to a large extent shielded from the direct impact of the 1973–74 decision because of the governmental practice of setting oil price levels below world prices. But with the decision in the 1977–78 budget to move toward import parity pricing and with the announcement of full import parity pricing in the 1978–79 budget, energy producers and their customers were subject to rising and fluctuating energy prices. Australia felt the full force of the 1979–80 OPEC decision.

The departure from 'normality' in the 1970s was significant also in that it bred confusion. And confusion led not only to the questioning of the accepted wisdom — Phillips-curve–Keynesianism — but encouraged a search for simplicities, 'basic truths', as the first stage in coping with the complex of new and altered relationships. Herein lay a key attraction of the neoclassical model. For the central message of the model was remarkably simple: the path to economic efficiency and to the restoration of 'normal' relationships was to let the market rule, to liberate the economy's inherent correcting mechanisms. It is interesting in this respect that in the 1973 survey, when the Treasury was beginning to ask whether the Phillips curve was dead, the department argued that inflation was a complex problem requiring the adoption of a variety of weapons to tackle it successfully. It declared: 'for practical people, concerned with reducing inflation, simplistic models and the simplistic prescriptions which flow from them are not helpful.'[4] By 1977, however, John Stone was advocating the use of what he referred to as 'simplicities' as a way of coping with the perplexing nature of the economic world. Stone confessed that 'the more I've had to live with the sort of situation we have been experiencing the more I have been driven to the view that one had better cling on to some simplicities if only because the more complex prescriptions are not particularly helpful'. He maintained that since 1975 there had evolved in the sphere of domestic policy 'a set of simplicities', described by some as oversimplicities, which had been 'broadly right'. Of these 'the most overwhelmingly simple simplicity' was the overriding need to reduce inflation and, as part of this, to reduce the size of the public sector.[5]

While the onset of confusion in the 1970s increased the attraction of neoclassicism, it served also to dampen the department's enthusiasm for the demand-management policies advocated by Keynesians. For the Treasury could argue that, quite apart from its familiar warnings about the problems of inflation, 'crowding out', and so on which expansionary policies were likely to cause, an active (discretionary) approach — which was at the core of Keynesian policy prescriptions — would almost certainly increase rather than reduce confusion. The department could support its case by pointing to the reaction to the 'kangaroo jumps' in policy (to use Michael Porter's term) which occurred during the Whitlam years. In a world of confusion and 'distortions' to traditional relationships, and uncertainty resulting from inflation and the growth of governmental regulation, the way to restore business confidence, so it seemed to the department and certainly to John Stone, was to pledge consistency and predictability in the use of policy tools. As Stone argued in 1981, a 'prime requirement' of economic policies 'is that they should promote a high degree of certainty as to basic philosophy and approach; there should be a public knowledge that certain courses will be pursued with determination and that an *ad hoc* and band-aid treatment will be abhorred'.[6] These sorts of ideas lay behind the Treasury's insistence on the importance of a pledge to achieve balanced budgets. They also lay behind the department's support for the announcement of conditional projection ranges for growth in M3. The Treasury argued in TEP no. 9: 'In a world characterised by high inflation and, partly related to that, instability and uncertainty, an appropriate and credible monetary projection provides an element of stability and certainty and a manifest [*sic*] of the anti-inflationary intent of policy — a "light" for the private sector to steer by.'[7] The point is, then, that the attraction of a neoclassical policy stance did not lie necessarily in it being any more logically sound than a Keynesian approach, but rather in that it seemed to the department, given its view of the attitudes prevailing in the private sector, the best way to restore business confidence.

Neoclassical policies seemed also the best way to restore discipline, something which was of great importance to the Treasury. For in the department's eyes there had been a persistent departure from 'reasonable' behaviour since at least the beginning of the 1970s. The first half of the decade, in particular, had been characterised by a pervasive indiscipline. Trade unions, for example, had been guilty of inordinate wage demands, excessive militancy and, in their push for shorter hours, of wanting to have their cake and to eat it too. On this last point the Treasury was arguing as early as 1972 that:

> Pressure for fewer working hours is much in evidence currently. So, for that matter, is resistance to moves for an increasingly competitive economic environment. All these manifestations work against economic growth and the raising of material living standards.
> Of course, if it were accepted that limitations on productive effort and moves towards increased leisure involved a taking out of productivity gains in that way rather than increasing real income, then the issue would resolve itself into a straight choice between different value judgments. It is, however, hard to see much evidence of an acceptance of, or even facing up to, the hard choice that is involved. That choice is, very simply, that the fruits of increased productivity cannot be garnered twice, once in real income and again in decreased productive effort or increased leisure.[8]

In a world in which inflation was rampant and in which there was an incessant clamour for higher wages and higher non-wage benefits, neoclassical economics became increasingly attractive to the Treasury. For neoclassical analysis offered order and obedience in a world which seemed to have become unusually wayward and unruly. Its underlying attraction was that it offered authority without having to resort to increased meddling by the state and the introduction of a plethora of controls. Indeed its message was that the arbitrary and irksome intervention of the state should be minimised and the self-equilibrating and disciplinary forces of the market be given much greater scope. To the Treasury the self-equilibrating market mechanism was the ultimate disciplinary force. Hence the department's persistent argument that one could try to override market forces but one would merely subject oneself to 'unnecessary costs', 'unnecessary pains'. 'Distortions' would not persist.

Inevitably, irresistibly, the department insisted, they would be corrected.

As with those pushing for higher wages, so too, in the Treasury's eyes, had governments been unwilling to make 'hard choices'. Governments had been guilty of indiscipline in the form of budgetary largesse, the main offenders being Gorton, McMahon in 1972, and worst of all, the Whitlam government. The 'loans affair' of 1974 stood in the Treasury's view as the supreme monument to governmental financial irresponsibility (given the sheer size of the proposed loan) and financial impropriety (given the underhandedness of the negotiations and the flagrant disregard for official channels). In pushing for the acceptance of balanced budgets the Treasury was pushing in part for an end to such behaviour. For governments, like those attempting to achieve both higher wages and increased leisure, would have to face up to the need for making 'hard choices' once they were committed to the goal of budget balance. It might be added that given these sorts of attitudes it was not surprising that a Keynesian view of the budget, one which saw its role as being to balance the economy, lost favour in the department. For in the Treasury's eyes such a view had and would continue to give licence to unrestricted government spending.

In pushing for balanced budgets and arguing against expansionary policies, the Treasury was hoping also to achieve a reduction in the relative size of the public sector — to the extent at least that budgetary equilibrium was achieved by reining in government expenditure. The aim here was not just to give the private sector 'more room' and to make possible taxation reductions but, once again, to unleash disciplinary forces. For, as we have seen, the Treasury view was that the vitality and efficiency of the private sector derived from the discipline which market forces imparted. To the Treasury, a larger public sector — something which would almost certainly result from the continuance of expansionary policies — was inherently undesirable because it would necessarily mean the increased employment of limited resources in uses not subject to the usual market disciplines faced by the private sector.

A longer-term view

Without denying its critical importance, it must nevertheless be admitted that there is a risk of overstating the significance of the economic experience of the 1970s as an explanation of the shift in the Treasury's outlook. In chapter 6 attention was drawn to the fact that since at least the mid-1960s the Treasury had been preoccupied with typically neoclassical concerns, something witnessed in particular by the elevation of the efficient use of resources to a major, if not to the pre-eminent, economic goal. Furthermore, by the mid-1960s the economy was being described as an inherently adaptable and flexible system; attention was being drawn to the critical role of relative prices in effecting economic change; criticisms were being directed at institutional arrangements which hampered the usually beneficent role of market forces; and emphasis was being attached to the need for economic decision-making to proceed on the basis of an explicit and careful evaluation of costs and benefits. All of these testified to the extent to which the department had moved toward a neoclassical viewpoint before the 1970s. Accordingly, the economic experience of the 1970s should be seen not as initiating the transition toward a predominantly neoclassical viewpoint but as hastening a pre-existing trend. There is a need, therefore, to search more widely for explanations of the change in the Treasury's outlook.

It would seem that the Treasury's traditional function of financial management heightened its interest in, and made it receptive to, a neoclassical viewpoint, in particular the importance of allocating resources efficiently. The Treasury declared in 1966: 'Just as the traditional budgetary Estimates procedure comprises a process of decision-making by governments, involving in effect problems of allocation within some relatively inelastic *financial* constraint, so the process as it is evolving today is increasingly coming to be looked at as involving problems of allocation of a growing total of *physical* resources so as best to serve national objectives.'[9] In other words, the traditional role of treasuries — which encompassed getting the best value for money and avoiding all forms of wasteful spending — blended easily with a desire for putting available goods and services to their best use and eliminating wasteful and inefficient economic activities. Furthermore, the department's traditional role predisposed it to the importance and desirability of exercising financial restraint: a department long used to demanding moderation from a spendthrift public service can be expected to have acquired an outlook wary of that which smacked of the excessive or the imprudent. And being responsible for advising on the means by which expenditure proposals could be financed, the Treasury's traditional function inevitably produced a wariness of budgetary imbalance.

But more important in shifting the Treasury's vision were the economic problems it faced. In chapter 6 emphasis was placed on the rapid rise in defence and others forms of public expenditure after 1963 in contributing to the transition in Treasury attitudes and interests. As early as 1964 the Treasury was arguing that 'to the extent that resources devoted to defence are provided (as in a fully employed economy they must be) by their diversion from the private sector, not only is private consumption likely to be affected but also the level of fixed investment, both public and private, may be lower than it would otherwise have been, probably with adverse effects upon the rate of growth'.[10] The department continued:

> Before the Second World War, when unemployment was considerably greater and more widespread than it is today, some increase in defence spending could stimulate economic activity generally and so increase growth, and, in those circumstances, it could not have been said with certainty that resources released from defence production or the armed forces would necessarily be taken up into other productive activities. There are, however probably no advanced economies of which this is true to any great extent today.[11]

There is here a point of fundamental importance: it was not defence expenditure as such which highlighted the question of resource allocation. It was, rather, the fact that the rapid rise in defence and other forms of public expenditure occurred in a situation of full employment. In this way the postwar period differed radically from the prewar world. As the Treasury itself noted in 1966,

> there is ... a notable difference, which cannot be too strongly stressed, between the pre-war period, when policies for full employment were far from being fully understood, and the post-war period, in which by and large most industrialised countries, including Australia, have maintained full employment with only relatively small cyclical variations from it... [B]y contrast with a pre-war position ... the post-war situation has generally been (and can be expected to continue to be) one in which labour in particular can only be used in producing one item by diverting it from its present use in producing another.[12]

A simple but important point emerges: the full employment of resources throughout the 1950s and 1960s and the increasing stress placed on resources by burgeoning public sector expenditure continually drew attention to the problem of economic scarcity. It was this, in turn, which directed the department's attention toward neoclassical concerns: the efficient use of resources, the importance of calculating opportunity costs, and so on.

The Treasury's characterisation of the postwar world in the passage above points to something else that explains the transition in Treasury thought: the generational factor. Minsky points out that 30 years without a financial panic or deep depression, such as occurred in the postwar years, can be expected to encourage the view

> that these anomalies are myths, or that what happened can be explained by measurement errors, human (policy) errors, or transitory institutional flaws which have since been corrected... That is, the view arises that the disturbing problem that established a need for a new theory 'never' really occurred. Thus an economic theory based upon a business cycle associated with a financial-instability view of how the economy operates can be replaced by theory with a steady-growth perspective, because the relevant considerations to substantiate the cyclical, financial-instability view cannot be made. This is what took place as the forties, fifties, and sixties spun their tales of war and apparent economic success — a success achieved without the aid of appropriate monetary and fiscal policy.[13]

It was pointed out in chapter 6 that the first half of the 1960s saw the rise of a new generation of Treasury officers to senior posts. It seems more than a coincidence that concurrent with these staffing changes was the publication of Treasury documents which revealed an upsurge of interest in neoclassical viewpoints and interests. While it would be obviously incorrect to claim that these 'younger' officers could ignore the great depression — the phenomenon which had such a marked impact on those at the top of the Treasury echelons, such as Wilson and Randall — the point remains that their world view was formed in a markedly different context to that of their superiors. For the context was one of full employment and, frequently, labour shortages; one of continued stress on available resources — something which reflected what was thought to be an apparently persistent tendency toward excess demand; one of continuous growth; and one of persistent inflation. While such conditions continued to underline the importance of aggregate demand as a determinant of economic activity, the Keynesian notion that the system was inherently flawed, in that there was no inherent tendency toward full employment, seemed increasingly tenuous. As described in chapter 5, 'depression' became an obsolete word during the 1950s. And the idea of a 'trade cycle' was replaced by the concept of a 'growth cycle'. Despite occasional (indeed infrequent) setbacks, such as in 1952 and 1961, there seemed every reason to take for granted the maintenance of a continuously growing and largely stable system.

John Stone was in fact well aware of the significance of the generational factor. In a 1969 address he argued:

> In the early post-war years, and indeed, albeit with diminishing force, until very recently memories of the 1930s lingered... Today, however, we are nearly 25 years into the post-war period, and nearly 30 years past those fearful pre-war years. Those whose minds were shaped by the experiences of those years, whether their personal experiences or those of their parents, are a steadily declining proportion of our communities. Quite literally, they are a dying race. Within the totality of decision-making small and great, which goes to shape the outcome within our private enterprise societies, the 'weights' have therefore been shifting steadily towards the new men (and increasingly, women) whose memories and expectations are quite different.[14]

And in a supplement to the *Treasury Information Bulletin* published in 1966, Stone and his fellow authors dismissed the depression experience as being 'no longer relevant' and went on to argue with some impatience that it was possibly because memories of the depression persisted in some quarters that the economy's basic adaptability was sometimes obscured.[15]

It needs to be remembered, however, that those Treasury officers who began to come to power in the 1960s and afterwards were a product not only of a particular economic context but of a particular intellectual context: one in which mainstream economics was dominated by the neoclassical synthesis (and hence one in which Keynes' chief theoretical heresies had been abstracted from); one in which the economics discipline was becoming increasingly mathematised; one in which partial equilibrium analysis was being replaced by an interest in general equilibrium analysis; and one in which leadership of the discipline had passed from Britain to the United States.

On this last point there can be no doubt that for the economics profession as a whole the neoclassical resurgence was linked with the domination of postwar economics by Americans. For what is notable about the United States is the reservation, if not sometimes outright rejection, with which Keynesianism (in particular its theoretical core) was greeted. What is notable also is the popularity there of diluted-Keynesian and anti-Keynesian brands of economics. It was in the United States that monetarism first gained in popularity and it was of course in Chicago that monetarism had its spiritual home. It was in the United States that the rational expectations school first appeared and gained the most adherents. And it was in the United States that benefit-cost analysis and PPB first began to be used extensively and whose theoretical underpinnings were first developed in depth.

The Treasury line

The growing influence of the United States on the trend of Australian economic thought is obvious. It can be seen, for instance, in the popularity of American economic texts in Australian universities (particularly at Monash and the Australian National University) and in the increasing popularity of undertaking postgraduate study in the United States. In the Treasury's case, the American influence was experienced not only indirectly but also directly. From the early 1960s onwards an increasing number of Treasury officers were seconded to Washington-based institutions such as the IMF and the World Banking Group. At the IMF Treasury officers were employed at a variety of levels, including executive director (Stone and O'Donnell being examples), alternate director, economist and technical assistant. And some of the younger officers have participated in the Young Professionals Programme of the IMF.

A 'Stone Age'?

This suggests that many factors have to be taken into account in trying to understand the transition in Treasury thought. No doubt, however, those whose knowledge of the Treasury is based solely on press reports, and especially those who are captivated by the 'great man' theory of history, might well be inclined to argue that the direction the Treasury line has followed since the early 1960s can almost entirely be explained in terms of John Stone's influence. Such a claim is not without some foundation. For certainly it is true that an interest in resource allocation became apparent in departmental publications following Stone's appointment in 1962 as head of the Economic and Financial Surveys Branch. And it is of course true that it was after Stone became deputy secretary (economic) in 1971 that the department's outlook became much more obviously neoclassical. Furthermore, it seems entirely reasonable to argue that Stone's early training in mathematical physics predisposed him, more so than other Treasury officers, to the deterministic, essentially mechanistic basis of the neoclassical model.

But none of these facts in themselves sufficiently justify the claim that Stone should be seen as the principal determinant of Treasury attitudes. The attraction of the 'great man' theory lies of course in its mono-causal simplicity and its exaggerated claims about the power of the individual. But this is also its main weakness, something which I hope will be obvious given the range of causal factors canvassed in this chapter. Without denying that Stone was a powerful intellectual force in the department and without denying the importance of his deep sympathies for the neoclassical model, Stone's position in the department is best seen not as a shepherd leading a flock of sheeplike Treasury officers but, to offer a more satisfactory metaphor, the zealot among the devout. For Stone's energies were directed primarily at converting those outside the department rather than those within. Indeed one reason why it is so easy to assume that he had a disproportionate influence within the department is because in his determination to enlighten others Stone has been willing, indeed almost anxious, to enter the limelight of public debate. In this way he contrasts markedly with the public reticence of departmental personalities such as Wilson, Randall and O'Donnell and it is easy to jump to the conclusion that his must have been a much more forceful presence.

A former senior officer in the department points out that Maurice O'Donnell's death in 1969 disturbed the projected succession in the department: 'Mr O'Donnell had been expected to be a short-term successor to Sir Richard Randall and to influence substantially further departmental leadership. His demise left a gap, and ultimately resulted in the McMahon Government appointing Sir Frederick Wheeler as Secretary, and his decision to appoint John Stone as Deputy Secretary.' 'In a sense,' he argued, 'this led to an enormous change in approach in the Department and the Wheeler/Stone leadership dominated it for the next fifteen years.' The meaning of 'enormous change in approach' is unclear. It would seem, however, that the officer was referring more to the administrative style of the department rather than its economic philosophy. For he continued: 'The present (or recent) image of the Department relates basically to the Wheeler/Stone style or styles, which contrasts considerably with that of Maurice O'Donnell.' The Wheeler/Stone era, he added, saw the Treasury 'almost continuously in conflict with politicians from both parties'.[16]

In understanding some of the differences in style between Stone and O'Donnell, it is instructive to consider Maximilian Walsh's tribute to the latter, published in the *Canberra Times* two days after O'Donnell died:

> It is perhaps appropriate that the death of Maurice O'Donnell should attract so little public attention beyond Canberra for M. O'Donnell was a man who was proud of the anonymity and integrity of the Australian bureaucracy. He epitomised all that was admirable in the system and he would have had it no other way [than] that his role in guiding the destiny of this nation was totally self-effacing and that his contribution was known and appreciated by a relatively small group within the community. I feel privileged to have known and respected Maurice O'Donnell. Although not of robust physique he was a prodigious worker who gave unstintingly of his considerable intellect. Despite the demanding nature of his position Maurice was a man of surpassing courtesy and inexhaustible patience. His manner was deceptively mild for a man who had such a steely dedication to his job and such an acute sense of responsibility. All who knew him realised he fought tenaciously for what he believed to be right and brought to his work a mind that was superb in both its analytical ability and its receptiveness to changing economic technology. He will be missed by the journalists of Canberra as well as the public service. However, Maurice O'Donnell left his own mark on the development of Australia and it is really the country at large, in its blissful ignorance of what Maurice's contribution was, that will miss him the most.[17]

Walsh's poignant prose serves as a reminder that the influence of Treasury personalities such as O'Donnell can easily be underestimated simply because, unlike Stone, they have preferred anonymity.

In his crusade against ignorance ('the greatest single danger to Australia's prospects for economic progress'), and in the name of promoting intelligent debate,[18] Stone, by contrast, has long made use of public pronouncements. The most obvious examples are his speeches while he was deputy secretary and secretary and the often politically embarrassing leakages of his letters and memoranda. But quite apart from these solo efforts, Stone secured the publication of a range of Treasury documents. It was here in particular that Stone's efforts were significant. It was while Stone was head of the Economic and Financial Surveys Branch that a spate of supplements to the *Treasury Information Bulletin*, prepared in that branch, were published. (Significantly, with Stone's departure for Washington in 1967 these special topic supplements ceased to appear, except for one on labour force projections.) And it was no mere coincidence that not long after Stone's return to Canberra, and his appointment as Deputy Secretary, two new vehicles were established to make public Treasury views: Treasury Economic Papers and the 'Statement No. 2' attached to the annual budget speech. In the more congenial political atmosphere of the second half of the 1970s 'Statement No. 2' steadily increased in length and TEPs proliferated. Furthermore, a whole host of other departmental publications appeared in the 1970s, including the Treasury Taxation Papers, supplements to the Treasury's *Round-Up of Economic Statistics*, as well as contributions to conferences and journals by individual Treasury officers, in particular by those engaged on the NIF model. All these documents can be seen as testimony to Stone's aim to disseminate Treasury views as widely as possible. Acknowledging that Treasury views became more prominent in the 1970s with much wider publication of departmental documents, Stone admits that 'I would have to plead guilty to having then probably been the strongest proponent of that course within the Department'. Those trying to understand the nature of the Treasury line can only be grateful for his efforts.

It is true that Stone played a major role in the writing of a number of Treasury documents. Referring to the supplements to the *Treasury Information Bulletin* published in the mid-1960s, Stone notes that 'I would certainly not claim to have written all (or any) of those papers but I did have a considerable hand — in some cases, a very considerable hand — in their presentation and the whole "editorial" tenor of them'. He also notes that he 'continued to be closely associated' with these documents when, after his return from Washington, they were reinstituted under the title of Treasury Economic Papers. It is also true that other Treasury documents have had principal authors. Richard Randall, for instance, was responsible for the annual surveys from 1956 until his promotion in 1966. But the point remains, as Stone would readily admit, that there has long been a tradition of teamwork in the production of departmental documents. Relevant here are the comments of one of the original members of GFEP:

> Within the FEP there was ... much interchange of views on current issues. It was ... an elite area staffed by highly qualified and intelligent people and they were encouraged to comment on and make contributions to documents as papers 'went up the line'. Any major documents which emerged from FEP would almost invariably have passed through several drafts and been scrutinised by a number of officers with an interest in the subject. Accordingly most of the work carried out in FEP in this period could rightly be described as *team* work. At the same time, FEP

was ... an integral part of the departmental machine and this meant that responsibility for many matters was finally taken by the more senior officers in FEP and in some instances, by the Permanent Head himself. The fact that this decision-making process was usually accepted by all concerned and that there was seldom any public disclosure of internal differences was probably due in large part to the efficacy of the consultation process which usually preceded the formulation of FEP advice on important matters.[19]

Although this description refers to the 1950s and 1960s, there would seem to be no reason why the emphasis on team work did not continue to apply to the production of Treasury documents in the 1970s and 1980s. Nor does there seem any reason to doubt the continuing veracity of the same officer's conclusion that 'it is extremely difficult, in most cases, to determine the extent and quality of the contributions made by individual officers'.

Three final points can be made about Stone's influence on the nature of Treasury thought. First, Stone's assessment is that the supplements to the *Treasury Information Bulletin*, with which he was so closely connected, 'did leave some slight mark not only on the quality of public debate (to which they were directed) but also, perhaps, on the course of debate within the Treasury itself'. Second, he argues that it is hardly necessary to point out that 'a strong belief in public debate (and an associated belief in the need to give the public some official basis for that debate)', two of the hallmarks of Stone's personal philosophy, do not in themselves provide evidence that he had a disproportionate influence on the nature of Treasury thought. Third, to portray Stone as the sole determinant of Treasury views is to insult the intellectual calibre of other officers in the department. Stone puts the point with his usual forcefulness:

> The Treasury contains what I sincerely believe to be the greatest collection of sheer intellectual talent in any institution in this country and on those grounds alone I think it nonsensical to suggest that people of the quality concerned would dream of surrendering their intellectual independence to any mere colleague (as I was in their eyes). Indeed, one of the very great qualities of the Department through my time there was what I might call the quality of its academic debate. The fact that most of that debate took place in-house merely contributed to its sharpness — indeed, at times, ferocity.[20]

Appendix:
The Treasury's NIF model

WHILE the Treasury's NIF model is but one of a range of tools used by the department in the formulation of economic advice and acts only as a supplement to the exercise of individual judgment, it needs to be recognised that the model has a special place in the history of macroeconomic modelling in Australia. Challen and FitzGerald have argued recently: 'Few would dispute the claim that the NIF project represents Australia's most sustained professional macroeconomic model-building effort, comparable with the major macroeconomic model-building efforts overseas, Certainly, NIF is the longest standing by far of Australia's general-purpose macroeconomic models.'[1] It would seem remiss, therefore, not to offer some comments on the Treasury's model-building activities and on the nature of the model.

'It would not be rash to assert,' Challen and Hagger have argued, 'that the most dramatic and significant development in economics since the end of the War has been the emergence of large-scale macro-dynamic econometric models.'[2] By 'macro-dynamic econometric model' they mean a system of numerical relationships which link the main economic aggregates (including GDP, aggregate employment and unemployment, the rate of inflation, the balance of trade, and the rate of change in the money stock) and which can be used to forecast the value of the aggregates (for say four to six quarters ahead) and/or to analyse the effect (over various time periods) of different policy proposals (simulation analysis). While model building gained in popularity in the United States and Britain from the early 1950s, it was not until the 1960s that attempts were made to model the Australian economy — the earliest attempt being that of J.W. Nevile in 1962. Another relatively simple and unsophisticated model was constructed in 1966 by J. Kmenta, while at about the same time a group of economists in the commonwealth public service attempted to apply a rudimentary forecasting model. This latter effort proved abortive.

The late 1960s, however, saw the beginning of what proved to be a sustained model-building effort in Australia, with the initial centres of activity being the Australian Bureau of Statistics (ABS) and the Reserve Bank. Chris Higgins attaches special importance to 1968, the year he returned to the bureau after graduate studies with one of the pioneers of macroeconomic modelling, Professor Lawrence Klein of the University of Pennsylvania. Higgins relates that early in that year

> I joined the small sub-section in the National Accounts area headed by Michael Keating, titled Investigation and Analysis. Among other tasks Keating participated, with several other Bureau officers, in the National Income Forecasting Committee (NIFC) and (mainly) Sub-committee. The procedures used by the Sub-committee involved separate estimates of income and expenditure aggregates, with subsequent reconciliation of the two sides of the production account by limited

Appendix

iteration among the participants ... Keating was working on inventories on two fronts: he was developing estimates of the stock valuation adjustment and experimenting with inventory equations using the Lovell specifications. I am not sure whether the statistical data estimates (required for other purposes as well) stimulated the econometric investigation, or vice versa; in any event the work was a joint product.[3]

While Keating worked on the interrelatedness of imports and inventories, Higgins worked on quarterly consumption functions. By the end of 1968, and despite the fact that the modelling and forecasting work 'was very much part time for us in those days', 'an econometric model was off and running in the NIFC processes'. Meanwhile work was proceeding apace at the Reserve Bank:

> Supporting the proposition that the developments I was involved in represented a tendency whose time was ripe, Bill Norton had returned from graduate studies (in the UK) at about the same time as I had, and was developing a quarterly model at the Reserve Bank. That research work went ahead rather more rapidly than ours in the Bureau of Statistics, and the model which Norton presented at the August 1969 ANZAAS Congress was already a good deal more elaborated than the NIF model was to become for several years. Norton had embarked, from the outset, on a larger design that would permit respectable policy analysis. That remained the emphasis at the Bank for some time, and it was not until later that the Reserve Bank participants in the NIF rounds brought competitive model-based forecasts to the meetings.[4]

Higgins notes that in the latter part of 1969 senior officers in the Bureau (including the Commonwealth Statistician, Keith Archer) were sufficiently impressed with the econometric work that it was decided to set up a sub-section. This sub-section, entitled Econometric Applications, was formally established in early 1970. Coincidental with these developments, Higgins joined the Treasury:

> At the end of 1969 an opportunity arose for me to move to the Treasury, which I did in early 1970, joining the also not-so-very-old Short-Term Forecasting Section under Dick Rye. [Vince] FitzGerald had come across from the Sampling and Methodology area of the Bureau to provide the nucleus of the new sub-section. Thus began the Treasury-ABS collaboration in the development of NIF. It was a most felicitous collaboration and in the next few years NIF progressed rapidly.[5]

After making its first public appearance in 1970, the NIF model increased rapidly in size and sophistication. Table A.1 provides a guide to the development of the model, listing the number of behavioural equations in the 1972 version (NIF-2), the 1976 version (NIF-6) and 1981 version (NIF-10). The major work in the period up to 1976, it can be seen, was the enlargement of the price and income-distribution sectors of the model. Work began on the detailed monetary sector in 1975 and was largely completed by 1977–78. The number of behavioural equations in the money and interest rates sector was enlarged from two in NIF-6 to 29 in NIF-10. Since 1977–78, as H.N. Johnston, the present leader of the NIF team, points out,

> the focus of the development [of the model] shifted to refurbishing those equations in the real sector which were starting to show their age. With the greater volatility of the economic experience in the 1970s, economic modelling the world over had become a more demanding but at the same time a potentially more rewarding undertaking as the greater variation in the data made for more effective testing of competing hypotheses; unfortunately, it also all too frequently showed the available explanations to be inadequate in some degree.[6]

Although the model had long been used for simulation purposes (for instance, in 1974 Caton, Evans and Johnston used the model in an analysis of the impact of different forms of wage indexation), it was not until the early 1980s that attempts were made to

The Treasury line

endogenise more sectors of the model and thereby improve its capacity for longer-term policy analysis — the simulation version being called NIF-10S.[7] However, the primary purpose of the NIF model remains that of short-term forecasting.

Table A.1 NIF model — behavioural equations

	NIF-2	NIF-6	NIF-10
Consumption	5	5	5
Investment	4	4	6
Imports	1	1	1
Labour market	3	3	3
Money and interest rates	1	2	29
Wages and prices	5	15	15
Incomes	1	10	13
Taxes and transfers	6	6	8
TOTAL	26	46	80

Source: Reproduced from Treasury *NIF-10 Model* p. 2

In a 1979 paper Challen and Hagger classified Australia's working macroeconomic models into three 'families': KK (Keynes-Klein), PB (Phillips-Bergstrom) and WJ (Walras-Johansen). They explained: 'The second name in each label is the name of the econometrician who produced the model we regard as the prototype — the father of the family, so to speak. The first name belongs to the theoretical economist who provided the vision — whose special way of looking at the working of the macroeconomy was taken over by the second-named and used as the framework for his prototype model.'[8] Challen and Hagger argued that the NIF model fitted squarely into the KK category. Commenting on the 1981 version of the model, Challen and FitzGerald explained the basis of the NIF model's classification: 'It is large (about eighty behavioural equations and 154 identities, involving 234 endogenous and 147 exogenous variables), non-linear, formulated in discrete time, stochastic and dynamic. It emphasises the determination of the major expenditure aggregates. The model is demand dominated and oriented to adjustment processes in disequilibrium.'[9]

The nature of an econometric model, and hence its classification, will of course reflect the purpose for which it is to be used. As we have seen, the NIF model was constructed and has mostly been used for forecasting purposes. Since its main purpose has always been to provide estimates of national income, it is perhaps not surprising that the model was constructed with a predominantly Keynesian flavour — where 'Keynesian' refers to the sorts of characteristics listed above: a model emphasising aggregate demand and one which is dynamic and concerned mostly with disequilibrium states.

Such is the complicated nature of the NIF model, however, that doubts have been raised about the usefulness and accuracy of categorising it as a KK model and indeed of the general adequacy of Challen and Hagger's criteria. One difficulty is that those models which were originally based on the prototype model — that presented by Klein in 1950 in *Economic Fluctuations in the United States 1921–1941* — have undergone much modification, particularly since the early 1970s. In the Treasury's case, for instance, much greater attention has been given to the supply side (in the wake of supply-side shocks) and the role of relative prices, and a well-developed monetary sector has been included, as well as a neoclassical formulation of business investment (on the grounds that it is the only framework which explicitly allows for capital-labour substitution). The result is an eclectic model: a product of modifying a predominantly Keynesian model by adding more and more neoclassical elements.[10] Johnston and his

Appendix

fellow members of the NIF team argue that while the early versions of the model had features which would classify it as a member of the KK family, 'the characterisation loses its crispness in its application to recent versions of the NIF model'. Further, 'the inevitable cross-breeding that occurs over the years can blur the family resemblance'. They also argue that while the model is certainly not monetarist, neither can it be described as Keynesian 'as that term has been popularly applied'. They conclude that 'the classification of a model of the scope and size of the NIF-10 model as monetarist, Keynesian, neo-Keynesian or some other label can be quite misleading'.[11] There is one sense, however, in which 'Keynes-Klein' seems a particularly apposite label for the NIF model. For Klein has had a direct influence on a number of the principal builders of the model. Higgins, as noted, was a Klein graduate. But as he points out, other members of the NIF team attended Pennsylvania to work under Klein, including Chris Caton and Neil Johnston. Higgins argues: 'While Klein's disciples have been many and have spread to many lands and many major modelling exercises, there has probably not elsewhere been as great and sustained a concentration as on the NIF project, at least outside the United States.'[12]

Notes

Preface

1 TEP no. 3, *Flexibility, Economic Change and Growth* Canberra: AGPS, 1978, p. 1
2 When figures were expressed originally in pounds these have been converted on the basis of £1 = $2

Chapter 1

1 C.B. Schedvin *Australia and the Great Depression* Sydney: Sydney University Press, 1970, p. 88
2 Quoted in L.F. Crisp 'Central Co-ordination of Commonwealth Policy-Making: Roles and Dilemmas of the Prime Minister's Department' *Public Administration* 26, 1, 1967, p. 36n
3 Quoted in ibid. p. 36
4 As in the remainder of this book, the modern terminology is used here in order to avoid confusion. In 1969 the Treasury accepted the conventions used in the rest of the Commonwealth public service and began to refer to branches as divisions. Divisions, then, are the chief administrative groupings within departments. Divisions are divided into branches, which are in turn divided into sections.
5 R.W. Cole 'The Economic and Financial Surveys Divisions of the Commonwealth Treasury' *Public Administration* 23, 2, 1964, p. 172
6 Bruce Juddery *At the Centre: The Australian Bureaucracy in the 1970s* Melbourne: Cheshire, 1974, p. 74
7 ibid., appendix, charts 5a and 5b
8 Treasury *First Annual Report 1978–79* Canberra: AGPS, 1979, p. 4
9 ibid. p. 5
10 pers. comm. to the author
11 S. Encel 'The Recruitment of University Graduates to the Commonwealth Public Service' *Public Administration* 12, 4, 1953, p. 228
12 Robert S. Parker *Public Service Recruitment in Australia* Melbourne: Melbourne University Press, 1942, pp. 269–70
13 D.B. Copland 'The Change-Over to Peace' in D.A.S. Campbell (ed.) *Post-War Reconstruction in Australia* Sydney: Australasian Publishing Co., 1944, p. 165
14 S.J. Butlin '"Of Course I Know No Economics, But —"' *Australian Quarterly* 20, 3, 1948, p. 40
15 'Memorandum on Treasury Organisation', 18 January 1946, J.J. Dedman Papers, National Library, Canberra
16 pers. comm. to the author
17 pers. comm. to the author; emphasis in the original
18 Patrick Weller and James Cutt *Treasury Control in Australia* Sydney: Ian Novak, 1976, p. 98
19 Graham Freudenberg *A Certain Grandeur: Gough Whitlam in Politics* South Melbourne: Macmillan, 1977, pp. 281–82
20 Geoffrey Hawker, R.F.I. Smith and Patrick Weller *Politics and Policy in Australia* St Lucia: UQP, 1979, p. 263

Notes

21 ibid. p. 265
22 Richard Randall 'Policy Co-ordination for the Service: The Role of the Treasury', quoted in L.F. Crisp 'The Commonwealth Treasury's Changed Role and Its Organisational Consequences' *Public Administration* 20, 4, 1961, pp. 317–18
23 RCAGA *Report* Canberra: AGPS, 1976, para. 11.3.13, p. 369
24 Quoted in Weller and Cutt *Treasury Control* p. 44
25 Crisp 'Central Co-ordination' pp. 38–39; emphasis in the original
26 Leon Glezer *Tariff Politics. Australian Policy Making 1960–1980* Melbourne: Melbourne University Press, 1982, p. 170
27 Ainsley Jolley *Macro-Economic Policy in Australia, 1972–1976* London: Croom Helm, 1978, p. 19
28 ibid. p. 21
29 'Memorandum on Treasury Organisation' paras 43, 46
30 M.W. O'Donnell 'Purposes and Practices of Treasury Policies and Controls', quoted in Crisp 'Treasury's Changed Role' p. 317
31 B.W. Fraser, The Australian Treasury — Tendering Economic Advice, paper presented to Royal Australian Institute of Public Administration, ACT Division, Canberra, October 1984, mimeo, pp. 5, 6
32 Glezer *Tariff Politics* p. 172
33 Paul Hasluck *The Government and the People 1939–45* Canberra: Australian War Memorial, 1952, p. 471
34 Quoted in L.F. Crisp *Ben Chifley* Melbourne: Longmans, 1961, p. 257
35 Cole 'Economic and Financial Surveys Division' pp. 173–74
36 H.C. Coombs *Trial Balance* South Melbourne: Macmillan, 1981, p. 132
37 ibid. p. 270
38 *Age* 20 January 1979

Chapter 2

1 See Joseph A. Schumpeter *History of Economic Analysis* New York: Oxford University Press, 1954, pp. 41–42, 561–62
2 J.R. Hicks *The Theory of Wages* 2nd edn, London: Macmillan, 1963, p. 306
3 J.R. Hicks *Value and Capital. An Inquiry into Some Fundamental Principles of Economic Theory* Oxford: Oxford University Press, 1939 p. 2
4 Léon Walras *Elements of Pure Economics or The Theory of Social Wealth* (1874), edition définitive (1926), trans. William Jaffé, Homewood: Richard D. Irwin, 1954, p. 48
5 ibid. pp. 224–25; emphasis added; words in square brackets added by translator
6 Georg Simmel *The Philosophy of Money* (1900), trans. Tom Bottomore and David Frisby, London: Routledge & Kegan Paul, 1978, p. 444
7 Walras *Elements* p. 84
8 Schumpeter *History of Economic Analysis* p. 974
9 William Jaffé 'Walras's Economics as Others See It' *Journal of Economic Literature* 28, June 1980, p. 530
10 Alfred Marshall *Principles of Economics. An Introductory Volume* 8th edn, London: Macmillan, 1920, p. 14
11 A.C. Pigou *The Economics of Welfare* 4th edn, London: Macmillan, 1948, pp. 6–7
12 Marshall *Principles* p. vii
13 J.R. Hicks 'Introductory: LSE and the Robbins Circle' in J.R. Hicks *Money, Interest and Wages*, vol. 2 of *Collected Essays on Economic Theory* Oxford: Basil Blackwell, 1982, p. 3
14 Murray Milgate *Capital and Employment. A Study of Keynes's Economics* London: Academic Press, 1982, p. 41
15 Marshall *Principles* pp. 349–50. This particular distinction between the short period and the long period is discussed more fully in Milgate *Capital and Employment* chs 3–5
16 ibid. p. vii
17 ibid. p. 710
18 ibid. p. 119
19 ibid. p. 356

20 ibid. pp. 5, 6
21 ibid. pp. 117–18
22 ibid. pp. 514–15
23 Lionel Robbins *An Essay on the Nature and Significance of Economic Science* 2nd edn, London: Macmillan, 1935, p. 16
24 J.R. Hicks 'A Reconsideration of the Theory of Value' (1934), reprinted in J.R. Hicks *Wealth and Welfare*, vol. 1 of *Collected Essays on Economic Theory* Oxford: Basil Blackwell, 1981, pp. 5–8
25 Vilfredo Pareto *Manual of Political Economy* (1906), eds Ann S. Schwier and Alfred N. Paige, trans. Ann S. Schwier, London: Macmillan, 1972
26 J.R. Hicks 'The Foundation of Welfare Economics' (1939), reprinted in *Wealth and Welfare* p. 62
27 A.C. Pigou *Economics in Practice* London: Macmillan, 1935, pp. 118–19
28 A.C. Pigou *Unemployment* London: William & Norgate, 1913, pp. 242, 243
29 A.C. Pigou *The Theory of Unemployment* London: Macmillan, 1933, p. 252
30 Murray Milgate and John Eatwell 'Unemployment and the Market Mechanism' in Eatwell and Milgate (eds) *Keynes's Economics and the Theory of Value and Distribution* London: Duckworth, 1983, p. 261; emphasis in the original
31 J.M. Keynes *The General Theory of Employment, Interest and Money* (1936), reprinted in *The Collected Writings of John Maynard Keynes* as vol. 7, London: Macmillan, 1973, p. 20n
32 Lionel Robbins *The Great Depression* London: Macmillan, 1934, p. 125
33 ibid. p. 185. The remaining quotations are from pp. 186–90
34 Pigou *Economics in Practice* p. 116
35 Pigou *Unemployment* p. 244; see also p. 254
36 Quoted in Mark Blaug *Economic Theory in Retrospect* 2nd edn, London: Heinemann, 1968, pp. 654–55
37 Keynes *General Theory* p. xxiii
38 All quotes are from J.M. Keynes 'Poverty in Plenty: Is the Economic System Self-Adjusting?' (1934), reprinted in *Collected Writings* vol. 13, pp. 485–93
39 Hyman P. Minsky *John Maynard Keynes* London: Macmillan, 1976, p. 57
40 Keynes *General Theory* pp. 249–50
41 J.M. Keynes 'The Multiplier' (1933), included in J.M. Keynes *The Means to Prosperity* American edn (1933), reprinted in *Collected Writings* vol. 9, *Essays in Persuasion* London: Macmillan, 1972, p. 350
42 Keynes 'Preface to the French Edition' in *Collected Writings* vol. 7, p. xxv
43 Keynes *General Theory* p. 313
44 ibid. p. 251
45 Keynes *Collected Writings* vol. 13, p. 395
46 ibid. p. 406
47 Keynes *General Theory* p. 254
48 John Eatwell 'Theories of Value, Output and Employment' (1979), reprinted in Eatwell and Milgate (eds) *Keynes's Economics* p. 97. See also Milgate *Capital and Employment* pp. 84–91
49 Keynes *General Theory* pp. 24–25
50 ibid. p. 27
51 ibid. p. 165
52 ibid. p. 213
53 ibid. p. 184
54 James Meade 'The Keynesian Revolution' in Milo Keynes (ed.) *Essays on John Maynard Keynes* Cambridge: Cambridge University Press, 1975, p. 82
55 See Robert Skidelsky 'Keynes and the Revolt against the Victorians' in Robert Skidelsky (ed.) *The End of the Keynesian Era. Essays on the Disintegration of the Keynesian Political Economy* London: Macmillan, 1977, pp. 1–9
56 J.M. Keynes 'An Economic Analysis of Unemployment' (1931), reprinted in *Collected Writings* vol. 13, pp. 354–55
57 J.M. Keynes 'The General Theory of Employment' (1937), reprinted in *Collected Writings* vol. 14, p. 121
58 J.M. Keynes 'The Theory of the Rate of Interest' (1937), reprinted in *Collected Writings* vol. 14 pp. 106–7; emphasis in the original

Notes

59 The phrase appears in J.M. Keynes 'My Early Beliefs' (1938), reprinted in *Collected Writings* vol. 10 *Essays in Biography* London: Macmillan, 1972, p. 447; all other quotations on uncertainty are from Keynes *General Theory* pp. 145–46, 149, 154, 161–63
60 Keynes *Collected Writings* vol. 14, p. 181
61 Keynes 'The General Theory of Employment' pp. 112–13
62 Sir Austin Robinson 'Impressions of Maynard Keynes' in David Worswick and James Trevithick (eds) *Keynes and the Modern World* Cambridge: Cambridge University Press, 1983, p. 260
63 Alan Coddington *Keynesian Economics: The Search for First Principles* London: George Allen & Unwin, 1983, p. 54
64 Keynes 'The General Theory of Employment' p. 114; emphasis in the original.
65 ibid. pp. 114–15
66 Quoted in Milgate and Eatwell 'Unemployment and the Market Mechanism' p. 262
67 E.J. Nell, review of Murray Milgate *Capital and Employment* (1982) *Contributions to Political Economy* 2, March 1983, p. 111; emphasis in the original
68 Keynes *General Theory* pp. 48–50
69 Keynes 'An Economic Analysis of Unemployment' p. 344
70 Keynes 'My Early Beliefs' p. 447; subsequent quotes are from pp. 448–9
71 R.F. Harrod *The Life of John Maynard Keynes* London: Macmillan, 1951, pp. 192–93
72 J.M. Keynes *A Tract on Monetary Reform* (1923), reprinted in *Collected Writings* as vol. 4, London: Macmillan, 1971, p. 147
73 Keynes *General Theory* p. 164
74 ibid. p. 379
75 ibid. p. 378
76 Nicholas Kaldor 'Keynesian Economics after Fifty Years' in Worswick and Trevithick (eds) *Keynes and the Modern World* pp. 1–2
77 ibid. p. 2

Chapter 3

1 Coombs *Trial Balance* p. 3
2 Crisp 'Commonwealth Treasury's Changed Role' p. 321
3 Quoted in 'Report from the Joint Select Committee on Public Accounts' CCP 1932–33–34, 4, p. 43
4 Percy Spender *Politics and a Man* Sydney: Collins, 1972, pp. 42–43
5 Prime ministerial broadcast, 8 November 1933, quoted in W.R. MacLaurin *Economic Planning in Australia 1929–36* London: P.S. King & Son, 1937, p. 177
6 *Full Employment in Australia* Canberra: CGP, 1945
7 CPD 182, 30 May 1945, pp. 2238–39
8 S.J. Butlin and C.B. Schedvin *War Economy 1942–1945* Canberra: Australian War Memorial, 1977, pp. 678–79
9 Roland Wilson 'The Economic Implications of Planning' in W.G.K. Duncan (ed.) *National Economic Planning* Sydney: Angus & Robertson, 1934, pp. 78–79
10 E.R. Walker *The Transformation of War-Time Controls* Realities of Reconstruction no. 3, Melbourne: MUP with OUP, 1943, p. 7
11 Crisp *Ben Chifley* p. 169
12 E.G. Theodore *Unemployment and Its Remedy* c. 1931, p. 4
13 H.V. Evatt *Post-War Reconstruction* Canberra: CGP, 1942, p. 57
14 Butlin and Schedvin *War Economy* pp. 626–27
15 R.G. Menzies *The Forgotten People and Other Studies in Democracy* Sydney: Angus & Robertson, 1943, p. 144.
16 Harold E. Holt 'The Role of Government in Maintaining Full Employment' lecture 6 in the Melbourne Junior Chamber lecture series 1949, *Boom and Slump: The Challenge to Private Enterprise*, p. 19
17 League of Nations *The Transition from War to Peace* report of the Delegation on Economic Depressions, Part I, Geneva, 1943, pp. 21–22
18 CDP 182, 30 May 1945, pp. 2238–39
19 Herbert Burton 'Principles for Post-War Policy' *Australian Quarterly* 15, 1, 1943, p. 34

20 L.F. Giblin 'Reconstruction: A Pisgah View' *Australian Quarterly* 15, 3, 1943, p. 6
21 Submission by Roland Wilson to the Joint Parliamentary Committee on Social Security, 23 July 1942, quoted in Selwyn Cornish, Full Employment in Australia: The Genesis of a White Paper, paper presented to the Post-War Reconstruction Seminar, Canberra, August–September, 1981
22 Coombs *Trial Balance* p. 4
23 Quoted in R.I. Downing 'Giblin as Ritchie Professor' in Douglas Copland (ed.) *Giblin. The Scholar and the Man* Melbourne: Cheshire, 1960, pp. 45–46
24 L.G. Melville 'The Place of Expectations in Economic Theory' *Economic Record* 15, June 1939, pp. 2–3
25 E.R. Walker *From Economic Theory to Policy* Chicago: University of Chicago Press, 1943, p. 71
26 See, for the correspondence between Giblin and Keynes, *The Collected Writings* vol. 13, *The General Theory and After: Part I. Preparation* ed. Donald Moggridge, London: Macmillan, 1973, pp. 414–19.
27 Colin Clark and J.G. Crawford *The National Income of Australia* Sydney: Angus & Robertson, 1938
28 D.B. Copland 'Development of Economic Thought in Australia, 1924–50' in D.B. Copland *Inflation and Expansion* Melbourne: Cheshire, 1951, pp. 16–17
29 Coombs *Trial Balance* p. 146
30 Robert Skidelsky 'The Reception of the Keynesian Revolution' in Milo Keynes (ed.) *Essays on John Maynard Keynes* p. 104
31 L.F. Giblin 'The "F. and E." Committee', February 1947, AA CRS A571, item 39/3251
32 Roland Wilson 'A Note on Economic Policy and Organisation for War', 12 September 1939, AA CRS A571, item 39/3251
33 Roland Wilson *Economic Co-ordination*, the Joseph Fisher Lecture in Commerce 1940, Adelaide: University of Adelaide at the Hassell Press, 1940, p. 25
34 Giblin 'The "F. & E." Committee'
35 S.J. Butlin *War Economy 1939–1942* Canberra: Australian War Memorial 1955, pp. 356, 357: See also Rodney Maddock and Janet Penny 'Economists at War: the Financial and Economic Committee 1939–44' *Australian Economic History Review* 23, 1, 1983, pp. 35–40.
36 Coombs *Trial Balance* p. 6
37 ibid. p. 4
38 Wilson 'Economic Implications of Planning' p. 60
39 ibid. p. 73
40 Roland Wilson 'Capitalism and the Second Effort' *Australian Quarterly* 4, 4, 1932, p. 58
41 Wilson 'Economic Implications of Planning' p. 74
42 H.C. Coombs *Problems of a High Employment Economy*, the Joseph Fisher Lecture in Commerce 1944, Adelaide: University of Adelaide at the Hassell Press, 1944, p. 35
43 H.C. Coombs 'The Economic Aftermath of War' in Campbell (ed.) *Post-War Reconstruction* p. 85
44 Copland 'The Change-Over to Peace' in ibid. pp. 124–25
45 D.B. Copland 'The State and the Entrepreneur', paper presented to a symposium of the Harvard Tercentenary Conference of Arts and Science, August-September 1936, reprinted in *Authority and the Individual* Cambridge: Harvard University Press, 1937, p. 49
46 Copland 'Change-Over to Peace' p. 125
47 ibid.; emphasis in the original
48 Melville 'The Place of Expectations' pp. 1–2
49 Walker *From Economic Theory to Policy* pp. 154–55; emphasis in the original
50 E.R. Walker *Australia in the Great Depression* London: P.S. King & Son, 1933, p. 137
51 E.R. Walker *Unemployment Policy with Special Reference to Australia* Sydney: Angus & Robertson, 1936, p. 170
52 E.R. Walker 'Sound Finance' *Economic Record* 15, April 1939, p. 63; emphasis in the original
53 L.F. Giblin 'Winning the War' AA, 1968/391, item 139
54 L.F. Giblin 'Unemployment' 17 October 1939, AA CRS A571, item 39/3799
55 L.F. Giblin 'Financing Full Employment' *Economic Papers* no. 5, 1945, p. 63

Notes

56 Tim Rowse *Australian Liberalism and National Character* Melbourne: Kibble Books, 1978, ch. 4
57 ibid. pp. 156–57
58 J.B. Brigden 'Economics and Ethics' *Morpeth Review* 2, 22, 1932, p. 20; emphasis in the original
59 J.B. Brigden 'Competition and Control' in G.W. Leeper (ed.) *Report of the Twenty-Second Meeting of the Australian and New Zealand Association for the Advancement of Science, Melbourne Meeting, January 1935* Melbourne: Government Printer, 1935, pp. 235–36
60 ibid. pp. 236–37
61 ibid. p. 239
62 Copland 'Change-Over to Peace' p. 122
63 Giblin 'Financing Full Employment' p. 61
64 L.F. Giblin 'Reconstruction in Australia' *Agenda* 2, 3, 1943, p. 217
65 Giblin 'Financing Full Employment' p. 62
66 Coombs 'Economic Aftermath of War' p. 78
67 Coombs *Problems* pp. 33–34
78 H.C. Coombs 'The Development of Monetary Policy in Australia' (1954), reprinted in H.C. Coombs *Other People's Money* Canberra: ANU Press, 1971, p. 9

Chapter 4

1 John Stone 'Inflation and the International Monetary System' *IPA Review* 23, 2, 1969, p. 58
2 D.B. Copland *Back to Earth in Economics: Australia 1948* Sydney: Angus & Robertson, 1948, p. 43
3 'Economic Trends and Prospects. Survey by the Investment and Employment Committee' 8 December 1947, AA CRS A571, item 47/1907, part 4
4 'Review of Economic Policy' 3 June 1949, AA CRS A571, item 47/1907, part 7
5 Butlin *War Economy* pp. 214–15. See also pp. 199, 316–17
6 Percy Spender *Politics and a Man* Sydney: Collins, 1972, p. 44
7 Coombs *Trial Balance* p. 7
8 Spender *Politics and a Man* p. 42
9 Quoted in Butlin *War Economy* p. 214
10 Paul Hasluck *The Government and the People 1939–1941* Canberra: Australian War Memorial, 1952, p. 470
11 Quoted in Butlin and Schedvin *War Economy* p. 627; emphasis in the original
12 'Memorandum on Treasury Organisation', Dedman Papers, National Library
13 H.C. Coombs 'Australia's Ability to Avoid Booms and Depressions' *Economic Papers* 8, 1948, p. 44
14 H.W. Arndt 'Control of Inflation through Fiscal Policy: A Reappraisal' *Economic Record* 36, December 1960, p. 505
15 CDP 201, 15 February 1949, pp. 241–42
16 Taxation Office *Taxation and the Economy* Canberra: CGP, 1948, p. 7
17 M.J. Artis and R.H. Wallace 'A Historical Survey of Australian Fiscal Policy 1945–66' in Neil Runcie (ed.) *Australian Monetary and Fiscal Policy* Hornsby: Hodder & Stoughton with University of London Press, 1971, pp. 414–15
18 'The Australian Inflation' *IPA Review* 3, 2, 1949, p. 39
19 *Sydney Morning Herald* 9 September 1948
20 ibid., 8 September 1949
21 A draft document, untitled, prepared for the Investment and Employment Committee, c. January 1949, AA CRS A571, item 47/1909, part 6
22 'Budget Prospects', 8 June 1950, AA CRS A571, item 50/1002, part 2
23 Artis and Wallace 'Historical Survey' p. 411
24 *Full Employment in Australia* Canberra: CGP, 1945, para, 30, p. 6
25 'Some Aspects of the Economic Situation' 8 May 1950, AA CRS A571, item 50/1003, part 1
26 'Economic Policy: May 1950', draft, 2 May 1950, AA CRS A571, item 50/1003, part 3
27 Coombs 'Australia's Ability' p. 44
28 ibid. p. 45

29 *Budget Speech 1949–50* p. 6
30 'Discussions on Economic Situation' 29 April 1950, AA CRS A571, item 50/1003, part 1
31 'Economic Policy: May 1950'. Note: by 'import surplus' the Bank meant running an unfavourable trade balance.
32 'Economic Policy' 8 June 1950, AA CRS A571, item 50/1003, part 2
33 D.A.L. Auld 'A Measure of Australian Fiscal Policy Performance, 1948–49 to 1963–64' *Economic Record* 43, June 1967
34 ibid., table 7
35 D.B. Copland, Structural Problems under Full Employment, paper presented to section G, ANZAAS conference, May 1951, mimeo, p. 7
36 Copland 'Development of Economic Thought in Australia'
37 G.G. Firth, Disinflation in Australia: A Democratic Dilemma, paper presented to section G, ANZAAS conference, May 1951, mimeo, p. 17
38 ibid. p. 12
39 ibid. p. 18
40 'The Prices Problem' 23 January 1951, AA CRS A571, item 50/1003, part 3
41 ibid.
42 See H.C. Coombs to A.W. Fadden, 20 February 1951, AA CRS A571, item 50/1003, part 3.
43 'The Prices Problem'
44 'Economic Policy — July, 1951' AA CRS A571, item 50/1003, part 4
45 Quoted in A.M.C. Waterman *Economic Fluctuations in Australia, 1948 to 1964* Canberra: ANU Press, 1972, p. 84
46 'The Budget, 1952–53' 21 July 1952, AA CRS A571, item 52/1768
47 'Some Thoughts on General Economic Prospects and Policy' 2 December 1952, AA CRS A571, item 52/1161, part 3
48 For a biographical sketch of Wilson, see John Hetherington *Uncommon Men* Melbourne: Cheshire, 1965, pp. 184–92. A revealing guide to Wilson's philosophy is his Giblin memorial lecture 1976, reprinted in *Search* 7, 7, 1976.

Chapter 5

1 *National Economy — Economic Measures* ministerial statement by R.G. Menzies, 14 March 1956, Canberra: CGP, 1956, p. 4
2 ibid. p. 15
3 H.W. Arndt 'Deflation through Wool' *Banker* 108, 1958, p. 660
4 Treasury *The Australian Economy, 1959* Canberra:CGP, 1959, p. 16
5 Treasury *Australia, 1956: An Economic Survey* Canberra: CGP, 1956, p. 12
6 ibid. p. 10
7 Treasury *1957 and Beyond: An Economic Survey* Canberra: CGP, 1957, p. 30
8 Treasury *The Australian Economy, 1958* Canberra: CGP, 1958, p. 24
9 Treasury *1957 and Beyond* p. 28
10 Treasury *Australia, 1956* p. 13
11 Treasury *1957 and Beyond* p. 27
12 ibid. p. 44
13 Treasury *Australian Economy, 1958* p. 26
14 Treasury *1957 and Beyond* p. 27
15 Treasury *Australian Economy, 1958* p. 25
16 *National Economy — Economic Measures* p. 6
17 Treasury *1957 and Beyond* pp. 27–28
18 D.B. Copland 'The Australian Economy: A New Look' *Economic Record* 33, August 1957, p. 143
19 Treasury *Australia, 1956* p. 11
20 H.W. Arndt 'The Australian Economy, September 1957' *Economic Record* 33, December 1957, p. 291
21 R.I. Downing 'The Australian Economy, March 1956' *Economic Record* 32, May 1956, p. 1
22 H.C. Coombs 'A Matter of Prices' *Economic Record* 35, December 1959, pp. 337–38, 348
23 P.H. Karmel 'Some Reflections on Inflation, Productivity and Growth' *Economic Record* 35, December 1959, p. 349

Notes

24 Treasury *Australia, 1956* p. 11
25 P.H. Karmel 'Australia's Economic Problems' *Australian Accountant* 26, February 1956, p. 56
26 T.W. Swan, Notes on Some Inter-Relations of Economic Policies (Employment, Balance of Payments, Spending, and Costs), paper presented to section G of the 1955 ANZAAS conference, reprinted as 'Longer-run Problems of the Balance of Payments' in H.W. Arndt and W.M. Corden (eds)*The Australian Economy: A Volume of Readings* Melbourne: Cheshire, 1963, p. 385
27 Treasury *Australian Economy, 1958* p. 21
28 Swan 'Longer-Run Problems' p. 394
29 ibid. p. 390
30 Treasury *Australia, 1956* p. 43
31 Karmel 'Australia's Economic Problems' p. 60
32 ibid.
33 Treasury *The Australian Economy, 1960* Canberra: CGP, 1960, p. 11
34 A.H. Boxer 'The Australian Economy, November 1959' *Economic Record* 35, December 1959, p. 319
35 Waterman *Economic Fluctuations* p. 164
36 Treasury *Australian Economy, 1960* p. 19
37 Treasury *1957 and Beyond* p. 32
38 Treasury *Australian Economy, 1959* p. 24
39 Tariff Board *Annual Report for Year 1958–59* Canberra: CGP, 1959, p. 6; Commonwealth Bank of Australia *Report and Balance Sheet, 1958* p. 5
40 Reserve Bank of Australia *Report and Financial Statements 1960* p. 20
41 Reserve Bank of Australia *Report and Financial Statements 1961* p. 20
42 Treasury *The Australian Economy, 1962* Canberra: CGP, 1962, p. 22
43 Treasury *Australian Economy, 1962* p. 19
44 Treasury *1957 and Beyond* p. 18
45 Treasury *Australian Economy, 1961* p. 13
46 ibid. p. 32
47 Waterman *Economic Fluctuations* p. 192. Some of the points made in the next three paragraphs are drawn from pp. 192–97 of Waterman's analysis.
48 H.W. Arndt 'Australia's Changing Financial Structure' in H.W. Arndt *A Small Rich Industrial Country* Melbourne: Cheshire, 1968, p. 58
49 H.F. Lydall 'The Australian Economy, February 1962' *Economic Record* 38, March 1962, p. 1
50 Waterman *Economic Fluctuations* p. 160
51 P.H. Karmel *Economic Policy in Australia — Ends and Means*, the G.L. Wood Memorial Lecture, August 1954, Melbourne: MUP, 1954, p. 6
52 Downing 'Australian Economy, March 1956' p. 26
53 James Meade 'The Price Mechanism and the Australian Balance of Payments' *Economic Record* 32, November 1956, p. 239
54 P.H. Karmel 'The Australian Economy, April 1957' *Economic Record* 33, April 1957, p. 19
55 See, for instance, E.L. Wheelwright 'Planning the Economy' *Quadrant* 6, 2, 1962
56 ibid. p. 52
57 A.R. Hall 'Investment Planning Will Have to Start Now' *Australian Financial Review* 8 May 1962
58 H.W. Arndt 'Five Contributions on Economic Planning' section 2, *Dissent* Spring 1963, p. 15, and 'Further Reflections on Long-Term Planning' (1962), reprinted in Arndt *A Small Rich Industrial Country*
59 Arndt 'Further Reflections' p. 91
60 R.W. Cole 'The Economic and Financial Surveys Division of the Commonwealth Treasury' *Public Administration* 23, 2, 1964, p. 173
61 Roland Wilson 'Increasing Deficit in the Balance of Payments' in *Australia: A Financial Times Survey*, supplement to the *Financial Times* 7 May 1962
62 Arndt 'Further Reflections' pp. 96–99. Further criticisms of the Treasury position are offered in Bruce McFarlane *Economic Policy in Australia. The Case for Reform* Melbourne: Cheshire, 1968, pp. 22–23

63 Treasury *Australian Economy, 1962* p. 19
64 Treasury *Australian Economy, 1961* p. 37
65 Keynes *General Theory* p. 380
66 ibid. p. 322
67 Treasury *Australian Economy, 1960* p. 27
68 Treasury *Australia, 1956* foreword
69 Treasury *Australian Economy, 1962* p. 31

Chapter 6

1 Most of this biographical material on Randall comes from Ian Fitchett 'From Woolsorter to Treasury Secretary' *Sydney Morning Herald* 2 November 1966.
2 'Maurice Walter O'Donnell' *Business Review* September 1969
3 For a brief biographical outline of Stone's career, see Paul Kelly 'Our Leading Public Servant' *National Times* 28 October 1978
4 Treasury *The Australian Economy, 1963* Canberra: CGP, 1963, p. 14
5 L.H.E. Bury 'Economic Management in the 1970s' *Australian Accountant* 40, December 1970, p. 502
6 AIPS *Economic Growth in Australia* Sydney: Angus & Robertson, 1962, pp. 136–37
7 Treasury *Australian Economy, 1963* pp. 25–26
8 Treasury *The Australian Economy, 1964* Canberra: CGP, 1964, foreword
9 W.M. Corden *Australian Economic Policy Discussion. A Survey* Melbourne: Melbourne University Press, 1968, p. 20
10 Treasury *Australian Economy, 1966* pp. 12, 23
11 J.O.N. Perkins *Macro-Economic Policy in Australia* 2nd edn, Melbourne: Melbourne University Press, 1975, p. 51
12 Treasury *The Australian Economy, 1967* Canberra: CGP, 1967, pp. 26, 27
13 *Investment Analysis*, supplement to the *Treasury Information Bulletin* July 1966, p. 5; emphasis in the original
14 ibid. p. 5
15 TEP no. 1, *Overseas Investment in Australia* Canberra: CGP, 1972, p. 119–20
16 *Investment Analysis* p. 26
17 ibid. p. 5; emphasis in the original
18 *The Meaning and Measurement of Economic Growth*, supplement to the *Treasury Information Bulletin* November 1964, p. 16
19 All quotations are from Treasury *Australian Economy, 1967* pp. 23–36
20 Russell Mathews *Public Investment in Australia. A Study of Australian Public Authority Investment and Development* Melbourne: Cheshire, 1967, pp. 29, 30
21 A.R. Prest and R. Turvey 'Cost-Benefit Analysis: A Survey' *Economic Journal* 75, December 1965, pp. 683–735
22 Quoted in *Investment Analysis* pp. 6–7
23 Mathews *Public Investment* esp. ch. 2
24 N.W.F. Fisher 'The Relationship between Benefit-Cost Analysis and Planning-Programming-Budgeting Systems' *Australian Accountant* 42, April 1972, p. 107
25 Weller and Cutt *Treasury Control in Australia* p. 118
26 Sir Frederick Wheeler 'Forward Estimates of Commonwealth Budget Expenditures' *Australian Accountant* 43, April 1973, p. 136
27 Weller and Cutt *Treasury Control in Australia* p. 144
28 Wheeler 'Forward Estimates' p. 134
29 Glezer *Tariff Politics* p. 12
30 *The Meaning and Measurement of Economic Growth* p. 5
31 *The Australian Balance of Payments*, supplement to the *Treasury Information Bulletin* February 1966, p. 5
32 *Projections of the Work-Force, 1963–76*, supplement to the *Treasury Information Bulletin* April 1965, foreword
33 *Report of the Committee of Economic Enquiry* vol. 1, Canberra: CGP, 1965, para. 17.100, p. 450

Notes

34 CPD H of R, 47, 21 September 1965, p. 1085
35 *Report of the Committee of Economic Enquiry* vol. 2, para. N.5, p. 1098
36 Glezer *Tariff Politics* p. 176
37 *The Meaning and Measurement of Economic Growth* pp. 13, 17
38 A.R. Hall 'The Australian Economy, August, 1961' *Economic Record* 37, September 1961, pp. 271–72
39 *The Australian Balance of Payments* p. 50
40 E.A. Russell 'Foreign Investment Policy — What Role for the Economist?' *Australian Economic Papers* 17, December 1978, pp. 198–99
41 Glezer *Tariff Politics* pp. 178–81
42 Treasury *Australian Economy, 1967* p. 23
43 J.R. Hicks 'Mr Keynes and the Classics' (1937), reprinted in Hicks *Money, Interest and Wages* p. 108
44 J.A. Trevithick 'Money Wage Inflexibility and the Keynesian Labour Supply Function' *Economic Journal* 86, June 1976, p. 329
45 Minsky *John Maynard Keynes* p. 38
46 J.R. Hicks 'Some Questions of Time in Economics' in Anthony M. Tang, Fred M. Westfield and James S. Worley (eds) *Evolution, Welfare and Time in Economics* Lexington: Lexington Books, 1976, p. 141. See also J.R. Hicks *Economic Perspectives. Further Essays on Money and Growth* Oxford: Oxford University Press, 1977, p. vii
47 See, for instance, John Fender *Understanding Keynes. An Analysis of 'The General Theory'* Brighton: Wheatsheaf Books, 1981, pp. 140–41.
48 Minsky *John Maynard Keynes* p. 51
49 Paul A. Samuelson *Economics. An Introductory Analysis* 3rd edn, New York: McGraw-Hill, 1955, p. 733. See also the definitions on pp. 11, 160, 569
50 ibid. p. 11; emphasis added
51 A.W. Phillips 'The Relationship between Unemployment and the Rate of Change of Money Wages in the United Kingdom, 1861–1957' *Economica* 25, November 1958
52 Paul A. Samuelson and Robert M. Solow 'Analytical Aspects of Anti-Inflation Policy' *American Economic Review* 10, May 1960
53 Axel Leijonhufvud *On Keynesian Economics and the Economics of Keynes. A Study in Monetary Theory* New York:Oxford University Press, 1968
54 Keynes to R.F. Harrod, 4 July 1936, reprinted in *Collected Writings* vol. 14, *The General Theory and After* p. 296
55 Keynes to R.F. Harrod, 16 July 1938, reprinted in ibid. p. 300
56 Sidney Weintraub 'Keynes and the Monetarists' *Canadian Journal of Economics* 4, February 1971, pp. 43–44
57 Peter Samuel 'Policies for Growth: The Vernon Report — A Review' *Australian Quarterly* 37, 4, 1965, p. 14
58 Bury 'Economic Management' p. 503
59 Tony Griffiths *Contemporary Australia* London: Croom Helm, 1977, p. 80

Chapter 7

1 Treasury *The Australian Economy, 1970* Canberra: CGP, 1970, p. 7
2 Richard Randall 'The Economy' in *Australia: An Economic and Investment Reference* Commonwealth of Australia, 1970, pp. 9–10
3 Treasury *The Australian Economy, 1969* Canberra: CGP, 1969, p. 8
4 Treasury *The Australian Economy, 1971* Canberra: CGP, 1971, p. 11
5 Jean Polglaze and C.S. Soper 'Wilfred Prest: An Appreciation' in J.P. Nieuwenhuysen and P.J. Drake (eds) *Australian Economic Policy* Melbourne: Melbourne University Press, 1977, p. xv
6 I am indebted to Mrs Marjorie Harper for these details. Mrs Harper was a tutor to the Melbourne students listed as graduating in 1949–52.
7 Treasury *The Australian Economy, 1968* Canberra: CGP, 1968, p. 12
8 J.E. Isaac, Wage Policy and the Commonwealth Arbitration Court, paper presented to section G of the 1955 ANZAAS conference, mimeo, p. 1
9 ibid. p. 1

The Treasury line

10 Treasury *Australian Economy, 1968* p. 13
11 Treasury *Australian Economy, 1971* p. 21
12 Treasury *The Australian Economy, 1972* Canberra: CGP, 1972, p. 19
13 ibid. p. 22
14 Treasury *Australian Economy, 1971* pp. 21–22
15 Treasury *Australian Economy, 1970* p. 11
16 Treasury *Australian Economy, 1971* p. 13
17 Treasury 'Statement No. 1 — Budget Estimates, 1968–69' attached to *Budget Speech 1968–69* Canberra: CGP, 1968, p. 3
18 ibid. 1969–70, p. 3
19 Alan Reid *The Gorton Experiment* Sydney: Shakespeare Head Press, 1971, p. 119
20 Treasury *Australian Economy, 1971* p. 18
21 ibid. p. 23
22 IAESR 'The Australian Economy' *Australian Economic Review* 4th quarter 1970, p. 4
23 ibid., 3rd quarter 1971, p. 4
24 ibid., 4th quarter 1971, p. 4
25 J.W. Nevile 'The Australian Economy, August 1971' *Economic Record* 47, September, 1971, p. 311
26 J.P. Nieuwenhuysen 'The New Inflation' in Nieuwenhuysen and Drake (eds) *Australian Economic Policy* p. 57
27 A.J. Hagger 'Inflation' in F.H. Gruen (ed.) *Surveys of Australian Economics* Sydney: George Allen & Unwin, 1978, p. 175
28 Quoted in Jolley *Macro-Economic Policy* p. 58
29 Treasury *Australian Economy, 1971* p. 31
30 Committee for the Economic Development of Australia 'Wage/Price Policies', supplementary paper no. 42, March 1972, address by B.M. Snedden, 18 November 1971, p. 7
31 Treasury *Australian Economy, 1971* p. 32
32 Treasury *Australian Economy, 1972* p. 22
33 P. D. Jonson 'Our Current Inflationary Experience' *Australian Economic Review* 2nd quarter 1973, p. 26
34 V. Argy and J. Carmichael 'Models of Imported Inflation for a Small Country — With Particular Reference to Australia' in W. Kasper (ed.) *International Money — Experiments and Experience, Papers and Proceedings of the Port Stephens Conference* Canberra: Department of Economics, Australian National University, 1976
35 J.W. Nevile 'Australian Inflation:Made at Home or Imported' in Kasper *International Money*
36 Treasury 'Statement No. 1 — Summary of the 1971–72 Budget', attached to *Budget Speech 1971–72* p. 2
37 William McMahon 'The PM versus the Bureaucrats' *Australian Financial Review* 3 June 1974
38 Nevile 'The Australian Economy, August 1971', p. 306
39 Treasury *Australian Economy, 1972* p. 42
40 Milton Friedman 'The Role of Monetary Policy' *American Economic Review* 58, March 1968. Some of the discussion here of inflationary expectations and rational expectations is based on J.A. Trevithick *Inflation*, 2nd edn, Harmondsworth: Penguin, 1980, chs 4 and 5.
41 Trevithick *Inflation* p. 82; emphasis in the original
42 Milton and Rose Friedman *Free to Choose: A Personal Statement* Harmondsworth: Peguin, 1980, p. 329
43 John Eatwell and Murray Milgate 'Introduction' in Eatwell and Milgate (eds) *Keynes's Economics and the Theory of Value and Distribution*, p. 13
44 F.H. Hahn 'Unemployment from a Theoretical Viewpoint' *Economica* 47, August 1980, p. 289
45 Treasury *Australian Economy, 1969* p. 14
46 Treasury 'The Economic Consequences of the National Wage Case Decision' *Incentive* 278, 25 June 1971, p. 3
47 Treasury *Australian Economy, 1971* p. 31
48 Treasury *Australian Economy, 1972* p. 24
49 Treasury *Australian Economy, 1969* p. 14

Notes

50 Treasury 'Economic Consequences' p. 3
51 ibid.; emphasis added
52 Treasury *Australian Economy, 1972* p. 23; emphasis in the original

Chapter 8

1 Samuelson *Economics* p. 212
2 J.W. Nevile and D.W. Stammer (eds) *Inflation and Unemployment. Selected Readings* Ringwood: Penguin, 1972, p. 9
3 Hagger 'Inflation' pp. 175–76
4 J.W. Nevile 'The Role of Fiscal Policy in the Eighties' *Economic Record* 59, March 1983, pp. 1–2
5 Barry Hughes *Exit Full Employment* Sydney: Angus & Robertson, 1980, p. 67
6 F.H. Gruen 'What Went Wrong? Some Personal Reflections on Economic Policy under Labor' *Australian Quarterly* 48, 4, 1976, p. 22
7 Hughes *Exit Full Employment* p. 75
8 Treasury *Australian Economy, 1973* p. 40
9 ibid. p. 12
10 ibid. pp. 37–38
11 Gruen 'What Went Wrong?' p. 25
12 Comments made at a seminar at Monash University, 12 December 1984
13 Treasury 'Statement No. 2 — The Budget and the Economy', attached to *Budget Speech 1975–76* Canberra: AGPS, 1975, p. 19
14 ibid. 1977–78, p. 31
15 ibid. 1976–77, p. 15
16 ibid. 1977–78, p. 21
17 John Stone 'Roundtable Discussion' in Michael G. Porter (ed.) *The Australian Monetary System in the 1970s* Monash University: Faculty of Economics and Politics, 1978, p. 242
18 Treasury 'Statement No. 2' 1978–79, p. 38
19 TEP no. 4, *Job Markets: Economic and Statistical Aspects of the Australian Market for Labour* Canberra: AGPS, 1978, p. 28
20 Treasury 'Statement No. 2' 1978–79, p. 39
21 TEP no. 4, p. 30
22 Treasury 'Statement No. 2' 1976–77, p. 15
23 ibid. 1977–78, p. 32
24 ibid. 1978–79, p. 38
25 TEP no. 4, p. 31
26 TEP no. 7, *Technology, Growth and Jobs: Treasury Submission to the Committee of Inquiry into Technological Change in Australia* Canberra: AGPS, 1979, p. 23
27 TEP no. 4, p. 37; this passage emphasised in the original
28 ibid. p. 33
29 ibid. pp. 34–35
30 C.I. Higgins 'Comment' in W.E. Norton and I.W. Little (eds) *Conference in Applied Economic Research* Sydney: Researve Bank of Australia, 1979, p. 346
31 TEP no. 4, p. 33n
32 C.I. Higgins, H.N. Johnston and P.L. Coghlan 'Business Investment: The Recent Experience' in W.E.Norton and D.W. Stammer (eds) *Conference in Applied Economic Research: Papers and Proceedings* Sydney: Reserve Bank of Australia, 1976, pp. 11–47
33 H.N. Johnston, R.B. Campbell and R.M. Simes 'The Impact of Wages and Prices on Unemployment' *Economic Papers* 60, December 1978, p. 32.
34 ibid. p. 36
35 F.H. Gruen 'Australian Economics 1968–78' in F.H. Gruen (ed.) *Surveys of Australian Economics* vol. 2, Sydney: George Allen & Unwin, 1979, p. 240
36 P.J. Sheehan and P.P. Stricker 'The Collapse of Full Employment, 1974 to 1978' in R.B. Scotton and Helen Ferber (eds) *Public Expenditure and Social Policy in Australia* vol. 2 *The First Fraser Years, 1976–78* Melbourne: Longman Cheshire, 1980, pp. 57–58
37 Treasury 'Statement No. 2' 1976–77, p. 23

38 ibid. 1978–79, p. 39
39 Higgins 'Comment' p. 344; emphasis in the original
40 H.N. Johnston 'Real Wages and Unemployment' *Australian Economic Review* 1st quarter 1979, p. 88; emphasis in the original
41 Stone 'Roundtable Discussion' p. 242
42 John Stone 'The Budget Deficit and the Economy' in *The Significance of the Budget Deficit* CAER paper no. 7, University of New South Wales: Centre for Applied Economic Research, June 1979, p. 25
43 Treasury 'Statement No. 2' 1979–80, p. 49
44 TEP no. 4, p. 2
45 Treasury 'Statement No. 2' 1977–78, p. 32
46 ibid. 1978–79, p. 39
47 ibid. 1979–80, p. 50
48 Treasury Taxation Paper no. 4 *Personal Income Tax: The Rate Scale* Canberra: AGPS, 1974, p. 19
49 TEP no. 9 *The Australian Financial System* Canberra: AGPS, 1981, p. 22
50 Treasury 'Statement No. 2' 1976–77, p. 10
51 ibid. 1978–79, p. 31
52 ibid. 1976–77, p. 23
53 Stone 'The Budget Deficit' p. 20
54 ibid. p. 27
55 ibid. pp. 28–29
56 Treasury 'Statement No. 2' 1976–77, p. 23
57 Stone 'The Budget Deficit' p. 25
58 TEP no. 9, p. 24
59 Treasury 'Statement No. 2' 1978-79, p. 22
60 ibid. 1979–80, pp. 46–47
61 CPD H of R, 98, 4 March 1976, p. 557
62 Hughes *Exit Full Employment* p. 139
63 TEP no. 2, p. 11; this passage emphasised in the original
64 ibid.; this passage emphasised in the original
65 ibid. p. 6
66 ibid. p. 33n
67 TEP no. 3, p. 2
68 TEP no. 7, p. 17
69 TEP no. 3, p. 38; emphasis in the original
70 ibid. p. 7; see also TEP no. 7, 1979, p. 19
71 TEP no. 3, p. 3n
72 TEP no. 7, p. 27
73 TEP no. 3, p. 43
74 TEP no. 4, p. 37
75 TEP no. 2, p. 26n
76 TEP no. 3, p. 43
77 TEP no. 5, *Energy Markets — Some Principles of Pricing* Canberra: AGPS, 1979, p. 6
78 Treasury 'Statement No. 2' 1979–80, p. 41
79 TEP no. 3, p. 43

Chapter 9

1 John Stone 'The Outlook for the Australian Economy' *Quarterly Review of the Rural Economy* 3, 1, February 1981, p. 30
2 Australian Treasury 'Statement No. 2 — The Budget and the Economy' in *Budget Statements 1981–82* Canberra: AGPS, 1981, p. 45
3 Stone 'Outlook' p. 33
4 Australian Treasury 'Statement No. 2 — The Budget and the Economy', attached to *Budget Speech 1980–81* Canberra: AGPS, 1980, p. 52
5 Treasury 'Statement No. 2' 1981–82, p. 10

Notes

6 ibid. 1980–81, p. 51
7 R.G. Gregory 'Some Implications of the Growth of the Mineral Sector' *Australian Journal of Agricultural Economics* 20, August 1976, pp. 71–91
8 John Stone, Australia in a Competitive World — Some Options, paper presented to the 21st General Management Conference of the Australian Institute of Management, Sydney, November 1979, mimeo
9 John Gorton 'I Did It My Way' *Australian*, 22, August 1971
10 Treasury *Australian Economy, 1963* p. 17
11 TEP no. 1, p. 1
12 John Stone 'Australia in a Competitive World: Some More Options' *Economic Papers* 1, 1, April 1982, p. 8
13 Treasury 'Statement No.2' 1981–82, p. 50
14 ibid. 1982–83, p. 48
15 ibid. p. 51
16 ibid. 1984–85, p. 32
17 Indecs Economics *State of Play 3* Sydney: George Allen & Unwin, 1984, p. 83
18 *Final Report of the Committee of Inquiry into the Australian Financial System* Canberra: AGPS, 1981, p. 1
19 Peter Sheehan 'The Campbell Report: An Overview' *Economic Papers* special edn, April 1983, p. 194
20 Andrew S. Carron 'The Australian Financial System' in Richard E. Caves and Lawrence B. Krause (eds) *The Australian Economy: A View from the North* Sydney: George Allen & Unwin, 1984, p. 208
21 Michael G. Porter 'Stabilization, Regulation and Misplaced Entrepreneurship' *Quadrant* 22, 9, September 1978, p. 15
22 John Stone '1929 and All That' *Quadrant* 28, 10, October 1984, p. 17
23 TEP no. 9 pp. 10, 12–13
24 ibid. p. 27
25 ibid. p. 101
26 ibid. p. 100
27 ibid. p. 90
28 ibid. p. 97
29 Treasury 'Statement No. 2' 1981–82, p. 49
30 ibid. 1982–83, p. 12
31 Paul Kelly *The Hawke Ascendancy* rev. edn, Sydney: Angus & Robertson, 1984, pp. 254–62
32 John Stone, Fiscal Policy 1985–86: the Prime Minister's 'Trinity', paper presented at Centre of Policy Studies, Monash University, December 1984, mimeo
33 Treasury 'Statement No. 2' 1983–84, p. 57
34 ibid. p. 62
35 ibid. 1984–85, p. 64
36 These are at 1979–80 prices.
37 Hughes *Exit* p. 154
38 Treasury 'Statement No. 2' 1976–77, p. 12
39 ibid. 1982–83, pp. 50–51
40 ibid. 1980–81, p. 63
41 ibid. p. 51
42 Stone '1929' pp. 16–17
43 Treasury 'Statement No. 2' 1982–83, p. 53
44 ibid.
45 ibid.
46 *Australian Financial Review* 13 February 1985
47 Kelly *Hawke* p. 104
48 Fraser, The Treasury — Tendering Economic Advice, p. 4
49 ibid. p. 12
50 John Stone 'What Kind of Country? In the Decade Ahead and Beyond' *Quadrant* 28, 12, 1984, p. 14

The Treasury line

Chapter 10

1. Higgins et al. 'Business Investment' p. 15
2. Higgins 'Comment' p. 347
3. ibid. pp. 342–43, 346–47; emphasis in the original
4. Treasury *Australian Economy, 1973* pp. 36–37
5. Stone 'Roundtable Discussion' pp. 240–41
6. John Stone 'The Outlook for the Australian Economy', supplement to *Quarterly Review of the Rural Economy* 3, 1, 1981, p. 33
7. TEP no. 9, p. 29
8. Treasury *Australian Economy, 1972* p. 41
9. *Investment Analysis* p. 27
10. *The Meaning and Measurement of Economic Growth* p. 19
11. ibid.
12. *The Australian Balance of Payments* p. 18
13. Minsky *John Maynard Keynes* p. 16
14. John Stone 'Inflation and the International Monetary System' *IPA Review* 23, 2, 1969, p. 61
15. *Balance of Payments* p. 46
16. pers. comm. to the author
17. *Canberra Times* 3 September 1969
18. See John Stone 'Australia in a Competitive World: Some More Options' *Economic Papers* 1, 1, April 1982, p. 20; Stone 'Outlook for the Australian Economy' p. 34
19. pers. comm. to the author; emphasis in the original
20. pers. comm. to the author

Appendix

1. D.W. Challen and V.W. FitzGerald 'Dynamical Features of the NIF-10S Model' in Treasury *Proceedings of the Conference on the NIF-10 Model* Canberra: AGPS, 1984, p. 186
2. D.W. Challen and A.J. Hagger *Modelling the Australian Economy* Melbourne: Longman Cheshire, 1978, preface
3. C.I. Higgins 'The Origins of the NIF Model: Some Personal Recollections' in Treasury *Proceedings* p. 280. For a useful insight into the development of Higgins' macroeconomic philosophy, see C.I. Higgins, Coming of Age in the 1970s. Reflections of a Practical Macroeconomist, paper presented to a symposium, Lessons from Recent European and Australian Macroeconomic Experience, Ottawa, June 1984, mimeo
4. Higgins 'Origins' p. 281
5. ibid. p. 282
6. H.N. Johnston 'Postscript on the Origins of the NIF Model' in Treasury *Proceedings* p. 285. On the development of the model, see also Treasury *The NIF-10 Model of the Australian Economy* Canberra: AGPS, 1981
7. See H.N. Johnston, C.W. Murphy and P.A. Perazzelli 'A Simulation Version of NIF-10' in Treasury *Proceedings* pp. 3–23
8. D.W. Challen and A.J. Hagger, Economy-Wide Modelling with Special Reference to Australia, paper presented to the Eighth Conference of Economists, Melbourne, August 1979, mimeo, p. 4.
9. Challen and FitzGerald 'Dynamical Features' p. 187
10. See C.I. Higgins 'Policy Relevant Models for the 1970s' *Australian Economic Review*, 1st Quarter 1979, p. 79
11. Treasury *NIF-10 Model* pp. 7, 13
12. Higgins 'Origins' p. 283

Bibliography

Treasury

Archival material

An extensive collection of Treasury documents is located in the Canberra Branch of the Australian Archives. Documents of the period up to and including 1953 were used in chapters 1, 3 and 4. The most important series is CRS A571. There is also material on the Treasury in the Dedman Papers in the Australian National Library, Canberra.

Annual surveys

These were published from 1956 to 1973, under the title *The Australian Economy* (the only exceptions being the first two surveys, which were entitled *Australia, 1956: An Economic Survey* and *1957 and Beyond: An Economic Survey.*)

Supplements to the Treasury Information Bulletin

The most useful are:
The Meaning and Measurement of Economic Growth (November 1964)
Projections of the Work-Force, 1963–76 (April 1965)
Private Overseas Investment in Australia (May 1965)
The Australian Balance of Payments (February 1966)
Investment Analysis (July 1966)
In the early 1960s the Treasury also began publishing a series of supplements entitled *National Accounting Estimates of Public Authority Receipts and Expenditure* which appeared at regular intervals (usually biannually) throughout the 1960s. Some of these contain useful sections on budgetary policy and the level of demand (see esp. section 5 of the August 1966 supplement).

'Statement No. 2'

In the second half of the 1960s the Treasury began publishing a cursory discussion of the economic context in 'Statement No. 1' attached to the annual budget speech. From the mid-1960s it began publishing 'Statement No. 6', which was a discussion of budget estimates in national account form. Statement No. 6 was to provide the basis for what became 'Statement No. 2 — The Budget and the Economy', first published in 1972. With the demise of the annual surveys after 1973, Statement No. 2 grew steadily in length and significance.

Supplements to the Round-up of Economic Statistics

The Treasury's *Round-up of Economic Statistics* replaced the *Treasury Information Bulletin* in the early 1970s. A number of important supplements to the *Round-up* have been published, mostly on technical topics. For a listing of the supplements see the *Round-up* of August 1984, p. 46

Treasury Economic Papers

These replaced the supplements to the *Treasury Information Bulletin*. In the period to 1984 the following had been published:

1 *Overseas Investment in Australia* (1972)
2 *Economic Growth: Is it Worth Having?* (1973)
3 *Flexibility, Economic Change and Growth* (1978)

4   Job Markets: Economic and Statistical Aspects of the Australian Market for Labour (1978)
5   Energy Markets — Some Principles of Pricing (1979)
6   NIEO: An Assessment of the Proposals for a New International Economic Order (1979)
7   Technology, Growth and Jobs (1979)
8   Resource Development: Maximising Opportunities (1980)
9   The Australian Financial System (1981)
10 Public Monopolies: Telecom and Australia Post (1983)

Treasury Taxation Papers

Between 1974 and 1975 the department published fifteen Treasury Taxation Papers, numbers 1 to 13 being submitted to the Taxation Review Committee during 1973 and 1974, and numbers 14 and 15 being submitted to the Comittee of Inquiry into Inflation and Taxation early in 1975. Two of the most useful are:

4   Personal Income Tax: The Rate Scale (October 1974)
14 Indexation of the Personal Income Tax System (July 1975)

Budget speeches and financial statements

A major source of information on Treasury attitudes is the annual budget speech and the various financial statements issued by the Treasurer. While the Treasury cannot be said to be responsible for the policy decisions announced in these documents (the responsibility must of course lie with the government of the day), it does have the responsibility for drafting the sections concerned with economic conditions. Budget speeches, financial statements and ministerial statements from the mid-1930s up to 1984 have been used extensively in this book.

NIF publications

The NIF-10 Model of the Australian Economy (1981) — includes a list of articles and papers by members of the NIF team
Proceedings of the Conference on the NIF-10 Model (1984)

Books

Arndt, H.W. *A Small Rich Industrial Country* Melbourne: Cheshire, 1968
Arndt, H.W., and W.M. Corden (eds) *The Australian Economy: A Volume of Readings* Melbourne: Cheshire, 1963
Butlin, S.J. *War Economy 1939–1942* Canberra: Australian War Memorial, 1955
Butlin, S.J. and C.B. Schedvin *War Economy 1942–45* Canberra: Australian War Memorial, 1977
Campbell, D.A.S. (ed.) *Post-War Reconstruction in Australia* Sydney: Australasian Publishing Co., 1944
Caves, Richard E. and Lawrence B. Krause (eds) *The Australian Economy: A View from the North* Sydney: George Allen & Unwin, 1984
Challen, D.W. and A.J. Hagger *Modelling the Australian Economy* Melbourne: Longman Cheshire, 1978
Coddington, Alan *Keynesian Economics: The Search for First Principles* London: George Allen & Unwin, 1983
Coombs, H.C. *Other People's Money* Canberra: ANU Press, 1971
Trial Balance Melbourne: Macmillan, 1981
Copland, D.B. *Inflation and Expansion. Essays on the Australian Economy* Melbourne: Cheshire, 1951
Copland, D.B. (ed.) *Giblin. The Scholar and the Man* Melbourne: Cheshire, 1960
Corden, W.M. *Australian Economic Policy Discussion. A Survey* Melbourne: Melbourne University Press, 1968
Crisp, L.F. *Ben Chifley* Melbourne: Longmans, 1961
Duncan, W.G.K. (ed.) *National Economic Planning* Sydney: Angus & Robertson, 1934
Eatwell, John and Murray Milgate *Keynes's Economics and the Theory of Value and Distribution* London: Duckworth, 1983
Freudenberg, Graham *A Certain Grandeur. Gough Whitlam in Politics* Melbourne: Macmillan, 1977

Bibliography

Friedman, Milton and Rose *Free to Choose. A Personal Statement* Harmondsworth: Penguin, 1980
Glezer, Leon *Tariff Politics. Australian Policy Making 1960–1980* Melbourne: Melbourne University Press, 1982
Gruen, F.H. (ed.) *Surveys of Australian Economics* Sydney: George Allen & Unwin, 1978
—— *Surveys of Australian Economics* vol. 2, Sydney: George Allen & Unwin, 1979
Harrod, R.F. *The Life of John Maynard Keynes* London: Macmillan, 1951
Hasluck, Paul *The Government and the People 1939–1941* Canberra: Australian War Memorial, 1952
Hawker, Geoffrey, R.F.I. Smith, and Patrick Weller *Politics and Policy in Australia* St Lucia: University of Queensland Press, 1979
Hicks, J.R. *Value and Capital. An Inquiry into Some Fundamental Principles of Economic Theory* Oxford: Oxford University Press, 1939
—— *The Theory of Wages* 2nd edn, London: Macmillan, 1963
—— *Economic Perspectives. Further Essays on Money and Growth* Oxford: Oxford University Press, 1977
—— *Wealth and Welfare*, vol. 1 of *Collected Essays on Economic Theory* Oxford: Basil Blackwell, 1981
—— *Money, Interest and Wages*, vol. 2 of *Collected Essays* Oxford: Basil Blackwell, 1982
Hughes, Barry *Exit Full Employment: Economic Policy and the Stone Age* Sydney: Angus & Robertson, 1980
Jolley, Ainsley *Macro-Economic Policy in Australia, 1972–1976* London: Croom Helm, 1978
Juddery, Bruce *At the Centre. The Australian Bureaucracy in the 1970s* Melbourne: Cheshire 1974
Kelly, Paul *The Hawke Ascendancy* rev. edn, Sydney: Angus & Robertson, 1984
Keynes, J.M. *A Tract on Monetary Reform* (1923), reprinted in *The Collected Writings of John Maynard Keynes* as vol. 4, London: Macmillan, 1971
—— *The General Theory of Employment, Interest and Money* (1936), reprinted in *Collected Writings* as vol. 7, London: Macmillan, 1973
—— *Essays in Persuasion*, vol. 9 of *Collected Writings* London: Macmillan, 1972
—— *Essays in Biography*, vol. 10 of *Collected Writings* London: Macmillan, 1972
—— *The General Theory and After, Part I: Preparation*, vol. 13 of *Collected Writings*, ed. Donald Moggridge, London: Macmillan, 1973
—— *The General Theory and After, Part II: Defence and Development*, vol. 14 of *Collected Writings*, ed. Donald Moggridge, London: Macmillan 1973
—— *The General Theory and After: A Supplement*, vol. 29 of *Collected Writings*, ed. Donald Moggridge, London: Macmillan, 1979
Keynes, Milo (ed.) *Essays on John Maynard Keynes* Cambridge: Cambridge University Press, 1975
McFarlane, Bruce *Economic Policy in Australia. The Case for Reform* Melbourne: Cheshire, 1968
Marshall, Alfred *Principles of Economics. An Introductory Volume* 8th edn, London: Macmillan, 1920
Mathews, Russell *Public Investment in Australia. A Study of Australian Public Authority Investment and Development* Melbourne: Cheshire, 1967
Menzies, R.G. *The Forgotten People and Other Studies in Democracy* Sydney: Angus & Roberston, 1943
Milgate, Murray *Capital and Employment. A Study of Keynes's Economics* London: Academic Press, 1982
Minsky, Hyman P. *John Maynard Keynes* London: Macmillan, 1976
Moggridge, D.E. *Keynes* London: Fontana/Collins, 1976
Nevile, J.W. and D.W. Stammer (eds) *Inflation and Unemployment. Selected Readings* Ringwood: Penguin, 1972
Nieuwenhuysen, J.P., and P.J. Drake (eds) *Australian Economic Policy* Melbourne: Melbourne University Press, 1977
Norton, W.E. and D.W. Stammer (eds) *Conference in Applied Economic Research: Papers and Proceedings* Sydney: Reserve Bank of Australia, 1976
Norton, W.E. and I.W. Little (eds) *Conference in Applied Economic Research* Sydney: Reserve Bank of Australia, 1979
Parker, Robert S. *Public Service Recruitment in Australia* Melbourne: Melbourne University Press, 1942

Patinkin, Don *Money, Interest and Prices: An Integration of Monetary and Value Theory* 2nd edn, New York: Harper & Row, 1965
—— *Keynes' Monetary Thought. A Study of Its Development* Durham: Duke University Press, 1976
Perkins, J.O.N. *Macro-Economic Policy in Australia* 2nd edn, Melbourne: Melbourne University Press, 1975
Pigou, A.C. *Unemployment* London: William & Norgate, 1913
—— *The Theory of Unemployment* London: Macmillan, 1933
—— *Economics in Practice* London: Macmillan, 1935
—— *The Economics of Welfare* 4th edn, London: Macmillan, 1948
Porter, Michael G. (ed.) *The Australian Monetary System in the 1970s* Monash University: Faculty of Economics and Politics, 1978
Robbins, Lionel *The Great Depression* London: Macmillan, 1934
—— *An Essay on the Nature and Significance of Economic Science* 2nd edn, Macmillan, London, 1934
Runcie, Neil (ed.) *Australian Monetary and Fiscal Policy* Hornsby: Hodder & Stoughton with University of London Press, 1971
Samuelson, Paul A. *Economics. An Introductory Analysis* 3rd edn, New York: McGraw-Hill, 1955
Schedvin, C.B. *Australia and the Great Depression. A Study of Economic Development and Policy in the 1920s and 1930s* Sydney: Sydney University Press, 1970
Schumpeter, Joseph A. *History of Economic Analysis* New York: Oxford University Press, 1954
Scotton, R.B. and Helen Ferber (eds) *Public Expenditure and Social Policy in Australia* vol. 2 *The First Fraser Years, 1976–78* Melbourne: Longman Cheshire, 1980
Skidelsky, Robert (ed.) *The End of the Keynesian Era. Essays on the Disintegration of the Keynesian Political Economy* London: Macmillan, 1977
Spender, Percy *Politics and a Man* Sydney: Collins, 1972
Trevithick, J.A. *Inflation* 2nd edn, Harmondsworth: Penguin, 1980
Walker, E. Ronald *Australia in the Great Depression* London: P.S. King & Son, 1933
—— *Unemployment with Special Reference to Australia* Sydney: Angus & Robertson, 1936
—— *From Economic Theory to Policy* Chicago: University of Chicago Press, 1943
Walras, Léon *Elements of Pure Economics or the Theory of Social Wealth* (1874), edition définitive (1926), trans. William Jaffé, Homewood: Richard D. Irwin, 1954
Waterman, A.M.C. *Economic Fluctuations in Australia, 1948 to 1964* Canberra: ANU Press, 1972
Weller, Patrick and James Cutt *Treasury Control in Australia* Sydney: Ian Novak, 1976
Worswick, David and James Trevithick (eds) *Keynes and the Modern World* Cambridge: Cambridge University Press, 1983

Articles, papers, reports, pamphlets and addresses

Arndt, H.W. 'The Australian Economy, September 1957' *Economic Record* 33, December 1957
—— 'Deflation through Wool' *Banker* 108, 1958
—— 'Control of Inflation through Fiscal Policy: A Reappraisal' *Economic Record* 36, December 1960
—— 'Australia's Changing Financial Structure' (1960), reprinted in H.W. Arndt *A Small Rich Industrial Country*
—— 'Further Reflections on Long-Term Planning' (1962), reprinted in Arndt *A Small Rich Industrial Country*
—— 'Five Contributions on Economic Planning' section 2, *Dissent*, Spring 1963
Artis, M.J. and R.W. Wallace, 'A Historical Survey of Australian Fiscal Policy 1945–66' in Neil Runcie (ed.) *Australian Monetary and Fiscal Policy*
Auld, D.A.L. 'A Measure of Australian Fiscal Policy Performance 1948–49 to 1963–64' *Economic Record* 43, June 1967
Boxer, A.H. 'The Australian Economy, November 1959' *Economic Record* 35, December 1959
Brigden, J.B. 'Economics and Ethics' *Morpeth Review* 2, December 1932
Burton, Herbert 'Principles for Post-War Policy' *Australian Quarterly* 15, 1, 1943
Bury, L.H.E. 'Economic Management in the 1970s' *Australian Accountant* 40, December 1970

Bibliography

Butlin, S.J. '"Of Course I Know No Economics, But —"' *Australian Quarterly* 20, 3, 1948
Carron, Andrew S. 'The Australian Financial System' in Richard E. Caves and Lawrence B. Krause (eds) *The Australian Economy*
Challen, D.W. and A.J. Hagger, Economy-Wide Modelling with Special Reference to Australia, paper presented to Eighth Conference of Economists, Melbourne, August 1979, mimeo
Challen, D.W. and V.W. FitzGerald 'Dynamical Features of the NIF-10S Model' in Treasury *Proceedings of the Conference on the NIF-10 Model*
Cole, R.W. 'The Economic and Financial Surveys Division of the Commonwealth Treasury' *Public Administration* 23, 2, 1964
Coombs, H.C. 'The Economic Aftermath of War' in D.A.S. Campbell (ed.) *Post-War Reconstruction*
—— *Problems of a High Employment Economy*, the Joseph Fisher Lecture in Commerce 1944, Adelaide: University of Adelaide at the Hassell Press, 1944
—— 'Australia's Ability to Avoid Booms and Depressions' *Economic Papers* 8, 1948
—— 'The Development of Monetary Policy in Australia' (1954), reprinted in H.C. Coombs *Other People's Money*
—— 'A Matter of Prices' *Economic Record* 35, December 1959
Copland, D.B. 'The State and the Entrepreneur', paper presented to a symposium of the Harvard Tercentenary Conference of Arts and Science, August–September 1936, reprinted in *Authority and the Individual* Cambridge: Harvard University Press, 1937
—— 'The Change-Over to Peace' in D.A.S. Campbell (ed.) *Post-War Reconstruction*
—— *Back to Earth in Economics: Australia 1948* Sydney: Angus & Robertson, 1948
—— 'The Limits of Social Control' *IPA Review* 5, September–October 1949
—— 'Development of Economic Thought in Australia, 1924–50' in D.B. Copland *Inflation and Expansion*
—— Structural Problems under Full Employment, paper presented to section G, ANZAAS conference, May 1951, mimeo
—— 'The Australian Economy: A New Look' *Economic Record* 33, August 1957
Cornish, Selwyn, Full Employment in Australia: The Genesis of a White Paper, paper presented to the Post-War Reconstruction Seminar, Canberra, August–September 1981
Crisp, L.F. 'The Commonwealth Treasury's Changed Role and Its Organisational Consequences' *Public Administration* 20, 4, 1961
—— 'Central Co-ordination of Commonwealth Policy-Making: Roles and Dilemmas of the Prime Minister's Department' *Public Administration* 26, 1, 1967
—— 'Politics and the Commonwealth Public Service' *Public Administration* 31, 4, 1972
Downing, R.I. 'Giblin as Ritchie Professor' in Copland (ed.) *Giblin*
—— 'The Australian Economy, March 1956' *Economic Record* 32, May 1956
Eatwell, John 'Theories of Value, Output and Employment' (1979), reprinted in Eatwell and Milgate (eds) *Keynes's Economics*
Eatwell, John and Murray Milgate 'Introduction' in Eatwell and Milgate (eds) *Keynes's Economics*
Edwards, John 'The Economy Game: Treasury and Its Rivals' *Current Affairs Bulletin* 51, 12, 1975
Encel, S. 'The Recruitment of University Graduates to the Commonwealth Public Service' *Public Administration* 12, 4, 1953
—— 'The Commonwealth Public Service and Outside Recruitment' *Public Administration* 14, 1, 1955
Final Report of the Committee of Inquiry into the Australian Financial System (Campbell Report) Canberra: AGPS, 1981
Firth, G.G., Disinflation in Australia: A Democratic Dilemma, paper presented to section G, ANZAAS conference, May 1951, mimeo
Fisher, N.W.F. 'The Relationship between Benefit-Cost Analysis and Planning-Programming-Budgeting Systems' *Australian Accountant* 42, April 1972
Fitchett, Ian 'From Woolsorter to Treasury Secretary' *Sydney Morning Herald* 2 November 1966
Fraser, B.W., The Australian Treasury—Tendering Economic Advice, paper presented to Royal Australian Institute of Public Administration, ACT Division, Canberra, October 1984, mimeo
Friedman, Milton 'The Role of Monetary Policy' *American Economic Review* 58, March 1968
Giblin, L.F. 'Reconstruction in Australia' *Agenda* 2, 3, 1943
—— 'Reconstruction: A Pisgah View' *Australian Quarterly* 15, 3, 1943

—— 'Financing Full Employment' *Economic Papers* 5, 1945
Gregory, R.G. 'Some Implications of the Growth of the Mineral Sector' *Australian Journal of Agricultural Economics* 20, August 1976
Gruen, F.H. 'What Went Wrong? Some Personal Reflections on Economic Policy under Labor' *Australian Quarterly* 48, 4, 1976
—— 'Australian Economics 1968–78: A Survey of the Surveys' in Gruen (ed.) *Surveys of Australian Economics* vol. 2
Hagger, A.J. 'Inflation' in Gruen (ed.) *Surveys of Australian Economics* (1978)
Hahn, F.H. 'Unemployment from a Theoretical Viewpoint' *Economica* 47, August 1980
Hall, A.R. 'The Australian Economy, August, 1961' *Economic Record* 37, September 1961
—— 'Investment Planning Will Have to Start Now' *Australian Financial Review* 8 May 1962
Hicks, J.R. 'A Reconsideration of the Theory of Value' (1934), reprinted in J.R. Hicks *Wealth and Welfare*
—— 'Mr Keynes and the Classics: A Suggested Interpretation' (1937), reprinted in J.R. Hicks *Money, Interest and Wages*
—— 'The Foundation of Welfare Economics' (1939), reprinted in Hicks *Wealth and Welfare*
—— 'Some Questions of Time in Economics' in Anthony M. Tang, Fred M. Westfield and James S. Worley (eds) *Evolution, Welfare and Time in Economics* Lexington: Lexington Books, 1976
—— 'Introductory: LSE and the Robbins Circle' in Hicks *Money, Interest and Wages*
Higgins, C.I. 'Comment' in Norton and Little (eds) *Conference in Applied Economic Research*
—— 'Policy Relevant Models for the 1970s' *Australian Economic Review*, 1st quarter 1979
—— 'The Origins of the NIF Model: Some Personal Recollections' in Treasury *Proceedings of the Conference on the NIF-10 Model*
—— Coming of Age in the 1970s. Reflections of a Practical Macroeconomist, paper presented to a symposium, Lessons from Recent European and Australian Macroeconomic Experience, Ottawa, June 1984, mimeo
Higgins, C.I., H.N. Johnston and P.L. Coghlan 'Business Investment: The Recent Experience' in Norton and Stammer (eds) *Conference in Applied Economic Research*
Holt, Harold E. *The Role of Government in Maintaining Full Employment* lecture 6 in the Melbourne Junior Chamber Lecture Series 1949, *Boom and Slump: The Challenge to Private Enterprise*
IAESR 'The Australian Economy' *Australian Economic Review* 4th quarter 1970
—— 'The Australian Economy' *Australian Economic Review* 3rd quarter 1971
—— 'The Australian Economy' *Australian Economic Review* 4th quarter 1971
Isaac, J.E., Wage Policy and the Commonwealth Arbitration Court, paper presented to section G, ANZAAS conference, 1955, mimeo
Jaffé, William 'Walras's Economics as Others See It' *Journal of Economic Literature* 28, June 1980
Johnston, H.N. 'Real Wages and Unemployment' *Australian Economic Review* 1st quarter 1979
—— 'Postscript on the Origins of the NIF Model' in Treasury *Proceedings of the Conference on the NIF-10 Model*
Johnston, H.N., R.B. Campbell and R.M. Simes 'The Impact of Wages and Prices on Unemployment' *Economic Papers* 60, December 1978
Johnston, H.N., C.W. Murphy and P.A. Perazelli 'A Simulation Version of NIF-10' in Treasury *Proceedings*
Jonson, P.D. 'Our Current Inflationary Experience' *Australian Economic Review*, 2nd quarter 1973
Kaldor, Nicholas 'Keynesian Economics after Fifty Years' in Worswick and Trevithick (eds) *Keynes and the Modern World*
Karmel, P.H. *Economic Policy in Australia—Ends and Means*, the G.L. Wood Memorial Lecture 1954, Melbourne: Melbourne University Press, 1954
—— 'Australia's Economic Problems' *Australian Accountant* 26, February 1956
—— 'The Australian Economy, April 1957' *Economic Record* 33, April 1957
—— 'Some Reflections on Inflation, Productivity and Growth' *Economic Record* 35, December 1959
Kelly, Paul 'Our Leading Public Servant' *National Times* 28 October 1978
Kregel, J.A. 'Economic Methodology in the Face of Uncertainty: The Modelling Methods of Keynes and the Post-Keynesians' *Economic Journal* 86, June 1976
Lydall, H.F. 'The Australian Economy, February 1962' *Economic Record* 38, March 1968

Bibliography

McMahon, William 'The PM versus the Bureaucrats' *Australian Financial Review* 3 June 1974

Meade, James 'The Price Mechanism and the Australian Balance of Payments' *Economic Record* 32, November 1956

—— 'The Keynesian Revolution' in Milo Keynes (ed.) *Essays on John Maynard Keynes*

Melville, L.G. 'The Place of Expectations in Economic Theory' *Economic Record* 15, June 1939

Milgate, Murray and John Eatwell 'Unemployment and the Market Mechanism' in John Eatwell and Murray Milgate (eds) *Keynes's Economics and the Theory of Value and Distribution*

Nell, E.J., Review of Murray Milgate *Capital and Employment* (1982) *Contributions to Political Economy* 2, March 1983

Nevile, J.W. 'The Australian Economy, August 1971' *Economic Record* 47, September 1971

—— 'The Role of Fiscal Policy in the Eighties' *Economic Record* 59, March 1983

Polglaze, Jean and C.S. Soper 'Wilfred Prest: An Appreciation' in Nieuwenhuysen and Drake (eds) *Australian Economic Policy*

Porter, Michael G. 'Stabilization, Regulation and Misplaced Entrepreneurship' *Quadrant* 22, 9, 1978

Prest, A.R. and R. Turvey 'Cost-Benefit Analysis: A Survey' *Economic Journal* 75, December 1965

Randall, Sir Richard 'The Economy' in *Australia: An Economic and Investment Reference* Commonwealth of Australia, 1970

RCAGA *Appendices* vols 1–4, Canberra: AGPS, 1976

Report of the Committee of Economic Enquiry (Vernon Report) vol. 1, Canberra: CGP, 1965

Robinson, Sir Austin 'Impressions of Maynard Keynes' in Worswick and Trevithick (eds) *Keynes and the Modern World*

Russell, E.A. 'Foreign Investment Policy—What Role for the Economist?' *Australian Economic Papers* 17, December 1978

Samuel, Peter 'Policies for Growth: The Vernon Report—A Review' *Australian Quarterly* 37, 4, 1965

Samuelson, Paul A. and Robert M. Solow 'Analytical Aspects of Anti-Inflation Policy' *American Economic Review* 50, May 1960

Sheehan, P.J. 'The Campbell Report: An Overview' *Economic Papers* special edn, April 1983

Sheehan, P.J., and Stricker, P.P. 'The Collapse of Full Employment, 1974 to 1978' in R.B. Scotton and Helen Ferber (eds) *Public Expenditure and Social Policy in Australia*

Skidelsky, Robert 'The Reception of the Keynesian Revolution' in Milo Keynes (ed.) *Essays on John Maynard Keynes*

—— 'Keynes and the Revolt Against the Victorians' in Robert Skidelsky (ed.) *The End of the Keynesian Era*

Snedden, B.M. 'Wage/Price Policies', address to Committee for the Economic Development of Australia, 18 November 1971, supplementary paper no. 42, March 1972

Stone, John 'Inflation and the International Monetary System', *IPA Review* 23, 2, 1969

—— 'Roundtable Discussion' in Porter (ed.), *The Australian Monetary System in the 1970s*

—— 'The Budget Deficit and the Economy' in *The Significance of the Budget Deficit*, CAER paper no. 7, University of New South Wales: Centre for Applied Economic Research, June 1979

—— Australia in a Competitive World—Some Options, paper presented to the 21st General Management Conference of the Australian Institute of Management, Sydney, November 1979, mimeo

—— 'The Outlook for the Australian Economy' *Quarterly Review of the Rural Economy* 3, 1, 1981

—— 'Australia in a Competitive World: Some More Options' *Economic Papers* 1, 1, April 1982

—— '1929 and All That' *Quadrant* 28, 10, October 1984

—— 'What Kind of Country? In the Decade Ahead and Beyond' *Quadrant* 28, 12, December 1984

—— Fiscal Policy 1985–86: the Prime Minister's 'Trinity', paper presented at Centre of Policy Studies, Monash University, December 1984, mimeo

Swan, T.W., Notes on Some Inter-Relations of Economic Policies (Employment, Balance of Payments, Spending, and Costs), address to section G, ANZAAS conference, 1955, reprinted as 'Longer-run Problems of the Balance of Payments' in Arndt and Corden (eds) *The Australian Economy*

Trevithick, J.A. 'Money Wage Inflexibility and the Keynesian Labour Supply Function' *Economic Journal* 86, June 1976

Walker, E. Ronald 'Sound Finance' *Economic Record* 15, April 1939

—— *The Transformation of War-Time Controls* Realities of Reconstruction no. 3, Melbourne: MUP with OUP, 1943

Weintraub, Sidney 'Keynes and the Monetarists' *Canadian Journal of Economics* 4, February 1971

Wheeler, Sir Frederick 'Forward Estimates of Commonwealth Budgetary Expenditures' *Australian Accountant* 43, April 1973

Wheelwright, E.L. 'Planning the Economy' *Quadrant* 6, 2, 1962

Wilson, Roland 'Capitalism and the Second Effort' *Australian Quarterly* 4, 4, 1932

—— 'The Economic Implications of Planning' in Duncan (ed.) *National Economic Planning*

—— *Economic Co-ordination*, the Joseph Fisher Lecture in Commerce 1940, Adelaide: University of Adelaide at the Hassell Press, 1940

—— 'Increasing Deficit in the Balance of Payments' in *Australia: A Financial Times Survey*, supplement to the *Financial Times* 7 May 1962

—— 'Labour and Industry, Trade and Finance in Australia' in *Australia: New Frontiers* New York: Chase Manhattan Bank, 1965

—— 'L.F. Giblin: A Man for All Seasons', the Gilbin Memorial Lecture 1976, reprinted in *Search* 7, 7, 1976

Index

accord, prices and income, 237, 245–46, 258
Amalgamated Metals, Foundry and Shipwrights' Union, 257, 259
Arndt, H.W., 90–91, 117, 124, 136–37, 139, 141
Artis, M.J., 92, 94, 117
Auld, D.A.L., 100–02
Australian Bureau of Statistics, 276
Australian Council of Trade Unions, 237, 246
Australian Institute of Political Science, 67, 74

balance of payments, deterioration in, 107, 112, 213; persistent deficits in, 111, 125, 127, 147–50, 177; recovery in, 115; surplus, 196, 207, 240–41; Treasury on, 111, 124, 149–50, 177
benefit-cost analysis, 159–61, 271; Treasury on, 155–60, 163, 175
Boxer, A.H., 131, 180
Brigden, J.B., 65, 75–78
Brophy, J., 11
budgetary policy, of Chifley government, 84–7, 90–96, 102; in 1949–50, 100–02; 1951; 'Horror Budget', 97, 104–07, 111; in 1952–55, 108–9; 1956 mini-budget, 111–12, 119, 124, 127, 133, 138; in 1956–60, 115–18, 132–34; November 1960, 131, 134–35, 138, 193; in 1961–64, 134–35, 150; in 1965–67, 152, 154, 156; of Gorton government, 186–87; of McMahon government, 173, 190, 192–94, 196; of Whitlam government, 15–16, 208, 215–17, 225; of Fraser government, 228–29, 236, 238–39, 246, 252; of Hawke government, 237, 252; Keynes on, 50–51, 171–72; in Full Employment white paper, 56; in 1930s, 53–55, 88; political difficulties with, 90–92, 95–96, 102–04, 108–09, 128; Stone on, 252; Treasury on, 87–90, 97, 105, 168, 185–88, 190, 193, 207, 213, 224–28, 238–39, 252–53
Burton, H., 60

Bury, L., 24, 62, 148, 178, 187–88
Butlin, S.J., 11, 55, 66, 88, 145

Cameron, R., 146
Campbell Committee, see Committee of Inquiry into the Australian Financial System
capital inflow, 101, 118, 131, 196–98; Treasury on, 242–43
capital-labour substitution, 219–21
Castles, I., 20, 180
Caton, C., 277, 279
Challen, D.W., 276, 278
Chifley, J.B., 6, 19, 22–23, 58–59, 65, 84–86, 90–93, 96
Chifley government, economic policies of, 90–96
Clark, C., 63
Coddington, A., 46–47
Cole, R.W., 7, 20–21, 147, 179–80
Committee of Economic Enquiry (Vernon Committee), 139, 147, 150, 160, 164–68, 175
Committee of Inquiry into the Australian Financial System (Campbell Committee), 247–49, 252, 259
Commonwealth Arbitration Court, 57, 101
Commonwealth Bank, 10–11, 57, 61–62, 84, 94–95, 97–100, 104–05, 107–10, 112, 132, 138
Commonwealth Conciliation and Arbitration Commission, 128–31, 152, 182, 185, 187; Treasury on, 185, 223–24, 256–57, 259, 263
consensus and cooperation, 74–79, 128, 142–43, 191–92, 215–16, 236–37; Treasury on, 143, 191–92, 258
Consolidated Revenue Fund, 54, 92–93, 105, 108
Consumer price index, see Prices
controls, direct, 85, 94–95, 105–06, 109, 149, 191; see also import restrictions
Coombs, H.C., 10, 23, 53, 61–66, 70, 78–79,

303

88, 95–96, 103, 106, 109, 124–25, 130
Coombs Commission, *see* Royal Commission on Australian Government Administration
Copland, D.B., 11, 62, 64–65, 70–71, 76–78, 83, 102, 106, 123–24, 126, 139, 180–81
Country Party, 19, 22, 97, 100, 197–98, 243
Craik, D., 179
Crawford, J.G., 19, 62–63, 145, 164, 166
Crawford Committee, 24, 231
Crean, F., 24, 178, 215–16
Crisp, L.F., 19, 53–54, 58
Cruise, H.F., 180
Cutt, J., 161–62

Daniel, R., 146, 180
Dedman, J.J., 6, 55, 60
deregulation, financial, 237, 246–51, 260
development, program 1950–51, 96–102; program 1950s, 123, 126; unbalanced, 86–87; *see also* immigration
Downing, R.I., 62, 124, 138, 180
Drought, 118, 153–54, 186, 244, 246

Eatwell, J., 41, 201
Economic and Financial Surveys Branch, 7, 23, 139–40, 146–47, 156, 179, 272, 274
economic decision-making, Stone on, 44; Treasury on, 144, 155–60, 220–244
economic growth, continuity of, 111–12, 176; desire in Australia for, 118–19, 121, 123, 157, 185; and inflation, 124–25, 184–85; slowing-down of; 148–49; Treasury on, 118–20, 123, 135–36, 148–49, 153, 157, 166–67, 176, 230
economic management, acceptance of during World War II, 5–6, 57, 59–60; confidence in, 127–28; limitations of, 95–96, 102–04, 108–09, 128, 141–42, 199–201, 225–27, 235; Treasury on, 128, 141–42, 168–69, 174, 202–04, 224–28, 232, 234–35, 238–39, 248–54, 262, 268
Economic planning, debate 1960–62, 138–39; Treasury on; 140–41, 162, 167–68
economic projections and forecasts, Treasury on, 141, 163–66, 173
economists, Australian, and economic education, 77–79, 102–04, 106, 128–29; and economic planning, 138–39; and 1951 'Horror Budget', 106; and import restrictions, 132; and inflation, 124–26; and Keynesianism, 53, 61–64, 79, 205; and neoclassical synthesis, 206–7; and saving ratio, 254–55; *see also* Financial and Economic Advisory Committee
economy, Australian, Treasury's confidence in, 116, 147, 167, 176–77, 179–80, 231–33; Treasury's vision of, 159–60, 233, 262, 268
Edgeworth, F.Y., 26, 46, 71
employment, growth in, 84–85, 218, 238, 246; *see also* Full Employment white paper; Labour market
Encel, S., 9–10
Evatt, H.V., 59
exchange, foreign, shortages of, 84–86; deregulation of, 247
exchange rate, alterations to, 100–01, 105, 154, 196–98, 212–13, 216, 229, 246, 265; arrangements, 1971–83, 249–50; flotation of, 237, 246–47, 251; Stone on, 242, 248–49, 251; Treasury on, 100, 197, 248–51
expenditure, defence, 94, 144, 150, 152–56, 163, 174–75, 269–70; private consumption and investment, 94–95, 111–13, 122, 129–30, 150–51, 153–54, 156, 186, 194–95, 209, 220, 238, 244, 246; public, 94–95, 108, 112–13, 116–18, 144, 150–56, 174–75, 186–87, 193–96, 208–9, 216, 229, 246, 251–52, 265
exports and export income, 84, 101, 107, 113, 115–17, 131, 134, 140–41, 149–51, 165, 177, 195–96, 207, 209, 220

Fadden, A.W., 19, 22–23, 97, 100–01, 104–06, 108, 115–18, 121, 138
Finance, Department of, 6, 230
Financial and Economic Advisory Committee, 65–66, 87–88, 128, 142; Keynesian philosophy of, 66–79
Financial Institutions Division, 7–9
Firth, G.G., 62, 102–04
Fisher, N.W., 161
FitzGerald, V.W., 276–77
Foreign Investment Division, 8–9
forward estimates, 161–62
Fraser, B.W., 21, 180, 237, 248–49, 260
Fraser, J.M., 20, 229–30, 236–37, 240, 244–45, 256
Fraser government, 6, 24, economic policies of, 228–30, 236–40, 244–45, 251–52; and Treasury, 228–30, 238
Friedman, M., 199–201, 203, 206, 223, 228
Full Employment white paper, 55–57, 60, 83, 89, 95
functional classification, 162

Garrett, J., 197
General Financial and Economic Policy (GFEP) Division, 16, 145–46, 156, 175, 223, 274–75; establishment, role and structure of, 6–9, 11, 89; qualifications of officers in, 14–15, 179–81; *see also* Economic and Financial Surveys Branch
Giblin, L.F., 61–63, 65–66, 73–74, 77, 88, 180
Glezer, L., 19, 21–22, 166, 168
Gorton, J.G., 19, 24, 178, 186, 242–43, 268
gross national expenditure, 113–14, 116, 130, 134, 151, 195, 208–09

Index

gross domestic product, 107, 113–14, 116, 138, 147, 150–51, 186, 195, 208–09, 217
Gregory thesis, 240–42
Gruen, F.H., 208, 213, 221–22

Hagger, A.J., 190, 206, 276, 278
Hahn, F.H., 201
Hall, A.R., 139, 167
Hasluck, P., 22, 88
Hawke government, economic policies of, 236–37, 246–47, 252
Hayden, W.G., 215–17
Heathershaw, J.T., 54
Hewitt, Sir Lennox, 19
Hicks, J.R., 26, 29, 33, 169–70, 181
Higgins, C.I., 180, 221–22, 264–65, 276–77, 279
Holt, H., 6, 22–23, 60, 137, 147, 150, 152, 154, 178
Holt government, economic policies of, 154
Howard, J.W., 237–38, 252
Hughes, B., 208, 210, 215, 229
Hyden, N.F., 180

immigration, 84, 86–87, 95–102, 123, 126, 148, 210–11; Treasury on, 97, 99–100, 109
'Imperfectionist' view, 35, 159, 201, 232
import restrictions, 94, 107, 109, 112, 118, 125, 127, 132, 150, 212, 216, 259; removal of, 131–32, 138
import surplus, 97–99
imports, 113, 140, 151, 208; flood of, 1951–52, 107–08; increases in, 109, 111, 120, 131, 134, 152–53, 195–96; shortages of, 84–86
Incomes-prices policies, 190–92, 206–07, 258, 264
industrial disputes, 101, 188–89, 211–12, 257, 265
inflation, 1945–49, 83–87, 92–96; in 1950s, 100, 104, 111, 115; in 1960s, 152, 154; in 1970s, 183–84, 198, 210–13, 217, 239, 265; and Australian economists, 124–26; causes of, 90, 94, 97–99, 100–01, 106, 141, 184, 192–93, 216; and community attitudes, 124–25, 141–43, 149; and saving ratio, 255; Stone on, 242; Treasury on, 99, 108, 111–12, 117–18, 123–25, 130, 135, 142–43, 149–50, 178, 183–85, 192–94, 207, 217, 229, 234, 239–40, 249, 251–52, 262–63, 266;
-unemployment nexus, 207, 217, 263–64
inflationary expectations, 199–202, 206; Treasury on, 201–04, 207, 215, 223, 226, 228, 253, 255–56, 264
instalment purchases, 136–37
Institute for Applied Economic and Social Research, 190

Institute of Public Affairs, 92
International Monetary Fund, 101, 131, 146, 272
international reserves, falls in, 107, 111–12, 115–16, 120, 127, 134, 150, 213, 229; increases in, 131–32, 187, 196–98, 207, 265
Investment and Employment Committee, 84–87, 100
Isaac, J.E., 182–83
'IS-LM' analysis, 169–71

Jackson Committee, 231–32
Jaffe, W., 28
Johnston, H.N., 221, 223, 277–79
Jolley, A., 20
Jonson, P.D., 192
Joyce, A.C., 11
Juddery, B., 7

Karmel, P.H., 125, 128–29, 137–38, 164
Keating, M., 276–77
Keating, P., 237
Kelly, P., 260
Keynes, J.M., 25, 35, 38–53, 58–59, 62–64, 66–67, 72, 105, 120, 129, 169–73, 181, 235, 271, 278; on economic decision-making, 44–48; on economic policy, 49–51; on methodology, 173
Keynesianism, x–xi, 3, 38–52, 142–43, 169–73, 201, 205; acceptance of in Australia, 1930–45, 53–79; acceptance of by Australian economists, 61–66, 79, 90; acceptance of by Treasury, 25, 89–90, 108–09; econometric models, 278–79; and Labor Party, 58–60, 90–93, 217; and Phillips curve, 172–73, 266; as basis of budgetary policy, 1950s, 105–06, 108, 117; in Treasury thought, 135, 235, 262; rejection of by Treasury, 178, 203–04, 224–28, 266–68, 271
Klein, L., 276, 278–79
Labour (and National Service), Department of, 23, 65, 84, 178, 193–94
Korean War, economic experience during, 100–02, 104–05, 107, 119, 124, 137, 254

Loan Council, 5, 57, 90, 175
Loan Fund, 92–93, 102
'Loans affair', 215, 268
Lynch, P., 228–29
Lyons, J., 54–55, 65

McBurney, S.S., 180
McEwen, Sir John, 19, 21, 22, 243
McFarlane, S.G., 11, 54, 88–89, 109
McMahon, W., 19, 154, 155–56, 178, 194, 198
McMahon government, economic policies of,

305

173, 193–94, 196–98, 210, 268; exchange rate dispute of, 197–98; electoral defeat of, 178
manufacturing; growth of, 84, 86, 177; malaise of, 231–32, 241
market discipline, Treasury on, 158, 178, 233–34, 244, 267–68
Marshall, A., 26, 28–33, 38, 46, 71, 169, 181; see also Neoclassicism
Mathews, R., 160–61
Meade, J., 43, 138
Melville, L.G., 61–63, 65, 71–72, 74, 145
Menzies, R.G., 19, 59–60, 88, 97, 101, 109, 112, 130, 143, 164, 174–75, 178
Menzies government, and development and migration program, 1950–51, 97, 101–02; and economic planning debate, 138–39; and 1961 election, 136, 175; economic policies of, 101–02, 104–09, 111–12, 113–17, 127–28, 130–35, 147–48, 150–54;
Milgate, M., 35, 201
Mills, R.C., 58, 61–62, 65, 145
minerals and mining, 96, 147, 149, 154, 176–77, 196–97, 240–41; exports of, 150, 165, 177, 196; see also Resources boom
Minsky, H., 39–40, 170–71
modelling, macroeconomic, 276–79
monetarism, 200–01, 206, 263, 271
Monetarism Mark II, see Rational expectations
monetary conditions, 107–08, 112, 132–34, 184, 187, 198, 207, 213, 265
monetary policy, of Chifley government, 95; of Menzies government, 99, 104, 106–08, 112, 132–34, 138, 150, 152; of Gorton government, 186–87; of McMahon government, 194; of Whitlam government, 207, 213, 216–17; of Fraser government, 228; Investment and Employment Committee on, 85; Treasury on, 99, 104, 186–87, 228, 248–51, 267; see also Committee of Inquiry into the Australian Financial System
Monaghan, J.V., 180

National Economic Development Council (UK), 139, 158
national income forecasting (NIF) model, 24, 274, 276–79
National Welfare Fund, 90–92
Nell, E.J., 47
neoclassicism, 3, 25–38, 51–52, 98, 70–71, 171, 205–06; and interest in resource allocation, 32–33, 51; policy prescriptions of, 35–38; compared with Keynesianism, 39–43, 45–47, 51–52; in Treasury thought, x–xi, 25, 122–23, 159–60, 169, 174–75, 178, 181, 207, 219, 223, 228, 232–5, 262, 264–72

neoclassical synthesis, 169–74, 205–07, 263, 271
Nevile, J.W., 190, 193–94, 205, 207, 276
Newton, M., 148
Nieuwenhuysen, J.P., 190
Norman, N., 213

O'Donnell, M.W., 20–21, 145–46, 179, 272–73
OPEC, 211, 239, 265–66
Ord River scheme, 161, 243
Overseas Economic Relations Division, 7–9, 179

Pareto, V., 26, 33, 71
Patinkin, D., 169–71
Perkins, J.O.N., 154
Phillips curve, 131, 172–73, 199–200, 206; Treasury on, 173, 203, 217, 266
Pigou, A.C., 26, 28, 34–35, 37–38, 46, 171, 181, 230
planning, programming budgeting, 161–62, 175, 271
Polglaze, J., 181
Porter, M., 248, 266
Postwar Reconstruction, Department of, 6, 10, 18, 65, 84, 89, 95, 102, 109
Prest, W., 181
prices, consumer price index (CPI), 86, 100, 107, 114–15, 130, 147, 150, 154, 182–83, 211, 217, 246; export, 84, 86, 101, 107, 111, 116, 131, 134, 207; import, 86, 211; oil, 211, 238–39, 265–66; see also inflation
Prices Justification Tribunal, 212–14
Prime Minister and Cabinet, Department of, 19–20, 109, 252; Economic Division, 6, 18–19, 22, 94, 100
private sector, Treasury on, 123, 158, 227, 244, 262, 268; see also public sector
productivity, 85, 182; and real wages, 127, 131, 182–83, 218–23, 264
profit squeeze, 213–14, 220, 222, 245, 256, 265
profits share, see Wages-profits share
Prowse, A.R.G., 180
Pryor, F.C., 10, 179–80
public sector, expansion of, 94, 160; vis-a-vis private, 144, 152, 155–56, 175, 216, 268; Treasury on, 144, 155–56, 158–60, 196, 244, 251, 254, 266, 268
public service, Commonwealth, economists in, 3, 9, 61, 65–66; recruitment policies of, 9–11, 65

Randall, Sir Richard, 7, 16, 24, 109, 147, 177, 270, 273–74; background and career of, 110, 145–46, 179
rational expectations, 200, 206, 226–27,

263–64, 271
Rattigan, G.A., 163
Royal Commission on Australian Government Administration (Coombs Commission) 13, 17–18; Task Force on Economic Policy, 24
real wage overhang, 221–24, 246, 264
recession, in 1952, 107–08, 116–19; 219; in 1961–62, 134–37, 154, 219; in 1971–72, 194, 196; in 1974–75, 213–14; in 1982–83, 236, 244–45
Reddaway, W.B., 63
referendum; 1944 and 1948, 60, 94; 1973, 190–91
Reserve Bank, 20, 110, 132–34, 150, 192, 198, 238, 247–48, 276–77; econometric model, 192, 276–77
resource allocation, Treasury on, 144, 156–60, 162, 166, 168–69, 174–75, 184, 191–92, 230–32, 249, 263, 269–70
Resource Allocation and Development Division, 231
resources boom, 236, 238–42, 244–45, 256
Robbins, L., 26, 32–33, 35–37, 52, 169, 173, 234
Robinson, A., 46
Rowse, T., 74–75
Royal Commission on Money and Banking, 58, 73, 247
rural industry, 84–85, 107, 116, 118–19, 128, 140–41, 153, 165, 177, 186, 244, 246; stabilisation schemes, 85, 95, 101
Rye, C.R., 180, 277

Samuelson, P.A., 169, 172–73, 205
saving ratio, 122, 254–56, 264; Stone on, 243; Treasury on, 120–23
Schedvin, C.B., 55
Schumpeter, J.A., 25, 28
Scullin government, economic policies of, 58–59
Shackle, G.L.S., 47
Sheehan, P.J., 222, 248
'Short, sharp shock' strategy, 15–16, 215
Simmel, G., 27
Skidelsky, R., 64–65
Smithsonian Agreement, 176, 197
Snedden, B.M., 178, 188, 190–93, 197–98
Solow, R.M., 172–73
Soper, C.S., 181
Spender, P.C., 54, 73, 88
stagflation, 190, 199, 202, 206
Stone, J.O., x, 4, 24, 259–60, 272; background and career of, 83, 146, 179, 237–39; and supplements to *Treasury Information Bulletin* 147, 156, 244, 274; on budgetary policy, 216, 226–27, 252, 266–67; on dollar float, 248–49; on exchange rate appreciation, 242; on generational factor, 271, on incomes-prices policies, 264; on inflation, 242; on profits share, 223; on public sector, 243–44; on rational expectations, 226–67; on resources boom, 241–42; on saving, 243; on tariffs, 242; on trade unions, 257, 259; on wages and wage fixation, 218, 223, 246, 257, 260–61; and influence on Treasury thought, 272–75
strikes, *see* Industrial disputes
structural change, Treasury on, 231–32, 253–54
Stuart, N.F., 10–11
Summit, National Economic, 237
Swan, T.W., 62, 125–27, 145

Tariff Board, 57, 132, 162–63
tariffs, 162–63; 25 per cent cut in, 198, 212, 214, 241–42, 265; Treasury on, 99, 159, 232, 234
taxation, increases in, 101, 105–06, 112, 134, 150, 152–53, 156, 186–87, 193; indexation, 225, 229; reductions in, 116–17, 130, 134–35, 187, 196, 216; Treasury on, 99, 122, 225, 229
Taxation Office, 92
Theodore, E.G., 58–59
terms of trade, 131, 153
Thomas, W.C., 11
Trade (and Industry), Department of, 19, 20–22, 154, 166–68, 175, 259
trade unions, 130, 141, 143, 183, 212; Treasury on, 178, 188–89, 192–93, 256, 258–59, 263, 267
Treasury, Department of the, role and responsibilities of, 4–6, 269; organisation and structure, 6–9, 179, 229–30; dominance of by accountants, 11; rise of economist in, 9–13, 89, 175; and Melbourne University recruits, 10–11, 146–47, 180–81; educational standards in, 12–14, 22–23; and the departmental line, 15–16, 88; unity in, 16–18; staffing changes in, 71, 145–47, 179–80, 270; dominance of in economic advising, 18–24; rivalry of with Department of Trade, 19–20, 154, 166–68, 175, 259; *see* under individual topics for Treasury views
Trevithick, J.A., 170, 200
Trust Fund, 92, 102

unemployment, 55, 84, 88, 107, 114–16, 129, 131, 134–35, 137, 187, 194, 196, 210, 214, 217–19, 236, 238, 244–45, 252, 264–65; natural rate of, 199–201, 223; Treasury on, 109, 143, 187, 210, 217–25, 245, 253, 255–57, 262
uniform taxation, 5, 64, 103

variable deposit requirement, 198, 212
Vernon Committee, *see* Committee of Economic Enquiry
Visbord, E.M.W., 20, 180

wage indexation, 101, 115, 130, 223–24, 246, 257–58
wages; increases in, 85, 95, 100–01, 105, 114–15, 120, 129–30, 150, 152, 154, 181–82, 185, 187–88, 190, 192–93, 207–08, 211–12, 214, 220, 236, 239–40, 245–46, 256–57, 265; 'explosion' 1973–74, 211–12, 214, 220, 265; moderation in, 131, 147; -profits share, 183, 217–18, 223; Treasury on, 130, 181–85, 187–88, 192–93, 210, 218–24, 240, 245, 256–59; *see also* Productivity and real wages
'wages pause', 1982–83, 245, 257–58
Walker, E.R., 57, 61, 62–63, 65, 72–74

Walras, L., 26–30, 71, 171, 201, 278
Walsh, M., 273
War Gratuity Reserve, 91–92
Waterman, A.M.C., 136–37
Watt, G.P.N., 109
Weintraub, S., 173
Weller, P., 15
Wheeler, Sir Frederick, 18, 24, 89, 97, 99–100, 161–62, 273; background and career of, 10–11, 109, 179–80
Whitelaw, R.J., 10
Whitlam, E.G., 20, 178, 215
Whitlam government, 15; economic policies of, 15–16, 198, 212–17, 225–26, 266, 268; and Treasury, 15–16, 24, 196, 213–17
Wilson, Sir Roland, 65, 76, 140, 147, 270, 273; background and career of, 11, 23–24, 106, 109, 145; early economic philosophy of, 57, 61, 67–71

more than the tour operator's offer of $20. Obtaining a translation of the tour operator's brochure could be invaluable in negotiations like this. The hotelier is also selling on higher satisfaction for the tour operator's clients and more repeat business rather than selling on price alone.

Although much more extensive, this is very similar to an actual meeting I attended **where** the tour operator finally agreed $28 per person.

> Concentrate on price and you have only one way to go – down. Switch from price to value and you have many paths all of them up.

One of the finest statements I have ever read on the whole subject of price and value was written over one hundred years ago and I have no hesitation in repeating it below.

Value . . .
It's unwise to pay too much, but it's unwise to pay too little. When you pay too much you lose a little money, that is all. When you pay too little, you sometimes lose everything, because the thing you bought was incapable of doing the thing you bought it to do.

The common law of business balance prohibits paying a little and getting a lot. It can't be done. If you deal with the lowest bidder, it's well to add something for the risk you run. And if you do that, you will have enough to pay for something better.

John Ruskin (1819–1900)

Very often in negotiating on price I have read this out and it has helped to win an argument.

Some hoteliers and sales executives automatically assume that the only way to clinch a major deal is to offer discounts. This could be the easy way out – in many situations the buyer would sooner have the proposition 'packaged' with a series of extras included, rather than having a reduction in the price. Many people say that the market is price sensitive today. What they mean is that the tour operators say the price is sensitive. Often research shows that the ultimate purchaser (the guest) may show an opposite reaction.

A leading sales executive said to me recently that the only right policy is 'pile 'em high – sell 'em cheap', quoting the famous policy statement by the founder of Tesco, a chain of supermarkets. But we are not selling cans of beans, and this attitude may well drive us out of business.

Send sales executives, receptionists and reservation staff out to look at competitors' rooms and list league tables of comparable tariffs. It might dawn on them that your quoted tariffs are not as high as they may seem. I have seen many sales staff and receptionists 'breathe in' as they quote the tariff for the room at $40, $60, or more, because they feel it is high. Once they have seen the competition's charges they will have much more confidence in selling their room rates.

Curiously enough, however sophisticated people become, everyone likes something for nothing. And if you include something in a package which appears to be free, people love it. In the Daula Hotel, Kano, Northern Nigeria, we introduced a rose for ladies leaving the dining room. The response was staggering. There are a mass of 'small' items which make people think you care and make them return. Too often we have a number of irritating add-ons. The small charge for a morning newspaper or – probably the worst – the cover charge in the restaurant. I know all the reasons for it, but it annoys the majority of customers. I rather like the idea of giving a departing guest a take-away gift which is associated with the area, like a selection of local cheeses, or a paperweight from a local stone, with your own name or emblem on the item or on the wrapping. I have a key ring, a leather coaster for my office desk, and a long shoe-horn which I use virtually every day – all reminding me of the hotels who gave them to me. Naturally the quality of the gift would depend on the style of hotel. Why give a departing guest just a receipted bill and a credit card slip when he leaves after spending possibly $2000 or more on a holiday?

It is a very good rule in obtaining repeat business to give guests something when they arrive and something when they leave.

In good or bad times there are always some people who will spend more money if you give them the chance. And there are always some companies or organizations who are selling a very expensive product, or trying to make a good impression on a product launch, where a hotelier can do the same. Usually the hotel costs are small compared to the overall costs of marketing, in relation to the development costs of a new product, and compared to the sales price of the product.

There is a place for discounts on quiet nights and periods of the year where the market is more price sensitive. Retrospective discounts to major buyers where they have given you more than a certain amount of business in the past years are also useful. But before hoteliers use discounts as a marketing weapon, first: